P9-AQN-579

Questions of Method in Cultural Studies

# Questions of Method in Cultural Studies

*Edited by*

Mimi White *and* James Schwoch

**Blackwell**
Publishing

Editorial material and organization © 2006 by Blackwell Publishing Ltd

BLACKWELL PUBLISHING
350 Main Street, Malden, MA 02148-5020, USA
9600 Garsington Road, Oxford OX4 2DQ, UK
550 Swanston Street, Carlton, Victoria 3053, Australia

The right of Mimi White and James Schwoch to be identified as the Authors of the
Editorial Material in this Work has been asserted in accordance with the UK
Copyright, Designs, and Patents Act 1988.

All rights reserved. No part of this publication may be reproduced, stored in a
retrieval system, or transmitted, in any form or by any means, electronic, mechanical,
photocopying, recording or otherwise, except as permitted by the UK Copyright,
Designs, and Patents Act 1988, without the prior permission of the publisher.

First published 2006 by Blackwell Publishing Ltd

1   2006

*Library of Congress Cataloging-in-Publication Data*

Questions of method in cultural studies / edited by Mimi White and James Schwoch.
p.   cm.
Includes bibliographical references and index.
ISBN-13: 978-0-631-22977-3 (hardcover : alk. paper)
ISBN-10: 0-631-22977-9 (hardcover : alk. paper)
ISBN-13: 978-0-631-22978-0 (pbk. : alk. paper)
ISBN-10: 0-631-22978-7 (pbk. : alk. paper)
1. Culture—Study and teaching.  2. Culture—Methodology.  I. White, Mimi,
1953–  II. Schwoch, James, 1955–
HM623.Q84 2006
306′.071—dc22

2005019316

A catalogue record for this title is available from the British Library.

Set in 11/13pt Bembo by
SNP Best-set Typesetter Ltd, Hong Kong
Printed and bound in Great Britain
by TJ International Ltd, Padstow, Cornwall

The publisher's policy is to use permanent paper from mills that operate a
sustainable forestry policy, and which has been manufactured from pulp processed
using acid-free and elementary chlorine-free practices. Furthermore, the publisher
ensures that the text paper and cover board used have met acceptable environmental
accreditation standards.

For further information on
Blackwell Publishing, visit our website:
www.blackwellpublishing.com

# Contents

# Contents

# Notes on Contributors

**Pertti Alasuutari**, Ph.D., is Professor of Sociology and Director of the Research Institute for Social Sciences at the University of Tampere, Finland. He is editor of the *European Journal of Cultural Studies*, and has published widely in the areas of cultural and media studies and qualitative methods. His books include *Desire and Craving: A Cultural Theory of Alcoholism* (1992); *Researching Culture: Qualitative Method and Cultural Studies* (1995); *An Invitation to Social Research* (1998); *Rethinking the Media Audience* (1999); and *Social Theory and Human Reality* (2004).

**Tim Anderson** is an Assistant Professor in the Department of Communication at Denison University. He has published in journals such as *Cinema Journal*, *The Velvet Light Trap*, and *American Music*. His book, *Making Easy Listening: Material Culture and Postwar American Recording*, is slated for publication in 2005. He is currently working on a project dealing with the early history of the American music program, *Soul Train*.

**John Caldwell**, a media studies scholar and filmmaker, is Professor of Film, Television and Digital Media at UCLA. His books include *Televisuality: Style, Crisis, and Authority in Contemporary Television*, *Electronic Media and Technoculture*; *New Media: Digitextual Theories and Practices*; and the forthcoming *Production Culture: Industrial Reflexivity and Critical Practice in Film/Television*. He is also the producer/director of the award-winning documentaries *Rancho California (por favor)*, and *Freak Street to Goa: Immigrants on the Rajpath*.

**Gini Gorlinski** has studied the musics of the Kenyah, Kayan, and other interior peoples of Indonesian and Malaysian Borneo for two decades. She has conducted four years of fieldwork, and returns to the island as often as possible to continue old projects, initiate new ones, and visit her adopted families and friends. She received an M.A. (Music/ Ethnomusicology) from the University of Hawai'i–Manoa in 1989, and a Ph.D. (Music/Ethnomusicology) from the University of Wisconsin-Madison in 1995. Her articles and essays have appeared in the *New Grove Dictionary of Music and Musicians, Ethnomusicology, Yearbook for Traditional Music, Borneo Research Bulletin, Journal of Musicological Research,* and *Encyclopedia of Popular Music of the World* (Continuum). Her current projects include an instructional Kenyah dance DVD/VCD, a *sampé* (plucked lute) audio CD, and a book manuscript, "From the Rock to the Rhyme: A Portrait of Society, Song, and Verse in Kenyah Community of Sarawak, Malaysia." Gorlinski teaches in the School of Interdisciplinary Arts at Ohio University, in Athens, Ohio.

**John Hartley** is a professor in the Creative Industries Research & Applications Centre, Queensland University of Technology, Australia. He was founding dean of the Creative Industries Faculty at QUT, and founding head of the School of Journalism, Media and Cultural Studies at Cardiff University in Wales. He has written many books and articles on cultural, media, and journalism studies, including *Creative Industries* (editor, Blackwell, 2005); *A Short History of Cultural Studies* (2003); *The Indigenous Public Sphere* (with Alan McKee, 2000); *American Cultural Studies: A Reader* (edited with Roberta E. Pearson, 2000); *Uses of Television* (1999); and *Popular Reality: Journalism, Modernity, Popular Culture* (1996). He is editor of the *International Journal of Cultural Studies.*

**Joke Hermes** teaches television studies at the University of Amsterdam (The Netherlands), and she is Professor of Public Opinion Formation at Inholland University. She is also co-founder and editor of the *European Journal of Cultural Studies.* Her research is on popular culture and cultural citizenship. Popular genres, media ethnography, and gender are recurrent topics in her published work. Her most recent book is *Re-reading Popular Culture* (Blackwell, 2005).

**Micaela di Leonardo** is Professor of Anthropology and Performance Studies at Northwestern University. She has written *The Varieties of Ethnic Experience* (Cornell, 1984); and *Exotics at Home: Anthropologies,*

*Others, American Modernity* (1998); edited *Gender at the Crossroads of Knowledge* (1991); and co-edited *The Gender/Sexuality Reader* (1997). She is currently writing *The View From Cavallaro's*, an historical ethnography of gender, race, political economy, and public culture in New Haven, Connecticut, and will be Residential Fellow at the School of American Research in Santa Fe, New Mexico, 2005–06.

**Sonia Livingstone** is Professor of Social Psychology and a member of the Department of Media and Communications at the London School of Economics and Political Science. She has published widely on the subject of media audiences. Her recent work concerns children, young people and the Internet, as part of a broader interest in the domestic, familial, and educational contexts of new media access and use. Books include *Making Sense of Television* (2nd edition, 1998); *Mass Consumption and Personal Identity* (with Peter Lunt, 1992); *Talk on Television* (with Peter Lunt, 1994); *Children and Their Changing Media Environment* (edited with Moira Bovill, 2001); *The Handbook of New Media* (edited with Leah Lievrouw, 2002); *Young People and New Media* (2002); *Audiences and Publics* (edited, 2005); and her current project, *Children and the Internet* (2006).

**Anna McCarthy** is Associate Professor of Cinema Studies at New York University. She is author of *Ambient Television* (2001) and coeditor, with Nick Couldry, of the anthology *MediaSpace* (2004). Her essays on television and other media have appeared in several anthologies and journals, including *October, The Journal of Visual Culture, The International Journal of Cultural Studies*, and *GLQ*. She is currently working on a study of television, culture and citizenship in the postwar United States.

**John Durham Peters** is F. Wendell Miller Distinguished Professor of Communication Studies, University of Iowa. He is the author of more than forty articles and book chapters, and over a dozen book reviews on the philosophy of communication, the intellectual history of communication research, democratic theory, and the cultural history of media. He has published *Speaking into the Air: A History of the Idea of Communication* (1999); and *Courting the Abyss: Free Speech and the Liberal Tradition* (2005); and has co-edited *Canonic Texts in Media Research: Are There Any? Should There Be? How About These?* with Elihu Katz, Peters, Tamar Liebes, and Avril Orloff (2003); and *Mass*

*Communication and American Social Thought: Key Texts, 1919–1968*, with Peter Simonson (2004).

**Andrea Press** is Research Professor of Communications and Women's Studies at the University of Illinois at Urbana/Champaign, where she is also Associate Director of Undergraduate Studies for the Communications College. She is the author of *Women Watching Television: Gender, Class, and Generation in the American Television Experience*; *Speaking of Abortion: Television and Authority in the Lives of Women* (with Elizabeth R. Cole); the forthcoming *What's Important About Communications and Culture?* (with Bruce A. Williams); and many articles about feminist theory and media culture. She is currently completing two projects, one focusing on adolescent girls' uses of new media, the other investigating how Americans discuss and organize around public issues in the new media environment. She has received grants from the National Science Foundation and the National Institute of Mental Health, and was an Associate of the Center for Advanced Study at the University of Illinois for the 2004–05 academic year. Professor Press co-produces the annual Roger Ebert Festival of Overlooked Films for the Communications College at the University of Illinois.

**James Schwoch** holds a permanent faculty appointment at Northwestern University, where he conducts research on media history, diplomacy and international relations, science and technology studies, and research methodologies. This is his fourth book, and he has also produced many articles and reviews. Agencies funding his work include the Ameritech Foundation; the Ford Foundation; the Fulbright Commission (Finland, Germany); the National Endowment for the Humanities; the National Science Foundation; and the Center for Strategic and International Studies (Washington DC), where he was a resident research fellow in 1997–8.

**Mimi White** is Professor of Radio/TV/Film at Northwestern University. She is author of *Tele-Advising: Therapeutic Discourse in American Television* and co-author of *Media Knowledge* (with James Schwoch and Susan Reilly). Her many essays on film and television have appeared in anthologies and journals, including *Screen*, *Camera Obscura*, *Cinema Journal*, and *Film and History*. In 2004–05 she was the Bicentennial Fulbright Professor in North American Studies at the Renvall Institute, University of Helsinki.

# Acknowledgments

Jayne Fargnoli at Blackwell first approached us with this book concept and guided us through the process with skill, wisdom, and patience. Ken Provencher at Blackwell joined us midway, and was instrumental and enthusiastic in helping bring the book to completion, as were the rest of the Blackwell staff.

We would not have a book without the contributors, whose essays comprise the bulk of this volume. They are the luminaries of this project, and share our highest accolades.

Questions of method in the context of interdisciplinary research became a central focus of James Schwoch's work through his convening an ongoing series of graduate workshops and seminars at Northwestern University in International Studies, funded by the Ford Foundation, between 1993 and 2000. We are indebted to the co-conveners of these methodology workshops and seminars, including David William Cohen, Charles Ragin, Micaela Di Leonardo, and Jane Guyer, as well as the many graduate students and visiting scholars from around the world who participated in these sessions. Mimi White and James Schwoch offered a graduate workshop on questions of methodology in the Department of Communication and Journalism at the University of Jyvaskyla in 1996, and we thank those participants, and especially thank Raimo Salokangas for his initial invitation and spirited collegiality. We also thank Dilip Gaonkar, who was our co-director in 2000 of a summer institute at Northwestern University on cultural studies, and extend our appreciation to the graduate students and visiting scholars who participated in the summer institute.

We thank Nick Brock and Margaret Aherne for their careful editorial oversight of this volume. As co-editors we gave *carte blanche* to the contributing essayists for the intellectual content of their individual essays, but acknowledge that any inadvertent changes to their essays introduced through our final copyediting and proofing are the sole responsibility of the co-editors and not the individual authors.

Finally, we acknowledge our utmost thanks to Travis White-Schwoch, our own in-house scientist, musician, critic, diplomat, and sage, who handled with his own unique and wonderful demeanor both of his parents working together to see this project through to completion, whether it be in workshops, seminars, conferences, airports, boats, taxis, trains, restaurants, or bars, from Evanston to Helsinki, beyond and back again, always, like everything else, yet another ever-present project in our home. Thanks, Travis – you are the greatest.

# 1

# Introduction: The Questions of Method in Cultural Studies

## James Schwoch and Mimi White

Cultural studies as an area of scholarly pursuit can arguably be traced all the way back to the early formation of a secularized European university system, but the main roots of the intellectual history of cultural studies are tied to developments in postwar Europe and the USA. From early efforts in the UK and Europe such as Richard Hoggart's book *The Uses of Literacy* and the eventual coalescence of a cultural studies center at the University of Birmingham, as well as broad and disparate work in the USA dealing with questions of mass culture (and some of that work undertaken by German expatriates associated with the Frankfurt School), cultural studies has, particularly since the 1990s, spread spatially around the globe and conceptually into a wide range of traditional fields and disciplines.

At various points in time, different traditional fields and disciplines have influenced cultural studies. For the most part, this influence, while important, does not seem to have brought about any obvious cohesion or unification to cultural studies. Many scholars celebrate and endorse the free-wheeling and extremely open nature of this area of intellectual pursuit, while others point to this openness as a sign of the relative intellectual weakness of cultural studies. While this ongoing debate in and of itself is ultimately meritorious (for it creates opportunities to reconsider a wide range of knowledge about the liberal arts), at the same time the debate has functioned in a way to discourage, and even prevent, careful and considered discussion about methodologies and cultural studies. As a result, cultural studies at the dawn of the twenty-first century looks like many different things, and the constitution of cultural studies remains indeterminate, highly subject to the unshared perceptions of individual observers.

This book sets out to explore whether cultural studies has a set of methodological assumptions, techniques, and models, and, if such an overall set exists, how various subsets do and do not work together. We expect this to be a controversial project. Practitioners of cultural studies, taken as a whole, seem to share little common ground. Yet if the range of work carried out in the name of cultural studies is vast, the work of cultural studies does share some common assumptions, and participates in a set of debates – including those regarding methodologies. Moreover, to the extent that cultural studies dodged embracing the question of method as an integral part of its project, methodology has been something of a structuring absence. Instead, cultural studies has largely defined its intellectual focus by invoking a broad (and at times even contradictory) set of overarching theories on the one hand, and the claims of discovering the vast array of cultural objects and practices that are studied (culture/everyday life/the popular/etc.), on the other.

The articulations of theory and objects/practices with the methodological trajectories that bring these together in ways that can be considered "cultural studies" as distinct from inquiry in a traditional discipline remains largely unexamined. Can cultural studies itself even fully be a distinct field of inquiry without eventually considering the questions of method? Although we are by no means convinced we have all the answers to this particular question, we do believe that the path for cultural studies to this distinction includes exploring questions of method. We also believe that this exploration of the path for cultural studies toward distinction is not merely an empty exercise, but a way of furthering the larger project of cultural studies.

We also draw a distinction – in this use of the term, a difference – between a theory, or theories, of cultural studies, and an exploration and articulation of the methodologies of cultural studies. This distinctive difference is important and bears further elaboration. To state it plainly, it is not the aim or goal of this book to explore methodologies as a way of generating and pointing toward an overall unified theory of cultural studies. We are not certain such a unified theory would even be possible or desirable. Setting aside this possibility, we recognize that some of the core assumptions of cultural studies practitioners include placing high values on the significance of concepts such as individual agency, identity, opposition and alternativeness, and resistance. With these values occupying such a prominent position in the core assumptions of cultural studies, the implications of delineating and articulating a general unified theory (which would likely mean looking for such values as parsimony, reductionism, objectivity, and universalism) are at such wide variance with the core values of cultural studies as to make "cultural studies" and "unified theory" indefinitely incommensurate. And perhaps this is not surprising, as the postwar emergence and later prominence of cultural studies was among other things a reaction to (and often against) scholarly trends which placed high value on parsimony, universalism, stability, and the elimination (or muting) of contentiousness. The historical trajectory of cultural studies in the academic world, its stable emergence in this context of Cold War intellectualism, and the implications of this formative crucible for methodological questions, are further discussed later in this introduction.

Since the mid-1980s, cultural studies has become firmly entrenched as a broad-based academic field of inquiry, both as a field or program in its own right, and in the context of more established scholarly disciplines. Firmly characterized as an interdisciplinary enterprise, and even at times as something of an "outlaw" interdiscipline, cultural studies developed in many different contexts and directions. In the process, work in cultural studies is united by a loose array of theoretical touchstones, an abiding concern with understanding power and resistance in culture, and an oscillating interest in sometimes drawing together, and other times pulling apart, approaches from the social sciences and the humanities. Because of the ways cultural studies has developed, and also because of its own historical roots, questions of method have not been posed in a general schematic, but rather have been fragmented into the context of specific disciplines and thus generally contained within those specific disciplines rather than articulated through cultural studies and across those disciplines. Thus most cultural studies scholars to date have argued against the possibility of methodological distinction for cultural studies, against privileging a given approach, and against the reducibility of method. In turn, these same scholars argue in favor of advocating all methodological possibilities and then proceeding into cultural studies fieldwork without first having a methodological outline in hand.[1]

Despite these valuable admonitions from experienced cultural studies researchers, this book directly raises questions about methodology in cultural studies work. It draws together scholars from different disciplines, and whose engagements with cultural studies are varied, to place the issue of method front and center. The goal is not to prescribe or delimit methods, but to explore questions of method in explicit terms.

What, if any, methods have prevailed in the interdisciplinary pursuits of cultural studies? In a field frankly shaped by borrowings from an array of fields (anthropology, art theory, linguistics, literary studies, media studies, philosophy, political science, and sociology, among others), what kinds of methodological choices are made, debated, attacked, and why? In what contexts are specific methodological choices privileged, and for what ends? The essays in this volume address these questions in different ways.

A book organized around the questions of method in cultural studies might strike some readers at first glance as fruitless, foolhardy, divisive, distracting, or simply an intellectual exercise akin to academic navel-gazing. One might ask why cultural studies scholars would even care about questions of method, since there is such an emphasis placed on pushing boundaries, constructing contexts, adapting theories and approaches for specific analyses, producing new readings, and positioning analysis in new discursive spaces not completely demarcated within the fields of dialog wholly contained within the ivy tower. Why would cultural studies even care about questions of method? In particular, why would cultural studies, of all fields, want to even think about the implications of method, particularly when the implications of method are often, accurately or not, associated with an imaginary scholar devoting an entire career to asking questions and deriving answers with the same methodological approach over and over again, regardless of topic, regardless of relevance?

While the "single-method-for-all-studies" scholar is an academic caricature, this caricature does beg a mild criticism of some scholars and some lines of thought in traditional disciplines: all fields and disciplines, old and new, gestating and declining, can benefit from regular examination, consideration and rearticulation of research methods. This is especially true at the turn of the twenty-first century, when an increasing attention to inter- and cross-disciplinary dialogs on the one hand, and advanced communication and information technologies on the other, are creating new research opportunities. One does on occasion wonder how carefully the rearticulation of method has accompanied these new opportunities. However, these conditions also suggest that this moment is a prime opportunity for cultural studies to benefit from its own foray into a methodological articulation: cultural studies is shaped by many disciplines and fields, cultural studies actively uses the texts, artifacts, and, on occasion, the infrastructure of advanced information and communication technologies to transform data into research, and the relative lack of methodological rearticulation in the traditional fields and disciplines gives cultural studies a unique opportunity to use the questions of method as a way of speaking back to those traditional fields and disciplines.

Even in those many cases where scholars have engaged a healthy articulation and rearticulation of method within the confines of their own field or discipline, the articulation and rearticulation of method within a discipline is not only an exercise that responds to the current flow of change at any given disciplinary moment. The articulation and rearticulation of method within a discipline is also akin to an act of intellectual history within that discipline. Cultural studies also deserves the benefit of such an intellectual foray for its own historical self-understanding, to be able to better understand its own triumphs, its own challenges, and its own disputes. We provide some of those investigations in the essays found in this volume, framed by a brief historical overview later in this introduction.

Rather than explore the question of methodologies in cultural studies in hopes of finding the route toward a general unified theory of cultural studies, we instead propose exploring the question of methodologies in hopes of finding what we would call a "management" or "negotiation" template of cultural studies methodologies for practitioners. By "management template," we aim with these essays to better delineate a general typology of methodological questions, considerations, assumptions and practices that can account for a wide range of individual work done in the area of cultural studies, as well as continuing to permit individual scholars invested in cultural studies to bring their own particularities and nuances – their individual agency – into the field. Much of the work produced in cultural studies has emphasized the *uses* of cultural texts and artifacts, and practices of everyday life in local and contingent contexts, often by a particular subset of a larger social system. Thus we believe that a methodological query of cultural studies should emphasize the possibilities of methodological usage – in other words, a template or matrix for the management of methodologies in cultural studies – rather than a single model which emphasizes or theorizes the boundaries of cultural studies. The editors of a recent compendium of cultural studies research remarked that methodology for cultural studies is not distillable into a single strain that one can outline, download, and take into the cultural arena.[2] We agree – and instead of looking for a single outline to download, we are more interested in sketching the parameters of a large spreadsheet with many reasonably possible cells to activate.

To round out this computer software analogy, our quest in this volume is not for the universal usability of a single cultural studies methodological outline, but instead to begin displaying the ongoing management and negotiation of a multi-celled cultural studies methodological spreadsheet. Such a spreadsheet might assist in the further navigation of common theories comprising the overall hypertext of cultural studies. Also, insofar as cultural studies is a multi-cross-interdisciplinary enterprise, there are multiple methodological histories that intersect but are not identical, depending on where scholars enter into the field. For example, in some fields, certain kinds of ethnographic inquiry were seen as a significant cultural studies contribution to a field focused on theory and texts, whereas in other fields, the introduction of textual theory served as a way of bringing qualitative specificity to their work. In other words, cultural studies in anthropology exhibits some distinct differences when compared with cultural studies in film studies. Therefore, with any cultural studies scholar at any given moment or in any given research project, the entire cultural studies spreadsheet is not likely to be visible on their "conceptual computer" page, or cultural studies methodological spreadsheet. The visible cultural studies spreadsheet cells are instead those that are germane to the operationalization of that specific project. But an important thing to remember is that non-visible spreadsheet cells in a given project still exist and are active elsewhere in the field as a whole, at any given moment. Scholars produce research over time and in trajectories. Here, the spreadsheet metaphor also assists in better understanding (to borrow from quantitative approaches) longitudinal analyses of the work of an individual cultural studies scholar, or a particular group of cultural studies scholars, over time and duration of a research career. While a single research project by an individual or group may occupy itself with a distinct (to borrow from semiotics) syntagm of the spreadsheet, the potential, over the course of a research career, to explore more of the full paradigm of the entire spreadsheet is genuine. Thus the spreadsheet metaphor for methodologies and cultural studies also helps to account for the trajectories of cultural studies researchers in the longer duration of a scholarly career.

The idea of a negotiated model, and the methodological metaphor of the spreadsheet, makes explicit that cultural studies often engages multiple methodologies, and that analyses of meaning and power in everyday cultural practices are advanced by drawing together methodologies from more than one traditional discipline, sometimes in ways that might be perceived as epistemologically antagonistic. At the same time, the methodological spreadsheet helps honor other approaches to cultural studies, especially those where a method strongly associated with one discipline is brought to bear on cultural objects and practices that are usually studied in another discipline using distinctively different methods. Both of these approaches involve cross- or interdisciplinarity, one of the familiar (if not trite) ways of characterizing cultural studies as a whole. The spreadsheet conception of methodological practice makes these claims explicit.

This approach also positions cultural studies as a site of innovation, since the idea of a negotiated method facilitates the development and response to social, cultural, and intellectual transformations; it proposes strategies of intellectual invention instead of disciplinary containment. Finally, a methodological spreadsheet conceptualization for the questions of method in cultural studies means that future innovation can be celebrated while past tradition remains respected: the spreadsheet itself is an open-celled computer software program, designed with the known quality of ever-expanding cells. Active spreadsheet cells are those visible on the screen and representative of those various approaches to method currently in play in the practice of cultural studies. While invisible until activated by future methodological innovations in cultural studies, the past and future cells suggest a continuum of historical engagement that represents an expanding self-knowledge for cultural studies.

This continuum of historical engagement representing an expanding self-knowledge we believe important: unlike some mainstream historical perspectives of other disciplines (thinking of the history of science and the work of Thomas Kuhn, for example), we reject conceptual frameworks that historicize cultural studies through the continual process of the cultural studies practitioner community as cyclically constructing, falsifying, and rejecting its own past intellectual paradigms. Instead, we see a history of cultural studies as a field of inquiry that continually seeks its situation through changing conditions of method, social context, topoi of inquiry, and objects of analysis, all the while never completely discarding its own past. The possibilities of this model mean that cultural studies is ready to take on new objects and think in new ways when it comes to both the future and the past. Indeed this perspective encourages a rethinking of the "history" of cultural studies as an academic field, which has traditionally been identified with the Center for Contemporary Cultural Studies (CCCS) at the University of Birmingham, and its specific British influences (Richard Hoggart, E.P. Thompson, Raymond Williams, et al.). This revision of the intellectual foundations of cultural studies also helps explain the diverse, multiple methodological influences that comprise the negotiated model we are proposing for thinking about questions of method in cultural studies.

## An Overview of Emergences of Cultural Studies: Intellectual History

The negotiation of the "method question" for cultural studies is intertwined with the conditions surrounding the emergence, or perhaps more accurately the "emergences," of cultural studies. The plural "emergences" is offered here to advance an historical reading which argues that since the end of the nineteenth century, bits of evidence suggesting the emergence of cultural studies as a component of a global intellectual landscape surfaced in several different intellectual and geographic locations. For various reasons, none of these emergences fully stabilized until the conditions which led to the emergence and initial stabilization of cultural studies in Britain after World War II. However, we have chosen to begin our brief historical recap of cultural studies at an earlier time, and chosen to work through a rubric of intellectual, rather than institutional, history.

In this historical overview, we have taken a self-imposed challenge to be both economic as well as eloquent, painting as best could reasonably be done a global history of the emergence of cultural studies in as concise a space as possible. Indeed, many histories of cultural studies start with the 1960s formation of the CCCS at Birmingham, and its immediate British influences and antecedents, bringing in continental European scholars second, as they were brought into consideration by this British Centre, and moving on to a basic institutional narrative explaining the global expansion of cultural studies. This is, albeit described by us here in overly simple terms, the standard institutional history with a "date-driven narrative" of cultural studies. Paradoxically, despite the well-known professed resistance to, or skepticism of, institutional analysis by many cultural studies practitioners, the standard cultural studies date-driven history is almost always also a standard institutional historical narrative. We see this standard institutional history of cultural studies as a paradox and a contradiction, and we are trying to do something about it with our historical narrative. Our alternative account does not conflict with the standard institutional date-driven historical narrative, but does, we believe, open new avenues of inquiry and consideration while also hopefully being more faithful to the professed values of many cultural studies researchers. Our historical overview is, therefore, a history with a difference by design. The historical narrative we offer is an important one, especially in terms of methodological implications. The historical overview grounds the idea that methodology – especially experimentation and expansion in cultural studies methodologies, akin to a spreadsheet – has always lurked in the global rise of cultural studies, and is directly related to a twentieth-century history of Western intellectual inquiry focused on exploring the cultural, conceptual, social, political and intellectual boundaries of Western societies. Our account helps set the stage for the individual essays which follow, framing our essayists in a long intellectual tradition.

The intellectual, political, economic, and social factors which were spurring various emergences of cultural studies can be seen as early as the late nineteenth century in the United States, with the growing concern for research on the new problems and challenges of mass, industrialized, and/or modern (you are free to choose or even add your own term to that list) society. These areas of new intellectual inquiry were emergent at both older private American universities, and also at the newer land grant universities, and took root across American university life in a number of ways. Thus, the intellectual projects which in the late nineteenth and early twentieth centuries stabilized into various schools and departments of communications or media at some American universities (Michigan, Northwestern, Wisconsin, for example), into sociology and social work at others (Chicago, Columbia, for example), or even public policy at still others (Harvard, Princeton, for example) shared some common ground with what we now consider cultural studies, albeit on the terms and conditions of a century ago. Like cultural studies, these new units were (and in many ways still are) often seen as a "methodological grab-bag," considered to be better understood as organized around their objects of inquiry rather than around a single theoretical precept, and, in their everyday existence within campus life, were more often than not marginalized, especially in their early years. These units could have, theoretically, "become" cultural studies units – they did not, but their origins and their areas of intellectual inquiry are not so distant and far removed from cultural studies that recognizing a little bit of common ground is impossible. So we might call these events one early emergence of cultural studies that, for various reasons, did not coalesce into a stable formation of cultural studies, but stabilized into other fields that now can reasonably be considered as useful and necessary ancillaries to cultural studies.

World War I and its aftermath also created conditions for emergences of cultural studies. Perhaps the two most pronounced cases in this regard are Weimar Germany and the Union of Soviet Socialist Republics. In the former case, the growth of the Institute for Social Research (the Frankfurt School) and its rigorous investigations of certain everyday experiences of mass culture produced some brilliant individual analyses as well as some strong theoretical disagreements. Beyond the Institute for Social Research, many other German universities during the Weimar period also pursued intellectual projects designed to study mass media. Intellectually the USSR was, if nothing else, relentlessly modern, and its state-led drive toward a universal scientific method – first Marxist, then Marxist-Leninist, then later Marxist-Leninist-Stalinist – had an incredible impact on shaping work within the USSR regarding the humanities and social sciences. However, in both the German and Soviet cases, the national turn toward authoritarianism in the political form of the state – National Socialism in Germany, and the over-Stalinization of Soviet scientific method (achieved in part by the simultaneous de-Trotskyization of Soviet scientific method) – severely limited the transnational applicability of these authoritarian modes of studying culture, with the minor exception of a few hard-line adherents scattered abroad, and the major exception of state-led imposition of these methods. The Soviet intellectual community was internally purged to construct a Stalinized standard Soviet scientific method, while the Institute for Social Research was physically fragmented; attempts to completely reconstitute its intellectual agenda as well as many of its practitioners diasporically scattered in safe havens (for example, the Princeton Radio Project of the late 1930s) were never fully realized.

The aftermath of World War I and its impact on attempted emergences of cultural studies is also evident in Europe beyond Germany and the USSR. In the turmoil of Eastern Europe, the national state emerged as the only realistic political alternative to a reconstituted

imperial relationship with Germany or Austria, the utterly shattered
Ottoman empire, or Bolshevism beyond the Soviet Union. These new
Eastern European states would add to the number of nations experimenting with culture and media in forging a relatively new practice,
the "massification" of national identity through such applications as
information dissemination, popular politics, fashion and cuisine, folk
arts, and media texts. (The massification of national identity in the
1920s and 1930s also took on its own variants in Western Europe, the
Western Hemisphere, and certain areas of Asia.) In the collapsed Austro-
Hungarian empire, Vienna would become an even more incredible
locale for cultural intellectuals than its lofty pre-war status; a city where,
for example, as youngsters Paul Lazarsfeld and Anna Freud would play
together while father Sigmund led Lazarsfeld's mother through psycho-
analysis, and a city which was at one point home to a vast number of
the most influential social and cultural scholars of the twentieth century
(virtually all of whom would exile themselves from Vienna in the years
after 1933).

While the geopolitics of the 1930s produced the conditions for what
might be called extremist cultural persuasion in the service of the
nation-state (the propaganda wars, the "Empire" radio services, the
national film councils, and so forth), the 1930s also marked the "intel-
lectualization" of mass audiences (the first maturing of a culture of
consumption in North America and Western Europe, with an emergent
culture of consumption in Latin America and certain areas of Asia,
contrasted with the politico-structural mass intellectual projects of
National Socialist Germany or the USSR) and also signs of an early
cosmopolitan cultural elite, consuming both high and low cultural
artifacts, in certain Third World cities with what might be called a
"colonial heritage" (or "proto-postcolonial metropoles"), such as Shang-
hai or Cairo. Radio networks, phonograph discs, travelling performers,
and sound cinema, now all in global circulation, had added the aural
to the complexity of understanding and analyzing the circulation and
consumption of visual and print-based media texts. World War II saw,
particularly in the USA but also elsewhere, an incredible state mobilization of cultural analysis, most prominent for the American case in
the Office of Strategic Services, but also discernible in the restructuring of universities themselves. This led, particularly in the USA, to the
postwar rise of area studies programs, yet another field of inquiry
sharing some common intellectual ground with cultural studies. During
the Cold War era, many of these USA area studies programs would

become politicized in the service of a national security state, most notably through the influence of research funding. This politicization of Cold War area studies also had implications for cultural studies – an implication of opposition, with cultural studies emerging in the 1960s and 1970s in part from an intellectual disdain for the overpoliticization of area studies (and certain components of the social sciences) during the Cold War.

It is the aftermath of World War II – the postwar period – that marks the first stabilization of cultural studies, its permanent emergence after five or more decades of scholarly cultural analysis sympathetic to the broad contours of cultural studies. While the institutional emergence of Richard Hoggart and the subsequent changes and growth of cultural studies in Britain and beyond are well-known and will not be recounted here, it is worth noting that the consequences of World War II for Britain – most notably, the loss of empire – had profound ramifications for the stable emergence of cultural studies. For example, anthropology in Britain before World War II had what might be called a significant "applied" component in its formation: British colonial officers in the field were routinely expected to gather anthropological data in the service of the colonial empire, and colonial field manuals often included basic instructions on how to gather anthropological data (including the provision of a ruler or scale on the front cover for accurately describing the size of objects and artifacts). Obviously, with the loss of empire, anthropology in postwar Britain would not be the same as it had previously been known.

The Allied occupation of postwar Germany was, among other things, a massive co-operative (and often contentious) experiment in building another nation's national culture, although one that clearly had a more or less fixed end-point. In short, cultural studies stabilizes in a postwar world coincident with the loss of empire, with an unprecedented emergence of new nation-states well beyond the scale and scope of the period after World War II, in reaction to and with partial contra-distinction against the Cold War politicization of area studies, and with a need for intellectual institutions to redefine themselves and their missions on new terms: domestic populations, new consumers, with higher education for the first time reaching significant segments of various populations heretofore deprived of access to higher learning. Of course, all the while, the world is experiencing yet another great expansion of circulating media texts and artifacts. Some of the early concepts, ideas, and teaching strategies of cultural studies were, in fact, extraordinarily well-suited to new pedagogical endeavors influenced by the theories of new thinkers such as Paulo Freire. This can be seen in the work of the Open University – where many students and programs simply could not afford expensive texts and other research materials, but did have easy access to popular media such as daily newspapers.

In the United States, postwar physical and intellectual restructuring and reconsideration in part saw an expansion of universities reaching out beyond the heretofore traditional student, as exemplified by returning veterans and a significant expansion of university infrastructure at a national level (for example, new branch campuses of major land grant universities). Rather than the loss of empire, the rise of the Cold War proved to be a more influential factor in restructuring the intellectual composition of American universities, with the postwar expansion of area studies programs and the expansion of the social sciences. The American experience also saw the rise to prominence of major philanthropic organizations such as the Ford Foundation, government funding programs such as the National Science Foundation or the National Endowment for the Humanities, and the increased influence of scholarly organizations such as the Social Science Research Council. These new (or renewed) American institutions wielded significant influence – particularly through program funding. The need to restructure and reconstruct intellectual institutions for a postwar world (restructured very differently in the USA, but nevertheless restructured), the remarkable expansion of educational opportunities to domestic populations previously excluded from the experience, the expansion and accessibility of media texts, and what in historical retrospect now appears to be the apex of a single-minded fixation of all nations acting in fee to their own national identity – in other words, the postwar Cold War period and its fixation on nations as a universally applicable unit of analysis – finally provided the necessary conditions for cultural studies to stabilize into sustained growth.

This brief overview of the intellectual history of cultural studies suggests that the roots of this field go back at least a century. As this history suggests, cultural studies might be productively conceived as a century of research aimed at articulating activities that mainstream academic and critical inquiry has left in the margins. In this sense, cultural studies is an academic field driven by a choice of "demarginalization." Cultural studies is driven by a choice to continually demarginalize, a choice exercised in many ways and through many intellectual projects now spanning over a century, in order to investigate important questions regarding modern society and culture. In other words, cultural studies chooses to go to the margins of society for its scholarly practice primarily in order to demonstrate the larger social significance of those margins and to consider those who are otherwise unacknowledged. This is not a demarginalization in the name of assimilation, homogeneity, or unified monoculture: it is a demarginalization in the name of appreciating the value of social and cultural difference in modern complex social systems.

The question of method for cultural studies, then, in both historical and contemporary terms, is also a question of how has this has been implemented in practice, or operationalized, in cultural studies research. This means that the question of method in cultural studies is a doubly crucial question. Not only is the question of method an avenue to historical self-understanding, it is also a key to understanding the successful demarginalization of certain segments of society and culture through cultural studies research and inquiry.

A range of questions are typically raised by considerations of methodology. What is the unit of analysis? How are data constituted, collected, analyzed, and disseminated? To what extent do cultural studies scholars constitute an intellectual community that shapes and reshapes its own identity; or, put another way, to what extent do cultural studies scholars demonstrate they are influenced by others in the field? At the same time, the "appropriate topic" for the application of cultural studies has spatially ranged from very local and specific subsets of social systems to global analysis, with everything in between. Similarly, the temporal configurations of cultural studies have ranged from very small slices of time to larger longitudinal studies. And, the question of space (and, to a lesser extent, time) has been a consistent theme in cultural studies research.

Finally, it is clear that a range of individual disciplines have had, and continue to have, an impact on cultural studies, just as cultural studies has tried to redefine traditional disciplines. These include but are not limited to modern literatures, comparative literatures, and literary criticism; anthropology; sociology; history; and political science. The essays in this volume variously address subsets of these issues. Because questions of space, time, and objects of analysis have loomed large in the field, the first set of essays addresses these issues in terms of method. The second section offers new perspectives on production and reception, in particular in the context of media studies. This is because media studies is an area that has significantly influenced, and has also been highly influenced by, cultural studies. Media studies, for example, provided inspiration in determining the range of objects for cultural studies analysis. Cultural studies, for example, presented itself to media studies as a corrective for redressing a too-narrow focus on the analysis of "texts" considered outside the social practices of production and reception. Cultural studies proposed that expanding the ways of approaching media enabled a better grasp of formations of power and resistance, especially in the everyday reception of media texts. The final section offers four case studies of the relation between cultural studies and other fields and disciplines.

## Notes

1  See, for example, Larry Grossberg, Cary Nelson, and Paula Treichler, eds., *Cultural Studies* (London: Routledge, 1992); Henry Jenkins, Tara McPherson, and Jane Shattuc, eds., *Hop on Pop: The Politics and Pleasure of Popular Culture* (Durham, NC: Duke University Press, 2003).
2  Jenkins, McPherson, and Shattuc, *Hop on Pop*.

# Part I

# Space/Time/Objects

# Introduction

The first section of essays examines several foundational issues and assumptions related to methodologies. In particular, these three essays interrogate how objects of study become recognized, explored, and constituted in the field of cultural studies. All three essays are exciting in many ways, not least in that they all consciously and carefully have moments where they push concepts and theories to their limits, a high-risk action in search of high rewards. This includes successful efforts in conceptually moving past the intellectual obstacles often evident in debates found in other books and volumes that first pit qualitative and quantitative methods as nothing but bipolar opposites, then advocate one approach to the exclusion of the other.

Anna McCarthy takes up the question of scalability regarding cultural studies. Scalability is a classic methodological question common to all fields and disciplines. For cultural studies, the question of scale not only connotes entrenched dichotomies between qualitative and quantitative research, but also raises questions of spatial concerns regarding the "geography" of a given topic of inquiry. This question also leads to a discussion of the "ordinariness" of many specific cultural studies inquiries. McCarthy uses scalability to invoke, among other concepts, the assumptions that positively correlate parsimony with useable theory. She also turns scalability into a useful concept for investigating the range of topics and objects that have garnered the attention of cultural studies researchers.

John Durham Peters begins developing his ideas about cultural studies and methodology in the very title of his essay: a careful, inspired reading of a single seminal text in cultural studies. Reminding us of the importance of understanding key texts, the value of close reading, and the need to recognize the impact of key texts upon a larger community of cultural studies scholars, Peters also uses Raymond Williams and his book *Culture and Society* to begin operationalizing – and therefore questioning, critiquing, supporting, and analyzing – questions about the value and influence of the concept of key texts for a community of cultural studies researchers, thus implicitly raising for interrogation the thorny but necessary question of canonical texts and competing visions for research in cultural studies. A model for how a single text can be re-read in a way that operationalizes the investigation of a broad sweep of texts and theorists in a given field, this essay is an accomplished example of how to structure an analysis from a single object or text outward into a vast and complex field of thought and literature.

John Hartley argues vigorously for the importance of text studies, and approaches understanding audience/reception studies as a kind of textual practice or production. Part of his essay explores the debates between "realist" and "constructivist" positions in cultural studies, including paying some attention to the ways in which his own position analyzing texts as discourse (and arguing that the studied audience is a discursive production) have been criticized to the point of parody by one camp of cultural studies scholars. He elaborates the implications of his position in terms of what it means to focus one's method on the analysis of texts of all kinds. This is not an argument for text analysis against audience studies. Rather, it concerns the constitution of objects for study. Like all three essays in this section, and most prominently on display in this essay, the author is taking high risks toward the goal of high rewards, pushing arguments and theoretical concepts to their outward limits. Hartley's essay, indeed all three of these essays, should also be read in recognition of the career output of each scholar, with each essay herein seen not only as a particular event, but also as part of their longer dialog built upon their own research trajectories. This same trend holds for all the essays in this volume.

# 2

# From the Ordinary to the Concrete: Cultural Studies and the Politics of Scale

## Anna McCarthy

*Cultural studies in the 1990s has begun to forget its commitment to ordinariness as a positive civic goal. (Hartley, 1999: 16)*

The word *scale* is a complex and highly abstract noun that expresses a number of different kinds of proportional relations, from the comparative size of physical phenomena to the mathematically calculable relationship between an object and its representation. Because the concept of *scale* is so abstract and far ranging, this essay violates some first principles of composition and begins with dictionary definitions, elaborating the history of *scale*'s usage in the human sciences. It will become apparent through this brief survey that although *scale* does not appear in Raymond Williams's *Keywords*, it certainly qualifies for keyword status. The problems of its definition, in other words, are "inextricably bound up with" the problems it is trying to describe (1976: 13). Exploring this conceptual richness and ambiguity, the following essay asks what the concept of scale means for methodology in cultural studies. Although the word is not a common one in cultural studies research, I will propose that a politics of scale has historically motivated cultural studies' interventions in the way knowledge is produced in the disciplines and spaces of higher education. As a political movement among intellectuals who are located within a variety of fields of inquiry, as well as in other institutions such as the arts and government, cultural studies has been defined by research agendas that vary widely from region to region as well as historically, in response to particular social conditions inside and outside the academy. However, it has consistently and persistently called attention to the broader political implications of scale-based methodological problematics such as the relationship between micro and macro social processes, or the establishment of valid conditions for empirical generalizability. Issues of scale, cultural studies research demonstrates, not only shape the forms and objectives of knowledge production but also serve as connections between intellectual activity and other forms of social practice. In giving readers an account of how the "problem" of scale, whether explicitly called that or not, has shaped descriptive terminologies and research programs within cultural studies, this essay offers a set of touchstones for evaluating how politicized work in the academy might find ongoing value in thinking about its agendas in terms of scale.

According to the second edition of the *Oxford English Dictionary* (1989; all references hereafter refer to the unpaginated online version) the first uses of the noun *scale* as a methodological concept appear in early modern taxonomy. They derive from the word's third meaning, the Middle English word for *ladder*, which endures in its current usage as a verb meaning *to climb*. The word's musical application, first documented in the sixteenth century, derives from this usage. In the early seventeenth century, a burst of usages associated with hierarchies of knowledge, abstraction and representation emerge out of this root meaning. By the seventeenth century, scale became conceived as a material idea akin to climbing a ladder into a new kind of service: as a model for conceptually rendering orders of being. This posits *scale* as "a succession or series of steps or degrees; a graduated series, succession, or progression; *esp.* a graduated series of beings extending from the lowest forms of existence to the highest" (*OED*, 1989: def 5a). Its earliest illustration is from Francis Bacon's 1605 *Of the Advancement of Learning*: "the speculation ... That all things by scale did ascend to vnitie" (1605, quoted in *OED*, 1989). Here we have *scale* referring to the kind of metaphysical hierarchy, culminating in some kind of plenitudinous unity, which Foucault (1970) identified in the taxonomic procedures of early modern human sciences.

At around the same time, the word *scale* also begins to express quantified and exact relations of proportion. Usages dating back to 1607 define the term as referring to "relative or proportionate size or extent; degree, proportion" (*OED*, 1989: def. 12a). This definition, bringing the mathematical operations of the ratio into play, assigns an additional kind of systematicity to the idea of scale as hierarchical order. If Bacon's 1605 usage makes scale an expression of where things or

beings are located on some predetermined metaphysical ladder, bringing *proportion* into the picture makes it possible to do away with the
ladder entirely. Scale as proportion allows an observer to grasp something's significance simply by comparing it to other things, without
reference to external standards of judgment. This ratio-based sense of
scale expanded over the course of the seventeenth century to include
quantified relations between objects and their representations. This
development, which seems closely linked to the direction of political
thought in the seventeenth century, defines *scale* as "the proportion
which the representation of an object bears to the object itself" (*OED*,
1989: def. 11a). From this definition is derived the adjectival expression
*to scale*, referring to a rendering "with exactly proportional representation of each part of the model" (*OED*, 1989: def. 11a).

This definition of scale as proportional representation might be
thought of as a Big Moment, for it has clear implications for the production of knowledge, specifically, in relationship to the rise of empiri-
cism. In proportional representation, relations between the referent and
the sign are exact and quantified. The sign is a faithful reproduction of
some key aspects of the referent (its proportions) and thus may be
treated as identical to the referent in certain circumstances. This is the
principle of scale in cartography, and, indeed, all of the examples supplied with this definition are cartographic, starting with a 1662 reference to a map of London. Relations of scale, this definition proposes,
are relations that can be relied on because they are mathematically
derived, thus guaranteeing a stable relationship between the representation and the real. This stability provides a model for empirical knowledge, in that the possibility of finding a mechanism of translation, or
mapping, which connects material things and their representations in
a precise, repeatable, and empirically known relationship extends to the
process of representation in *thought*.

However, simultaneous usages of the concept of scale, extending
beyond the mathematic applications and into the subjective realm of
judgment and analysis, point to the methodological conundrum that
scale continues to introduce into the research process. Early modern
usages of scale as "a standard of measurement, calculation, or estima-
tion" (*OED*, 1989: def. 13) apply not only to physical appraisal but also
to the process of reasoning, specifically, to the conditions under which
reason can move from the particular to the universal. The *OED* offers
as an example of such usage a statement about methodology from
Bacon's 1626 *Sylva Sylvorum, or A Naturall Historie*: "Definite Axiomes

are to be drawn out of Measured Instances; And so Assent to be made to the more Generall Axiomes, by Scale" (cited in *OED*, 1989: def. 13). Here, the concept of scale helps stabilize a necessarily murky dichotomy: the relationship between physical observation and mental speculation in inductive reasoning. Bacon uses scale to explain how theoretical propositions are derived, showing them to be large-scale syntheses of smaller, discrete empirical phenomena. To earlier uses of *scale* as an expression of orders of hierarchy (the ladder) and relations of proportion (the map) this methodological proposition adds the far more complicated idea of scale as an expression of relations between physical specificity and theoretical generality, in other words, as degrees on a conceptual continuum spanning from materiality on one end to abstraction on the other. In constructing a thread between the two, *scale* regularizes the process of knowledge production by implying that there is a proportional relation between the datum, the definite axiom, and the general axiom.

With this final sense of scale as, in a sense, a conceptual pathway between the physical and the mental, early modern uses of the word solidify its current power as a methodological precept. Scale becomes a concept capable of managing dichotomies in multiple epistemological dimensions, disciplining the production of knowledge by regularizing procedures of physical measurement, quantified representation, qualitative evaluation ("order of being"), and intellectual abstraction. But this very elasticity is also a liability. Bacon's explanation of inductive method is interesting for the way it illustrates the *slipperiness* of scale as a technique of dichotomy management. In this statement, he manages to asserts the existence of universals (Generall Axiomes) while simultaneously acknowledging the necessity of convention and arbitrariness, if only rhetorically: it is the cultural, indeed electoral, process of "assent" that forges the metonymic connection between "Generall Axiomes" and "Definite" ones, and a metaphorically physical process ("drawing out") connects the latter to the measured, empirical world. Bacon's statement implies no definite break between the material world and consciousness, between particulars and universals, the concrete and the abstract. Although it might distinguish them from each other, it simultaneously offers the scale-based reasoning of induction as a thread of action and rhetoric actively connecting thought and thing, observation and speculation. This makes orders of scale seem fundamentally arguable, always open to judgment and dependent on relativism.

From this etymological excursion it should be clear that while decisions based on judgments of scale are clearly central to methodological
conventions in modern intellectual inquiry, these procedures seem
entangled and slippery when we consider them closely. The kinds of
relationships designated by *scale* go beyond the simple physical sense of
size. They straddle the qualitative/quantitative divide, enabling conceptual movement between argument and evidence, generality and specificity, concreteness and abstraction. It is because of this slipperiness that
orders of scale perform so many basic epistemological tasks within the
modern apparatuses of knowledge production within the academic
disciplines. Taken individually, the various methodological procedures
that organize research through scale are crucial for managing uncertainties about how to link conceptual and/or material objects that are of
different degrees of size and abstraction. Orders of scale establish standards and priorities in research. Conceptions of appropriate scale determine the limits of case studies. They carve up research agendas in space
and time, in relationship to geographical regions and temporal period-
ization. Less obviously, a sense of scale shapes relations between primary
and secondary materials – a relation which is not only temporal, as the
terms imply, but also a relationship between two conceptual scales: the
particular and the general. They establish fields and subfields of inquiry
(e.g. micro- and macroeconomics), and they help distinguish between
theory and method in empirical research. E.P. Thompson's words are
exemplary here: "methodology is [sometimes] used in place of theory.
[But] there is such a thing as methodology, which is the intermediate
level at which a theory is broken down into the appropriate methods
you are going to use ... to test that theory, and equally at which
empirical findings are brought up to modify the theory" (1984: 14).
Thompson's use of the term *level* to describe these forms of abstraction
and generalization indicates the persistence of Bacon's schema in locating theory in a conceptual relationship to observation and recording.
It implies that what might be called the "general axioms" of theory
are formed from what would correspondingly be the "specific axioms"
of method. It is a relationship in which method is at once the elemen-
tal "stuff" out of which theory is formed and, in its specificity, something fundamentally *other* to theory.

An order of scale also plays a key role in defining terms *within*
methodology; specifically, it manages the distinction between *method*
and *technique*. The latter term, two historians note, refers to the routine
processing of evidence (note-taking, counting, etc.), whereas *method*

defines the more general process of reflection upon conditions of knowledge production (Karsten and Modell, 1992: 1–2). Orders of scale are thus active in defining methodological problems within and across the disciplines. Historians, literary critics, sociologists, biologists, and economists must all endeavor to reconcile the different levels on which their research proceeds, balancing the scope of their conclusions with the size of their data, and articulating the kinds of knowledge that are enabled by the range of their research.

As this might suggest, orders of scale also provide the disciplines with a ready-made framework within which to launch a critique of particular research projects. Whenever a project's methodology deviates from conventional scales of analysis, it can be disciplined, corrected, and even discounted through appeals to the kinds of evidence that are produced on other scales of analysis. You can attend a panel of world system historians in the morning and chide them for the absence of "voices" in their accounts, and then criticize a panel of ethnomethod-ologists and microhistorians for disregarding the big picture in the afternoon. In each instance, what you are calling for is an impossible thing: a research stance that affords a total view, and which is able to move effortlessly between scales. You are asking, in other words, for a researcher who embodies the ideal liberal subject, capable of synthesiz-ing all forms of knowledge, and a research program capable of absorb-ing all epistemological perspectives (Tinkcom, 2002). Thus Peter Burke, questioning the value of microhistory's "human interest stories," calls for historians to "link the microsocial and the macrosocial, experiences with structures, face-to-face relationships with the social system or the local with the global. If this question is not taken seriously, microhis-tory might become a kind of escapism, an acceptance of a fragmented world view rather than an attempt to make sense of it" (Burke, 2001: 116–17). It should be noted that this desire for an impossible holism is not limited to the viewpoints of professional historians. In sociology, Randy Martin notes, the quest for totality is evident in the Parsonian legacy: "For the system-theoretic model, [the ethnomethodologists'] alternate sociologies were relegated to occupying the place of the micro in the very syntax they were meant to disturb" (2001: 65). Functional-ism, with its smoothly working scale models of the social world, thus serves as a kind of disciplinary superego, generating rote critiques that make it impossible for the "local" simply to *be* local – it has to be situated as typical, or not typical, of some kind of non-local, non-concrete phenomenon.

# Orders of Scale in Cultural Studies

Having laid out the origins of scale as a methodological concept and sketched some of its currently central functions in methodological thought and debates within the disciplines, I want to turn to what the concept means for cultural studies. But first this means asking what methodology might mean outside of a disciplinary context, within an intellectual movement responsive primarily to political conditions both within and outside the academy, and only secondarily to the protocols for the production of knowledge that are established within conventional fields of research. If the construction of a method, regardless of disciplinary status, is part of all research and, moreover, if all research necessarily involves selections and assessments based on orders of scale, then what guides these procedures within cultural studies? I will argue in this section, assuming the leftist agenda that has historically defined cultural studies as a movement, that these procedures are – indeed *should* be – guided by particular political considerations. And, moreover, I will suggest, the complexity of scale as a concept makes it a particularly rewarding way of defining methodological interventions in the disciplines from outside. The slippery relativism of orders of scale – always open to the possibility of adding one more degree of size or magnification, one more level of concreteness or abstraction, always producing continuities between things and ideas, between universals and the particulars that produce them – makes them highly heuristic thinking tools for cultural materialists.[1]

On a very general level, you can observe the consistence presence of a politics of scale in cultural studies' agenda-setting across the broadest of disciplinary breaks, disciplinary contexts, and "generational" arguments. A basic suspicion of generalized abstractions is one of the most obvious connections, although it is also an intellectual tendency that leads to the occasional conflation of cultural studies and postmodernism in North America. This suspicion is evident in one of Raymond Williams's most frequently cited dictums: pedagogically invaluable for media studies teachers, that "There are in fact no masses; there are only ways of seeing people as masses" (1958: 300). It is equally present in Marianne de Laet's assertion that the anthropology of science and technology shares with cultural studies a commitment to "tracing *how*, exactly, particulars become universals" (2001: 101). However, the politics of scale in cultural studies' methodological debates goes beyond antifoundationalism. In the realm of critique, a concern with the power relations of scale is evident both in those attacks on cultural studies projects from outside, and in those aimed at modifying them from the inside. In the latter camp, Austral and non-Western cultural studies scholars note that their work is governed by a "West and the rest" geopolitics. Thus, for example, doing cultural studies in Hong Kong means ignoring one's local audience in favor of an accrediting international and universalized English-language readership (Ma, 2001: 271). A similar orientation toward non-local readerships means that Australian cultural studies must engage generalized theoretical constructs like "'difference,' 'pleasure,' 'subversion,'" rather than studies of national media texts in order to avoid being "pushed for *methodological* reasons into the 'dead zone' of the *too* specific . . ." (Morris 1992: 457, original emphasis. See also Grossberg, 1997: 298). Meanwhile, Occidental critics charge that cultural studies celebrates the local, fetishizes the specific, and exaggerates the power of the individual at the expense of other, structural forces, like economic oppression (Garnham, 1995; Maxwell, 2001). The debate is endless; feminists (rightfully) rejoin with the provocation that perhaps masculinist visions of totality make critics unable to see the forms of noncapitalist activity that define people's everyday movements through capitalism (Gibson-Graham, 1996). For those who see the choice between political economy and cultural studies as an "either/or" one, the two movements are irrevocably divided by axiomatic differences in the scale on which they construct models of social change.

The various critiques of cultural studies as having an inappropriate sense of scale clue us into some differences between methodology within cultural studies and methodology in the disciplines. These differences are important: if Dennis Dworkin's excellent and appreciative history of British cultural studies must repeatedly offer a cautionary criticism of various researchers' apparent refusal, or inability, to generalize, then clearly some things need to be set straight (1997: 84–5, 162, 189). One way to think about the difference is to say that, within disciplines, methodology is formed not only to govern and reflect upon the production of knowledge, but also to police entry and enforce sometimes reactionary notions of "standards" in the service of "pure" knowledge production (Miller, 2001). The "threat" of cultural studies is its disrespect for disciplinary orthodoxy. Not being a discipline, cultural studies does not have the same kinds of standards to police (which is not the same thing as saying that it is incapable of surveillant or disciplinary acts). But if it aims at producing provisional, rather than eternal knowledge (Nelson et al., 1992: 6) this does not mean that cultural studies has no method, as is sometimes claimed (ibid.: 2). Indeed, its practitioners have regularly engaged in debates over particular methods, for example, the value of "cultural critique" versus "cultural policy." Indeed, it has seemed at times that debates leading to programmatic statements about the direction of the field have been the most visible work in cultural studies. Clearly, cultural studies has a long history of methodological thought. But what distinguishes its methodological reflection from more disciplinary ones?

The difference becomes evident when we contrast a disciplinary approach to orders of scale, such as Burke's previously cited critique of microhistory as merely "human interest stories," with one delineated in cultural studies. A good example of the latter is the explicit discussion of methodology and scale in Stuart Hall's famous "Two Paradigms" essay (1980). The essay intervenes in the argument between the empiricist, micro-oriented, resistance-minded "culturalists" (e.g. Thompson and Williams) and the "structuralists" (theoretical, anti-empiricist, Althusserian) that took place in the 1970s. These arguments are largely about scale and determination in Marxist models of culture, binarized as a choice between commitments: to theory and to structural explanation on the one hand, to empirical research and careful analysis of practices on the other. For Hall, this is a false dichotomy. Cultural studies' mission is not to choose one or the other, but rather to follow a Gramscian path and attempt "to think *both* the specificity of different practices and the forms of the articulated unity they constitute" (Hall, 1980: 72). Now it might seem that here Hall constructs a methodological model, based on the synthesis of different scales, structurally comparable to the liberal subject's totalizing viewpoint articulated by Burke. But whereas Burke assumes the existence of the "macro" as an actual, material level of the social, Hall's model characterizes the macro-level – the totality – not as a material entity, but as a form of abstraction.

Hall bases this model on Marx's dialectical method in *Capital*, articulated in a quote, apparently from the *Grundrisse*: "In the analysis of economic forms, neither microscopes nor chemical reagents are of assistance. The power of abstraction must replace both" (67–8). In his exegesis of Marx's method, Hall introduces two metaphors for the viewpoint of the cultural studies researcher: the microscope and, more implicitly, the map. Note that in the quotation above, Marx invokes the microscope's material process of visual scale manipulation in *opposition* to the mental process of abstraction. Hall's analysis, however, twists this opposition into an analogy. Marx's method, he notes,

> rests not on the simple exercise of abstraction but on the movement and relations which the argument is constantly establishing between *different levels* of abstraction: at each, the premises in play must be distinguished from those which – for the sake of argument – have to be held constant. The movement to another level of magnification (to deploy the microscope metaphor) requires the specifying of further conditions of existence not supplied at a previous, more abstract level: in this way, by successive abstractions of different magnitudes, to *move towards* the constitution, the *reproduction* of "the concrete in thought." (68, emphasis in original)

Whereas Marx referred to the empirical process of observation associated with microscopy as an illustration of what the process of dialectical abstraction is *not*, Hall transforms the optical process of moving between different levels of magnification into an analogy *for* the dialectical method.

Hall compounds the metaphorical reversal by invoking a different sense of scale immediately after citing Marx's microscope. This is his restatement of the goal of the dialectical method as the "reproduction of the concrete in thought." This phrase compares dialectical analysis not to shifts in perspective achieved through optics, but rather to the process of representation or creative activity, via the notion of "reproduction." Hall's proposal for a unified cultural studies is based on relationships of scale insofar as its invocation of the concrete implies that the final product of the dialectical method is something like the perfect – and impossible – map, a map which aims at the reproduction of a terrain at a scale of 1:1. Hall thus explains the simultaneous necessity and contingency of abstraction by comparing it on the one hand to the idea of optical scale, shifted by lenses placed between subject and object, and on the other hand to the idea of representational scale, the proportional reproduction of an object.

What's important here is the way Hall's twist on Marx's microscope makes abstraction a material process of scale manipulation on a par with optics and proportional representation. His inversion of Marx's metaphor might therefore be thought of not simply as an attempt to render a difficult concept easier to grasp, but also as an attempt to synthesize another key insight from the *Grundrisse*, namely, Marx's radically relativizing assertion that *abstraction is always a material production*: "[E]ven the most abstract categories, despite their validity – precisely because of their abstractness – for all epochs, are nevertheless, in the specific character of the abstractions, themselves likewise a product of historic relations, and possess their full validity only for and within these relations" (1973: 105). In other words, nothing is transcendent for all time. Abstractions (and, by extension, expressions of concreteness) are historically rooted and thus variable from epoch to epoch.

Together with the material processes invoked in the metaphors of microscope and 1:1 map, as ways of manipulating the concrete through abstraction, this radically relativizing and historically contingent understanding of what stands as "generality" – indeed, as *theory* – signals the difference between cultural studies' methodological commitment to moving between macroanalytic and microanalytic scales and the meaning of this analytical movement in the disciplines (a meaning I am admittedly singularizing by using Burke as its straw man). In the latter, scale shifting is understood as the reconciliation of different, but equally stable and consistent levels of empirically derived knowledge about the social. It is the correct procedural technique for the production of the researcher as knowing liberal subject. In this context, it is hardly coincidental that particularly influential micro-methodological interventions in the disciplines, like Carlo Ginzburg's *The Cheese and the Worms* (1980), take as their subject matter the historical conditions under which particular, subjective models of abstraction (i.e. Menocchio's cosmology) are formed (on this point cf. Foucault, 1970). In cultural studies at the moment Hall is describing it, scale shifting is understood not as a movement toward greater positivist knowledge but rather as an acknowledgment of the limits of all knowledge claims, their grounding in particular material circumstances, mediating technologies, and metaphors. Moving between levels of abstraction is a way of relativizing knowledges, revealing their origins in particular material conditions, not of striving toward all knowingness.

This might sound like a reduction of cultural studies to antifoundationalism or postmodernism, but there are important differences. What Hall is attempting to articulate for cultural studies is a politicized understanding of social totality on which to base a research methodology. He therefore refuses a Foucauldian model of concreteness for cultural studies on the basis of a commonly held assessment of Foucault's epistemological position: "Foucault so resolutely suspends judgment, and adopts so thoroughgoing a skepticism about any determinacy or relationship between practices, other than the largely contingent, that we are entitled to see him ... as deeply committed to the necessary non-correspondence of all practices to one another. From such a position neither a social formation, nor the state, can be adequately thought" (71). As this last sentence might suggest, Hall's commitment to the development of "a properly materialist theory of culture" lies in the need to understand culture in terms that might expand forms of social praxis. He opposes this to Foucault's project, although the recent applications of Foucault's later work on govern-mentality – a literature I will address presently in relationship to the cultural policy "push" in cultural studies – points to an area of significant overlap. Indeed, it is interesting to note that both Hall and Foucault were grappling with neoliberalism's ascendancy at the same moment in the late 1970s.

Cultural studies' broader commitment to political practice is evident in its commonplace characterization as an antidisciplinary formation, guided by progressive left politics rather than knowledge production. The methodological implications of this point are elaborated in Jennifer Darryl Slack's proposition that "the commitment is always to be able to adapt our methods as the new historical realities we engage keep also moving down the road" (Slack, 1996: 114). Method, this suggests, might better be thought of in terms of knowledge and theory production oriented toward a debate, or consensus, about what the left needs to know about culture at a particular moment; it is a particular way of relating theory to praxis. A well-known passage from Engels describes praxis as the goal of theory because, after all, "the proof of the pudding is in the eating"; moments of methodological reflection might therefore best be understood as ways of devising recipes for the pudding of praxis, however it is defined at the time. This "peculiar condition" has led to the characterization of cultural studies' method as a changing *bricolage* of self-reflexive techniques. Indeed, Lawrence Grossberg suggests that cultural studies "has to be made up as it goes along. Thus cultural studies always reflects on and situates itself and its claims, limits its field, acknowledges its incompleteness" (1997: 285. See also Willis, 1980: 95).

This is a useful definition of cultural studies' methodological impro-visation, but there is a certain idealism in the image of "making it up as we go along." This image can only stand for methodology in a very abstract, un-institutional sense, projected outside of the messy, fraught context of professional norms and power relations in higher education. The key word in Stuart Hall's proposition that cultural studies took shape in Birmingham as an institutional practice "that might produce an organic intellectual" (1992: 281) is surely *produce,* as it calls attention to the material conditions of academic work, conditions which, as Grossberg notes elsewhere in a discussion of the Americanization of cultural studies, bring cultural studies into alignment with complex problems of professionalization, academic class politics, and disciplinary "turf" (1997: 297–8). Thus, although the improvisatory model may accurately describe the ideal conditions of research in cultural studies, namely its responsiveness to political questions of the moment, any attempt to account for shifts in the methodological horizons of cultural studies must emphasize not only how such shifts have emerged from particular historical and political circumstances (e.g. Thatcherism), but also how they have followed a logic of autocritique within the movement and in some kind of interaction with the disciplines.[2] Although the process of recognizing, querying, and building on an intellectual history and an institutional trajectory may not be as coherent, evolutionary, or authorized as it seems to be within disciplines, it is nevertheless part of the movement of cultural studies. Methodological shifts in cultural studies, at least those oriented around problems of scale, can definitely be tracked as responses to existing research agendas, and ongoing systems for valuing and accrediting the work of professional academics.[3]

With this in mind, the next section of this essay traces some of the ways cultural studies has sought to politicize academic knowledge, and frame politics outside the academy, by scrutinizing the power relations encoded in conventional orders of scale within which this knowledge is produced. The threatening unmanageability of scale as a concept means that I will only address one thread of its emergence in cultural studies: the formation of, and crisis in, "ordinariness" as a research topic. The crisis must be seen as continuous with the political commitments of postwar British intellectuals that led to the emergence of the ordinary in the first place, interests which shifted the focus of discussions of culture from the idea of a pure and abstract good to the concrete and material frame surrounding such abstractions. "Ordinariness," like Marx's abstraction, is historically specific; what gets counted as ordinary can shift radically over time. As Charlotte Brunsdon notes, reflecting on the legacy of the work in television studies conducted at Birmingham in the 1970s, "ordinariness has unquestionably changed" (2001: 57). However, as I will suggest, even though what counts as "ordinary," and "concrete" or as "exceptional" and "abstract" is different in each case, one can nevertheless discern an ever-increasing insistence on the inescapably material conditions of knowledge production in the discussions that constitute cultural studies across a range of arenas.

## Ordinariness in British Cultural Studies

"Ordinariness" is arguably the first attempt of cultural studies to manipulate disciplinary assumptions of scale in order to call attention to particular political goals. In their writings in the 1950s and 1960s, Richard Hoggart, E.P. Thompson, Williams, and other New Left cultural critics, historians, and sociologists fashioned ordinariness into a deliberately small-scaled conceptual object that was not only to be studied but also lobbed over the walls of the disciplines and institutions of higher learning. *Ordinariness* is an abstract noun, but what it designated in the early days of cultural studies was, in some ways, the embodiment of concreteness: the sediment of practices that make up everyday life on the small scale of lived experience. However, ordinariness is also incredibly large scale. As a concept, its place within a managed dichotomy is marked out in opposition to the extraordinary, the remarkable, the special, the valuable; if the latter are scarce, rare, and "out of the ordinary" phenomena, then the ordinary is a resource in abundant supply. But, paradoxically, it is so immediate and ubiquitous that it is also invisible, ineffable, ephemeral. As a concept, *ordinariness* thus served a political purpose within academic research programs by disrupting conventional assumptions about scale and value, generality and importance. The paradoxical orders of scale contained and defined within the concept of the ordinary were, for the postwar British intellectual left, endemic to the material analysis of culture. As Williams wrote, in *Culture and Society*, "the difficulty about the idea of culture is that we are continually forced to extend it, until it becomes almost identical with our whole common life" (1958: 256).

In some respects, analyzing ordinariness might seem comparable to analyzing "the everyday;" as Luce Giard notes in relation to the latter, it "is doomed to an incessant coming and going from the theoretical to the concrete and then from the particular and circumstantial to the general" (1998: xxiii). However, there is a crucial difference between the French legacy of the everyday and ordinariness in early British cultural studies. In the latter, the commitment to the concrete experience of the ordinary erupts from working-class politics and demands for the redistribution of cultural capital in higher education, whereas the French Situationist everyday and its afterlives expresses more diffuse political commitments, arguably more bourgeois, undoubtedly more *avant-gardist*. Ordinariness in early British cultural studies reflects a desire to speak about working people's lives, necessarily lived in local contexts, and the ways in which individual biographies add up to class trajectories, helped or hindered by particular institutions for the dissemination and consumption of culture. This desire becomes immediately clear to anyone who pages through volumes of *Universities and Left Review* from the 1950s. One encounters a striking array of articles, documentary photo-essays, and film and television reviews oriented around questions of changes in the institutions and experiences of everyday working-class life in postwar Britain. This interest reflects political and intellectual questions being asked on the left in this period, as a response to social conditions within and outside of the academy, among them apparent forms of class mobility opened up by consumption, shakeups in international socialism, and the intellectual maturation of a new generation of working-class scholars (on these factors, see Dworkin, 1997: 1–124). From within the latter group, both Williams's pronouncement that "culture is ordinary" and Hoggart's 1957 *Uses of Literacy*, described by Hartley (1999: 16) as a founding text in a "semio-history of ordinariness," helped define the methodological "lowering" of sights from "high" to "ordinary culture" as a political gesture. According to Frank Webster, Hoggart's microscopic attention to detail and cadence distinguished the *Uses of Literacy* from sociological studies of working-class life: "you can hear the voices of flesh and blood people and feel their presence, you can *be there* in a way in which most Sociology sadly misses" (2001: 81, emphasis in original).

In the work of Hoggart, in particular, we can see a complex mediation between orders of scale, from micro to macro, to produce a concrete sense of working-class people's culture and their resources for survival. Like Ginsburg, Hoggart addresses issues of scale not only in his methodological framing but also in his subject matter, showing how the "macro" space of the nation is inaccessible to the working people of the North (a tactic Marx used to great effect in Chapter Ten of *Capital*, vol. 1). As Gibson and McHoul note, Hoggart's method was highly interdisciplinary. He essentially invented the "*bricolage*" method of cultural studies, combining "literary studies, sociology, and auto-biography;" to replace "big literary history" with "the detail of the little histories of ordinary life" (2001: 25, 23. See also Dworkin, 1997: 85). This mixture was not merely a set of choices made in the interests of rhetorical effect. It also reflected the institutional arrangements circum-scribing the position from which he spoke – that of the scholarship boy, whose curious insider/outsider perspective made him a figure who could be taken "as standing for nascent cultural studies itself" (24–5). But Hoggart's mediated perspective does more than make possible a mobile narrative technique, moving easily from one scale of analysis to another to produce both textured renderings and distanced judgments. It also leads him into a discussion of orders of scale as expressions of material power. In a section of *The Uses of Literacy* (19) entitled "the personal and the concrete" he notes that working-class conceptions of "us" and "them" are founded in a lack of access to non-local scales of social experience: "The question of how we face 'them' (whoever 'They' are) is, at last, the question of how we stand in relation to any-thing not visibly and intimately part of our local universe" (72). For Hoggart, the worldview of his working-class neighborhood was prem-ised on the impossibility of abstractions and translations in scale, such as "the needs of the state" or "good citizenship" (73). It took his own mobility through the British education system, and the class injuries incurred along the way, to gain a more "aerial" perspective, a perspec-tive which included an awareness of the class-delineated horizons of abstraction, knowledge, and macro-level access within which bourgeois models of political life are formed. Hoggart's technique, incorporating his own travel between scales, thus embodies the kind of abstraction Hall identified, via the metaphor of the microscope and the 1:1 map, as cultural studies' dialectical mandate: reproducing the concrete in thought.

However, over the course of the next few decades, critiques within cultural studies as a movement would begin to question the politics of knowledge, the models of the social, and the assumptions about uni-versal subjectivity that came to be encoded in the concept of ordinari-ness as advanced by Hoggart and others. Originally serving as a heuristic tool within higher education, forcing debate around hier-archies of culture, and calling attention to the ordinary people affected by these hierarchies, the ordinary itself became a problem, constructing hierarchical scales of its own. As cultural studies developed and insti-tutionalized at Birmingham in the 1960s and 1970s, figures other than the scholarship boy came to stand for cultural studies, and wreak havoc with the "ordinary" on which its theories of culture rested. In the process, more diversified scales of analysis entered the cultural studies repertoire of methodologies, as expressed both in research projects at the Centre for Contemporary Cultural Studies (CCCS) and in its theory seminars.

Perhaps the first challenge to the ordinary came in the highly visible form of the youth cultures emerging in the 1960s and 1970s, cultures which, in their disaffection, marginality, and extraordinary forms of display fashioned in kinship and conflict with Black British style, placed pressure on self-evident, homogenous connections between working-class culture and ordinariness. In the encounters between intellectuals and youth taking place in this period, new research models were formed. A renewed understanding of power relations and judgments of scale played an important role in their development. Youth cultures brought spectacular visibility and new forms of social collectivity onto the research agenda, raising new questions about the direction of working-class and national culture in Britain. In 1959, writing in the last issue of *ULR*, Hall proposed that "The revolt and iconoclasm of youth today arises because of the contradictions between the true and the false elements in their culture: because the wave of post-war prosperity has raised them to cultural thresholds which offer rewards unequal to the expectations aroused" (quoted in Hartley, 1992: 6). Youth culture, in this formulation, was one of many symptoms of working-class disappointment in the postwar promise of opportunity. To grasp these changes, researchers drew on small-scale research tech-niques, like ethnography and participant observation, to supplement the more formal interviewing techniques which had characterized earlier sociological experiments, like the *ULR* reports on life in "New Towns." These techniques kept the researcher on the same scale as his or her informants, so that no total "aerial" vision of cultural traditions could be gleaned. Thus, what *Resistance Through Ritual* (Hall and Jefferson, 1976) and *Subcultures* (Hebdige, 1979) produced was not a holistic vision of culture composed of layers of infinitesimal ordinariness, but a rather more complexly scaled vision of generational conflict, racial heterogeneity, and modes of cultural consumption within the homo-genous designation of class. Ordinariness became a parental ideology, a tradition in crisis.

However, it would take interventions by feminists and scholars working on issues of race and ethnicity in British culture to fully demolish the rule of ordinariness, revealing the assumptions upon which it was based (Hall, 1992; see Brunsdon, 1996, on the problematic assumptions underlying narratives of the history of CCCS as a series of "interruptions" by feminism and black activism). Certain kinds of people's lives and cultural activities were coming to represent the ordinary at the expense of others, specifically women's activities. These ordinaries, it seemed, were simply *too* ordinary to capture the attention of researchers. Following feminist interventions in the Centre's research agendas, the "housewife" became the site of the thickly described, participatorily observed forms of ordinary culture with which cultural studies research was concerned. (On this figure, see Brunsdon, 1999. See also Dworkin, 1997: 176–80.) Around the same time, normative subjects and universals took on a different challenge, as scholarship on race and ethnicity within British cultural studies threw the entire centrality of the ordinary as an object of study into question. Ordinariness came dangerously close to the concept of Englishness, a form of exclusion emerging from historical conditions of empire and immigration. For some Britons, ordinariness was never an option. This scholarship reframed concerns with specificity and concreteness away from the routines of the ordinary and toward the ongoing crisis of race relations in Britain, a crisis formed at the end of the decade in the concurrence of Thatcher's victory and a series of incidents of uprising and racial violence (Dworkin, 1997: 180). In this climate of what Hall would later call "authoritarian populism," designations of ordinariness, of Englishness, of "we" became problematic concepts. They were revealed as ongoing expressions of power, marking some experiences as universal and others as specific and partial.

According to Hall (1992: 283), these interventions, and the "linguistic turn" prompted by continental theory, shaped the direction of methodological discussions at the CCCS under the direction of Richard Johnson in the second half of the 1970s. The (implicitly white, male) focus on the "ordinary" understood as the working-class culture gave way to complex, highly theoretical models of power and oppression, including racism and sexism, in which class struggle was only one of several factors. In methodological terms, this had several consequences. First, it brought other theoretical figures, like Fanon, into the pantheon of cultural studies (Stam, 2001). Secondly, it brought non-popular media forms into the conceptual orbit of cultural studies, specifically, the experimental film essays of the Black film collectives (Pines, 1996). And thirdly, by insisting on the historical specificity of race, "in order to see how it articulates – or not – with other social relations" (Solomos et al., 1982, quoted in Dworkin, 1997) scholarship on race and ethnicity made it impossible for models of culture to be structured according to simple hierarchies of significance, anchored in an economic "last instance." This insistence on *specificity* disrupted any easy identitarian equivalencies that might be made under terms like "women's history" (Carby, 1982/1996). Much as ordinariness had revealed the value systems of traditional approaches to culture in higher education a few decades earlier, these interventions on the level of race and gender exposed ordinariness as a concept that naturalized certain hierarchies of scale, rendering one kind of experience general, primary, and national and marginalizing others to the zone of the contingent and the specific in the process. Once a way of communicating materiality, ordinariness now worked to efface it.

## Post-ordinary Cultural Studies: Articulation and Policy

What replaced ordinariness in British (or Anglophone) cultural studies? If the term represented a methodological insistence that the act of calling something or someone "ordinary" was a judgment of scale inseparable from social structures of class (or race and gender), the subsequent research agendas of cultural studies shifted the question of the politics of scale away from the ordinary and toward the more abstract concept of concreteness (this shift is embodied in the summary turn of Stuart Hall's 1980 "Two Paradigms" article). In the 1970s, an engagement with Gramscian theory and Althusserian structuralism led many on the culturalist side to articulate their sense of the politics of research in less historical, and more theoretical terms. However, questions of scale, in different ways, remained central to the research agendas that developed from this shift. Emblematic of the change is Raymond Williams's work following the "linguistic turn," in which the structural place occupied by ordinariness is now claimed by a theoretically-informed notion of *materiality*. Guided by a continued suspicion of abstractions, Williams's exemplary and influential discussion of base/superstructure models in *Marxism and Literature* (1977) offers a thoroughgoing critique of dichotomous theories based on a bourgeois distinction between the material and the immaterial. Williams found Gramsci's concept of hegemony vital as a way of thinking about how material life – institutions and practices of culture – served as an arena for domination and subordination (111). While acknowledging the contributions of Althusserian structuralism to marxist cultural theory, particularly the role of ideology in the reproduction of relations of production, Williams refused to see the base/superstructure relationship in Althusserian terms, that is, as an opposition between the material world and the world of ideas oriented toward the perpetuation of the relations of material production (93). Rather, everything is material; it is the designation of certain phenomena as non-material that is the characteristic ideological move of bourgeois philosophy. In an essay on the sociology of culture, Williams similarly criticized the "bourgeois concept of 'mass communication' and the tied radical concept of 'mass manipulation'" as "inadequate to the true sociology of these central and varying institutions" (136). Instead of the study of the diffuse psychological phenomenon of media effects, he advocated the study of "the complex sociology of [media] producers, as managers and agents within capitalist systems" (137). This emphasis on materiality maintained the focus on people that had initially brought ordinariness into the spotlight as a research topic. But now, following the "linguistic turn" in cultural studies, the people whose activities together comprise the institutions where culture is *produced*, rather than those who consume culture, defined Williams's sense of cultural materialism.

This turn toward cultural production anticipated the ideas about the politics of scale emerging in cultural studies' research agendas in this period, ideas that would implicitly reevaluate and reinterpret existing notions of the concrete, the ordinary, and the material in the movement. The two that I will examine here seem at first to be radically opposed to each other in their understanding of intellectual activism. One, the concept of articulation, extended cultural studies in a theoretical direction, whereas the other, cultural policy advocacy, eschewed theory in favor of administrative action. Both, however, sought to untangle the political meanings of *concreteness*. In reckoning with scale as an expression of degrees of materiality, these new directions in cultural studies may have challenged the underlying assumptions of ordinariness as a primary subject matter but they nevertheless maintained contact with the theoretical interventions previously done in its name. Like the small-scale, micro-level processes designated by the concepts of the ordinary and the popular, both the identity formations described by articulation theory and the practical, managerial work of cultural policy making sought to uncover the material origins of the abstractions generated by the idea of culture at a particular moment. In tracing the political meanings of methodology in both articulation and policy as materially oriented projects, this essay moves toward its concluding speculations on the ways that an awareness of the politics of scale might continue to serve as a valuable tool for intellectual activism whether or not it is carried out under the banner of cultural studies.

The theory of articulation inaugurated a methodological shift in cultural studies − from ordinariness to crisis, from class to multiple structures of difference. How might the social experiences and structuration of race and/or gender, and/or sexuality at a particular historical moment mediate and even determine political economy, researchers asked − acknowledging as much as possible the mutability of such categories as they emerged as forms of social knowledge. The theory of articulation was the solution. According to Jennifer Darryl Slack, articulation emerged as a model through which researchers in cultural studies might maintain a materialist perspective on culture for as long as possible, resisting overly reductive abstractions associated with existing Marxist concepts of culture and determination (Slack, 1996: 116). As Slack's genealogy of the term points out, *articulation* often served as a kind of placeholder for a non-reductive position in late 1970s and early 1980s British marxist discussions about culture, signifying the possibility of "theorizing the elements of a social formation and the relations that constitute it not simply as relations of correspondence . . . but also as relations of non-correspondence and contradiction . . ." (117). Issues of scale were implicit in all of these discussions, oriented as they often were around the Althusserian concept of "a complex totality structured in dominance . . . made up of a relationship among levels" (ibid.). These discussions borrowed from Marx the idea that such relationships were not predestined by the mode of production but rather "produced within specific conjunctures [which] come to be seen as historically specific articulations of concrete social forces" (117). Hall, drawing on Ernesto Laclau and Antonio Gramsci, brought the model of articulation into cultural studies where he proposed it be understood as a particular kind of concrete process: "An articulation is thus the form of the connection that *can* make a unity of two different elements, under certain conditions. It is a linkage which is not necessary, determined, or absolute for all time. You have to ask, under what circumstances *can* a connection be made?" (1986 interview with Grossberg published in Morley and Chen, 1996: 141).

For Hall, there were tangible stakes in his proposal of articulation as a methodological assumption for work in cultural studies. It was a concept that could disarm overly hierarchical models of power, not only those which placed relations of production at the prioritized top (or controlling bottom) of the scale, both as abstract structures operating on material life, if only at "the last instance," but also those which had placed a particular kind of (white, male) ordinariness at the vanguard of political change in cultural studies. In 1980, outlining the methodological principles ("theoretical protocols") that could be derived from the concept and which "must govern any ... proposed investigation" into the pressing phenomenon of racism under Thatcher, Hall prioritized "the premise of historical specificity" in which "racism is not dealt with as a general feature of human societies, but with historically specific racisms" (1980/1996: 50). Racism, in short, is an articulated structure in that it cannot be explained "in abstraction from other social relations" (51). Articulation thus set a methodological agenda for cultural studies in that it required, Hall noted, that research start "from the concrete historical 'work' which racism accomplishes under specific historical conditions – as a set of economic, political, and ideological practices, of a distinctive kind, concretely articulated with other practices in a social formation" (52).

The concept of articulation thus promised to re-order the orders of scale that had remained implicit in cultural studies' suspicion of universals, by making the temporally scaled down limits of "specific historical conditions" more central. And in its recognition of multiple intersecting practices, articulation seemed capable of transforming the materialist approach to culture into a flexible and historically responsive, and complexly scaled, theory of power. In the insistence on (*pace* Althusser) no necessary correspondence between "levels" of social life, and in the refusal to name stable causes and ultimate determinants *a priori*, the theory of articulation replaced both "vulgar" and "structuralist" Marxist explanatory paradigms with a Gramscian insistence on the concrete. As Hall notes, "Gramsci's work often appears almost *too* concrete; too historically specific, too delimited in its references, too 'descriptively analytic,' too time and context-bound" (1986/1996: 413). For Hall, the (Althusserian) critique of Gramsci as "untheorized" errs in mistaking the nature of Gramsci's debt to Marx. For while he certainly worked with key marxist concepts (mode of production, forces and relations of production), he recognized them as abstractions. "Gramsci understood that as soon as these concepts have to be applied to specific historical social formations ... the theorist is required to move from the level of 'mode of production' to a lower, more concrete, level of application" (414). Concreteness, in short, restored the historical materialism to Marx's method and, via the concept of articulation, made it possible to take specific forms of power like racism into account in any analysis of capitalism, and vice versa.

As Nick Couldry points out in relation to "connectionism," articulation's legacy in cyberculture studies, insisting on infinite forms of determination has limited use as a methodology, as it blocks attempts at "thinking concretely about what the complexity of culture might mean and how to investigate it" (Couldry, 2000: 94). And indeed, although the term *articulation* has become a crucial element of the vocabulary of cultural studies, it is by no means clear that anyone doing research on culture in the 1980s ever knew exactly how to translate it into a method, or a set of techniques. It is telling, indeed, that Slack's essay on "the theory and method of articulation" illustrates the concept's promise as a method by tracing how it might alter practices of theorizing communication (123–7). Janice Radway suggests that articulation might serve as the basis of a "reworked" ethnography, one that takes as its object not texts and their relations to readers, as her influential *Reading the Romance* did, but rather "the fluid process of articulation ... the process whereby the historical human subject is constructed through the linkage, clash, and confluence of many different discourses, practices, and activities. Such an ethnography would have to begin with the everyday, not with texts" (1996: 245). This proposal reinstates the ordinary in its return to the small scale of the everyday. However, it does not get at the more complexly scaled elements of articulation foregrounded by Hall, namely, the ways in which conjunctures are formed between different "levels" of social life.

This suggests that, rather than focus solely on one scale of existence, the individual, or the social group, or the practice of consumption, a methodology based on articulation would need a more mobile relationship to modes of abstraction and concreteness. But this recognition does not move the methodology much further toward a set of techniques. In a critique of the concept of articulation as a model for the political methodology of cultural studies, Tony Bennett (1996: 83) argues that the very "fluidity" of the process makes the praxis of cultural studies lean heavily toward discursive registers. This, he notes, is a big problem with the Gramscian tradition in cultural studies. Against the latter, which, in a somewhat idiosyncratic reading, he sees as locating its model of non-deterministic social relations in processes of representation, Bennett proposed a Foucauldian model, emphasizing the contingency of the social in material rather than discursive terms. This model, for Bennett, would better encourage "us to focus on the detailed routines and operating procedures of cultural institutions . . . the business which culture is caught up in, looked at in these terms, goes beyond the influence of representations on forms of consciousness to include the influence of institutional practices, administrative routines and spatial arrangements on the available repertoires of human conduct and patterns of social interaction" (82). This proposal hearkened back to Williams's call for a sociology of culture; it took one step further in assigning a more active sense of praxis to the researcher, one that moved him or her beyond the world of representations and into the world of institutions.

Bennett's proposed application of Foucault as a model of praxis, offered in response to the discursivity of articulation theory, was part of a broader push toward cultural policy, as a way of rethinking political praxis in cultural studies (Bennett, 1998: 7; O'Regan, 1993; Cunningham, 1992). Like articulation theory, it emerged in dialog with state and governmental power structures in a particular national context. But whereas the former responded to the political problem of Thatcherism, cultural policy emerged from a politically progressive national context, specifically, the governmental initiatives in culture associated with the uninterrupted rule of the Labor Party in Australia from 1983 to 1996. The arguments for cultural policy advocacy as the proper work of cultural studies reunited the concrete and the ordinary, but not as a return to the originary white working-class ordinary. Using Foucault's later work (1979/2001) on governmentality as a model, Bennett, Ian Hunter, and others shifted the locus of ordinariness from the object of cultural studies research to the identity of the researcher. It was no longer radical to study the ordinary and the insignificant, bringing popular culture in all its microbial forms into the academy. Rather, the policy advocates suggested, the radical gesture was to *be* ordinary and insignificant, assuming the modest, practical guise of the government worker (Bennett, 1992, quoted in O'Regan, 1993: 195). The movement's political potential, they suggested, lay not in terms of its ability to produce cultural critique, even if it did so in the service of ordinary, small-scale forms of everyday culture, but rather in its ability to *be* ordinary, instrumental, "hooked in" with institutions rather than disdainfully condemning them and their managerial populations from an illusory position of transcendence. Cultural studies practitioners were the ones who needed to become ordinary, as ordinary as the material, organizational social networks in which culture is produced, regulated, disseminated, and reformed. The bureaucrat, Morris (1992: 466) notes, became cultural studies' ideal figure.

This cultural policy "push" in Australian scholarship was a materialist intervention in that it sought to ground the history of the study of culture in modes of governance. The progressive political value of such a move, according to Ian Hunter, was that it broke with what he saw as the romantic, aesthetic approach to culture, implicitly predicated on a separation of intellectuals from the object of study, whether in the service of contemplative disinterest or dialectical withdrawal: "the imperative to abstain from direct political activity until the reconciliatory moment of the dialectic brings the time to ripeness." Using work by Terry Eagleton as an example, Hunter (1992: 355) suggests that "the notion that the work of art cannot be known directly and definitively finds its correlate in the idea that society cannot be immediately subjected to administrative reason and intervention." In arguing that cultural studies' methods needed to mirror the concrete and pragmatic work of the cultural technician, Hunter and others invoked a politics of scale as they sought to redirect the movement away from "ethical grandiloquence, in which massive, world-historical problems are debated on such a level of generality that they cannot possibly be solved, and posed in ways which do not, will not, and cannot ever connect to agencies by which actual social futures may be given a 'definite shape'" (Morris, ibid.). In other words, the policy advocates inverted the sense of scale on which understandings of politics and methodology were predicated. Becoming banal, in short, was a way to avoid the "banality of cultural studies" that Morris, in an oft-cited zinger, defined as the endless repetition of statements about culture as "complex and contradictory" (Morris, 1990: 24).

As O'Regan notes, the acrimonious, either/or tenor of the policy intervention in cultural studies methods was to a large degree a reflection of institutional circumstances in higher education at that moment in Australia, "where the injunction to be socially relevant has been given a significant, alternative, and much more specific ... definition" by virtue of an increasing movement toward economic rationalization in the formation of cultural policy (197). O'Regan himself ultimately refused to accept the either/or terms wholeheartedly, proposing instead "an alternative view of policy," or a Latourian tone in which policy is understood as "information handling" (199). Rather than merely reversing the positions occupied by cultural critique and cultural policy on the hierarchical scale of political relevance, and determinism, as Bennett and others had sought to do, O'Regan rejected this order of scale altogether, noting

> I don't think policy ... is the structural engine room which powers everything else. Policy is a particular kind of informational practice with its own limitations, potentialities, and linkages to other kinds of public discourse, including cultural criticism and journalism, over which it holds no necessary pre-eminence. (ibid.)

In this move, O'Regan proposed an even more radical understanding of policy as ordinary, and of the politics underlying methodological choices as contingent upon concrete circumstances: "there are no *a priori* principles for choosing policy over cultural criticism. Nor can any presumption be made about social utility and effectiveness as necessarily belonging to one or the other" (201). In this call for a pragmatic sense of cultural studies as a field of social actions, O'Regan radically relativizes the scale of cultural studies, seeing it as one among many forms of knowledge work carried out on the small-scale world of governmental institutions. O'Regan's call for a pragmatic and flexible, rather than doctrinaire, understanding of cultural policy work is an important move, as it initiates a convergence between the theory of articulation as a social process and the practice of cultural policy work. Both refuse the "macro" perspective and insist that intellectual practices "articulate" with other practices in a broader cultural plane. Toby Miller, translating this mandate into a blueprint for approaching particular cultural texts, characterizes this method as the analysis of cultural citizenship produced "where the popular and the civic brush up against one another" (1998: 4). In such formulations, a sense of the importance of specific moments of articulation in defining the project of cultural studies as a form of civic practice returns.

In conclusion, I want to ask how this persistent interest in situating the work of cultural studies within increasingly material frames of reference leads, perhaps inexorably, to a more relativist and material understanding of higher education as both a professional sphere and a workplace. This entails, I suggest, a reprise of ordinariness as a concept in cultural studies' intellectual activism.

# Conclusion: Academic Labor as Ordinary Work

Policy studies' recognition of the work of professional academics as existing on a continuum with other, governmental modes of knowledge work is evident in one current focus of intellectual activism in the United States: responses to the apparent rise of the "corporate university." Invigorated by recent National Labor Review Board (NLRB) decisions sanctioning graduate student labor organizing at private institutions, a movement is emerging based on the managerial, governmental functions of the professoriate. A large part of this movement is predicated upon the unavoidable recognition of the university's increasing dependence on a pool of flexible, temporary, under-remunerated laborers in an ever-expanding set of euphemistic employment categories. In the words of adjunct faculty organizer Vincent Tirelli (1998: 181), "the nation's higher education faculty have not been immune to the trend toward low-paying, part-time, and temporary work." If ideologies of the distinctiveness of academic work practices often rest on hierarchical scale models of meritocracy and apprenticeship, then one aspect of the call for equitable labor practices in higher education is the replacement of these models with a more transparent one, in which academic labor exists on a continuum with, rather than to the side of, other forms of "ordinary" work (Juffer, 2001: 268–70; Tirelli, 1998: 193–4). The difficulty in organizing around this idea lies, Andrew Ross (2000: 6–7) notes, in the fact that the production of culture, whether by educators or artists, is a form of labor traditionally discounted by those selling it. The problem, he suggests, is that "artistic and academic traditions extol sacrificial concepts of mental or cultural labor that are increasingly vital to newly important sectors of the knowledge industries. No longer on the margins of society, in Bohemia or the Ivory Tower, they are providing a rationale for the latest model of labor exploitation in core sectors of the new industrial order, and pioneering the workplace of tomorrow" (2). Cultural studies at this particular moment is, interestingly, less affected by these changes than the disciplines are, given that the highest levels of exploitation can be found in the disciplines and vocational sectors of the institution rather than in cultural studies *per se*. Cultural studies is not part of the education production line staffed by adjuncts and graduate student employees at the American university; rather, this line is made up of teachers of languages including "English as a Second Language," music, written composition, media production, and continuing education – the latter an extremely lucrative source of income for large private urban universities. Yet at the same time, as was the case with cultural studies, these "extramural" sites of higher education, the university's "outposts" marking the points where it meets the world beyond the campus, serve as the locus for new forms of political action and radical thought.

A recent article by Jane Juffer (2001) demonstrates the ongoing importance of close reflection upon the methodological assumptions underlying critiques of the political economy of higher education. Orders of scale, she implies, remain relevant to the politicized work of cultural studies within the disciplines. As a critique of the critics of the corporate university, the essay exemplifies the ongoing relevance of articulation, in the sense of awareness of the linkages formed at concrete historical moments, as a first principle of intellectual activism. Detailing the contradictions and obstacles facing Latino studies in this moment in higher education, Juffer asks what kinds of intellectual practice Latino/a cultural studies should adopt, to best serve students whose entry into the university, after all, is made possible through corporate models of managed diversity – models in which "diversity" serves the purposes of job training in multiple dimensions. Many critics bemoan the corporatization of higher education. But, under current conditions, Juffer asks, is an abstracted understanding of culture as "a space of opposition that is most effective when it is pure" (268) the best place from which to launch a critique? After all, many critiques betray a nostalgia for a past when it was possible to believe that the university was free from the contamination of the market (and, she implies, the people who came in with the market.) In these critiques, "as in corporate diversity discourse . . . the subject is granted an autonomy which exceeds material conditions, indeed, in which material conditions are assumed to be impediments to truth" (285). Both the sacrificial model of academic labor as a vocational calling and the purist model of liberal culture as resistance to commodification are abstractions that conceal their origins in the material conditions of the university as an institution. Rather than mount an activist politics on this basis, Juffer calls for a practice of Latino cultural studies in the institution which *acknowledges* "the corporate university's material commitments" rather than disdaining them, "and hence the students and faculty who gained entry on the basis of these commitments" (285; cf. Miller, 2003). In arguing for a model of academic work that accepts the idea of the professor as manager, and which tries to actualize the political agency within this identity, Juffer demonstrates the continued relevance of ordinariness as a "civic virtue" more valuable than liberal exceptionalism in cultural studies.

Juffer's remarks illustrate the continued need for cultural studies to reflect on the political assumptions underlying judgments of ordinariness and transcendence. Encoded in the phrase "Culture is Ordinary" is the imperative to understand the work of the scholar as part of a tradition of ordinary practices in cultural labor – teaching, reform, activism, policy work, administration. Increasingly, I have tried to show, cultural studies is itself ordinary. Political activism in the academy, whether it calls itself cultural studies or not, can draw on this sense of ordinariness as a methodological resource that focuses attention on the material conditions of knowledge production, and guards against the easy acceptance of foundational abstractions. Although "cultural studies" may not always matter very much as a discipline or a single, coherent set of research techniques, its methodological insistence on situating knowledge production within the concrete, small-scale world of everyday life, from spaces of leisure to the workaday world of institutions, ensures its continued relevance for political reflection within higher education.

## Notes

1  The illuminating work on the politics of scale in the discipline of geography lie outside the confines of this essay. However, I must note that my own thinking on this issue is strongly influenced by the work of geographers, particularly the writings of Doreen Massey (1994), Neil Smith (1992), and David Harvey (1996). For an excellent overview, written by a geographer specializing in media, of the ways that scale has shaped thinking on media and politics see Clive Barnett, "Neither Poison nor Cure: Space, Scale, and Public Life in Media Theory" in Nick Couldry and Anna McCarthy (eds.), *MediaSpace: Place, Scale, and Culture in a Media Age* (London: Routledge, 2004). An account of the conceptual work of scale in cultural research would look differently again were it written from the disciplinary perspective of anthropology – a point raised collectively by Birgit Meyer, Charles Hirschkind, Mattijs van der Poort and Steve Hughes in response to a draft of this paper presented at the Research Centre in Religion and Society, Department of Sociology and Anthropology, University of Amsterdam in 2003. Their generous feedback is much appreciated; any errors in the essay are my own.

2  We can see evidence of cultural studies' status as a "formation" rather than a coherent discipline in the fact that many of the cultural studies researchers who made important contributions to ethnographic studies of audiences have not continued

in ethnography. The historical and geographical moment within which such audience studies took shape has been succeeded by a different set of political agendas. The work of David Morley is emblematic in this regard. One can trace a research arc from his classic *Nationwide* audience study, published at the beginning of Thatcher's prime ministership in 1980, to the more recent *Spaces of Identity* co-authored with Kevin Robins, a study of the role of media in the formation of national identities in Europe at the threshold of union. This shift in emphasis corresponds closely to the changing political questions facing British, and later European, subjects in this period.

3   The need to situate methodology within an order of scale that includes the conditions of knowledge production in the academy is easily grasped when one considers that a contradictory set of class relationships can be shored up under the methodological rubric of interdisciplinarity. On the one hand, the faint outline of a "global subject" comes into view in the ideal inter- or un-disciplinary *bricoleur* of cultural studies, described by some as a figure possessing the ability and resources – or "charismatic authority" (Bennett, 1998: 58) – to rise above disciplines and their methods. There may be an institutional division within the profession, at least in the United States, between those who are interdisciplinary and those who, for reasons that might have a lot to do with teaching demands, curricula, tenure status etc., are not. But, on the other hand, interdisciplinarity describes a relationship to the institution which is in no sense a "rising above." In postwar Britain, cultural studies' interdisciplinarity reflected the marginal class and institutional status of those scholars, like Hoggart and Williams, who shaped its emergence (Gibson and McHoul, 2001: 24–5). In the United States, the kinds of academic appointments that institutionalize interdisciplinarity are fraught with problems of workload and performance evaluation. Most obviously, people who work in women's studies, black studies, and various area studies often hold joint appointments in one or more departments and/or "programs," a situation which can double the amount of service work and administration one must do, to say nothing of the thorny promotion and retention issues involved in navigating not only more than one departmental "culture," but also the concerns of more than one professional audience for one's work (Wissoker, 2000). Methodologies are as shaped by these circumstances as they are by the questions being posed by the historical moment.

## References

Barnett, C. (2004) "Neither Poison nor Cure: Space, Scale, and Public Life in Media Theory," in Nick Couldry and Anna McCarthy (eds.), *MediaSpace: Place, Scale, and Culture in a Media Age* (London: Routledge), pp. 58–74.

Bennett, T. (1992) "Putting Policy into Cultural Studies," in Grossberg et al. (eds.), *Cultural Studies* (New York: Routledge), pp. 23–33.

Bennett, T. (1998) *Culture: a Reformer's Science* (London and Thousand Oaks, CA: Sage Publications).

Brunsdon, C. (1996) "A Thief in the Night: Stories of Feminism in the 1970s at CCCS," in David Morley and Kuan-Hsing Chen (eds.), *Stuart Hall: Critical Dialogues in Cultural Studies* (London: Routledge), pp. 276–86.

Brunsdon, C. (1999) *The Feminist, the Housewife, and the Soap Opera* (New York: Oxford University Press).

Brunsdon, C., C. Johnson, R. Moseley and H. Wheatley (2001) "Factual Entertainment on British Television: the Midlands TV Research Group's '8–9 Project'," *European Journal of Cultural Studies*, 4(1): 29–62.

Burke, Peter (ed.) (2001) *New Perspectives on Historical Writing* (University Park, PA: Pennsylvania State University Press).

Carby, H. (1982/1996) "White Woman Listen! Black Feminism and the Boundaries of Sisterhood," in Houston A. Baker Jr. et al., *Black British Cultural Studies: A Reader* (Chicago: University of Chicago Press), pp. 61–86.

Couldry, N. (2000) *Inside Culture: Re-imagining the Method of Cultural Studies* (London and Thousand Oaks, CA: Sage Publications).

Cunningham, S. (1992) *Framing Culture: Criticism and Policy in Australia* (North Sydney, NSW, Australia: Allen & Unwin).

Dworkin, D. (1997) *Cultural Marxism in Postwar Britain: History, the New Left, and the Origins of Cultural Studies* (Durham, NC: Duke University Press).

Foucault, M. (1970) *The Order of Things: An Archaeology of the Human Sciences* (New York: Vintage Books).

Foucault, M. (1979/2001) "On Governmentality," in Michel Foucault, James D. Faubion et al., *Power: Essential Works of Foucault, 1954–1984*, vol. 3 (New York: The New Press), pp. 201–22.

Garnham, N. (1995) "Political Economy and Cultural Studies: Reconciliation or Divorce?," *Critical Studies in Mass Communication*, 12(1): 62–71.

Giard, L. (1998) "Introduction," in Michel de Certeau, Luce Giard, and Olivier Meyrol, *The Practice Of Everyday Life,* vol 2: *Eating and Cooking* (Minneapolis: University of Minnesota Press).

Gibson, M. and A. McHoul (2001) "Interdisciplinarity," in Toby Miller (ed.), *A Companion to Cultural Studies* (Cambridge, MA: Blackwell), pp. 23–35.

Gibson-Graham, J.K. (1996) *The End of Capitalism (As We Knew It): a Feminist Critique of Political Economy* (Cambridge, MA: Blackwell Publishers).

Ginzburg, C. (1980) *The Cheese and the Worms: the Cosmos of a Sixteenth-Century Miller*, trans. John and Anne Tedeschi (Baltimore: Johns Hopkins University Press).

Grossberg, L. (1996) "On Postmodernism and Articulation: an Interview with Stuart Hall," in David Morley and Kuan-Hsing Chen (eds.), *Stuart Hall: Critical Dialogues in Cultural Studies* (London: Routledge), pp. 151–73.

Grossberg, L. (1997) *Bringing it All Back Home: Essays on Cultural Studies* (Durham, NC: Duke University Press).

Hall, S. (1980) "Cultural Studies: Two Paradigms," *Media, Culture, and Society*, 2: 57–72.

Hall, S. (1980/1996) "Race, Articulation, and Societies Structured in Dominance," in Houston A. Baker Jr. et al., *Black British Cultural Studies: A Reader* (Chicago: University of Chicago Press), pp. 16–60.

Hall, Stuart. (1986/1996) "Gramsci's Relevance for the Study of Race and Ethnicity," in David Morley and Kuan-Hsing-Chen, *Stuart Hall: Critical Dialogues in Cultural Studies* (London: Routledge), pp. 411–40.

Hall, Stuart (1992) "Cultural Studies and Its Theoretical Legacies," in Grossberg et al. (eds.), *Cultural Studies* (New York: Routledge), pp. 277–94.

Hall, S., and Jefferson, T. (1976) *Resistance Through Rituals: Youth Subcultures in Post-war Britain* (London: Hutchinson).

Hartley, J. (1992) *The Politics of Pictures: the Creation of the Public in the Age of Popular Media* (London and New York: Routledge).

Hartley, J. (1999) *The Uses of Television* (London: Routledge).

Harvey, D. (1996) *Justice, Nature and the Geography of Difference* (Cambridge, MA: Blackwell).

Hebdige, D. (1979) *Subculture: The Meaning of Style* (London: Routledge).

Hoggart, R. (1998/1957) *The Uses of Literacy* (New Brunswick, NJ and London: Transaction Publishers).

Hunter, I. (1992) "Aesthetics and Cultural Studies," in Grossberg et al. (eds.), *Cultural Studies* (New York: Routledge), pp. 347–67.

Juffer, J. (2001). "The Limits of Culture: Latino Studies, Diversity Management, and the Corporate University," *Nepantla*, 2(2): 265–93.

Karsten, P. and J. Modell (eds.) (1992) *Theory, Method, and Practice in Social and Cultural History* (New York: New York University Press).

de Laet, M. (2001) "Notes on the Traffic between Cultural Studies and Science and Technology Studies," in Toby Miller (ed.), *A Companion to Cultural Studies* (Cambridge, MA: Blackwell), pp. 101–15.

Ma, E. (2001) "Peripheral Vision: Chinese Cultural Studies in Hong Kong," in Toby Miller (ed.), *A Companion to Cultural Studies* (Cambridge, MA: Blackwell), pp. 259–74.

Martin, R. (2001) "The Renewal of the Cultural in Sociology," in Toby Miller (ed.), *A Companion to Cultural Studies* (Cambridge, MA: Blackwell), pp. 63–78.

Marx, K. (1973) *Grundrisse*, trans. Ben Fowkes (London: Penguin Books).

Massey, D. (1994) *Space, Place, and Gender* (Minneapolis: University of Minnesota Press).

Maxwell, R. (2001) "Political Economy in Cultural Studies," in Toby Miller (ed.), *A Companion to Cultural Studies* (Cambridge, MA: Blackwell), pp. 116–38.

Miller, T. (1998) *Technologies of Truth: Cultural Citizenship and the Popular Media* (Minneapolis: University of Minnesota Press).

Miller, T. (2001) "What it is and what it isn't: Introducing ... Cultural Studies," in Toby Miller (ed.), *A Companion to Cultural Studies* (Cambridge, MA: Blackwell), pp. 1–22.

Miller, T. (2003) "Governmentality or Commodification? US Higher Education," *Cultural Studies*, 17(6): 897–904.

Morris, M. (1990) "Banality in Cultural Studies," in Patricia Mellencamp (ed.), *Logics of Television Essays in Cultural Criticism* (Bloomington: Indiana University Press), pp. 14–43.

Morris, M. (1992) "On the Beach," in Grossberg et al. (eds.), *Cultural Studies*. New York: Routledge, pp. 450–78.

Nelson, C. et al. (1992) "Cultural Studies: An Introduction," in Grossberg et al. (eds.), *Cultural Studies* (New York: Routledge), pp. 1–16.

O'Regan, T. (1993) "(Mis)taking Policy: Notes on the Cultural Policy Debate," in John Frow and Meaghan Morris (eds.), *Australian Cultural Studies: A Reader*. Urbana: University of Illinois Press: pp. 192–208.

*Oxford English Dictionary Second Edition* (1989). Online (subscription only) at http: dictionary.oed.com.

Pines, J. (1996) "The Cultural Context of Black British Cinema," in Houston A. Baker Jr. et al., *Black British Cultural Studies: A Reader* (Chicago: University of Chicago Press), pp. 183–93.

Radway, J. (1996) "The Hegemony of Specificity and the Impasse in Audience Research," in James Hay, Lawrence Grossberg, and Ellen Wartella (eds.), *The Audience and its Landscape* (Boulder, CO: Westview Press), pp. 235–46.

Ross, A. (2000) "The Mental Labor Problem," *Social Text*, 18(2): 1–31.

Slack, J. (1996) "The Theory and Method of Articulation in Cultural Studies," in David Morley and Kuan-Hsing Chen (eds.), *Stuart Hall: Critical Dialogues in Cultural Studies* (London: Routledge), pp. 112–30.

Smith, N. (1992) "Contours of a Spatialized Politics: Homeless Vehicles and the Production of Geographic Scale," *Social Text*, 33: 55–81.

Stam, R. (2001) "Cultural Studies and Race," in Toby Miller (ed.), *A Companion to Cultural Studies* (Cambridge, MA: Blackwell), pp. 471–89.

Thompson, E.P. (1984) "Interview," in Henry Abelove (ed.), *Visions of History* (New York: Pantheon).

Tinkcom, M. (2002) *Working Like a Homosexual: Camp, Capital, Cinema* (Durham, NC: Duke University Press).

Tirelli, V. (1998) "Adjuncts and More Adjuncts: Labor Segmentation and the Transformation of Higher Education," in Randy Martin (ed.), *Chalk Lines: The Politics of Work in the Managed University* (Durham, NC: Duke University Press), pp. 181–201.

Webster, Frank (2001) "Sociology, Cultural Studies, and Disciplinary Boundaries," in Toby Miller (ed.), *A Companion to Cultural Studies* (Cambridge, MA: Blackwell), pp. 79–100.

Williams, R. (1958) *Culture and Society, 1780–1950* (London: Chatto & Windus).

Williams, R. (1976) *Keywords: a Vocabulary of Culture and Society* (New York: Oxford University Press).

Williams, R. (1977) *Marxism and Literature* (New York: Oxford University Press).

Willis, P. (1980) "Notes on Method," in S. Hall, D. Dobson, and P. Willis (eds.), *Culture, Media and Language* (London: Hutchinson), pp. 88–95.

Wissoker, K. (2000) "Negotiating a Passage Between Disciplinary Borders," *Chronicle of Higher Education,* April 14, p. B4.

# 3

# *Raymond Williams's* Culture and Society *as Research Method*\*

## John Durham Peters

Questions of method are always self-reflexive. Even the term *method* conceals the ancient Greek word *meta*, as *methodos* is a contraction of *meta hodos*, meaning a following after. Reflections on method are always meta-reflections, both in the twentieth-century sense of *meta* as an inquiry that implicates itself and the ancient sense of *meta* as *after, across*, or *among*. Reflections on method are almost always post hoc reconstructions. Method's owl takes flight only at dusk. Despite its inflation in some of the more militant branches of the twentieth-century sciences into epistemological technique, method is more richly understood as an existential, even ethical, problem of how to enter into a relationship with one's material. In historical inquiries, the method delivers the past: method is the gatekeeper of the spirit-world. Method regulates what messages can pass between the living and the dead. Method is too interesting a topic to abandon to those who see it only as a set of techniques. One of the great defenses of humanistic inquiry in the later twentieth century, Hans-Georg Gadamer's *Truth and Method* (1989), so vehemently opposes the scientific notion of method as technique that the book might more properly be called *Truth **or** Method*. For Gadamer, properly humane studies are ones that require no technique at all, and by letting method be identified with scientism, he lets his enemies define the problem. A position far less radical, and more helpful, recognizes method more richly as a question of the inevitably political and moral attitudes we take toward

\* Revised version of "Retroactive Enrichment: Raymond Williams's *Culture and Society*," in *Canonic Texts in Media Research: Are There Any? Should There Be? How About These?* Ed. Elihu Katz et al. (Cambridge: Polity Press, 2003), pp. 217–30.

the past, the world, and other people. Raymond Williams, in his germinal book *Culture and Society* (1958), knew this well. In discussing the method of *Culture and Society*, as I propose to do in this essay, one must also exemplify it.

*Culture and Society* is one of several texts to define an intellectual framework for analysis of the social, cultural, and political setting of media. It is not only a fountainhead of British cultural studies, but also shows striking and rarely noted affinities with both German critical theory and mainstream American media sociology. Together with the other founding works of leftist analysis of culture and society in postwar Britain, Richard Hoggart's *The Uses of Literacy* (1957) and E.P. Thompson's *The Making of the English Working Class* (1963), as well as Williams's own sequel *The Long Revolution* (1961), *Culture and Society* is made more richly and diversely intelligible by the work that emerged in its wake, much of it directly on media texts, audiences, and institutions, most famously at Birmingham but also with other branches in Leicester, Milton Keynes, London, Chapel Hill, Sydney, Taipei, etc. *Culture and Society* exemplifies the hermeneutic principle of retroactive enrichment. (*Methodos* is what follows after.) It reinvented a tradition of British thought and literature by rereading, and as a text itself, it has grown in meaning. Descendants can give life to their ancestors. Sentences in Williams now resonate to frequencies unheard when it was written. What were small streams in 1958 can be reread nearly 50 years later as the sources of mighty intellectual rivers (just as Williams found in debates between Burke and Cobbett the seeds of later arguments about culture and democracy). Subsequent history can be kind or cruel to human works, and *Culture and Society* has enjoyed a rather blessed afterlife. It would be much less resonant without what has been said since. As a source (at least carrier) of much of the intellectual DNA still reproducing in media and cultural studies, *Culture and Society* deserves its place in the canon.

The literary origins of British cultural studies are well known. In the United States, sociology had long served as a chief academic field for social criticism since its institutionalization in the late nineteenth century, but the intellectual scene in Britain was different, for sociology was far less prominent in both university and more general intellectual life. Literary studies in Britain served as a major outlet for social-political inquiry and criticism, and Williams's work, including *Culture and Society*, is an outstanding example of the ways in which questions of literary quality and aesthetic taste were turned into questions of social power and cultural access. As Terry Eagleton (1984) notes, the function of literary criticism in Britain had long been to intervene in the public sphere of political debate. But *Culture and Society* marks the beginning of something more unique and rare about Williams's work: the treatment of words as a peculiar kind of material full of markings of historical consciousness and political struggle. Williams was one of the great lexicographers of our age and he saw that attention to words and their histories are inseparable from theoretical inquiry and political critique. Cultural studies *à la* Williams requires erudition of its practitioners.

*Culture and Society* is, at the most obvious level, an extended study of intellectual life in Britain from the late eighteenth century to the mid-twentieth century. No potted history of ideas, it is rather an engagement with, even invention of, a tradition of reflection on and criticism of the social and cultural transformations of modern British life. Williams's coverage of such figures as Edmund Burke, the Romantic poets, J.S. Mill and Thomas Carlyle, Matthew Arnold, D.H. Lawrence, T.S. Eliot, and George Orwell may look now like a standard syllabus, but as Williams notes (1990: v–vi), there was no self-conscious category in British intellectual life as a culture-and-society tradition when he wrote it. *Culture and Society* is remarkably willing to recruit thinkers with conservative credentials – Burke, Coleridge, Carlyle, Lawrence, Eliot – to the cause of a common culture and as indigenous resources for cultural criticism, a reclamation project shared by other 1950s British intellectuals on the left (Mulhern, 2000: 67). (Williams's readiness to engage right-wing thinkers has an affinity with Walter Benjamin's notion of *rettende Kritik* or redemptive criticism, and the best thinkers of the twentieth-century left, from Lukács and Gramsci through Adorno and Habermas and Williams and Hall, have never been cowed by political litmus tests.) The intelligence, subtlety, and often productive ambivalence of his readings of diverse figures make *Culture and Society* still a useful primer on the history of social thought in Britain as well as on Williams's own thought.

Williams's history of the idea of culture is itself a cultural and political project. The German translation of *Culture and Society* is called *Intellectual History as Social Theory* (*Begriffsgeschichte als Sozialtheorie*), a title that concisely captures the book's aim and method. "*Culture and Society* is a work which, in the very act of 'placing' a tradition, places itself within it" (Eagleton, 1976: 26). Williams was doing a title search for his own practice as a cultural critic, especially in the book's splendid "Conclusion." Here Williams writes as a socialist concerned for democracy, a humanist concerned for the quality of expression, and as a moralist concerned with the adulteration of human possibilities. The Conclusion's announced "effort at total qualitative assessment" recalls Arnold and Mill, Burke and Cobbett, Eliot and Leavis – indeed, the group of thinkers the book comments on. The Conclusion serves as Williams's own assimilation of and installment in the culture and society tradition; in it he appears "as the latest figure in the lineage he traces, a character within his own drama" (Eagleton, 1976: 23). Here he speaks as voice, not as commentator, with diverse echoes from the treated authors both topically and tonally.

It might be a surprise from the description thus far to discover that the Conclusion is in large part a wrestle with the meaning of mass communication. *Culture and Society* is one of several works in an international moment (or "conjuncture" as Williams would later say) that grappled with the political, social, and cultural meaning of the mass media. In the United States, 1950s media sociology can be symbolized by Paul Lazarsfeld and C. Wright Mills studiously ignoring each other at the water cooler in the Columbia University Department of Sociology. Lazarsfeld's work was empirical, quantitative, externally funded, and politically mainstream. It was in tune with the view of democracy as a functioning system which did not require active articipation of citizens but rather a consensual balance among various interest groups, a position explicit in the conclusion to Berelson, Lazarsfeld, and McPhee's *Voting* (1954). Lazarsfeld largely neglected the industrial or technological context of media in his work, though not in his thinking, as can be seen in essays with Robert K. Merton (1948) and in Lazarsfeld (1948). By showing psychological and sociological barriers to mass media influence, Lazarsfeld's Bureau of Applied Social Research offered a kind of defense of the capacity of ordinary people to think, talk, and associate for themselves. By showing how people interpret, filter, ignore, or even resist media influence, Elihu Katz and Paul Lazarsfeld's *Personal Influence* (1955) serves, as Simonson (1996) notes, as a democratic apologetic. Katz and Lazarsfeld argued that people still talk and have social relations; selectivity and interpersonal relations damped the threat of the big bad media (Frankfurt School) or the hope of big good media (Chicago School). In a brilliant piece of data-reduction Katz argued that these two outlooks, however opposed they may seem, in fact agree that media have major effects; both are in thrall to visions of mass society.

In contrast, Mills, ultimately drawing on both Chicago and Frankfurt sources, as well as the legacy of John Dewey and Walter Lippmann, painted a much gloomier picture. In his draft analyses of the 1944 fieldwork he directed in Decatur, Illinois, and which would later become the basis of *Personal Influence*, Mills wrote of power as well as influence, social structures as well as group ties. More pointedly, in chapter 13 of *The Power Elite* (1956), Mills unfurled a theory of mass society which is a clear intramural skirmish with Lazarsfeld and specifically with *Personal Influence*, a battle that would continue with his attack on Lazarsfeld's "methodological inhibitionism" in *The Sociological Imagination* (1959). In *The Power Elite*, Mills argued that media do not simply shape people's voting, fashion, movies, or shopping choices, but provide ordinary people with their aspirations, identities, and even experiences. Clearly for Mills media effects (not a term that he featured) were pervasive, not rare. To be sure, Mills's views of media were embedded within a much broader historical account of the structural transformation of the modern public, an account that owes something to both Walter Lippmann and John Dewey: media fill the historical gaps left open by modern personal alienation, social uprooting, and the retreat of educational and other institutions. Mills called for a critical – and empirical – sociology that would draw on biography and history as its chief sources and have as its object the growth of reason and the emancipation of humanity, and, in this, he shared much more than he wanted to admit with Lazarsfeld's own vision (Sterne, 2005). The task of sociology he believed (like Raymond Williams) was historically continuous with the novel: to bring modern social order to an imaginative self-clarification, resulting in a heightened responsibility to fact and experience.

Mills vs. Lazarsfeld in the 1950s, just as Adorno vs. Lazarsfeld in the 1940s, became cemented in the historical self-consciousness of mass communication research in the late 1970s (Gitlin [1978] taking the Adorno–Mills side, Morrison [1978] taking the Lazarsfeld side) as the divide between critical and empirical research, a division first named by Lazarsfeld himself. These debates offered dualisms that are unfortunately still with us as historical and political categories for describing media studies and its history, even if the best work of the past two (and maybe six) decades has transcended them: minimal vs. strong effects; optimism vs. despair about popular consciousness; quantitative vs. qualitative methods; affirmative vs. radical politics. For too long, it was assumed that choosing one side of the dichotomies was a package deal: if you believe in the wisdom of ordinary people, then you must also take an affirmative stance to the culture industry and engage in survey research. Clearly the terms on each side do have an elective affinity, but there is nothing naturally given about them.

This is one lesson of Williams's Conclusion. Its position on mass communication is a stunning arbitration of positions that in the 1950s and after were largely polarized in the United States. Again, it belongs to an international moment that is clearer retrospectively than it was at the time. The year of publication of *Culture and Society*, 1958, also saw the appearance of Hannah Arendt's *The Human Condition* and Aldous Huxley's *Brave New World Revisited*. A year after Williams's *Long Revolution* (1961) came Jürgen Habermas's *Structural Transformation of the Public Sphere* and also the founding manifesto of the New Left in the United States, the Port Huron Statement (1962). In the year 1962, a great outpouring of work in a wide range of fields converged on the problem of communication (Peters and Simonson, 2004). Among Marxists, independent radicals like Mills, and humanist centrists like Arendt and Huxley, there is a concern for communication as cure and disease of modern life, with the mass media playing a particular role in each text, sometimes as villain. These works all deal with the threat of mass society, of lonely crowds, and seek ways to rebuild a more vital democracy. They were all composed in the light of the rise of the New Left: the effort to build a program of humane, progressive, coalition-based social justice. To twist Gitlin's title (*The Twilight of Common Dreams*, 1995), these texts reflect the dawn of common dreams. Habermas's public sphere, Arendt's realm of speech and action, or Williams's common culture all envision vibrant, democratically engaged politics, however much these thinkers differ on details, histories, politics, and even principles. All of them have a catholic, nondogmatic sensibility, and no strict standard of political or intellectual rectitude. All of them have an interest in classic works, however that lonely term is defined, and are willing to work with unfashionable or at least historically deep intellectual methods and objects. (This is in sharp contrast to the tone of most later cultural studies, which is, whatever else one might say, always relentlessly hip.)

Though attempts at canonization are always partly acts of will or imagination, it requires no leap to see Williams's Conclusion as being about mass communication theory. Williams reads old texts in order to build his own story; we may do the same with his texts. The terms and questions are plain for all to see, as in the section titled "Mass-communication" (pp. 300–5) and the one titled "Communication and Community" (pp. 313–19). Williams both mediates late 1950s debates (with the salutary effect of forcing a rethinking of the critical-empirical divide) and offers an original vision of his own. Williams is perhaps best known in media studies for his 1970s work on television and Marxist cultural theory, but a reading of *Culture and Society* will also place him, appropriately, among a different generation, as one of the sanest voices speaking amid the din and loathing of the mass culture debates of the late 1950s.

In Williams, Arendt, and Habermas alike, there is a strong working conviction that words serve as secret records of social transformations. Words like *culture*, *public*, or *Öffentlichkeit* end up, in their works, revealing entire histories of human struggles and societal changes. Indeed, one of the many genres of writing that Williams worked in – along with history, criticism, novel, theory, and essay – was the dictionary, and his *Keywords* (1976, rev. ed. 1985) grows out of the project begun in *Culture and Society*. For Williams, the history of words can serve as a kind of geological record of changed structures of feeling. To him, no less than for Habermas or Arendt, intellectual history is no leap from mountaintop to mountaintop but, rather, a tracing of social struggles. Lexicography serves as social and cultural history: as in Arendt and Habermas, words offer privileged access to seismic changes in human experience. Ways of seeing, for Williams, are socially conditioned in a strong way, as in his famous phrase, there are no masses, only ways of seeing people as masses (*Culture and Society* [hereafter *C&S*], 300). Our modes of vision are saturated with social experience, but also help, in turn, to shape possible relationships with others. Whether they come in literature, journalism, and drama or social science, history, and statistics, stories are ways of both imagining and enacting social worlds.

Hence Williams's positive evaluation of entertainment, at least as a potential form of social connection. Though he clearly recognizes that most of what is on offer by the postwar culture industries is cheap, silly, or escapist, the sheer abundance of drama available to people in the twentieth century enriches our possible modes of mutual connection, a claim finding its greatest statement in Williams's 1974 inaugural lecture at Cambridge University, "Drama in a Dramatised Society" (O'Connor, 1989). As "any real theory of communication is a theory of community" (*C&S*, 313), scholarship, as one of many imaginative labors, has a privileged role in social description and criticism: "To take a meaning from experience, and to try to make it active, is in fact our process of growth" (*C&S*, 338). "In every problem we need hard, detailed inquiry and negotiation" (*C&S*, 338). "Inquiry plus negotiation" defines Williams's method well, both political and intellectual, one he shares with Mills, Arendt, and Habermas. *Culture and Society* belongs to a moment in which the best scholars blended methods of social science and humanities – a call Katz (1959) was also making at the same time.

Williams's account of mass communication takes pains to avoid technological determinism or contempt for audiences. Williams is decidedly not a medium theorist. "The techniques, in my view, are at worst neutral" (*C&S*, 301). At best, new technologies alter the emphases of extant social activities and relations, but never revolutionize them. Technologies themselves are shaped by the context of use and social decisions about their deployment, a point that anticipates his *Television: Technology and Cultural Form* (1974), which includes a blistering attack on McLuhan. To take technology as a determinant is for Williams to risk freezing a particular social practice into something natural rather than historical. The mere fact that many of the media of mass communication are impersonal and involve one-way flows does not imply that the audience is anesthetized. "Reception and response, which complete communication, depend on other factors than the techniques" (*C&S*, 302). Mass communication, he argues, is really multiple transmission, a means of distributing symbols that emerged first with the printing press and grew into broadcasting. The social meaning of multiple transmission is also at least ambiguous. He finds it ironic that historical developments that gave millions unprecedented access to cultural materials are largely interpreted as harming those people; for him, the very notion of mass communication participates in the depreciation of audiences by painting them disparagingly as *masses*. The key question is not the forms in the abstract, but the intentions of communication practices and the social relationships they sustain. Williams is not closed to empirical or qualitative methods here, and his respect for the intelligence of actors, as in Hoggart's *Uses of Literacy*, opens up this possibility (though he does not pursue it in *Culture and Society*). In *Television* (1974), Williams even performs a bit of content analysis, carried out apparently during a bored and lonely semester as a visiting professor at Stanford University.

Like *Personal Influence*, but with a much clearer political program, Williams is opposed to the mass-society notion of audiences as dupes or dopes. His claim that "Communication is not only transmission; it is also reception and response" (*C&S*, 313) could be the motto of 40 years of British cultural studies with its interest in how people receive and reply to, appropriate and abuse, media matters. Like the Columbia tradition, he opposes the notion of powerful media, though his formulation again has a sharper critical twist – the danger is a "dominative" habit in thinking about communication (*C&S*, 313). The media are only one among many sources in the formation of minds: "ideas and feelings are, to a large extent, still moulded by a wider and more complex pattern of social and family life" (*C&S*, 308). The effort to register an impact on the mass mind "has failed, and will continue to fail, when its transmissions encounter, not a confused uncertainty, but a considered and formulated experience" (*C&S*, 313). The mass media cannot manufacture conviction out of thin air. While it would clearly be a mistake to exaggerate the affinity between the overall visions and programs of Williams and Lazarsfeld, the structure of their argument about audience resources for resisting media influence is quite similar. Where the Columbia school refers to psychological selectivity, canalization, and primary groups, Williams talks about experience, practice, and social relations. Williams's vocabulary is politically and culturally richer, as Lazarsfeld's is scientifically more replicable. The common enemy to both is mass society theory (something that rarely existed as a positive program, but rather more often as a construct in the hands of its detractors). *Culture and Society* and *Personal Influence* both distrust cultural pessimism, the vision of people as "hollow men" without souls, and see such thinking as an artifact of a bad set of spectacles, not as the real nature of social experience.

Williams's account of the rise of mass culture undercuts the historical decline narratives that underlie mass society theory without substituting a happy account of progress as an alternative. Williams suggests that belief in an earlier golden age – for instance, the eighteenth century as the highpoint of the English novel – owes in large part to the selective preservation of the historical record. Novels that are still read today from the eighteenth century tend to be good ones, while many lousier ones have been long forgotten; today, in contrast, we live in a historical mix in which a consensus on taste has not yet been reached and in which lots of hackwork is available. Williams is no cultural Darwinian who thinks works compete and survive on the sole strength of their aesthetic virtues: his point, rather, concerns the problem of historical framing. (Here again Williams's method treats the past not as given but as a set of artifacts whose selective survival is the first item to be accounted for.) To describe modern culture as decline, one has to choose a beginning point, and this choice always has specific consequences. One can start in 1870 or 1740, or, as he notes in chapter 2 of *The Country and the City* (1973), one can trace the ever-receding horizon of a whole and happy rural life back to Eden. Williams is highly sophisticated about historiographical deck-loading: to say that modern life involves a fall in taste is a proposition that must first account for the differential afterlife of texts, the choice of starting points, and, above all, the obvious fact that modern life has seen an expanding, not contracting, culture. Like Lazarsfeld and Merton, Williams takes care to distinguish relative and absolute changes: "In every case, certainly, the proportions [of serious culture] are less than we could desire, but they are not negligible" (*C&S*, 308). Perhaps even more heretically for a thinker of critical sympathies, Williams's common sense does not wilt before the lure of the commodity. About the charge that consumerism has wholly bought off political radicalism, he replies: "It is wholly reasonable to want the means of life in such abundance as is possible" (*C&S*, 324). People who acquire refrigerators and radios are not necessarily becoming spoiled; they are gaining "objects of utility" (*C&S*, 323). Again, Williams is not a happy capitalist, proponent of progress, or anti-green celebrant of consumerism, but he is someone who treats modernity with a differentiated gaze. Unlike some of his disciples, he is very slow on the draw to dismiss an intellectual position. Intellectually, he is not a picky eater.

His refusal of despair, nostalgia, and celebration – a common emotional palette for media critics – is reflected in his criticism of both what he calls "old democrats," who have a touchingly virginal faith in the goodness and intelligence of the people, and "the new skeptics," who are so aware of the constraints and conditions of modern democracy that they abandon hope in it. Both of these attitudes – which strikingly resemble those of Dewey and Lippmann respectively, or more recent debates between communitarians and realists—Williams believes, leave the door open for con-artists and cultural hucksters. In contrast to Berelson, Lazarsfeld, and McPhee's *Voting* (1954) or Lippmann's *Phantom Public* (1925), Williams takes the deficiencies of public interest and information themselves to be political and historical, not natural, facts: interest and inertia derive from the organization of society (*C&S*, 310); sullenness is a social product, not a simple reflection of bovine inertia in human nature or the masses (*C&S*, 316). And yet, as in Columbia work, Williams despises cynicism: "there is a huge area of general suspicious disbelief, which, while on particular occasions it may be prophylactic, is as a general habit enfeebling" (*C&S*, 316). Williams warns us against the dangers of both realism (cynicism) and blind faith (folly) in democratic attitudes. The stand-off between innocence and experience only leaves the political field open for exploitation by the hard-headed opportunist, and Williams calls for a realism grounded in hope.

The grounded sociological sense shared by Williams and the Columbia tradition also shows up in the account of audience interpretation of media texts. In *Culture and Society* he has not yet developed the more complex scheme of "Base and Superstructure in Marxist Cultural Theory" (1973), a piece that sees the interpretation of artifacts as a kind of productive labor allowing for a variety of interpretive strategies while also sowing seeds of an interest in subculture. "Active reception, and living response, depend in their turn on an effective community of experience" (C&S, 316). His defense of working-class culture as, to use terms developed by Paul Willis, an elaborated rather than restricted code suggests the importance of communities of interpretation in decoding. Working-class culture, he argues, does not lack ideals: rather, it has a different one – that of solidarity – instead of the middle-class ones of individualism or service. Working people do not lack creativity or intelligence; they simply express it in alternative ways. Williams wants to pluralize modes of knowing so that literate and educated ones do not steal all the prizes. Gardening, carpentry, and organizing can also be modes of intelligent human activity. For Williams, as for Hoggart in *The Uses of Literacy*, the defense of working-class culture (indeed, the very notion of working-class *culture*) is shaped by his warm extended family background; both are defending their aunts and uncles, not crusading for bloodless abstractions. The defense of subculture, the notion of collective interpretation, the defense of intelligence as something exercised in response or practice as much as in literate utterance are all principles that resonate in work in Williams's broad wake, in Hall, Hebdige, Brunsdon, Morley, McRobbie, Ang, Fiske, and many others. Indeed, as James Curran (1990) pointed out, the celebration of active audiences in cultural studies was in many ways an unwitting recreation of the central finding of the Columbia tradition.

British cultural studies, like the Columbia tradition, has long taken pride in offering a more subtle take on popular capacities than that offered by the Frankfurt School. For the latter, at least in its worst moments, the culture industry was apparently an apparatus that had its terminus in the head of every person. Horkheimer and Adorno could write sentences portraying the petit-bourgeois schmucks at the movies as incipient fascists or infantilized sadists, though they could also write sentences hinting at the possibility of popular redemption and resistance, though their readers – especially in Anglo-American cultural studies – have tended to ignore their more nuanced sentences and the dialectical nature of their prose (Peters, 2003). Williams, in contrast, manages a clear criticism of the concentrated power to communicate without also flirting with the idea that the people are suggestible zombies. He thinks of his family, himself, in the audience, not as others. Indeed, in one of his famous lines, itself reflecting the famous line from Sartre that "hell is other people," he said: "Masses are other people" (*C&S*, 300). His point is to criticize the alienating abstraction of assuming the observer's rather than the participant's role. The Columbia tradition, in turn, rarely concerns itself directly with culture industries as such, but does offer in its way a defense of the dignity of audiences, who, it is claimed, still talk and still read despite the coming of radio and television; effects research certainly reveals the intermediate steps between the media's messages and the audience's attitudes. Williams stands between these two options, offering a critical theory with a heart, a theory of the culture industry that is not also a theory of the consciousness industry.

The Columbia school rarely offered normative solutions; prior to Habermas, the Frankfurt School considered explicit political and ethical norms vain (and Habermas's life's work has been to correct this lack); but Williams has a positive program for reorganizing channels of communication. What is needed is "a different attitude to transmission, one which will ensure that its origins are genuinely multiple, that all the sources have access to the common channels" (*C&S*, 316). Here are all the key leftist principles of a transformed media system: diversity of channels, alternate sources, popular access. Like Mills (1956: 301), Williams laments the disjunction between distribution and contribution – that is, the gap between the ability to hear (possessed by many) and the ability to be heard (possessed by few). Williams, of course, has a critique of mass culture, but it is more thoroughgoing than many in the late 1950s who predictably blasted away at degraded taste; his critique extends to the concept of mass itself. Williams denies the Olympian view of the critic, showing the politics of the ready-made categories of cultural critique. And he gives more resources of hope than the vision of mass deception. Williams sees the cultural industry not as a totally closed system like vertically integrated Hollywood, but as a reformable set of arrangements. His analysis of media industries is perhaps too dismissive of organizational culture or structural constraints within the culture industries, however – he seems to believe that new management and popular control would be sufficient (a replacement of the "cheapjacks" who are currently in charge), a view he would complicate in "Means of Communication as Means of Production" (1980).

Williams's attack on low cultural quality is insistently ethical and political: that is, a defense of the intelligence of the receiver, and a critique of cultural machinery that is so frankly elitist and exclusive. His attacks on media are never exclusively aesthetic. He is not shy to condemn most of what is on offer, but the condemnation turns not only on poor quality but on organizational exclusion and governance, a lack of popular access to the "training" (*C&S*, 310) to interpret culture, a point reminiscent of Bourdieu's cultural capital. Indeed, Williams is both an ethical and a political critic, whereas most of his followers drop the ethical dimension. Stuart Hall, for instance, has a politics but not an ethics: I do not mean the person, who is one of the most splendid human beings of our times, but as a developed program of intellectual analysis and center of gravity. In this Williams learned a great deal from the authors he criticized: Burke, Coleridge, Mill, Arnold, Lawrence, Orwell, and, of course, Leavis. Cultural studies today largely lacks an ethics; or, rather, it has let ethics be completely subsumed by politics. Williams knew the difference.

Nations, like canons, are modes of organizing disparate materials: the task of both is to establish relations between the living and dead. And new relations with the dead enable new relations among the living. Much of my interest in Williams concerns the way he enriches and resolves debates that came to an apparent impasse in the United States in the late 1950s and have continued since: a widened canon provides resources for escaping from false dichotomies that come down from the past. In the US it is striking to find a leftist thinker in the formative postwar era who takes a nuanced look at the social consequences of the mass media – most intellectuals at this point were lamenting the spurning of their leadership by the industries of popular culture (as Lazarsfeld and Merton [1948] also note). Just as the 1989 translation of Habermas's *Structural Transformation of the Public Sphere* gave a blast of fresh air to Anglophone media studies by showing that as early as 1962 a critically-minded scholar was engaging in historical and empirical mass communication research at the highest level, Williams's Conclusion, if read as a partner in a transatlantic conversation on the meaning of mass communication, is astonishingly relevant for our debates today. Williams reads smartly if placed in dialog with his fellow late 1950s worriers about modernity. His historical method resembles Arendt or Mills or Habermas; his view that media audiences are insulated by social relationships from media influence and insulted by elitist intellectuals resembles Katz and Lazarsfeld; and his analysis of the economics, class-basis and concentration of media power resembles Mills or Adorno. Among the immortals dialogs can be arranged that never took place in life. One point of canons is to orchestrate the concourse of the spirit-world – which is precisely what Williams did, in turn, in *Culture and Society*. *Culture and Society*, which will shortly celebrate its fiftieth anniversary, should become a site for dialogue among Chicago, Columbia, Frankfurt, Toronto, and British cultural traditions.

Both nations and canons offer frames of interpretation, and I want to conclude by suggesting that *Culture and Society* may be a richer text today abroad in the US than at "home" in the UK. This difference may reflect a difference in the place of media in the US and Britain, one of many curious differences in the intellectual life of the two countries, as Corner (1995: 159–60) points out. In late 1950s within the US, after the quiz show scandals, most intellectuals abandoned the relatively new medium of television, a desertion that might also reflect the transformation of television from a regional, New-York-City-based medium carrying "quality" dramatic programming for an elite audience, to a national, Los-Angeles-based system in the late 1950s. FCC Commissioner Newton Minow gave television its sealing malediction in 1961 as a "vast wasteland," coolly deploying one of the great pessimistic tropes from modernist literature, T.S. Eliot's *The Waste Land*. The TV field was abandoned to a new breed of pop thinkers like Marshall McLuhan (Peters and Simonson, 2004: 268–73). In Britain, the story was different: many intellectuals maintained a constructive engagement with the medium as critics, consultants, and script-writers, Williams himself being a good example of all three, and the BBC retained a commitment, however paternalistically executed in practice, to the troubled category of "quality" programming. In England, the long-standing basis of mass-cultural criticism from Leavis to Hoggart was print culture, not television: in *Culture and Society*, as in *The Uses of Literacy*, television hardly rates a mention. In the US, one way to sell lots of books is to blame television for some social ill and praise print as the cure; the television jeremiad is a well-recognized and remunerated genre. In contrast, pioneering studies touching on television written in the UK such as the 1960s writings collected together by O'Connor as *Raymond Williams on Television* or Stuart Hall and Paddy Whannel's *The Popular Arts* (1964) are written discriminatingly, always seeing the possibility of genuine experience or art together with the dangers of stupefaction or exploitation.

If, in an American setting, *Culture and Society* gains contemporaneity as the rearranger of the entire historical legacy of media research by combining the best of what hitherto seemed embattled traditions, in Britain today the text has a certain obvious lack: its monocultural vision of the nation. In its status as official predecessor to British cultural studies, *Culture and Society* neglects gender, race, and sexuality, though there is class and nation and even a brief mention of imperialism; subculture is implicit, though built on class lines rather than on other sorts of affiliation; resistance, too, is implicit in the notion of experience as the first court of appeal when facing a media text. *Culture and Society* offers no close engagement with media artifacts, which ought not to be surprising for a programmatic statement – certainly as a television and theater critic, Williams did enough of that (O'Connor, 1989). For some critics (for example, Paul Gilroy [1991: 49–51]), Williams's Achilles' heel is his vision of race and nation: calling himself a "Welsh European," Williams's vision of the political and intellectual dissident was typically the white male British working-class hero. For today's conventional wisdom, it's remarkable that *Culture and Society* claims to be a history of British thought in the nineteenth century while barely noticing the colonial and imperial context in which ideas of culture were applied, with the British empire covering over one-fifth of the habitable earth in the same period. Problems of culture and society from 1780 to 1950 were not insularly British but global in their elaborations and effects. To be fair, Williams later explicitly acknowledged these absences (1979: 113ff) and regarded *Culture and Society* with the alienation that serious authors almost always have for their earlier work. At a time when Britain is rethinking itself as a multicultural and multiracial nation, in which the empire strikes back in curry, language, fashion, people, and music, the island-based, white-guy character of *Culture and Society* is perhaps the part that requires the most interpretive generosity today. When past and present meet, they cast light on each other's potentials and each other's lacks. This – together with the attention to words and their histories, political and intellectual openness, an implicit ethical sensitivity, and respect for the resources of tradition – is perhaps the greatest lesson in method *Culture and Society* offers to cultural studies today.

# References

Arendt, Hannah (1958) *The Human Condition* (Chicago: University of Chicago Press).
Berelson, Bernard, Paul F. Lazarsfeld, and William McPhee (1954) *Voting* (Chicago: University of Chicago Press).
Corner, John (1995) *Television Form and Public Address* (New York: Edward Arnold).
Curran, James (1990) "The New Revisionism in Mass Communication Research: A Reappraisal," *European Journal of Communication*, 5:2–3: 135–64.
Eagleton, Terry (1976) *Criticism and Ideology* (London: NLB).
Eagleton, Terry (1984) *The Function of Criticism: From the Spectator to Post-structuralism* (London: Verso).
Gadamer, Hans-Georg (1989) *Truth and Method* (New York: Continuum, 2nd revised edition).
Gilroy, Paul (1991 [1987]) *There Ain't No Black in the Union Jack* (Chicago: University of Chicago Press).
Gitlin, Todd (1978) "Media Sociology: The Dominant Paradigm," *Theory and Society*, 6:2 (September), 205–53.
Gitlin, Todd (1995) *The Twilight of Common Dreams* (New York: Metropolitan).
Habermas, Jürgen (1962) *Structural Transformation of the Public Sphere* (Cambridge, MA: MIT Press, 1989).
Hall, Stuart and Paddy Whannel (1964) *The Popular Arts* (New York: Pantheon).
Hoggart, Richard (1957) *The Uses of Literacy* (New Brunswick, NJ: Transaction, 1992).
Katz, Elihu (1959) "Mass Communications Research and the Study of Popular Culture: An Editorial Note on a Possible Future for this Journal," *Studies in Public Communication*, 2: 1–6.
Katz, Elihu and Paul F. Lazarsfeld (1955) *Personal Influence* (Glencoe, IL: Free Press).
Lazarsfeld, Paul F. (1948) "Communication Research and the Social Psychologist," *Current Trends in Social Psychology,* ed. Wayne Dennis (Pittsburgh: University of Pittsburgh Press).
Lazarsfeld, Paul F. and Robert K. Merton (1948) "Mass Communication, Popular Taste, and Organized Social Action," *The Communication of Ideas*, ed. Lyman Bryson (New York: Cooper Square).
Lippmann, Walter (1925) *The Phantom Public* (New York: Macmillan).
Mills, C. Wright (1956) *The Power Elite* (New York: Oxford University Press).
Mills, C. Wright (1959) *The Sociological Imagination* (New York: Oxford University Press).

Morrison, David E. (1978) "*Kultur* and Culture: The Case of Theodor Adorno and Paul F. Lazarsfeld," *Social Research*, 45: 331–55.

Mulhern, Francis (2000) *Culture/Metaculture* (London: Routledge).

O'Connor, Alan (1989) *Raymond Williams on Television* (New York: Routledge).

Peters, John Durham (2003) "The Subtlety of Horkheimer and Adorno: Reading 'The Culture Industry,'" *Canonic Texts in Media Research: Are There Any? Should There Be? How About These?*, eds. Elihu Katz et al. (Cambridge: Polity Press), pp. 58–73.

Peters, John Durham and Peter Simonson (2004) *Mass Communication and American Social Thought: Key Texts, 1919–1968.* (Boulder, CO: Rowman and Littlefield).

Simonson, Peter D. (1996) "Dreams of Democratic Togetherness: Communication Hope from Cooley to Katz," *Critical Studies in Mass Communication*, 13 (December): 324–42.

Sterne, Jonathan (2005) "C. Wright Mills, the Bureau for Applied Social Research, and Meaning of Critical Scholarship," *Cultural Studies <=> Critical Methodologies*, 5: 65–94.

Thompson, Edward P. (1963) *The Making of the English Working Class* (New York: Pantheon).

Williams, Raymond (1958) *Culture and Society* (London: Chatto & Windus, 1990).

Williams, Raymond (1961) *The Long Revolution* (London and New York: Columbia University Press).

Williams, Raymond (1973) *The Country and the City* (London: Hogarth Press, 1993).

Williams, Raymond (1974) *Television: Technology and Cultural Form* (New York: Schocken).

Williams, Raymond (1976) *Keywords: A Vocabulary of Culture and Society* (revised edn. New York: Oxford University Press, 1985).

Williams, Raymond (1979) *Politics and Letters: Interviews with New Left Review* (London: NLB).

Williams, Raymond (1980) "Means of Communication as Means of Production," in Raymond Williams, *Problems of Materialism and Culture* (London: Verso), pp. 50–63.

# 4

# "Read thy self": *Text, Audience, and Method in Cultural Studies*

## John Hartley

*There is a saying much usurped of late, That* Wisedome *is acquired, not by reading of* Books, *but of* Men. *Consequently whereunto, those persons, that for the most part can give no other proof of being wise, take great delight to shew what they think they have read in men, by uncharitable censures of one another behind their backs. But there is another saying not of late understood, by which they might learn truly to read one another, if they would take the pains; and that is,* Nosce teipsum, Read thy self.

Thomas Hobbes[1]

The "method" of cultural studies has had a controversial history, since from the start cultural studies was regarded by proponents and critics alike as an *avant-garde* enterprise – innovative or upstart, depending upon where one stood. As an interdisciplinary meeting ground there was no one "method." Cultural studies itself became a site for debates about important issues that confronted knowledge institutions more generally. The mutually untranslatable disciplinary languages of literary criticism, Marxism, anthropology, psychology, and the social sciences found they had incommensurate protocols about what counted as evidence, how it was collected, and whether it could be generalized.

As an interdisciplinary colloquy, cultural studies caused continuing methodological turbulence. How to analyse spoken and written language, visual images, and mediated audiovisual sequences for their cultural meanings? How to produce evidence of causal sequence connecting the world of meaning with the world of power? How to connect questions of structure (economy, class, etc.) with questions

71

of agency (individual subjectivity, creativity, etc.)? How to bring to bear on those questions new theoretical, philosophical or political ideas, including feminism, structuralism, post-structuralism, post-modernism, postcolonialism? These were all significant and disputed issues.

An even more fundamental doubt suffused cultural studies, or perhaps even explained (i.e. caused) it. This was the question of the nature of the *real*, and more particularly about the status of *knowledge* of the real. It wasn't that anyone doubted that something was out there (as they say) and that it was real. No one really fell for the scholasticist absurd-ities to which unsympathetic observers loved to reduce the debate. But still the question of the status of the real was both profound and banal.

At the deeper level, cultural studies was but one site where doubts were expressed about the extent to which nineteenth-century notions of science, based on the natural sciences, could be extended into cultural, sociopolitical and textual matters. In the human sphere, things that had been granted the status of self-evident truths in the expansionist phase of Western modernism were turning out to be contingent or "relative" after all. The "facts" of scientific progress, freedom, and rationality proved to be neither timeless nor universal, but historical and culture-bound. Culture could not be explained by a discourse that was itself a symptom of that culture – certainly not without the implications of explanation from within being taken seriously.

No one claimed that "the real" could be understood in some "Alice-in-Wonderland" way as comprising "whatever I say it is." But what people, individually and in collectivities both formal (institutional) and informal (cultural), said and thought, was also a material phenomenon with material effects. Discourses organized practices. What was *taken to be* self-evidently real, what *counted* as true, had both important causal force and also important blind-spots. In short, researchers could be completely committed to *truthfulness* while doubting the imperial truths of the era. Indeed, the "method" of root-and-branch skepticism, for which postmodernism, deconstruction and postcolonial theory became notorious, was fundamental to scientific inquiry itself. These were not "romantic" outbursts seeking to assert the supremacy of individual subjectivity over the material forces of nature. Cultural studies was fundamentally rational – it posed "methodological" problems about knowledge, how it was got, and for whose benefit. What looked like "the bleeding obvious" in one context proved to be no more than the expression of particularistic class, gender, or racial supremacy in another. It was no more than basic scientific thinking to refuse to prejudge such issues.

At the banal level, claims of access to the real could result in material benefits for those whose claims were given most credence. Disciplinary turf wars sometimes had a whiff of self-interest about them. Greater access to "the real" might result, for the successful method and its "knowing subject," in greater access to government research funding (and thence influence on public policy), or greater access to business (and thence to investment or consultancy). Trashing the po-mos was good sport for those who wanted to convince their own funding agencies that they were a no-nonsense outfit with "can-do" credentials. Cultural studies, as a "critical" rather than a "research" discipline (to use a distinction of Meaghan Morris), at least in its earliest years, was slow to catch on to the politics of discourse in this respect. For longer than was required by the need to "think outside the square," its luminaries continued to attempt to "say new things in new ways" by saying them in a kind of impenetrable theoreticist jargon that only aficionados could read. It was easy to mock such stuff; hard to get it past the funding bodies and mass-circulation editors.

But where and how was "the real" to be found? Cultural studies had a foot in more than one camp. Some proponents were devoted to the naturalistic description of things, i.e. to empirical studies of cultural practices, media audiences or the economic performance of cultural industries. Of these, some retained even more fundamentalist notions of science, seeking only to describe behaviors that might test hypotheses about causal sequence in phenomena; e.g. psychological investigations into media "effects," abstracted entirely from context, and reduced to measurable variables, whatever violence such methods did to the "real" lives of audiences.

Others sought to understand underlying structures, of which surface details were perhaps but symptoms or expressions. These included followers of structural anthropology and linguistics – Lévi-Strauss, Lotman, Saussure – who were pretty sure there were *universals* at work in the structures of language and other meaning-generating systems. Communication, kinship, and the economy were all thought to be instances of universal laws of circulation – of signifiers, women, and money. It was predicted that studying these might lead to an understanding of the "human mind."

The "methods" inherited by cultural studies therefore included both *realist* and *constructivist* versions, and often strange amalgams of the two. Indeed, cultural studies *became* a strange amalgam. Its earliest proponents were "empiricists" and "realists" – people like Richard Hoggart and even Raymond Williams were keen to *describe* the life of ordinariness in the history of national cultures. Then cultural studies went through a major "constructivist" period, via the marxist structuralism of Stuart Hall, and also by encounters with the psychoanalytical and formalist work of *Screen* theory, via feminism, and increasingly also via continental philosophy, whether the original writers regarded themselves as structuralists or not (e.g., successively, Lacan, Althusser, Foucault, Irigaray, Derrida, Deleuze, Lyotard, Baudrillard).

The upshot of this history – the more so as cultural studies migrated to America – was that a highly *constructivist* agenda was increasingly regarded as mere empirical fact. In fact "the real" turned out to be just what a constructivist amalgamation of Marx, Foucault, Barthes, Freud, and Hall said it was: namely, an *effect of power*. Indeed, the "deep structure" that produced "empirical" phenomena was increasingly thought to *be* power (variously defined, in sociological, marxist, feminist, or Foucauldian terms).

Oddly, both realist and constructivist positions were recognizably *modernist*; one derived from Kuhnian "normal science"; the other from (among other sources) "high" modernist literary and visual art. Both were dedicated to a correct conceptualization and understanding of the real. Scientific realism had its influence in the sociological and social science reaches of cultural studies, plus early semiotics ("the science of signs") and some versions of "scientific" Marxism (Althusser), as well as anthropology, both ethnographic and "structural." But the "constructivist" method certainly attracted more attention – if not notoriety – to the field. Relativism, postmodernism, textualism, and theoreticism all seemed to point *away* from engagement with the real, said the critics, toward an "anything goes" methodology where truth was abandoned. However, the "constructivist" method originated in claims to a *superior* realism over mere naturalistic description.

Meanwhile the most militant proponents of "the real" – those who regarded it as "the bleeding obvious" – concurred happily with the constructivists that the *meaning* of the real was all about power. But the realists wanted to know why cultural studies couldn't find out about power by going out and investigating its empirical effects. For instance, why not talk to "real" audiences, then check out the "real" ownership and control of media corporations? In reply, cultural studies could flaunt its theoreticism by asking how such a requirement would have advanced the natural sciences. An understanding of, say, the power of electricity could never have been secured by such methods. What would be learnt about electricity by interviewing people about its effects, such as lightning and static? What would knowing that Benjamin Franklin, inventor of the lightning conductor, was also a power-broker of the political kind, add to the understanding of electrical power? Was it possible to advance knowledge of electrical circuits by asking consumers how it felt to change a light-bulb? Could electromagnetic force be understood by knowing who owned and controlled the copper mines of Katanga? Of course not. Any real understanding of textual power required: (a) curiosity about how textual systems work as such, what their capacity might be; and (b) some sustained effort to determine what was meant by power. Any such understanding would have to set out from recognizing the *reality* of "textuality" itself, not seeing communication as a transparent medium through which meanings flow unchanged.

These currents, and the turbulence caused by their confluence, were especially noticeable in audience studies. The study of modern audiences was simultaneously an empirical science using quantitative and positivist methods and a site of some troubling questions about "the real." Audiences were very large demographic "facts," but knowledge of them was always and only indirect. Media audiences were too big, too diffused into everyday life, and too context-dependent to attain even the fictional coherence of other large demographic communities such as nations. But the indeterminacy of media audiences didn't stop people wanting to speak on their behalf. Politicians, issue-advocates, media entertainers, and commercial organizations were experts at knowing what audiences liked, would stand for, or wanted.

Power was certainly at stake here, because those who wanted either political or commercial power had to "know" their audiences. But in cultural studies it was important for analysts to recognize that claims made *on behalf of* audiences were a ruse to power, even when they were made by scientists. Audiences' "real interests" tended to be described in ways that suited the survival of the institutions that spoke on their behalf. In these circumstances, to claim scientific knowledge of an audience's wants or needs could appear megalomaniacal and self-serving, rather than testable and falsifiable. It was important for academic researchers *not* to claim objective knowledge of audiences' "subjectivity," since there was no such thing as a subjective audience – persons had subjectivities and engaged in audiencing practices – but such individuated activities did not amount to large-scale self-consciousness as such. Audiences were not "knowing subjects." They were only ever *imagined* communities.

Unknowable they may have been, but audiences had to be known to guarantee the continuation of important social institutions.

- Claims about audience *size* were central to the orderly conduct of important industries – television, cinema, recorded music, newspapers, magazines, etc.
- Claims about audience *behavior* were crucial to policy formation and government regulation of popular media.
- Claims about the "*effects*" of media on audiences were at the very heartbeat of the twentieth century, with a modernist desire for comfort and freedom counterbalanced by fear of manipulation and inundation (by "others" from within as well as by external "threats").

In relation to "effects," audiences *had* to be influenced for free markets and democratic politics to survive, for both commercial and political campaigns to have any meaning. But simultaneously they *must not* be influenced to behave or believe improperly. Violence, communism, passivity, dumbing-down, bad language, bad taste, bad diet – these were unlooked-for "effects" of media consumption that had (where they were agreed by politicians and "public opinion" to have occurred) to be minimized. These preoccupations inevitably led to periodic outbursts of interest in how knowledge of audiences was arrived at, and, more fundamentally still, what an audience *was*.

Hitherto, textual analysis had been applied mostly to the "high" arts that were thought to be morally uplifting. With cultural studies, not only were literary and artistic techniques applied to non-canonical creative works like television shows and newspapers, but they were also available to prise open "texts" that had no creative intentions whatsoever, including official and industry discourses and documents, and even academic "texts" themselves. So it became possible to analyze textually what those who spoke on behalf of audiences were saying, as if it were fictional, and to interrogate claims made about audiences as *discourse*, not "science." Science itself became merely more "text" that needed explanation, not a privileged part of the framework of explanation.

What if audiences were in need of neither correction nor protection, but were already living in a "meaning democracy" where their desires, fears, behaviors, and influences were theirs, not literally the business of profit- or power-seeking agencies? And what if the only way that audiences could be known was via *textual* rather than *behavioral* evidence? And what if "the audience" was as "constructed" a "reality" as any other – an indeterminate, contingent, contentious outcome of governmental, corporate, scientific, and discursive strategies, not a "thing" with the properties of "the bleeding obvious"?

This was where I came in. In an article published in 1987, I argued that television audiences were only ever encountered as representations.[2] In addition, my work in cultural and media studies centered on "*reading*" texts, especially popular mediated ones. Apparently these two facts meant that:

- I don't believe in reality,
- I contend that anything goes,
- One could say whatever one liked about the object of study without bothering to investigate it empirically,
- Any method of investigation is as good as any other since they're all discursive.

These criticisms in fact came from Greg Philo and David Miller, in a report called *Cultural Compliance: Dead Ends of Media/Cultural Studies and Social Science*, published by the Glasgow University Media Group, of which Philo was the director. They wrote:

> Some theorists have gone over the edge into the twilight world where only the discursive is real while others hover on the cusp of the real and the discursive. In the former camp, Hartley has argued that there is no such thing as an empirical audience.[3]

They called this position "radical constructivism" (evidently borrowing the term "constructivist" from David Morley),[4] and they didn't like it. I was one of the "dead ends" of their title.

Why?

1  Because they wanted to insist that there's a real world beyond discourse.
2  Because they worried that, "if we can only know through discursive practice and the questions we ask 'determine' our results, then any piece of empirical research is as good as any other and is not 'evidence' for or against a particular proposition." Their contrary preferred view was that "in fact, the meaning of events is not infinitely negotiable" (p. 24).
3  They wanted discourse to be an effect as well as a cause: "discourse can be undermined when it comes up against changed material realities and public disbelief."
4  The "key difficulty with [my] 'discursive practice' approach is that discourse is itself part of the real world which can best be judged in the same way as the rest of reality through experience and evidence about how it really works" (p. 25).

So much did I agree with their conclusion that "discourse is itself a part of the real world" that I spent a lengthy publishing career trying to find adequate ways to "judge ... how it really works," using textual and discursive evidence. Their "key difficulty" was therefore "*no problemo*" for me. I was also fairly certain that there was a "real world beyond discourse," although, for reasons advanced above, I was never confident that *knowledge* could be encountered outside of language, and here I didn't follow Derrida so much as the philosopher of science Karl Popper.[5] Nor did I have a problem about discourse changing in response to changes in "material realities." Again, it was a claim I tried to substantiate in my own work.

That only left their second objection as a point of difference between us. They wrote that if knowledge was discursive, then "anything goes." "Any piece of empirical research is as good as any other." They illustrated the point by allowing their imaginations to run riot:

> Let us suppose for a moment that three cultural theorists (two exponents of discursive practice and one constructivist) find themselves in a darkened attic. They have been unable to change the light-bulb and are discussing the location of the hole in the floor which is the exit. The first two agree that the hole is just in front of them. In this sense "reality" is constructed for them by discourse, which has real consequences on the direction of their steps. The constructivist meanwhile, true to his radical constructivism, subverts the preferred meanings offered by the other two and wanders around randomly in another part of the attic.

> The other two theorists [*sic*] assessment of where to walk is, however, immediately revised when they hear the shout and thud which the constructivist makes as he falls through the (real) exit and hits the floor.[6]

I presume I must have been that "radical constructivist," shouting and thudding as I unexpectedly encountered the real. "Reality," please note, took the shape of an unpleasant, inanimate adversary, balefully lying in wait for the foolish textualist, who was so impractical he couldn't even change a light-bulb. But while I was in fact given credit for discovering the whereabouts of the real, my "method" was dismissed as "random wandering" – not purposeful empirical exploring of the bracingly realist kind no doubt undertaken each morning by Messrs Philo and Miller.

A similar approach to that of Philo and Miller was adopted by Jim McGuigan, in a critique of my work in the *European Journal of Communication*. Apparently I was an "anything-goes" postmodernist, so it was OK to have some fun at my expense by making up pretend scenarios as "evidence" of the ludicrousness of the textualist position. McGuigan wanted to send up what he (sarcastically) called my "courageous defence of 'the Essex girl'":

> Roughly speaking, to paraphrase Hartley: "So what's wrong with Essex girls, you stuck-up male intellectuals? They/we like kissing!" I, personally, have no axe to grind against Essex girls. Live and let live, I say. But, what is the connection between the Essex girl and Tom Paine, who is, according to Hartley, his hero? Hero and heroine kissing behind the hedge in the suburban south-east of England. It's a postmodern image, indeed, but I am not at all sure what it tells us. Nothing, I suspect. Just a bit of fun.
>
> Let's get real. I have taken liberties with Hartley's text; and presumably, that is allowed, or else there is no consistency here at all.[7]

For reasons that would have been evident within its pages, I took two paragraphs in a 250-page book to argue that the figure of "the Essex girl" was a personalization of "suburban, feminized, consumerist ordinariness."[8] Elsewhere in that book I took the political philosopher and democrat Thomas Paine to represent the possibility that political emancipation could be popularized via journalism. As for kissing, I analysed various examples of it in the pictorial media, and also discussed how the very notion of "kissing" might describe certain cross-demographic relationships, between textmakers and audiences, for instance. "Kissing" is arguably a more appealing metaphor, certainly a better teaching device, for such contact than the more familiar combative language (like grinding axes "against" Essex girls) based on notions of power, domination, and struggle.[9]

An image of Tom Paine from Sussex kissing an imaginary girl from Essex could indeed stand for cordialized cross-demographic communication between political theory and ordinary people. So by all means let them kiss. Such a prospect was less risible than the spectacle of self-proclaimed "progressive" critics who wanted to spread the (Painite) message of popular sovereignty among the "masses," while treating contemporary ordinariness as a mere bit of fun, signifying nothing (and, in the name of "consistency," extending the same treatment to my work). I argued in *Uses of Television* that this dislike of the ordinary – the refusal to see politics in everyday life, or progressive potential in pleasure – has been a long-standing failure of the British and perhaps the international intellectual left, where *democracy*, especially any sign of it emanating from the demos itself, was taken as a *defeat*.[10]

Meanwhile, in Australia, a very heated public debate was led by Keith Windschuttle, who was at the time entering a phase of professional controversialism (he later migrated from this topic to an even more widely controversial denial of the extent of atrocities against Aboriginal people during Australia's settler history). The fuss on this occasion was about the relations between cultural studies and journalism education.[11] In an article published in at least five different versions across three continents, he attacked the same 1987 article of mine as had been criticized by Philo and Miller:

> The logic of Hartley's approach is that all these editors need to do is simply adopt a different methodology to measure the audience or a different definition of what the audience is, then give themselves whatever ratings, circulation and revenues they choose.[12]

Although that was a "logic" never proposed by me, it may in fact have been what Karl Popper used to call a "bold hypothesis" – it was "falsifiable" by testing it empirically and against the historical record. But Windschuttle wasn't that much of an empiricist; he wasn't about to test anything. It was enough for him that editors and broadcasters "have to believe there are real people out there in the world." Indeed, but that belief did not determine the quality of what was known (or "believed") about audiences, nor the means used to find out.

To assess how different methodologies did in fact produce "different" audiences, it was necessary only to observe what happened when an established method changed. This happened when the people-meter displaced the diary system in TV ratings. It happened to music when the pop music charts were reformed, and to publishing when sales-tracking software was introduced. Suddenly there were indeed different bestsellers, different hit songs, different top-rating shows. And beyond these occasional disruptions to "business as usual," a routine demonstration of the power of different methodologies to produce "different" audiences was on show all the time, when rival pollsters sampled the same population.

Windschuttle's "realist method" of pointing to the "bleeding obvious" (just kick the table-leg as proof of its reality) was also adopted by David Morley. In his book *Television, Audiences and Cultural Studies*, he praised my "valuable corrective" to "naïve realism," but then shifted the argument from "epistemology" to "ontology" (he reckoned I'd got them mixed up) in order to retain *his* version of realism:

> Naturally, any empirical knowledge which we may generate of television audiences will be constructed through particular discursive practices, and the categories and questions present and absent in these discourses will determine the nature of the knowledge we can generate. However, this is to argue, contra Hartley, that while we can only know audiences through discourses, audiences do in fact exist outside the terms of these discourses.[13]

But the problem wasn't solved this way. Once Morley had agreed that "we can only know" through discourse, it ought to have followed that we can't know what and how things "exist outside discourses." Slipping in an emphatic "in fact" ["because I say so"?] wouldn't make it come true. Conversely, my insistence that audiences were "invisible fictions" – discursive products – was not an assertion that *nothing exists* beyond such constructions, only that whatever knowledge is produced and circulated about audiences is discursive, and none the less real for that.

Even if he were to concede this epistemological point, Morley was not prepared to go the extra ontological mile. He was "contra" my argument that there was no "actual" audience beyond its production as a category. Here my point was not that there were no *people* out there, nor that "we" could think or do whatever we liked. I was much less willing to make assumptions about what audiences are, do, or think than were my critics, nor did I claim to speak on their behalf.

Here's what I actually wrote in 1987:

> [Television audiences] are the invisible fictions that are produced institutionally in order for various institutions to take charge of the mechanisms of their own survival. Audiences may be imagined empirically, theoretically or politically, but in all cases the product is a fiction that serves the needs of the imagining institution. In no case is the audience "real", or external to its discursive construction. There is no "actual" audience that lies beyond its production as a category, which is merely to say that audiences are only ever encountered *per se* as *representations*.[14]

The modern TV audience was not like an "audience" in a traditional context – say an audience with the Pope or royalty, or an audience in a theatre. The "modern" media audience was already "postmodern." It was not self-present as such, not an assembly, not known to itself by mutual gaze and encounter, and it did not behave as a crowd or mob. Its existence wasn't actual but virtual. The TV audience didn't exist *as such*. Instead, "the audience" was a discursive construct of (among others) media organizations, government regulators, and academic criticism. All of these extended the traditional idea of the audience as a self-present assembly, and applied this metaphorically to aggregations of mutually unconnected populations of, for instance, individuals-in-families at home. Those who constructed audiences in this way went on to use what they "knew" about them to authorize acts undertaken in institutions from which audiences-as-people were routinely excluded, including government, media, and academic/critical institutions.

Audiences were not people – not the whole of any person, not the same as "the people." People occupied the position of audience from time to time, and were tutored in how to do that by the media themselves. But the "I" that watched TV was also:

- *more* than "the" audience: "I" am also consumer, citizen, reader, parent, professor, etc.;
- *less* than "the" audience: "I" am not entirely what audiences are taken to be by any given imagining institution – from their point

of view "I" might be the wrong age, nationality, gender, or I might exhibit the wrong attitudes, tastes, behaviors;

- *other* than "the" audience: When am "I" audience, and when not? Am I audience only when attending to the screen with active engagement? Whenever my TV set is switched on whether I'm watching it or not? When I'm showing TV-clips in a classroom or conference hall? When I subsequently buy goods, express opinions, or vote for parties that have been promoted on TV? When I am "me" – as influenced by TV directly, wittingly, or otherwise.

- *"better"* and *"worse"* than "the" audience: "I" behave in ways not predicted by audience research – for instance, I don't beat up old ladies after watching action-drama; I don't buy cola or hamburgers, no matter how often they're advertised; I don't drive more slowly after watching *World's Wickedest Police Chases* or a public safety campaign.

- The "I" that watches TV always *both exceeds and falls short* of what "audiences" are routinely supposed to be like – this two-sided truth is perhaps the founding premise of *The Simpsons*.

"The audience" was an "invisible fiction" – never encountered as such, whole, being itself, speaking for itself. It was not a knowing subject. It could therefore only ever be an object of knowledge.

But it was a *discursive* object. Historically, the TV audience was produced most often and powerfully as an object of modernizing, progressive knowledge. It was only important to most researchers because it stood for the population at large, and was investigated in order to answer important questions about the populations of modern countries. Will they revolt? How will they vote? What will they buy? How can they be rendered civil?

These questions were not reckoned important across the whole range of media, but only in relation to the currently most popular or "mass" medium. Few researchers outside of book retailing were interested in "the audience" for literature – the literary reading public was simply not imagined as an aggregate of living, empirical people who had to be surveyed every 15 minutes of each evening as to what page of what publication they were on. Audience research was not a highly developed branch of literary, theatrical, or musical studies. Paradoxically, real audiences – people who actually assembled as *the audience* of plays, shows and musical performances – were surveyed rather infrequently compared with the stay-at-home "audience" of TV-viewers. This was because social science was interested only in audiences *as populations taken to be objects of knowledge* – specifically, of commercial, governmental, or critical knowledge. Such audiences did not exist *in themselves*, never mind *for themselves*. They existed only *in knowledge*.

The ideal-type of modern science preferred knowledge to be entirely objective, impersonal, and independent of the investigator (as hinted by Morley, above). But knowledge of TV audiences could not take this pure objective form, not only because investigators themselves were almost always *part* of an audience in some way, but also because audiences were only encountered *textually*. There were different aspects to the textuality of audiences:

1   the epistemological issue of the textuality of scientific knowledge itself – the extent to which what was "known" arose from the mode of its representation as knowledge, rather than from its own physical properties;
2   the textualization of audiences by knowledge-seeking institutions – converting people into ratings, for instance, where they often took the mute form of the statistic;
3   textual address to audiences within media discourse itself – that part of media texts devoted to relations between themselves and their "readers."

Textual analysts had for many years grappled with the latter issue, via the problem of what Umberto Eco called the "reader's position."[15] Much work was done on the textually "implied reader" of literature (Iser) and the textually "preferred reading" of media (Hall et al.); on "reception" and "reader-response" theory (Radway); on "open" (literary) and "closed" (popular) texts (Culler); and on "interpretive communities" (Fish).[16] All this betokened a very fuzzy boundary between "text" and "reader" – each reaching out to the other with strategies from the semiotic to the psychic, designed to "get across" the gap between meaning and identity.

Textmakers had tried every trick in the book to turn those *people* out there into *readers* by hailing, interpellating, positioning, addressing, preferring, appealing, seducing. It was clear that such issues needed to be taken into account when audiences were investigated. There remained a very real requirement for decent textual analysis to be undertaken right at the heart of empirical audience research. How did texts, including truth-claiming journalism, establish *relations* with their readers as well as *representations* of whatever their subject matter might be?[17] This question remained, no matter what actual readers might have had to say about their experience of the encounter.

At the same time, it was important to distinguish the implied reader, which could be identified by *empirical analysis of objectively existing text*, from critical wish-fulfilment, in which audiences were simply presumed to be what a given observer would like them to be. Alan Sinfield and others inveighed against literary critics who liked to *invoke* "the reader" or "the audience" as thinking or feeling a particular response to a given text. These responses all too often turned out to be mere projections of the personal desires and readings of the critic, who "proceeds blithely with an un-situated 'reading,' thereby effacing the possibility of readers from subordinated groups."[18] The politics of this went beyond personal bad faith. It was just this kind of projection that I identified at the *institutional* level as the "invisible fiction" of the audience – the projection on to "the audience" of the needs, purposes, fears, or desires of the imagining institution, be that commercial, governmental, or critical.

But empirical social science took a further epistemological step. It took the institutionally produced audience to be the *same thing* as "*the people*" – the population as a whole. The TV audience was routinely equated with "the nation," for instance. This kind of projection was not frowned on at all; in fact it was required in the name of "generalizable" data, by means of which universalizing statements could be made about populations on the evidence of what was known about textualized audiences. David E. Morrison went so far as to dismiss as "inconsequential" the entire enterprise of cultural studies on the grounds that it refused, according to him, to produce generalizable (quantitative) data. In the course of this critique he gave a revealing account of what a *social-science reader* actually did in the act of reading other people's research:

> If generalisation [of focus group findings] is not given then the results become so meaningless that the reader is "forced" to give meaning to them by making the generalisation themselves through an assumed general applicability to wider populations. Without this assumption the research makes little sense, or is so trivial as not to be worthy of serious reading. Why bother reading the accounts of a few people drawn from the general population, if there is nothing special about them? They are ... ordinary people who derive their status of interest by what they may tell us about people generally.[19]

What if "what they may tell us about people *generally*" was nothing? Are "people" in themselves merely inconsequential? Morrison had no concept of *self-representation* by ordinary people. He reckoned, for instance, that "to know how some people incorporate television into their lives remains at the level of the inconsequential unless it is known whether they speak for more than themselves" (p. 158). Audiences were only interesting *at all* if they stood for something that they were not. That required data about sufficient numbers of "ordinary people" to support statistical analysis. Clearly, the way the investigator textualized the audience produced the form of the knowledge: in Morrison's case, knowledge was permissible only in the form of quantitative data. However, a researcher from a different tradition may have "known" "the audience" not as a community at all, but as an appeal by textual address. It was a "you," not a "they" (much less an "it").

Nevertheless, textual appeals by media and other agencies could be *"peopled"* in various ways. The extent to which this happened was a legitimate question for empirical research. For instance, in response to political or commercial campaigns, people came out on the streets for good or ill, or they voted, bought, or watched in particular intensities. Equally, despite the best efforts of political and commercial campaigners, they decided not to do what was desired of them. But no one knew in advance how any of this would turn out, if at all, which is why advertising or publicity was needed before an event, polling during it, and audience research after it. The reason was simple: "audiences" and "people" are not the same thing. There's a gap. It was unsafe to equate a common sense notion of "people" to audiences. Conversely, it seemed much safer to propose a convergence between "texts" and "readers."

Intrepid researchers who sallied across the gap between audiences and people in search of the (representative and quantifiable) "real" would still find only textuality. But the Enlightenment fantasy of the pre-semiotic *enfant sauvage* continued to haunt empirical research. A disciplinary desire persisted to define "real" in opposition to "textual" and to find in "the real" such things as opinions and attitudes, behaviors and structures, power and struggle, in a natural state, unsullied by semiosis. But "people" were semiotically impure (in the anthropological sense); they were muddied in meanings long before the audience researcher waylaid them in the mall, or called them from the phone-center, or trooped them off to the lab and the focus-group meeting room.

Socially oriented research needed to take both the textualization of everyday life and the practices of vernacular reading much more seriously, and to think in terms of "reading" (a practice) rather than "the audience" (a thing). What audiences *did* when they "read" media texts was not frequently investigated. Empirical audience research usually began at a place quite far downstream of this, when people had already processed their reading practices into further textual performances, such as diary completion, filling in of questionnaires, participating in focus groups, etc. In short, the audience as "reader" was seldom caught in the act. What was converted into "knowledge" was the bit where people *produced* rather than "consumed" text.

For some researchers, that banal institutional impediment to accepting that audiences were a textual phenomenon remained in play. Those who did empirical research wanted to be able to get on with it. They relied on the self-evident, naturalized, independent existence of audiences prior to the act of investigation. And they needed such audiences to stand directly for even larger populations, so that conclusions about particular samples could be generalized. At some level, this was a funding matter; researchers wanted to protect their scientific credentials in the face of funding councils or endowments that were willing to support "science," but had difficulty with "postmodernism."

There were, however, various problems with this kind of de-textualized "empirical" audience research as evidence:

- First, the investigation of such populations was always undertaken from the point of view of the investigating institution, not from that of the audience "itself." Far from being respectful of the audience's point of view, such research wanted to conclude something about audience "behavior" that would lead to policies (governmental, commercial, or critical) designed to *change* it.
- Second, it was individualist and behavioural – tending to associate people's practices as audiences with their personalities and situation as individual "subjects." Another perspective on audiences would investigate the actions of "being" an audience as a kind of literacy, not a kind of person.
- Third, the "experience" of being an audience said very little about the "textual system" that audiences encountered.[20] The semiotic and institutional power of a textual system such as journalism, drama, or advertising could not be investigated by talking to audiences (or readerships), since these phenomena were the *product* of such systems.

Asking people how they felt would reveal something about the people, but very little about the *system*. Discursive institutions could not be explained out of individual experience.

Strangely enough for a realist empirical researcher, Greg Philo wasn't all that interested in television as a textual system, or in the concepts of text, discourse, or even audience. He was interested in politically partisan campaigning – not in *understanding* the audience, but in *changing it*. In a publication called *Dispatches from Disaster Zones* he reported on the kind of empirical work that he did with the Glasgow Media Group:

> What is the relationship between what is being said in the media and what the mass of the people actually believe? What the mass of the people see when they look at the news on Africa is a panorama of epidemics, deaths, babies crying, refugees, bodies: what they conceive of as an enormous mess. I asked people in the focus groups that we were using, do you remember Rwanda and all the fighting and all that? "Oh yes, yes", they said, "we remember that". What do you remember? "Oh, dead bodies, oh a lot of refugees, you know." What caused it, I said, do you remember what caused any of this? "Oh, it was a lot of tribes fighting, wasn't it?" If I say the word "tribes" to you, I said, what comes into your head? "Men in grass skirts", they said, "men in grass skirts with spears."
>
> So I say to you that the worst of what we imagine to be tabloid journalism, and the worst of the colonial or post colonial clichés that we can imagine in our own heads, are what is in the heads of very many people in the population ...We need to break the way in which people think about Africa: to break the idea of men in grass skirts ...You need to ...attack the template. You need to identify moments of information which will shatter the basic way in which people think about Africa.[21]

While claiming transparent access to the real, this type of empirical research had no intention of leaving that reality as it found it – there was no desire here to "live and let live." Essex-girl had to be "*broken*." Her beliefs had to be "*attacked*," her thinking "*shattered*."

Such a line of thinking led Philo and Miller to an extraordinary inversion of the original purpose of the Glasgow Media Group. It was set up in the 1970s to analyse the gap between media reports and reality, and therefore to hold the media to account for bias, distortion, and lack of objectivity. It was designed to be the scourge of *journalism*.

But by the time Philo and Miller had taken over the agenda, it was presented as the scourge of *media studies* (of which it nevertheless remained a part). News media were not only let off the hook; journalists became the salvation of the same radical politics that had previously campaigned *against* journalism *in the name of* media studies. Philo and Miller, from an avowed leftist stance, reproduced the very same argument against academic media research that had been advanced from a rightist stance by Keith Windschuttle. They applauded journalism itself as the only critical, progressive, modernist discourse left after the ravages of the po-mos:

> The abdication of responsibility by academics means that it is left to journalists to do the hard work of uncovering the truth and revealing corruption and abuses of power. Many of the most penetrating critiques of developments in areas such as government information management, the new PR and promotional industries and political corruption, state secrecy and surveillance, journalistic practice, editorial control, censorship and news reporting of conflict, the tabloid press, media empires and satellite broadcasting, the problems faced by women in the news media, gendered politics and culture, on racism and on children, childhood and youth, have been written not by academics but by journalists.[22]

"If the point is to change the world," say Philo and Miller, "then such work [i.e. media and cultural studies] is pointless" (p. 48). What made it pointless was not that it had nothing to say about media, culture, textuality, and the like, nor even that it failed to produce objective knowledge by appropriate disciplinary methods. Its deficiency was that it was not a sufficiently "penetrating critique" to "change the world" in a direction approved of by the Glasgow Media Group.

Textualists "abdicated academic responsibility," apparently, if we failed to *reform* audiences. Taking them as one found them in order to understand what they were, or teaching them directly, or teaching students and intellectuals about them, were not acceptable markers of *academic* responsibility for Philo and Miller. Trying (as I have) to elaborate a critical position that was located at the audience's "point of view" was anathema, unless it was accompanied by an attempt to "penetrate" the poor blighters with a "penetrating critique." If you didn't want to *improve* the popular, then you were dismissed for "celebrating" it, and in the residual culture of miserablist lament for a lost politics of Revolutionary Rupture, "celebrations" were populist, dangerous and depoliticizing. At the same time, "breaking," "attacking," and "shattering" the object of study were somehow understood to be part of "empirical" science. Writers who found something positive in television were contrasted pejoratively with those journalistic heroes who did the "hard work" of "uncovering the truth." Academics who used their teaching position to *teach* were merely failing to "reveal corruption and abuses of power."

So how can audiences be investigated? Whenever I hear the word "audience," I reach for my "reading" (see Figures 4.1 and 4.2).

David Morrison wrote (in a passage quoted above): "Why bother reading the accounts of a few people drawn from the general population, if there is nothing special about them? They are ... ordinary people who derive their status of interest by what they may tell us about people generally." The half-serious, half-playful musings of an anonymous day-release student about chrysanthemums and the mining industry make a full enough reply to Morrison. But to do justice to the "account" of the ordinary person who produced this text requires not a pro-forma psychological test but a *poetics* of the everyday. It marks the irreducibility of the ordinary. It is not easily converted into "data" for population management by militant activists, whether radical or reactionary. It needs to be *believed*, not bean-counted. It even has its uses as a "teaching text" – it certainly taught me something. In fact I found it discarded at the Polytechnic of Wales (the former Glamorgan School of Mines) when I arrived there for my first academic job in 1975. I've kept it ever since to remind me of the extent to which "ordinariness" exceeds in reach and grasp, beauty and power, the rather tawdry prying of some types of social science inquiry.

Whoever Julian B. Rotter (the "Author" of the blank psy-form) may have been, his copyrighted promptings simply failed to provoke anything in this "subject" other than poetry. As *psycho-data* it must have been pretty valueless, which is why it ended up in the bin where I found it, but as *text* it could hardly be richer. Its real "author," an apprentice mining engineer who dutifully exceeded the instruction to express his "*real feelings*," was being encouraged to "respond" in the most individualized and behaviorist way possible. But he actually managed to create out of these banalities a powerful sense of family, community, industry, and region, not to mention personal qualities from wit to compassion.

24: The future of coalmining, lies between the lines 1-40.

INCOMPLETE SENTENCES BLANK – ADULT FORM

Name ... (blanked out) ... Sex ... Male ... Age ... 29 ... Marital Status ...
Married
Place ... Brynhyfryd, Glynneath, Neath [South Wales] ... Date ... 8th
Jan 1975

Complete these sentences to express <u>your real feelings</u>. Try to do every one.
Be sure to make a complete sentence.

I like growing chrysanthemums because it relaxes me.
The happiest time I have is when I potter around with
chrysanthemums.
I want to know more about the basics of chrysanthemum growing.
Back home after a holiday is the era of another holiday.
I regret that fishing licences will cost more this year.
At bedtime I should sacrifice sleep and consentrate [sic.]
on swotting.
Men whom I work with help each other in their daily work.
The best holiday I have had was in Spain '74.
What annoys me most is people talking on the catch when I
throw darts.
People who annoy me most are people who talk on the catch
when I throw darts.
A mother whom I know well carries on with a father whom I
know well.
I feel sometimes that the night shift inventor should be
made to work days regular.
My greatest fear is of all my chrysanthemum cuttings failing.
In school we are given blank sheets which are to be filled in
with data.
I can't understand how some people can be rough with children.

Ψ

Copyright 1950 The Psychological Corporation
All rights reserved (etc.) No part of this blank may be reproduced in any form of
printing or by any other means, electronic or mechanical, including, but not limited to,
audiovisual recording and transmission, and portrayal or duplication in any
information storage and retrieval system, without permission in writing from the
publisher. See Catalog for further information.
The Psychological Corporation, 304 East 45th Street, New York, N. Y. 10017

JULIAN B. ROTTER, AUTHOR
Printed in U.S.A.  71-181AS

*Figure 4.1* Blank form *recto*

Sports `like chrysanthemums really do interest me.`
When I was a child `I wish that I had'nt take up mining as a`
`career.`
My nerves `are on edge when I have to pick the darts team.`
Other people `whom I work with feel that night shift should be`
`banned.`
I suffer `day fatigue when I work night shift.`
I failed `my first driving exam due to a puncture and hitting`
`another car.`
Reading `if taken as an adjective is this side of London.`
[Refers to town of Reading]
My mind `goes blank when j notation is thrown at me.`
The future `of coalmining, lies between the lines 1-40.`
I need `at this very moment a nice cold Guin[n]ess.`
Marriage `brings the best out of man.`
I am best `when I am in the glasshouse with the`
`chrysanthemums.`
Sometimes `on my way to the college I feel like carrying on`
`to London.`
What pains me `most is to see my daughter in pain.`
I hate `peeling potatoes for dinner.`
This place `often reminds me of the past, dark and dreary.`
I am very `fond of gardening because it proves to be very`
`relaxing.`
The only trouble `with when I catch a big fish, someone's caught`
`one larger.`
I wish `that I could have health, wealth and another three`
`wishes.`
My father `said yesterday that he was waiting for his first`
`big pools win.`
I secretly `wish that I can pass the Colliery Engineers`
`Certificate Exam.`
`I, the above signed state that the above to be true to my`
`knowledge.`
Dancing `like night shift do not go down to[o] well with me.`
My greatest worry is `that mortgage repayments will be completed.`
Most women `who talk to me want to know how my wife and`
`daughter are.`

*Figure 4.2* Blank form *verso*

This was clearly "true" and as stated was something to be proud of. But the subsequent history of that future – strikes, pit closures and the de-industrialization of the South Wales coalfield – gave the text a poignant dimension its author could not have imagined at the time. To re-read it over a quarter of a century later is also to encounter *self-representation* by someone (an "unrepresentative" ordinary person) in the very moment of their being positioned in that gap between social-science knowledge and their own personal lives as people. That gap is spanned by *text* – not a text abstracted from everyday life but one precisely expressing it, by one of those whose life it was. The extent to which this miner's "real feelings" escaped the intentions of the Psychological Corporation of New York, and expressed imaginative truths about the historical period and community in which he lived, is the exact measure of how far short of "reality" any de-textualized empirical social science research must necessarily fall.

However, social science research remained very hostile to the prospect of a textualized audience. For instance, the anthropologist Mark Hobart criticized the leakage of the concepts of "text" and of "reading" into places he thought they shouldn't go:

> Academics' reverence for texts not only enshrines closure, but also a singular form of superiority. What proportion of people in Italy, England or, say, Bali spend much of their time reading texts? My guess is that it is forms of popular culture and mass media which occupy most peoples' time and attention in many parts of the world. The idea that people might escape textual closure is so horrendous that we have two related fields, cultural and media studies, the self-appointed task of which is to textualize shopping and fashion, film and television. Just consider the title of Fiske and Hartley's analysis of television, *Reading Television*. Watching television and film or shopping may well involve textuality in complex ways. It does not mean that such activities are texts. By textualising the world academics have condemned themselves to be even more irrelevant than they already are.[23]

This is probably a case of shooting the messenger. Jon Klancher, Thomas Richards, and others have shown that the process of textualizing the world in order to control it had a history not only among academics, but more widely among an emerging knowledge class, going back to the needs of a bureaucratizing power-structure in nineteenth-century imperial Britain.[24] In other words, *the world has been textualized*, not least in media forms within whose terms such publics as can be imagined have their existence.

Hobart castigated cultural and media studies academics for finding "the idea that people might escape textual closure" to be "horrendous." But here he was disingenuous at best. Much of cultural and media studies, including my own work, was trying to do just the opposite of this, as McKenzie Wark has argued:

> The concepts of "reading" and "readership" that Hartley advances are crucial for any genuinely democratic approach to thinking about this unspeakable majority who come together as a public ...What is refreshing about Hartley's approach is that it takes seriously the idea that it is not just the talking heads who know how to read, but that silent suburbans also know a thing or two about how to make meaning out of a text. Both "reading" and "text" might apply as much to television and pop songs and movies and journalism as to the novel. Acts of reading that take place with the telly on in the suburban living room, or while listening to the radio in the car on the commute, are what constitute the actual public culture of the nation. It might not be the ideal "public sphere" imagined by political theorists, but unlike the latter, it actually works.[25]

Thus, the politics of the issue went beyond my personal position. Wark pointed out how my approach to reading and readerships went against the grain of the "caricature" of cultural and media studies such as that advanced by Hobart. Wark wrote:

> Ironically, what Hartley is doing here is the opposite of the usual caricature of cultural studies. According to that put-down, cultural studies brings trashy pop culture into the refined world of the literary classroom. But what Hartley does is go looking for the reading practices of the literary classroom out in the common world. He goes looking for examples of the way people read, and by reading, become a public. The public are a "reading public", and they read voraciously – movies, books, magazines, TV shows. And out of what they read, the public decide who they are, what they believe, what the common world is like, what ideas of the "fair go" to pursue.[26]

In short, it is necessary to make a "sympathetic and constructive reading of the way reading itself works in everyday life" (p. 135). That remained the goal; its purpose, to describe what might be called "meaning democracy."

Having said that, there is still legitimate force in Hobart's reluctance to give "text" and "reading" too free a rein as metaphors for what happens when ordinary people pay attention to media and engage in cultural activities. This is because of the overly "top-table" provenance of textual analysis itself, as a disciplinary discourse. Literary studies has had a very long history, with medieval antecedents in sermonizing, the homily, and biblical exegesis − "teaching the laity" in short. Its later (modernist) prestige was at least partly based on the use of the high literary canon as the moral center of the school curriculum and as an antidote to the infections of new, popular, and mediated culture. Was it therefore wise to found the study of new, popular, and democratizing media on a "textual tradition" that was rooted in a desire to inoculate the population against demo(cra)tic culture? Was it appropriate to make literary exegesis − originally designed as a technique for inculcating collective discipline and individual self-management in popular classes − into the very tool of popular analysis? Was popular narrative itself, from news and soap opera in particular to "public service" media in general, in the end little more than a pedagogic mechanism for "popularizing" the moral code of those whose own consciousness and consciences were formed by (too) much literary reading?

It is not wise for any critic to impose on "the people" a moralizing message from anywhere, least of all from on high. But at the same time, *teaching* is an *anthropological* activity (unlike *schooling*, which is historical and institutional), crossing epochs from pre-modern to post-modern societies − without it human "society" couldn't be social. Likewise cross-demographic communication, gathering populations together despite their different interests, remained a constant requirement. In the modern era, popular sovereignty could not be exercised without large-scale communication, transmitting text to the public on the issues of the day for their consideration, and feeding back textualized "public opinion" to the representatives in the political sphere. The imperfections of that communicative process from day to day (where there remained a need for both vigilance and reform) were less important than the more fundamental issue of its necessity to public life in the first place.

A significant aspect of any such two-way process was teaching; employing the oratorical, rhetorical, persuasive, hortatory, and other skills of *discourse*. Such teaching was not all ideology and populism. Cross-demographic communication was more than ever necessary in conditions where "the public" (like "the Left") could no longer be assumed to be "speaking the same language" as each other. Democratization needed to be extended through *different* groups and identities, not imposed from above by means of a uniform message or belief-system. The extension of democracy relied quite crucially on a two-way process of "teaching" by and of those who occupied knowledge-producing positions within an economy based increasingly on information and culture. "Critical reading" as a *practice* needed to be cultivated among different sections of the overall population, "for themselves" and in their own idiom.

Hence it did seem that the concept of text was useful, precisely to understand the conditions (and the very form) in which cross-demographic communication took place and the techniques by means of which it was done – including narrative, drama, entertainment, and journalism. It was equally useful, as Wark pointed out, to imagine the ordinary citizen as a citizen-reader, "voraciously" reading texts from all sources as part of the activity of self- and community-formation. This squared with Abercrombie and Longhurst's idea of the diffusion and dispersal of audiencehood into everyday life, such that the idea of separable categories of "people" and "audience" became ever more problematic, no matter how important the conceptual distinction between them (as argued earlier). To trace and analyse textuality in everyday life, and to grasp the activity of audiencing, required a mode of analysis that certainly had literary origins. But – and here's the answer to Hobart's qualms – the need and purpose was to *democratize the technique* (to "generalize" it *among* populations, not to generalize *about* them), and not to make the object of study into "literature."

It followed, therefore, that the notions of "text" and "reader," not to mention that of "teaching," have all evolved radically beyond their original usage in literary exegesis.[27] Media analysis itself has become old. Forty-odd years after *Uses of Literacy* it was even something that people had retired from (my old colleague from the Polytechnic of Wales, John Fiske, for one). In that time it developed a public colloquy, a body of work, a set of interdisciplinary tools, which would outlive any given practitioner. The concept of text was stretched and transformed. It needed to be used, criticized, and modified as part of a process of historically changing working definitions, not as an absolute category.

People trained in media and cultural studies have something very helpful to offer those trained in social and political theory and empirical media studies. As political economists engaged with media technologies, or audience ethnographers investigated the place of media in people's everyday lives, they too necessarily performed feats of textual analysis as they proceeded. But they didn't always like to admit that they were even doing textual work, or that "serious reading" (Morrison) was more than a process of gathering up sociological generalizations. But given the inter-permeation of media textuality and everyday life, not to mention "content" as economic sector, and (textual) analysis as an important control and management tool, then clearly social scientists, journalists and policy makers need better training to improve their own practices and self-reflexivity as textual analysts. Perhaps they needed to come up to the standard of critical reading already attained by some of those "silent suburbans" (never mind the hapless "constructivists").

But while that true interdisciplinarity remains still in the process of becoming (or not; the triumph of textually unsophisticated "social science" that allows lazy statements about reading to go unchallenged seems for the moment to be ascendant), there remain some issues that have been forgotten while everyone's been taking pot-shots at the glass houses of their methodological neighbors. *Caveat lector! Nosce teipsum!*[28]

- *First, methodological debate.* Cultural studies itself has a history of what I call "walking away syndrome" when confronted by difficult problems of method or the politics of its own knowledge. Problems were not worked through. Challenges were issued, then everyone started to think about something else. As a disciplinary discourse with a history, cultural and media studies needed to extend, defend, and revise their own textual practices. The fluctuating fortunes of textual analysis were not a function of the object of study. Rather they resulted from the use of media and cultural studies themselves as political hot potatoes in the politics of knowledge. This was the "field" on which battles between modernism and postmodernism were fought. But after the sound and fury died away, there was still *text* to analyze.[29]
- *Second, legitimacy of knowledge.* The adversarial tone taken in some writings toward textual analysis in both academic and journalistic outlets suggested that there was more at stake than a method; anxieties stalked those who denounced, as well as their chosen targets. Indeed, the social sciences, even science as a whole, as well

as journalism itself, face the *same* crisis of legitimacy that their "militant tendencies" have delighted to find in media studies. There is a crisis of legitimacy in the realm of knowledge, and members of the knowledge class[30] continue to vie with each other in public to cause their own particular brand to prevail, i.e. to retain some "power to command" in the name of disciplinary truth.

It seemed that the dreadful textualists, with their relativism, postmodernity, constructivism and abstraction from the real, were at the forefront of those who would undermine the foundations of knowledge, and who, therefore, at all costs, had to be stopped. But even if all the textualists in the world were rounded up and loaded onto a truck and sent to, let's see, Coventry, the problems associated with knowledge wouldn't go away. There would remain what all this was but a symptom of – problems of legitimacy, and the need for inter- or even post-disciplinary research to understand the social production and circulation of truth.[31]

Look, for example, at a routine piece of popular journalism from a randomly chosen mass circulation British daily newspaper[32] – a glimpse into the popular rhetoric, if not the demographics, of truthfulness, in which the "truth ratings" were as tabulated in Figure 4.3.[33]

It was a mixed blessing for someone with my job – a professor with interests in journalism – to find that *journalists* were believed by 79 percent of the sample *not to tell the truth*, while exactly the same percentage believe that *university professors* "*can* be trusted" to tell the truth. Perhaps more sobering was the finding that "scientists" enjoyed scarcely more credibility than the "man in the street." In fact, the legitimacy of all branches of the knowledge class, but especially the most public ones, was treated with skepticism by the public in whose name they operated. Journalism, politics, and government seemed to need as much help with their truth-image as did cultural, media, and textual studies.

- *Third, textualization of public life.* There was a growing convergence between three great "social functions" that had been organized since classical times (when they were more integrated) into separate, mutually suspicious institutions: Government, Education, Media. These "three Ds" – of democracy, didactics, and drama – converged right on the site of media textuality. Government and Education used the mechanisms of Media (drama) to gather populations, to communicate across demographic boundaries, to administer and

**'79% THINK JOURNALISTS TELL PORKIES'**

Who Can Be Trusted

Percentage of people who believe various professions can be trusted to:

| | TELL THE TRUTH | NOT TELL THE TRUTH |
|---|---|---|
| Doctors | 91 | 7 |
| Teachers | 89 | 7 |
| Priests | 80 | 14 |
| Professors | 79 | 10 |
| Judges | 77 | 16 |
| Newscasters | 74 | 17 |
| Scientists | 63 | 27 |
| Police | 61 | 31 |
| Man in Street | 60 | 28 |
| Pollsters | 49 | 35 |
| Civil Servants | 47 | 41 |
| Union Officials | 39 | 47 |
| Business Leaders | 28 | 60 |
| Government Ministers | 23 | 70 |
| Politicians | 23 | 72 |
| Journalists | 15 | 79 |

[Figures from a poll commissioned by the British Medical Association]

*Figure 4.3* From *The Mirror*, January 26, 1999, p. 12

teach the people. If the two-hundred-year-old technologies of modern democracy were to be renewed and extended in the era of interactive multi-media, and of the integration of the technologies of broadcasting, computing, and telecommunications, then attention to textuality would have to be more vigilant than ever. What a "text" comprised in these new circumstances was open to empirical investigation, as were the issues of the "audience," "citizen," and even who and what "we" might be, either as disciplinary knowing subjects or as persons. But exactly this sort of rethinking was timely, and would be assisted by scrupulous textual analysis, rather than by the abandonment of the technique.

- *Fourth, readers became writers.* In formal knowledge and popular participation alike, a gap that was common since early modern times between (near-universal) reading and (demographically restricted) writing appeared to be closing. In the world of formal academic knowledge it was quite possible that the situation was already reversed: there are more writers than readers. Commentators in the academic press have complained that "too much" was being published. Everyone wanted to contribute to the scholarly journals, but fewer wanted to subscribe (I know; I'm the editor of the *International Journal of Cultural Studies*). Doctoral theses were produced in increasing numbers, but were not widely read beyond their examiners. The Research Assessment Exercise (RAE) in the UK stimulated the production of ever more "original" knowledge, but confined the concept of dissemination to publishing alone. In addition, also it downgraded *strategic* publications that might explain or envision a whole field to the status of (mere) teaching textbooks (not funded). In academic work, writers were privileged over readers. It was both honorific and economically advantageous to *speak* but not to *listen*. Even to *debate*, as in the present essay, which resulted from a "reading" of criticisms of my own published texts, was of dubious standing (i.e. it may not be "RAE-returnable"). Since the democratization of Higher Education in the 1970s (earlier in the US, of course), there have been far more speakers around. The result was increasingly that senior staff set their own work as course reading, and junior staff were too busy writing books to read them.

Meanwhile, in public life, the same trend could be discerned. Interactive communication technologies were at last extending the power of public address to Jo/e Public. Everyone had the right to *speak* in a democracy, but that right was "inconsequential" unless it involved the possibility of being heard – it needed to aspire to the status of *communication*, not just *expression*. "Freedom of speech" on an industrial rather than an individual scale was always, in fact, freedom to *write*. However, the "mass" print and broadcast media were always rather clumsy instruments when it came to offering that particular freedom to the population at large. They did it with "letters to the editor," talkback radio, TV chat shows, and indirectly via surveys, polls and vox pops. But the new digital media like the Internet were much more efficient in this respect. The right of everyone to speak in public was turning into a practical reality. But if everyone was speaking, writing, hollering, disclosing, commentating, reviewing, leaking – if, "in a democracy everyone is a journalist," as Ian Hargreaves has argued[34] – then who was "the reader"; the "audience"? In public life as in formal knowledge, then, the relations between addresser and addressee were changing. Media communication was privatizing – turning from public inscription to private writing.

In these circumstances it remains important to attend to the consequences of the social-scientific obsession with producing "objective" knowledge about audiences while neglecting their "textual" dimension. Reading is not a natural talent that matures unconsciously either in academics or in wider populations. Pouring "empiricist" scorn on textualists during an unprecedentedly textualizing period in history is unwise to say the least. Instead, efforts are needed to understand what has happened to the social relations of textuality. An effort is also needed to promote a high standard of critical reading and textual analysis – a *textual practice* in short – not only among audience-publics, but also among knowledge-class professionals from academic researchers to governmental policy makers.

Finally, returning to that *Mirror* poll (Figure 4.3), it could be pointed out that in the legitimacy stakes it wasn't the truth-seeking journalist or scientist who won the trust of the public (even by their own empirical standards, using their preferred statistical method). It was the *rhetorical* teachers, doctors, priests and professors who were trusted to "tell the truth." The public remained disposed to trust pre-modern professions more than modern ones, to accept the *bona fides* of medieval exegesists (priests, professors, and teachers) above militant modernists (journalists, politicians, ministers, business leaders, scientists). Perhaps they were on to something beyond nostalgia for mere "legacy systems."

*John Hartley*

Perhaps they knew that "text" and "audience" could only be *made* one and the same via the mechanisms of "transmodern teaching" and popular critical reading.

What, then, of "method in cultural studies"? If a "policy recommendation" for scientists, journalists, realists, textualists, and the rest of cultural studies were to arise from this essay, it would take as its text the words of transmodern Thomas Hobbes: "*Nosce teipsum*, Read thy self."[35] *Caveat lector!*

## Notes

1 Thomas Hobbes, *Leviathan*, ed. C.B. Macpherson (Harmondsworth: Penguin, 1968 [first published 1651]), p. 82.
2 John Hartley, "Invisible Fictions: Television Audiences, Paedocracy, Pleasure," *Textual Practice*, 1:2 (1987): 121–38.
3 Greg Philo and David Miller, *Cultural Compliance: Dead Ends of Media/Cultural Studies and Social Science* (Glasgow University: Glasgow Media Group, February 1998), p. 23.
4 David Morley, *Television, Audiences and Cultural Studies* (London: Routledge, 1992), p. 178.
5 See John Hartley, *Tele-ology: Studies in Television* (London and New York: Routledge, 1992), chapter 7.
6 Philo and Miller, *Cultural Compliance*, p. 25.
7 Jim McGuigan, "Review of *Popular Reality*," *European Journal of Communication*, 12:2 (1997): 251–4, this quotation, p. 253.
8 John Hartley, *Popular Reality: Journalism, Modernity, Popular Culture* (London: Arnold, 1996), pp. 166, 168.
9 Hartley, *Popular Reality*, pp. 4–6 for the kissing methodology; p. 12 and chapters 4 and 5 for the politics of kissing. See also Mark Gibson, "Richard Hoggart's Grandmother's Ironing: Some Questions About 'Power' in International Cultural Studies," *International Journal of Cultural Studies*, 1:1 (1998): 25–44, especially p. 40.
10 John Hartley, *Uses of Television* (London and New York: Routledge, 1999), chapter 9. See also John Carey, *The Intellectuals and the Masses* (London: Faber & Faber, 1992).
11 See *Media International Australia incorporating Culture & Policy*, 90 (1999), "Media Wars" themed section, edited by Terry Flew, Jason Sternberg, Cratis Hippocrates, pp. 1–90.
12 Keith Windschuttle, "Cultural Studies versus Journalism," in M. Breen (ed.), *Journalism: Theory and Practice* (Sydney: Macleay Press, 1998), pp. 17–36, this quotation, p. 28.
13 Morley, *Television, Audiences and Cultural Studies*, p. 178.
14 Hartley, "Invisible Fictions," p. 125; see also *Tele-ology*, p. 105.

15  Umberto Eco, *The Role of the Reader: Explorations in the Semiotics of Texts*. (London: Hutchinson, 1981); see also Yuri Lotman, *The Structure of the Artistic Text* (Ann Arbor: Michigan University Press, 1976), pp. 295–6.

16  See, for instance, Wolfgang Iser, *The Act of Reading: A Theory of Aesthetic Response* (Baltimore: Johns Hopkins University Press, 1978); Stuart Hall, Ian Connell, and Lydia Curti, "The 'Unity' of Current Affairs Television," *Working Papers in Cultural Studies*, 9 (1976): 51–93; Janice Radway, *Reading the Romance: Women, Patriarchy and Popular Literature* (Chapel Hill, NC: University of North Carolina Press, 1984); Jonathan Culler, *The Pursuit of Signs: Semiotics, Literature, Deconstruction* (London: Routledge, 1982); Umberto Eco, *The Role of the Reader* (Bloomington: Indiana University Press, 1979); Stanley Fish, *Is There a Text in this Class? The Authority of Interpretive Communities* (Cambridge, MA: Harvard University Press, 1980).

17  See Hartley, *Tele-ology*, chapter 5.

18  Alan Sinfield, *Cultural Politics – Queer Reading* (London: Routledge, 1994), pp. 51–3, 62–9; see also Jonathan Dollimore, "Bisexuality, Heterosexuality, and Wishful Theory," *Textual Practice*, 10 (1996): 523–39.

19  David E. Morrison, *The Search for a Method: Focus Groups and the Development of Mass Communication Research* (Luton: University of Luton Press, 1998), p. 159.

20  For the concept of a "textual system," see John Hartley, *Popular Reality: Journalism, Modernity, Popular Culture* (London: Arnold, 1996), pp. 31–4 and *passim*.

21  Greg Philo, "The Content of Media Coverage," in Don Redding (ed.), *Dispatches from Disaster Zones: The Reporting of Humanitarian Disasters* (London ECHO [European Community Humanitarian Office], 1998), pp. 44–5; see also Crisis pages at www.alertnet.org.

22  Philo and Miller, *Cultural Compliance*, p. 47.

23  Mark Hobart, "Ethnography as a Practice, or the Unimportance of Penguins," *Europaea: Journal of the Europeanists*, II-1 (1996): 3–36 this quotation p. 9.

24  See Jon P. Klancher, *The Making of English Reading Audiences 1790–1832* (Madison: University of Wisconsin Press, 1987); Thomas Richards, *The Imperial Archive: Knowledge and the Fantasy of Empire* (London: Verso, 1993).

25  McKenzie Wark, *Celebrities, Culture and Cyberspace: The Light on the Hill in a Post-modern World* (Sydney: Pluto Press Australia, 1999), p. 134.

26  Wark, *Celebrities*, p. 135.

27  See Hartley, *Uses of Television*, chapters 4, 5, and 11, for a discussion of the notion of text/reader relations in the popular media as "transmodern teaching."

28  *Caveat Lector*: "Let the Reader beware"; *Nosce teipsum*: "Read thy self".

29  See John Hartley, *A Short History of Cultural Studies* (London: Sage Publications, 2003).

30  For this term see John Frow, *Cultural Studies and Cultural Value* (Oxford: Clarendon Press, 1995).

31  I discuss this issue more fully in John Hartley, "What is Journalism? The View From Under a Stubbie-Cap," *Media International Australia incorporating Culture & Policy*, 90 (1999): 15–33.

32  This paper originated as a talk at the School of Oriental and African Studies, London University, on Australia Day, January 26, 1999; the *Mirror* was "today's paper" on that day. I'm grateful to Mark Hobart for the invitation.

33  In Figure 4.3, "porkies" = "lies," from rhyming slang "pork pies = lies."

34  Ian Hargreaves, "The Ethical Boundaries of Reporting," in Mike Ungersma (ed.), *Reporters and the Reported: the 1999 Vauxhall Lectures* (Cardiff: Centre for Journalism Studies, 1999), pp. 1–15; this quotation, p. 4.
35  Hobbes, *Leviathan*, p. 82.

# Part II

# Production and Reception: The Politics of Knowledge

# Introduction

The essays in this section revisit questions about studying production and reception, with a particular emphasis on media. The study of production has often been identified with the studies of media industries, and in particular with political economy. From this perspective, cultural studies, despite its interests in the negotiation of power and resistance, has frequently been considered to be at odds with another significant approach to the critical study of media industries in political economy. So one point from the previous section these essays more thoroughly investigate are questions regarding economics, politics, and culture. Additionally, this section also offers inquiries into the tensions between theory and practice, and between text and infrastructure. In addition to these aforementioned themes, the essays in this section explore relationships between textual systems, institutions, and audiences.

In "Cultural Studies of Media Production: Critical Industrial Practices," John Caldwell argues for the importance of critical work on the cultures of media production. He proposes an approach to understanding the media industry and its production practices as a mode of theoretical, aesthetic, and critical discourse, or a form of "lay theory." Caldwell incorporates an ethnographic approach that is more commonly associated with the study of audiences and reading and reception practices than it is with the bastions of capitalist media privilege and practice. Caldwell demonstrates the complexity and heterogeneity of the individuals who participate in media production and their everyday practices. He opposes his perspective to those who see "the industry" and its products (popular media texts) as a hegemonic monolith whose messages of domination can only be deconstructed and exposed through academic cultural analysis, or resisted through the reading practices of readers outside the industry. In the process, he offers new methods of analysis and new ways of thinking about theory and production. His canny analysis is an invitation to reassess production and production cultures in their complex self-reflexivity.

The next essays in this section turn to questions of reception and popular culture. In cultural studies approaches to media in particular, Stuart Hall's "encoding/decoding" has become a guiding essay in the development of studies of reception, bolstered by the work of other theorists, especially Antonio Gramsci and Michel de Certeau. The study of reception and audiences has been considered a significant way of understanding specific, located interpretive strategies, often seen as a way of resisting the power of dominant cultural texts.

In "Feminism and the Politics of Method" Joke Hermes reviews the motives and strategies for feminist engagements with ethnographic approaches to readers/viewers of popular culture. She reminds us that the turn to reception was a strategic move, rooted in a feminist political agenda. At the same time, she explores some of the contradictions that have characterized feminist studies of audience reception. Hermes recognizes that, as she writes in her essay, "the impetus behind audience research is precisely motivated by the wish not to speak on behalf of others even though, as a researcher, one does exactly that." Hermes also discusses some of the limits of this approach, such as the absence of socially "powerful" informants (i.e. white men), and her own experiences in dealing with a study of texts with audiences that included women and men.

Andrea Press and Sonia Livingstone explore issues that emerge in audience research methods when brought to bear on new media. They elegantly review the use of audience studies in relation to television, and recent efforts (of others as well as their own) to study computer and Internet users in this context. They draw a distinction in audience research methods between what they call reception and ethnographic studies, offering an important corrective to the tendency to conflate these distinctive methods and emphases within the field. In striving to combine these, they also note the problems in balancing the relative influence, in theoretical and methodological terms, of structural constraints and inequalities versus individual agency and transformation. Their essay helps situate possibilities for future work in relation to the ways in which audience research has been conducted over the past three decades.

# 5

# Cultural Studies of Media Production: Critical Industrial Practices

## John Caldwell

*"Nobody knows anything."*

William Goldman (1983) summing up the theoretical and intellectual incompetence of Hollywood

*A dull and tedious tome ... Downright silly ... Most of it could have been put together by any Hollywood correspondent in two weeks.*

*Variety* mocking the naïvety of academic Hortense Powdermaker's (1950) anthropological study of Hollywood (Bierstadt, 1951: 124)

It would be difficult to imagine a more resolute institutional divide than that which recurs between academic culture on the one hand, and the cultures of media production on the other. The agitated skewerings of Goldman and *Variety* above are merely the tip of a very extensive historical and rhetorical iceberg, one comprised of rifts, write-offs, and accusations whenever academics try to "seriously" study Hollywood, or when industry players publicly imagine themselves to be prescient theorists. Part of this rift is based on anxieties about who knows what in Hollywood (and what can be known about the place); and part of it results from an overdetermined cultural "mystique" that continues to assign to the industry an almost medieval authority, fashioned over decades, about how the industry works and what it means. Yet other cultures and tribes and industries and social groups also deploy and cultivate mystiques, but this fact has seldom derailed serious cultural studies research in the way that Hollywood has managed to do.

As I demonstrate in the essay, part of the reason for the distance between cultural studies formulations of the industry – and the industry – has to do with the fact that media industries themselves invest tremendous resources in producing knowledge (and critical knowledge) about the industry. Viewing this kind of industrial knowledge production, furthermore, as mere public-relations, marketing, bumpf, promotion, context, or even backstory is shortsighted and misguided given the extensive and convoluted nature of the contemporary mediascape. In this essay, and in the larger study from which it comes (forthcoming), I examine such meta-critical knowledge as "critical industrial practice," and consider ways that the layers of industrial self-theorization provide both challenges for cultural studies research and distinctive opportunities for more fully understanding the ideologies and behaviors at work in something as convoluted, contradictory, heterogeneous, and as ostensibly monolithic as "*the* industry."[1]

The account that follows may seem a little ecumenical to some, since it includes as many references to popular and industrial studies of the industry as it does to academic research on the same phenomenon. This breadth is valuable for a number of reasons. Given the relative lack of critical work on the cultures of media production available today, and the ways that knowledge about the industry is reflexively postulated, managed, and interrogated in the commercial sphere, these reflexive industrial accounts stand in fact as forms of what I have termed "low theory" (1993), "industrial semiotics" (1994, 1995), and "theorizations-in-practice" (2000). These terms are very close to Ellen Seiter's (1999) concept of the critical competencies of audiences as forms of "lay theory." Yet because media production industries, unlike audiences, are by nature comprised of professionals, the term "lay" seems less adequate as a qualifier here than other frameworks, including Phil Agre's (1997) formulation from AI and computer and cognitive science of "critical technical practice." The relative absence of a sustained tradition of cultural studies research on contemporary media industries means that the field would benefit from opening up the very models that have dominated it since its aggregation around and following the influential work of the Birmingham Centre and (what has come to be known as) British cultural studies research in the 1970s. In this tradition, cultural studies has generally focused on cultures of reception and consumption (on audiences, users, subcultures, the working class, publics, or "the people") while less extensive work has been undertaken in the systematic study of media production cultures. This inclination has resulted in part from the field's theoretical launch as a reaction against top-down theories of culture and the Frankfurt School's model of the culture industry in the 1970s (Horkheimer, Adorno), Raymond Williams's work (1974) on the history of "social uses" of technologies and the nature of "mobile, privatized consumption," Louis Althusser's (1971) theory of "ideological state apparati" (ISAs) as understood through spectatorial/subject "interpellation," and Stuart Hall's (1980a, 1980b) notion of "resistant" and "negotiated readings," all located largely outside of the corporate and industrial sphere.

Even field-setting applications of Gramsci's (1971) theory of "hegemony," while articulating the role of the state, also placed a renewed emphasis on the role of subjects, citizens, and consumers in the creation of consent – and in the misconstrual by subjects that audience and industrial interests are congruent. Ethnography emerged in media studies outside of anthropology departments during this period as a privileged and useful methodology appropriate for the analysis of cultures of domesticity and consumerism (Morley, Brunsdon, Gray, Gillespie, and Seiter, among others). However, ethnography has not achieved the same sort of success and visibility in the study of media production cultures. Nor has any other research paradigm for that matter. I intend to consider this lack and provide suggestions about how cultural studies might more effectively engage media production and the industrial formation.

Despite the radical, interdisciplinary, boundary-crossing objectives of its formative years, cultural studies has emerged (in many universities) as a dominant, sanctioned, and bounded scholarly discipline. In achieving this institutional inertia, various attempts have been made to "map the field" of cultural studies. Considering but one of these projects – the ambitious international cultural studies conference at Urbana in 1990 and its resulting publication (Grossberg, Nelson, and Treichler, 1992) – makes unavoidable questions about the absence of media industry studies. Of the 40 chapters in this important work, only one dealt substantively (albeit indirectly) with a culture of media production – Jody Berland's "Angels Dancing: Cultural Studies and the Production of Space." This contributon built on the work of Hennion (1990) on interactions in a French recording studio. All of the other contributors placed far more emphasis on meta-theorizing cultural studies, and reflecting on the problematic of cultural studies methodologies, agency, and significance.

The binary categories that cultural studies deployed in forming the field – even beyond the subject-user emphases of Hall, Althusser, Williams, and Gramsci – may also have legitimated a working disinterest in media industry. The easy and repeated caricaturing of "aesthetics" as antithetical to cultural studies stands as but one example. John Fiske (1986: 254) defined cultural studies, for instance, as a "political" framework, something set in polar opposition to a study of culture's "aesthetic" products; something that concerns a "way of living." Ian Hunter drives home the same founding principle: "The cultural studies movement conceives of itself as a critique of aesthetics" (Hunter, 1992: 347). While nineteenth-century aesthetics is an easy mark, contemporary aesthetic practice is not. One of the inevitable, but perhaps unintended, consequences of this field-defining anti-aesthetic is that the field looked beyond the very *cultures* and *lived communities* that produce and circulate aesthetic media forms. The anti-aesthetic straw-man imagines that objects are still the chosen target of aesthetic analysis. Yet contemporary aesthetic practice has been theorized in much more inclusive terms, and is comprised and perpetuated by a complex aggregation of social communities and professionals; practitioners that are guided by codified patterns of behavior. Their interactions and cultural commitments together form temporarily consensual alliances that are regularly deemed "the industry." Even as we grant that cultural studies concerns "ways of living," scholars must not overlook the fact that "ways of living" also define media professionals and their various industrial subcultures.

This situation suggests several potentially valuable correctives for cultural studies. If the anti-aesthetic helped blind cultural studies to industry, then the incomplete application of new methods in historiography, from works like E. P. Thompson's *Making of the English Working Class* (1963), caused scholars to only partially apply what it means to study cultures "from the ground up." Media practitioners also make culture "from the ground up"; and media practitioners can be productively studied "from the ground up." The material that follows also suggests other shifts in approach: that producers are also audiences; that encoders are also decoders; that industries are also cultures; that practitioners, like audiences, have agency; that commercial practitioners, like audiences, can and do employ strategies of resistance and negotiation. The constellation of behaviors and competencies invoked here – considered broadly under the view of industry as a lived and theory-driven culture – can be usefully considered as forms of critical industrial practice. With decades of scholarship invested in research on the "production of culture" – usually (and ironically) considered from the perspective of its impact on subject-users – cultural studies would benefit by considering more fully as well the specificities of "cultures of production."

## Methodologies/Faultlines

*I want to convey not only how and why I think the networks do what they do, but a sense of the ambience and texture of the industry's life-as-it-is-lived.*

Todd Gitlin (1983: 14), on his method of interviewing and studying Hollywood television

*The least satisfying feature of the book is that the material on the program creators reads like network press releases. I know all too well that that most producers are essentially salesmen, liable to begin sentences with "Can I be honest with you on this?" They are also capable of creating their own mythology and spreading the myths with joy.*

Lawrence Laurent (1993: 88) criticizes the naïvety displayed by an academic book of interviews with primetime producers

As television critical and cultural studies were formalizing their presence in the academy in the 1980s – by synthesizing feminist, psychoanalytic, and ideological theory with audience and textual analysis – a few books attempted "industrial" interventions into the ways that television is studied (Gitlin, 1983; Newcomb and Alley, 1983; Marc and Thompson, 1992). All three works made available to readers lengthy interviews with scores of primetime television producers, creators, and/or executives. This was novel stuff for a field that had grown out of literary and cinema studies, and imported European "high theory"; but it was also (apparently) suspect material. For to "allow producers to speak for themselves about the making of television art" (Brown, 1984: 53), seemed to give the high-ground back to the very people who were responsible for perpetuating the dominant ideology on television. The books seemed, that is, to be a reversion to older forms of "top-down" formulations of the culture industry. I recall being corrected a few years back, when I remarked on the laudable "thick description" of Gitlin's work, and the valuable access to "behind-the-scenes" discourses he provided to readers and scholars. Todd Gitlin merely came to LA, I was told, and "was taken to lunch." Producers and executives take people to lunch for a living, and do so everyday. That's their profession. They spin and legitimize their decisions as they talk and socialize, and even socializing is part of the professional craft. According to this view, Gitlin didn't realize he'd been hustled by self-serving myths.

Granted, perhaps Gitlin *was* "fooled" by his informants, even as sociologist Leo Rosten had been fooled by his informants in 1938 and anthropologist Hortense Powdermaker had been fooled by her Hollywood "insiders" in 1946. Laurent, in the epigraph above, nearly likens the culture of primetime producers to sales in a used car lot, where admissions of "honest" and "from-the-heart" disclosure actually mean just the opposite, and *caveat emptor*. Yet Gitlin himself raised this issue when he remarked that the industry works by "telling" (14) and by "taking meetings." In fact many of the early efforts to study the industry included evidence and awareness of knowing reflexivity. Powdermaker defended herself in print by noting that she – unlike trade writers, who always seemed to have a job application or screenplay in their back pockets – was not in anyway secretly interested in employment or stature in the industry (Powdermaker, 1950: 3–4; Kent, 1992: 2). Newcomb and Alley, far from simply providing an anthology of un-edited interviews, couched their producer texts within a three-part theoretical model of television as a cultural forum and the participatory, interactive process of industry–audience "liminality." Although any interview may be problematic, these were not just press releases scammed on earnest outsiders.

Surveying the littered trail of industry studies like these over the past half-century shows a repeated pattern: access granted, stories told, behind-the-scenes knowledge made available, scholar challenged or written off. One did not have to go to Derek Freeman's indictment of Margaret Mead's lifework to find the pattern. What began to interest me, however, was not the issue of truth or falsity of informants, or motives, or vested interests, or the "truth" behind the screen and its spin – but the *process* of informing, the workaday *narrative forms*, the interpersonal *rituals* used to establish moral high-ground, the *genres* of disclosure, and the *regulatory structures* that managed critical knowledge about the industry and its players. The fact that the write-offs of scholarly studies were typically so agitated and unequivocal suggested that these scholars had stepped into a minefield; had uncovered, that is, industrial concerns of great importance and investment. I would argue from this that it is these processes, forms, rituals, genres, and regulatory structures that offer keys to contemporary media industries. These forms of mediation should not be viewed as mere flak for the truth-bound ethnographer digging for some deeper key to industry. As I hope to show in what follows, in many ways these mediations *are* the industry.

Media ethnographies emerged as an antidote to the abstractions of media and cultural studies that had been built on acutely delimited forms of textualism or provocative (but always slightly suspect) theoretical speculations. Ethnography promised scholars more concrete conditions for analysis, "real" versus interpellated or positioned spectators, and engagement with lived identity and class formations rather than purely (or casually) theorized ones. As they flocked to the audience, the new media ethnographers of the 1970s and 1980s characterized other methodologies, either implicitly or explicitly, as forms of "naïve textualism" or speculative and naïve theorization (Morley, 1992: 122). Yet I would argue that the kind of media industrial practices that I have broached here place the "common sense" assumptions of ethnographic method (at work even in ethnographies framed by the complications of post-structuralism) similarly in doubt. "Naïve ethnography," that is, proves to be as problematic as naïve textualism in accounting for cultures of media production. Having access, and informants, and backstory information on industry may by themselves position the industry scholar as a "text" being written by the industry – for this is the very same relationship that characterizes the industry's relationship with its vast audiences. After all, in the age of digital and via ubiquitous forms of "multi-purposed" content these audiences also daily seek out critical knowledge about the industry.

To fully engage the deep practices of the media production industry, cultural studies scholars would do well to consider the perspectives of other scholarly traditions of research that are active in the same hunt. Since the 1970s industrial studies have emerged from vastly different intellectual traditions, and have seldom acknowledged any direct linkage to the field of cultural studies per se. Political economists (Schiller, 1999; McChesney, 1999; Balio, 1996), sociologists (Gitlin, 1983; Streeter, 1997), humanities scholars (Newcomb, 1974; Newcomb and Alley, 1983; Marc, 1985), and mode of production historians (Neale and Smith, 1998; Bordwell, Thompson, and Staiger, 1985; Schatz, 1983, 1988; Alvey, 1997; Anderson, 1993) stratify production culture in very different ways; many times from distant vantage points provided by archives, financial reports and records, trade accounts, and/or on-screen texts and narratives. Even a cursory sojourn through the industry (whether as an ethnographer, journalist, intern, or production assistant) quickly shows the importance of these perspectives and materials. That is, as I have argued elsewhere (Caldwell 1995, 2000, 2001, 2004), it is impossible in the digital era to talk of industrial cultural or aesthetic practices without talking about the stuff of political economists and sociologists: marketing, economics, conglomeration, professional practices, and community formation. Although they are not "determining," such things now arguably are involved in "authoring" contemporary media texts. Likewise, it is now impossible to talk about marketing or distribution or the global economy without also talking about how industries creatively produce semiotic and aesthetic forms of difference (the traditional province of humanities scholars). And it is impossible to talk about media content without considering the industry cadres involved in demographic, marketing, and audience research (the stuff of quantified social science research).

Part of the resistance to effective analysis of the production culture is due to the fact that the industry (far from being an inert, locatable object for analysis) excels at publicly generating over-arching metaphors, figurative paradigms, and master narratives that constantly frame and re-frame the production industry. The commercial age of digital, for example, now promotes and sanctions three new and resilient master narratives for both industry and culture: conglomeration, globalization, and convergence. While these are posed and hyped pervasively as neat and ostensibly inevitable outcomes, they are far from it. In fact, the more "total" the paradigm, the more the industry must work discursively, narratively, and socially to marshal the heterogeneous aggregation of interests it represents into consensus. In the same manner, there can of course be no credible master narrative for cultural studies research of the production industry as well. But the mode-of-production historians, mentioned earlier, do offer some useful possibilities for making even contemporary industrial fieldwork more viable. The stratified and diversified nature of the classical Hollywood system that Neale and Smith, Schatz, Bordwell, Thompson and Staiger, Anderson, and others detail is *not* the same system as contemporary transnational media conglomeration, but there are a number of points of continuity and congruence alongside the cultural and industrial breaks that have occurred over the past five decades. Studio system and mode-of-production studies (although historical rather than contemporary) provide more holistic models of interaction, along with terms and perspectives from which the contemporary mediascape can be engaged and better understood. Yes, print and moving image archival sources, trade and professional publications and codes, studio structures, labor practices, marketing, and distribution and professional rituals shore up these histories, but such things also inevitably inform the decisions of contemporary practitioners, whether they are informants, interview subjects, or objects of workplace participant observation. Ignoring the logic of such factors is a failing that contemporary cultural studies of the production industry need not make.

Since the 1990s a series of new works suggest that a broader-based dissatisfaction with the reception/consumption bias in cultural studies has emerged. Several books on television provide potential models for the analysis of production culture. In *Watching Race* (1995), Herman Gray further developed and situated the interviewing mode of Newcomb and Alley, Marc, and Gitlin by integrating the insights of producers across his critical, theoretical, and textual readings of racial formation in American television. Jostein Gripsrud's *The Dynasty Years* (1995) drew both from interviews with producers of the American primetime soap series and from personnel in the Norwegian television industry that programmed the series as components of his transnational study (the series in international distribution), and for his evaluation of critical theoretical practices in the field. Julie D'Acci's *Defining Women* (1994) represents a model for television scholarship, as it adds access to the development process and producers' meetings, and participant observation to a wider discussion of gender politics in American culture of the 1980s, and the logic of feminism for primetime programmers. Whereas D'Acci examines these dimensions in the rise and fall of a single series, Jane Shattuc's *The Talking Cure* (1997) uses many of the same methods – interviews, access to producers' meetings, site observations, and an emphasis on the construction of femininity – as a way of clarifying insights from a vast textual sample of an entire genre: daytime talk and tabloid television of the 1990s. Barry Dornfeld's *Producing Public Television* (1998) adds a dimension to this emerging oeuvre of industry studies given that he served two simultaneous roles in the production of the series: he was both an academic researcher for the producers and a production assistant for the production company. This dual role was criticized as counter-productive and possibly self-defeating by some scholars (see, for example, Curtin, 2000), but it raises again the issue broached earlier in this essay: how does access and insider knowledge either enhance or compromise analysis? Justine Cassell and Henry Jenkins' *From Barbie to Mortal Kombat* (1998) creates a multi-authored work on gender and experience in computer games, and features in-depth interviews with professional computer game developers. Many of the more recent studies and the methodologies that underpin them are listed in Table 5.1.

This brief summary indicates just how important three impulses have become in recent studies of production culture: first, to provide space for producers to "speak for themselves" (via interviews or transcripts); secondly, to integrate more "empirical" forms of fieldwork of into critical cultural analysis (site observation, audience participation); and thirdly, to maintain reflexivity and critical distance in analysis. Some of the writers collect industrial data and critically integrate it from critical positions outside of the industry (Gray, D'Acci, Shattuc). Others work to cooperatively author accounts by allowing informants/practitioners to have some say over the final form of the study (Dornfeld). Unlike some earlier studies, all of the studies cited here would, I believe (because of various forms of reflexivity and disclosure), fulfill the kinds of parameters that Seiter (1999) has articulated for "situated ethnographies." Yet what I find most interesting in this group is the extent to which site access usually depends upon a (high-level) producer or executive contact (essentially a corporate gate-keeper), a situation that inevitably raises the issue of how much and to what extent the researcher is beholden to that producer. It is worth considering more closely two of the studies in this regard, *Making and Selling Culture*, and *From Barbie to Mortal Kombat*. Both books are multi-authored and multi-vocal, and both books involved inviting or luring key figures from their respective producing cultures (industrial spaces) to academic spaces and symposia. What results are much livelier forms of disclosure, avowal and disavowal, than one might find in an industrial space. Elizabeth Traube (1996) and Michael Curtin's (1996) critical summaries are particularly good at placing the kind of animated dialog and divergent talk that ensues at these university forums into meaningful cultural and political-economic contexts respectively. I think what is particularly good about the above studies is the way they all attempt to "triangulate" industrial analysis from several discrete methodologies, and the fact that each of the scholars is adept at textual analysis.

One way to build on these works is to find ways to gain access to industry other than the executive or "producer's gate" (which inevitably brings with it top-down perspectives and pressures). In many

*Table 5.1*  Recent production culture studies and their methodologies

| Recent production culture studies | Integrated methodologies |
| --- | --- |
| *The Producer's Medium* (1983) | Interviews framed by theoretical introduction and critical essays used to comment on interviews. |
| *Designing Women* (1994) | Site observation and practitioner interviews in study of cultural construction of feminism in programming. |
| *Watching Race* (1995) | Interviews integrated into societal/industrial study of racial construction as programming strategy. |
| *Televisuality* (1995) | Observation of technical and production practice integrated with textual and cultural analysis of industry. |
| *Dynasty Years* (1995) | Practitioner interviews as background in transnational media study and critique of theory. |
| *Making and Selling Culture* (1996) | Practitioner interviews in academic space, interposed with critical texts from academic colloquium. |
| *The Talking Cure* (1997) | Site observation and practitioner interviews integrated with extensive textual analysis of genre. |
| *Producing Public Television* (1997) | Ethnographer as practitioner in industrial space. Participatory authoring with company oversight of account. |
| *Barbie to Mortal Kombat* (1998) | Practitioner interviews in academic space, interposed with academic texts from symposium. |
| *Latinos, inc.* (2001)[a] | Ethnographer in commercial, advertising sphere, tied to critical race theory and transnational economics. |

*Table 5.1*   Continued

| Recent production culture studies | Integrated methodologies |
| --- | --- |
| *Consuming Youth* (2003)[b] | Scholar's multiple roles include community worker, ethnographer, and alternative media production. |
| *The Other Woman* (2005)[c] | Scholar integrates "below-the-line" interviews, with labor/gender analysis, and imaginative workshops. |

a   See Arlene Davila, *Latinos, inc.: The Making of a People* (Berkeley: University of California Press, 2001).
b   See Vicki Mayer, *Consuming Youth, Producing Dreams* (New Brunswick, NJ: Rutgers University Press, 2003).
c   See Miranda Banks, "The Other Woman: Gendered Production Work and the Female Action Hero," dissertation, UCLA, 2005.

cases the "below-the-line" crafts, professional associations, and ancillary work-spaces provide a better – or at least different – understanding of the complex fabric of the production culture. A second way to build on these recent developments in industrial scholarship is to consider forms other than the word-driven rhetorical interview for analysis. Practitioner artifacts, technologies, spatial utilization, professional practices, studio design schemes, and workplace organization all help break the interview-centric predilection of critical scholars seeking access. Third and finally, enough industrial work has been completed that scholars would benefit from "comparative" ethnographic and workplace studies. For example, while both Shattuc and D'Acci examine some of the same broad issues, they do so from very different genres, practitioners, and dayparts; and both of these "worlds of production" are vastly different from the "public intellectual" aspirations of Dornfeld's PBS producers and academic researchers. Likewise, Ohmann and Traube reveal a far more skeptical and/or contentious interchange between the high-end film and television producers and academics in their project, than Cassell and Jenkins reveal in their interchanges between computer game developers and critical academics. Why is this? What are the institutional differences between the videogame world and motion pictures that encourages differing valuations of critical knowledge? All three of these broad issues (forms of access and identification, forms of evidence and data, and reflexive meta-critical analyses of industrial study as a field) inform my proposal that follows for research on "critical production practice."

Some very good work on the media production culture has also emerged from outside of film and television studies. This work helps inform the analysis that follows, and it is to this work that production culture studies might profitably look. Considering research on "non-media" workplace cultures, that is, allows one to mitigate the institutional inertia that has built up within the disciplines of both film mode-of-production studies and British cultural studies. Research on the social construction of scientific practice and the "actor–network" theory (Latour, 1986) on workplace "cultures of computing" by communications technology scholars (Starr, 1995), on AI, computational technologies and human experience (Agre, 1997), on "situated" and "distributed cognition" (Clancey, 1997), on regional and comparative studies of high technological industries (Scott, 1988, 1993; Scott and Soja, 1996), and on aesthetic and cultural geographies and public policy (Storper and Salias, 1997; Moloch, 1996) offer particularly good models that might profitably inform a film/television production culture researcher. Together such projects suggest ways to approach the culture industry *on terms other than its own – even as one acknowledges fully the extent and force of industrial critical figuration.* I will return to these possibilities in the pages that follow.

## Critical Industrial Practice

*Having been a marketing analyst in Hollywood before becoming an academic professional, Justin Wyatt is especially well qualified to examine the rise and dominance of high concept filmmaking in Hollywood.*

Tim Coleman (1995: 653) on the "insider" authenticity of "outsider" academic Justin Wyatt (1994)

*He has always worshipped the people about whom he has written. . . . After interviewing Dawn Steel in her office, he is still so transfixed that he barely got home without hyperventilating; she has the intensity of a star.*

Nicholas Kent (1992: 2) on the "outsider" inclinations of "insider" veteran trade writer Paul Rosenfield

Many studies of production culture, including those cited above, raise the issue of authorial identity vis-à-vis the industry. Sometimes this is done via self-disclosure (the author an "insider" or "outsider"). At other times industrial studies are criticized for lofting generalizations from the outside (the academic as amateur or naïve). Some industrial accounts are taken to task as missives from the "sour-grapes" genre, which account for their skewed perspectives (yes, an insider, perhaps, but with an axe to grind). Other accounts are lashed – in an industry noted for its obsession with accelerated change, cyclical fashions, ageism, and twentysomething management trainees – for their obsolescence (the author as over-the-hill and out-of-touch, an obsolete and now-marginalized "player"). These forms of disclosures and outings are, of course, obligatory in modern, post-structuralist anthropological writing as well, which requires reflexivity in method and text (Clifford and Marcus). But such self- and othered-disclosures are also part and parcel of Hollywood – the way that wannabes, and up-and-comers work cocktail parties and receptions, or hustle agents or producers to take meetings. The scholar may disclose (as an effort at authenticity or legitimacy) the presence of his or her own media experience and "credits" or not. The industrial informant on the other hand – inevitably well-versed in scanning name-tags while working a room or a market in order to quickly move and gauge the mobility-potential of any contact – will also consider the value that this interrogator may have for their own career or fortunes. While the "any news is good news" notion does not satisfactorily explain informant requests to go "off-record," or threats made to deny disclosures after interviews, industrial informants know that scholars now ply their wares on an extensive, web-like landscape of meta-media discourse, one that includes many of the same publishing and public forums frequented by their own marketing departments.

Because insider knowledge is *always* managed, because spin and narrativization define and couch any industrial disclosure, and because researcher–practitioner contacts are always marked by symbiotic tensions over authenticity and advantage, cultural studies must move beyond restrictive and bounded forms of textualism *and* ethnography. The layers of discursive and semiotic management at work in the culture of production mean that researchers would benefit by shifting emphasis to what I term the contemporary *industry's "deep" texts, rituals, and spaces*. My aim in this section is to find and suggest concrete ways by which cultural studies can reconsider itself in the face of an

*Table 5.2*  Critical industrial practices

---

1 **Deep Texts** (tools, technologies, artifacts, icons)
2 **Emic Interpretations** (industrial narratives, genres, self-portraits)
3 **Critical Industrial Geographies** (sanctums, borderlands, contact zones)
4 **Liminal Industrial Rituals** (mentoring, pitching, summits, retreats, trades, mergers/marriages, divestitures/divorces)

---

industry that is increasingly preoccupied with *"embedded" forms of critical and cultural analysis.*

## 1  Deep texts (tools, technologies, artifacts)

*Most cameramen are not used to talking without a tool in their hands ... One way or another (Willis) has tamed his tools ... He talks like a lion tamer – eyes wary, whip in hand, always sensing the animal (the film emulsion) sensing him.*

DP [Director of Photography] Gordon Willis' primal tool talk (Mcdonough, 1985: 68)

*When he speaks of the "literature of light", shoptalk turns lyrical. His interview is impassioned, semi-mystical; you can smell the steam rising from his neglected plate of pasta.*

DP Vitorio Storaro's theorizations on cinematography (Mcdonough, 1985: 69)

How do material objects in the production culture convey meaning? How do practitioners deploy and rationalize their artifacts and tools? Comprehensive answers to these questions, and an exhaustive account of critical industrial practice in the production culture is, of course, beyond the scope of this chapter. I would like, however, to introduce symptomatic examples in each of the four parts of this model (a framework that delineates material, narrative, critical, and ritualistic forms of "embedded knowledge"). The first strata in this scheme – "deep texts" – includes a variety of contemporary material artifacts, including: (1) production tools; (2) user-iconographies (imagery and texts that manage use); and (3) cultural technical-encasements (like demo tapes).

1(a) *Technical Encasements.* In reaction to the totalizing theories of the "cinematic apparatus" in the 1970s (Baudry, 1974; Comolli, 1986), critical studies scholars have largely abandoned or de-emphasized studies of production technologies. Yet local technologies, and the specific uses to which they are put, suggest a range of embedded cultural investments. I would like to reopen questions of the technical apparatus, not as an "ideological" "one-size-fits-all" straightjacket, but as a form of *material* critical and cultural practice. Here I take as models the work of both Clifford Geertz and Sally Hacker. Geertz (1985: 4) raises the possibility of viewing media machines as forms of embedded knowledge: "Sorting through the machinery of distant ideas, the shapes of knowledge are always ineluctable, local, indivisible from their instruments and their encasements." Hacker (1990: 213) suggests how the design and use of machines should be seen as part of an entire network of social relations and identity: "Some think that technology refers merely to machinery (as sexuality might refer to genitals), while others insist it means the entire set of social relations within which the machinery is designed, developed, and used."

Although seldom considered in the same context, issues of both sexual identity and political economy animate the world of contemporary film/television production technology and practice in workaday ways. My interest in how such factors inform and regulate the production community and its technical culture follows from a set of basic assumptions. First, although far from being determining or causal, industrial and institutional relations do in fact work to predispose and cultivate specific kinds of screen experience through widely circulated promotional icons and Geertzian technical "encasements" (machine artifacts that serve as "local" forms of knowledge). Secondly, industrial iconography – secondary representational texts (demo tapes, editorial photographic illustrations, photographs of machines) – function in the proprietary world of television and new media to conceptualize technologies, to normalize specific user interfaces, and to invest in and privilege certain modes of production. Finally, the "machines" of the technical culture can also be viewed in a sociological sense as "machineries for status ranking." Locked in a symbolic tension with eroticism (at least since the Neolithic era according to Hacker), technologies have been used to gender, organize, and maintain relations of power in society. The technical cultures of film, television, and new media are simply among the flashiest and most adept at leveraging mere media machines into social machineries of status, power, and subordination. They are also, however, social worlds managed by public performances of sentiment and heart; group behaviors that critical theorists and political economists tend to ignore.

Television's current technical practice – from highly fluid and mobile stylistics in cinematography to painterly and montage work in digital effects (fx) – is now marked by the accelerated development of new technologies across the full range of production uses. Mapping this kind of technical practice along the registers that Geertz and Hacker propose – as social and psychic geographies – raises several general questions. Is there, for example, a meaningful relationship between the micro-geographies of the *production* culture – now geared to a "probe aesthetics" that is characteristically invasive and immersive – and the "pipeline"-obsessed "push" programming now championed in electronic media *distribution*? Secondly, what social and political-economic factors might help explain the recent shift in technical and production practice toward "probe aesthetics" and "push programming"? The general preoccupation by media cultural studies with audience pleasures and identities (to the exclusion of industrial ones) can only be justified if one disregards the flood of discourses that introduce and greet each new media technology on- and off-screen today. It seems time, that is, to reconsider media machineries as both highly privileged and socially instrumental cultural and psychological constructions as well. So to Patricia Mellencamp's (1992) thesis about television (as now imbricated in the repetition and contradiction-induced compulsive "anxieties" of consumer culture), I want to raise the issue of the social psychology of industry – as it is evident in the stressed, and compulsive social practices of a very "anxious" culture of production. To Lynne Joyrich's (1997: 69–98) theorization from screen form and spectatorship of "critical and textual hypermasculinity" I'd like to suggest, in the section that follows, two other kinds of performance: "industrial and technical hypermasculinity."

1(b) *Iconographic User-Manuals.* The introduction of new production tools has upset traditional models of work and crew relations. It has also, I would argue, exacerbated the sense of uncertainty that has historically defined the production culture (at least since the advent of subcontracting as a governing principle). In this regard, it is worth considering more closely the nature of specific technical encasements via the iconographic practices that accompany the technologies. First, an entire genre of ancillary video production circulates in and around the production world in the form of "demo tapes"; theses are calling cards, if you will, used to snag projects, make bids, sell equipment, and pitch services. Every DP, editor, and effects artist worth his or her salt hawks these, as do the specialty production boutiques that offer individual services, looks, and stylistic sensibilities. If the whole point is to individuate and differentiate, then these demo tapes are crucial forms of currency in a system of exchange that has little time for the rituals of pre-electronic business: face-to-face meetings or the patient screening and review of complete sample works.

Demo tapes, however, are more than just advertisements that connect unique looks to names. They are also "primers" of new videographic technique; "user-guides" that explicate stylistic options for each new type of production technology; and "lexicons" that schematize and conjecture on meanings and uses. Demo tapes, at least in the sense that scholars like Andrew (1976), Agre (1997), Clancey (1997), Stam et al. (1992: 123), and Hayward (1996: 380–4) have defined "theory," are essentially workaday forms of theorization about the medium. As practitioners jockey for position and compete for projects they also circulate knowledge and figurative analogies about stylistics in a semiotic sense. Demo tapes show the industry constantly speaking to itself; boasting about stylistic prowess even as demo producers struggle to legitimize themselves. Leverage depends on establishing a consciousness of "influence" among practitioners, and each new demo tape that circulates reacts to those that are already stacked in producers' offices and post-production suites. The business and merger "synergies" that litter the trades (e.g., project-specific linkages between Disney, PDI, Pixar, ILM, etc.) really mirror the atomization and "boutique" individuation that now rules the production world as a whole. Demo tapes, in effect, codify corporations and individuals as synergistic "chunks."

Structural changes in the corporate world make demo tapes far more pervasive in the industry today than they were two decades ago. This has as much to do with the important role that the commercial advertising industry has had on television as anything else. Commercial spot production along with music television, as I have argued elsewhere (1995), has "taught" network television in more ways than one: it is a hungry proving ground that rewards new, risk-taking production talent; it provides *de facto* research-and-development of new production technique and technologies; and it has taught television to conceptualize in stylistically intense short-form segments, all this even as it works to "de-narrativize" much that issues from the multi-channel spectrum. The demo tape is part of the lingua franca that facilitates these levels of exchange.

1(c) *Cultural Technical Encasements: the Military–Identity Complex.* Both historical precedence and new manifestations in contemporary practice predispose the mode of Hollywood television production to character-izations of "militaristic" masquerade. The marshaling of crew and cast on soundstage or location by autocratic directors, at least since Eric von Stroheim, has been a legendary part of the gloss on Hollywood. Consider the ways that the production industry continues to militarize its professional rituals and identities: Location shooting literally involves rapid mobilization, and the occupation of territories in submissive neighborhoods. Armed guards cordon off high security areas. Studio film and television carries its own war-like semiotic, housed as it is behind fortress-like walls with armed sentries. Even as the vertical structure of labor relations map a command-and-control scheme on the creatives, the rhetoric of those in the hierarchy suggests hardened sacrifice. DPs, for example, talk proudly of "coming up through the ranks." Evidence of a semiotic "war-footing" is everywhere. Militaristic production tropes stand as the most aggressive symbolic figures for claiming cultural space, for defining the production enterprise, and for establishing a spatial relationship and logic between the production cadres on the one hand and the world and its filmic subjects on the other. This symbolic marshaling is encased both in machines, and announced in secondary promotional theorizations.

For Panavision, one of the leading suppliers of motion picture tech-nology for primetime television and film, production *is* war. Panavision marketed its prowess in 1993 by reference to the bloody Iwo-Jima flag raising in World War II.[2] The production struggle in this icon is waged in a completely homosocial space by anonymous, hardened bodies and teamwork. Feature film origination on Panavision evokes primetime. Marshaling the Panavision "way" (a dedicated team struggle, by a highly competent technical cadre, doing it the "hard way") flags cinematic programming above other, more mundane, video forms. Even for non-Panavision users – journeymen and assistants in camera departments everywhere – the imagery aims to stroke a sense of professional pride; a battle cry for quality. *Semper Fi* Panavision.

Field production, and electronic news gathering – more like search-and-destroy missions – offer smaller tactical efforts than 35 mm film origination. Yet video equipment manufacturers sell the process, and the practitioners, on the use of heavy armor. Sony mounted its Betacam SX campaign with explicit linkage to military field armor, boasting that Sony offered "the best weapon in the field." High technology electronics, here, in the age of smart weaponry, are offered with the "go-anywhere" portability of all-terrain warfare. Firepower tropes extend from production field tactics to the bunkered world of the post-production suite, as well. Quantum marketed its heavyweight hard drives (actually very small metal boxes used in non-linear editing systems) as large-scale incendiary threats. This tableau – a fantasy stretch of the corporate technical community – is informed by both the big-screen production values of an action-pic, and the (crash-prone, disk-error) iconography of violent carnage. Beneath its breath, Quantum seems to intone: "We are not the lightweight keepers of digital data that we may seem."

Wescam is a diversified production technology company that packages the variants of its "projectile eye" for features, for primetime, for reality shows, and for local news. It markets its gyroscopically controlled airborne cameras with tropes more typical of an airborne assault than simply descriptions of axis movements and "coverage." Consider the helpful, dystopian, critical rhetoric in its demo tape: "The city ... at night ... exciting ... a dark haven for criminals ... infrared surveillance from 3,000 meters above earth." From the symbolic construction of electronic culture as a Darwinian landscape, to the call to master and mount the space with immersive technologies, probes, and ocular projectiles, comes the explicit and unabashed call-to-arms of those that rent and sell the tools and weapons like Wescam. Militarism still serves as the time-honored trigger to corporate media success, studio reputation, and market dominance. Acute representations of gender are also ground up in the militarized/masculinized enclave of the technical culture.

## 2 Emic interpretive frames (industrial narratives, genres, self-portraits)

*A poor Jewish boy growing up in Texas, Spelling was regularly beaten up until he had a nervous breakdown at age nine. That gave him the opportunity to read, which he says led directly to a career in television. Poor childhood out of the way, Spelling takes a stab at just how rich he is today.*

Aaron Spelling's "life story by justification" (Cooper, 1996: 1873)

*In jaunty Tom-Swift prose, Walker writes a careening, gee-whiz, one-after-another narrative. Here he is warming to the story of his 1919 expedition to the wilds of Northern Canada ...*

DP Joseph Walker's narrative of technological development (Mcdonough, 1985: 69)

Industrial knowledge is regularly narrativized and generically framed in accounts like the ones cited above. The "big" public statements in memoirs and tell-alls drag out the usual narrative-structure suspects: Horatio Alger, Tom Swift, rags-to-riches, "dues-paying" sojourn-in-the-wilderness-before-making-it, phoenix-from-the-ashes (or -rehab or -studio layoff), score-settling revenge, or primal scream therapy. Far more ubiquitous than these master genre arcs is the workaday deployment of anecdotal exchange. To some degree quantification in the form of box-office, ratings, and revenues does play a role in promotional narratives and attributions of status, but the authenticity of any "players" is established not simply through the accounting department's numbers, but rhetorically, through a process of storytelling, one involving short-form anecdotal "chunks." "Pitching" (the process of distilling feature-length narratives to 2–3 punchy sentences) is, after all, what film/TV practitioners must do to land projects, agents, gigs, and development deals. The "pitch aesthetic" (Caldwell, 2004: 57–9), that is, is far more than a summary device used in the world of screenwriting and producing. Anecdotes set the tone of meetings, mark territory and credibility and status in the pecking order, and establish common ground for "deals" before the "suits" are brought in to finalize legal contracts in print.

Examining the short- and long-form narratives that circulate around production practice provides what linguist Kenneth Pike (1954) would refer to as an "-emic" (internal or subject) rather than "-etic" (external or analyst) understanding of such practices (as in the difference between "phonemic" and "phonetic"). Sociologists would refer to this as a focus on meaning inside the group, as the "ethno-logic" of the social subjects being studied. This subject-centered logic is, of course, something that anthropologists have nearly always valued. In the production culture, narrative provides keys to the ethno-logic of media practitioners, and does so in ways that conscious disclosures by "indigenes" or "informants" cannot. Consider how the following secondary accounts quickly de-construct the narrative structure and meaning of one recent, and grandiose, industrial summa by an entertainment writer:

> It will come across rather like a collection of anecdotes on index-cards...Again and again Biskind will tell a story: x fires or curses at or beats up or pulls a gun on or bankrupts or sodomizes y. And then will follow his little disclaimer: "x has no memory of the event." Or,

> sometimes, "y has no memory of this event." At times this may literally
> be true, since all the major figures in this history seem to have been
> drugged up to the frontal lobe most of the time. (narrative structure of
> Biskind's *Easy Riders, Raging Bulls* [Bowman, 1998: 78])

> Biskind can work without acknowledgment from his tightly-wound-
> Eastern-Jews-coming-undone-in-California template. (ethnic genre
> definition of industry in Biskind's tell-all trade history [Kent 1998:
> 65])

Academic industrial research – as my earlier survey of the diverse academic disciplines that pursue it suggests – produces results that are
sometimes difficult to generalize from. "Trade" publications (along with
memoirs, autobiographies, and "behind the scenes" looks), on the other
hand, suggest just the opposite, that the industry is generalizable, and
do so in an overdetermined way. Trade narratives also serve to promote
and validate the "aura" and notion of an elite space inside the locked
worlds of Universal, Time-Warner, and Spelling. The relative believ-
ability of the inner-space constructed in such texts functions to anoint
and authenticate such accounts. Anecdotal practices and autobiographical accounts tend to shift the focus on production culture from
the spatialized world of industrial relations to the temporal logic (and
narrative arc) of the authoring personality. While such tales establish
the myth of a player's value based on cross-corporation human/career
development and potential, such accomplishment is usually situated
within an off-limits space (the corner executive office, parties, the
studio lot at Sony, etc.).

Emic self-interpretations also inform industrial visual iconographies.
Less narrative arcs or plots than self-conscious depictions of an ideal
or "alternate world" (one prerequisite for narrative), visual tableaus in
equipment ads and trade promotions key the reader/viewer into favored
practitioner interpretations. There is, for example, an acute investment
in "working" identity and disclosure even in corporate production
logos and brands. Many of these play upon a favored trope: that the
age of digital and the cyber-production artist is also, somehow, like the
industrial age of the manual worker. An array of corporate production
logos – from the Film Worker's, Serious Robots, and Horizons – all
utilize the same rock-chiseled, primitive effect: chunky production
man-locked-in-geometric-form. The Horizons company brands itself,
for example, as chiseled-man holding planet. The Modern Digital

company leaves no doubt as to the implications of this iconographic trend. Its corporate promotion for computer imaging apes the (apparently?) allied task of 1930s-era steel construction workers. The WPA stock footage company also goes retro. It represents itself in Stalinist-inspired social realism: as a well-muscled foundry worker pounding steel with a sledge and anvil. The Center City Film/Video company uses a similar 1930s graphic to show itself as King-Kong like; as both technically strong, and (somehow) "sensitive." Other trades show video effects editors, locked into head-gear (à la *Clockwork Orange*) as slaved worker-machines. The digital audio company Sonic Foundry, in both its logos and trade promotions, builds its corporate image around the primordial molten magma and flying sparks of a steel-mill and forge.

What traits do these icons share? A tremendous urge to physicalize a creative task that has become essentially cerebral. But why? There is, then, a persistent conceptual compensation at work here, given the actual task of pushing buttons or stylus. But lest we denigrate the fantasies of concrete productivity here (in a world that produces only "symbolic" or entertainment capital), it is important to note that these practices also evidence a desperate affirmation, and legitimacy, of the workers' tasks. Even if their final product is purely visual or fleeting, it is nevertheless produced by real human labor.

The desperate attempt to affirm digital work-for-hire as somehow concrete, muscular, and productive – and as somehow involving sweat and sinew – has a darker side as well. Much of the iconography evokes "performance anxieties" and physical masochism. A whole series of current production and technical images suggest that this iconography is produced for an "anxious" industry; one fueled by masculinist anxieties. In one want-ad campaign in the technical trades, for example, multinational giant Sony solicits their vision of the engineer of the future: a Caucasian, cyberman lost in angst-meditation. Illustrated technical advertisements, for example, depict single male figures, pulling and twisting frames, or – under headline imperatives that bark: "Get Real" – being propelled at high speed. One post-production house calmly boasts that "We can do anything"; a capacity ironically illustrated by a classical engraving of a man locked into a Rube Goldbergesque torture contraption. The Bogen company launched the marketing campaign for its "Avenger Grip Equipment" using photos of raging men on steroids, exerting extreme physical pressure in an attempt to destroy the product. Other companies exploit Edward Muybridge's sequence photographic studies to draw analogies between their performance as media artisans, and the semi-nude men trapped in Muybridge's experimental cages. The fat and traumatized bodies of men people other technical ads. One shows a "before" picture of a grotesque, fleshy, male body, followed by an ironic, hand-washing, company "after": "We won't promise you ..." Anxiety, isolation, stress, and rage permeate explicit representations of production work and products.

However, contemporary industrial iconography is not limited to masculine physical anxieties and mental stress. There is also a recurrent genre in the technical trades that exploits masochism and mutilation in order to explain the production task. Since all of the icons, images, and discourses that I am examining are forms of self-representation, this tendency to symbolic self-mutilation is worth considering in more detail. In what is surely a strange marquee for corporate promotion, the operative iconographic truisms at work here are violence and bodily pain. Non-linear hard-drive manufacturer Quantum symbolizes its technical capacities in full-color spreads of incendiary apocalypse that hurtle male victim-bodies through the air. Trades like *Digital Video* featured articles mouthing fairly common clichés from production trade shows: "Serial Ports on Steroids." Such references to production gear and testosterone are illustrated with editorial images celebrating sado-masochism: men in cable-choked bondage, with pectorals and jugular veins bulging. The S&M genre runs a gamut of variations, with strapped-down and tortured production boys loaded to the gills with logistical paraphernalia and technology. The Toronto Film Commission lures work north of the border with the torqued body and pavement-placed head of a wannabe-director scouting with a viewfinder. Micropolis hawks its products by showcasing a trapped geek-boy. Qualcomm marketed itself in 1997–98 with huge, dismembered and distorted eyeballs. Non-linear giant Avid keyed its marketing campaign for the new Xpress with the promise "Xpress yourself," against which young male bodies (in mismatched primary-colored plaids) torque and twist in airborne trauma. The Sound Forge company further developed the "launched" male body trope by thrusting its model-man through the plastered walls of its illustrated masonry studio. While the projectile-bodies of Avid and Sound Forge evoke an extreme and deadly pain (ostensibly bordering on production pleasure), other corporations celebrate and extend the trope temporally as torture. Copy for the digital device Houdini, for example, verbally touted its "flexibility," but showed off such prowess by twisting the legs and arms of its user into impossible (and dislocating) configurations behind his head and back. Heavyweight Boss Studios made sure the torture/mutilation genre carried its own explicit critical interpretation. Their user-artist holds high-voltage electrodes to either side of his balding and aging skull; promising to "jump-start" the creative process through suicide by electrocution. An editorial illustration in *New Media* cracked the male skull open even further, to show creative shots (applications) exiting the brain's gray matter into the bloodless world of the atmosphere. Performance anxieties, compulsive work-habits, and stress in the lower levels of the technical iconography here face a far less ambivalent but no less recurrent obsession. Male masochism and bodily mutilation now apparently stand as accepted public symbols of technical creativity and corporate advantage.

An overdetermined performance of identity pervades these industrial discourses, technical encasements, icons, and promotional rituals mentioned here. Such practices ratchet up symbolic aggression, hypermasculinity, and the tortured male body as keys to understanding the technical demands of the production enterprise. Since these practices are located in industry trades and technical literature, this kind of performativity functions less as an attempt to persuade the culture at large (viewers, spectators, or consumers), than as a way in which the industrial community speaks to itself; makes sense of itself; critically positions itself and members of the tribe.

An aesthetic of force seems to drive contemporary production practice. One the one hand, "probe technologies" (Wescam, Steadicam, jib-arms, fiber-optic finger lenses, etc.) are identified with the mode of cinematic television (primetime and commercial production) and arise out of what many might still deem the "old-boys" network of Hollywood television production. In this milieu, bankable production value is now tied to an aesthetic of invasive spatial practice, and force; typically rendered or depicted as if in real locations and landscapes and stages; typically produced by groups of laborers working in dedicated, hierarchical teams. Digital and videographic television, on the other hand, stands as a kind of "new-boys network"; a homage to the myth of the isolated male artist locked to his computer-imaging workstation. His anxiety with work, and physical pain, is visualized as a component of his isolation; and a key to his creativity. The trope of the long-suffering male artist finds in the digital age an update: the surging, torquing, self-mutilating – but always hip – artist on electronic steroids.

*John Caldwell*

## 3 Critical industrial geographies (sanctums, borderlands, contact zones)

*My field techniques had some similarities to and some differences from those I had used on an island in the Southwest Pacific ... I took the inhabitants of Hollywood and the South Seas seriously, and this was pleasing to both.*

Anthropologist Powdermaker (1950: 3–4) on studying the natives of Hollywood

*Travel for (the director) becomes an adventure that no tourist can buy. Wherever he goes, he becomes involved with the natives at the locations.*

TV Commercial Director Ben Gradus on contact with non-professional "natives" (Gradus, 1981: 4)

It may come as a surprise to some that "distanciation" and analytical "estrangement" are cultivated not only by critical theorists and social scientists (like Brecht and Powdermaker) but also by practitioners (like TV director Ben Gradus). Of course, the practice of distancing – of making the locals strange and exotic – is not just about attributing interpersonal *identities* to those on the outside of the respective professional circles of either the anthropologist or director. The practice seems also to reinforce an institutionalization of *space*. Following the work of Lefebvre (1984), Foucault (1977, 1979), and Soja (1989), these industrial geographic predilections provide keys to the play of power and pleasure in the production culture as well.

*Insides, Outsides, Access, Borderlands.* Because the corporate sphere is proprietary, access for research has generally been difficult to achieve, and scholarship frequently suspect because of the vested interests that manage access. A graded hierarchy of access has emerged along practitioner caste lines. Since the production culture is fueled by socioprofessional "networking" relationships among and between these castes, space is constructed in socially symbolic ways. Consider the spatial metaphors that inform both sociological and industry accounts:

> Hollywood is comprised of three concentric circles. The largest circle embraces all of the thirty thousand movie workers and movie makers; the middle circle encompasses the movie makers alone ("the movie colony"), the producers, actors, directors, and writers who participate in Hollywood's social and professional life; and the smallest circle, the one

at the center of power and prestige, encloses the movie elite, some two hundred and fifty persons ... (sociologist Leo Rosten's [1941: 33] cultural geography: the concentric space of the Hollywood "colony)

Club Rule Fifteen: To succeed in the club and to last, you need more than one dimension. (trade writer Paul Rosenfield's [Kent, 1992: 2] geography: the rule-governed, limited access "club")

Anthropologist Powdermaker viewed Hollywood as an "island," sociologist Rosten viewed Hollywood as a "colony," and trade writer Rosenfield viewed Hollywood as a "club." These diverse paradigms perhaps make sense given the roots that inform each analysis: respectively, ethnography, sociology and economics, and gossip journalism. Despite the differences dramatized between the approaches – Professor Rosten's supporters savaged Professor Powdermaker in academic journals (Bierstadt, 1951: 124; Raglan, 1952: 44); and competing show-biz writers ripped Rosenfield in print (Kent, 1992: 2) – all three paradigms are very much alike in terms of their formulations of and dependence upon notions of space. Island, colony, and club are, that is, all spatialized social phenomena, bounded and cut-off from surrounding groups and cultures. All three metaphors, furthermore, heighten the importance of tropes of interiority, the center, and the (island/colony/club) elite. By extension, all three metaphors also thereby invest significance into: (1) possibilities for access into these bounded worlds; and (2) travel between the regulated zones, from outside to inside. I would argue that this kind of spatiality actually dominates many workplace, industry, and professional practices today as well. But while many industry chroniclers and analysts perpetuate these same spatial metaphors, most such accounts (including these three) "say very little" (Rosten, 1941: 33) about the ubiquitous worlds of media production work (the "outer circles") in order to expose the social significance of the elites, the powerful, and the "players" (of the "inner circle"). While this emphasis may have made some sense during the studio era in film, and the network era in American television, it misses the mark and fails to account for the culture of production in the age of multi-media and mergers. The outer rings of the concentric paradigm – the "below-the-line" crafts, unions, digital boutiques, manufacturers, dot-com alliances, and socioprofessional interactions – make available to scholars provocative avenues of research into contemporary technological, cultural, and economic changes. All sorts of cultural practices – the performance of identity,

*John Caldwell*

desire, hybridity, alterity, resistance, negotiation, and sexual politics (the traditional foci of cultural studies) – are daily "acted-out" in these outer and intermediate zones of the production culture.

In arguing this approach, I build on and respond to the important, recent work of both Nick Couldry (2000a), and Anna McCarthy (2001), on media space. Couldry is particularly good at demonstrating the flaws of postmodern theory, which tended in figures like Baudrillard (1983), to "erase" space as a meaningful category. A close examination of the deep spatial texts from industry that I've referred to above underscores, to use Couldry's terms, media's "complexification" – rather than "erasure" – of space as a meaningful category. Far from offering mere simulations, industrial rituals and demo tapes betray an obsession with space and place, often reinforcing the notion that production spaces are physical, tangible, robust, and demanding. Whereas Couldry (2000b) elaborates the physical boundaries, symbolic boundaries, edges, and journeys by lay audiences to and from industrial space, I take as my focus the faux- and modified public and private spheres that are constructed for professional community members "inside" those boundaries and edges. McCarthy's work, in turn, serves to unseat the traditional privilege given the domestic sphere in accounting for television by showing how site-specific uses of television outside of the home transform and mediate audiences in ways that complicate gender, class, and consumption. The kinds of industrial, spatial, and textual practices that I examine more fully elsewhere similarly complicate viewership and agency – but do so for *practitioners* rather than lay audiences.

Recurrent professional rituals, workplace practices, and exchanges of industrial texts and icons all, in some way, theatricalize the production space for practitioners. They also regularly negotiate what it means to make media, what it means to form alliances, and what and how changes in economy, technology, and public taste stand both as threats to career and corporation, and as forces that can be "leveraged" by foresighted and resilient artisans. Space and depictions of space invariably serve as terms used to rationalize, understand and make sense of change.

As a starting point, it is useful to recall the recurrent metaphor and practitioner self-representation examined in the preceding section: the sense that the media and digital artisan labors alone, in the darkness, in anonymity; cut off from human contact, and driven to anxiety by long hours of desperation. A number of demo tapes ("Blue," 1997,

136

"Tektronics/Lightworks," 1997, "NAB Convention TV," 1997, "Promax," 2001) bring this spatial "self-portrait" to life. The "digital sweatshop" topoi at work in these tapes is but one in a wide range of spatializing self-representations. The narrative contexts and arcs emerge from and help demarcate a graded taxonomy of social spaces – a geography of the production culture, if you will. This geography, which is more fully articulated elsewhere (Caldwell, 2003: 35), can be summarized as follows, and includes a series of highly stratified – but interconnected and self-bounding – spatial worlds.

- The *highly proprietary private sphere* of the pitch and the development meeting.
- The *therapeutic private space* of the corporate retreat.
- The *faux-private space of the workplace* or studio, or soundstage, whereby constant discursive interventions from management create instability through implicit surveillance.
- The *faux-public space*, or the *sequestered public sphere*, created at professional trade shows, conventions and meetings where ostensible contestation and celebration is staged for professionals in the community as if they were witnessing and participating in a public sphere.
- The *semi-public spaces of professional events* awards shows, season preview meetings, and press junkets where a place for access is extended from the industry to sanction audience consumption from a specific, regulated vantage point. The public nature of these "stages" as ocular key-holes is overproduced by public-relations, even as the aura of consensus covers over severe contestation and dissensus in the industry.
- The *contact-zones for mentoring* emerge at moments in which those with insider knowledge venture out to half-way spaces to share personal insights on making it in Hollywood, how the business works, and how to start a career.

Having established an inside – outside binary as the central ideology delineating these zones, travel or movement between zones is set-up and hyped as key or crucial moments via industrial rituals, framing narratives, and visual iconographies. These theatricalized moments of professional movement are promoted as interventions during which the industry (or its players) consciously intends to negotiate the very boundaries and barriers they have previously established and sanctioned. This staging of industrial space and travel – in order to traverse it – gives the geography of the production culture a self-fulfilling dynamic.

## 4 Liminal rituals (mentoring, pitching, summits, retreats, marriages, divorces)

*You'll never eat lunch in this town again.*

Socioprofessional downside of Julia Phillips's (2002) "slash-and-burn" industry genre

*When a studio executive says "I love your work!" it means "Who let you past the guards." "We're going to make your movie!" means "Six months from now you'll read in Variety that we're making a cheaper movie just like your idea." And "This is the best first draft I've ever seen!" means "You're fired."*

Summary of screenwriter William Goldman's theory of meetings and industrial communications (Friend 2000: 134)

*Cultivation Rituals.* Ex-producer and executive Julia Phillips and screenwriter William Goldman presuppose, as have many others before them, that activity in the culture of production is facilitated and governed within the slippery world of meetings, face-time, and conversational rhetoric. Understanding the significance of these forms of social inter-action means considering the structure of the industry and the stakes of its players. The film, television, and digital media industries, for example, are characterized by an extreme stratification and division of labor, and "winner-takes-all" business plans. Yet many of the favored industrial rituals act blind to the group-based contestation that defines the enterprise, and work instead to promote the idea that the industry is unified, personal, and humane. Yet the industry is far from user-friendly, unified, or monolithic. To achieve the illusion of access, unity, and consensus, therefore, the industry makes overdetermined efforts: first, to imagine and underscore the many critical "private" moments and spaces that drive effective producing and content development; and secondly, to bring those critical moments of privacy "out into the daylight" in enabling gestures intended to "help" others in the field. That is, the appetite for "behind-the-scenes" information and "secrets" are not unique to fandoms and show-biz reports on *Entertainment Tonight, Extra*, or *Inside Hollywood*. Rather, the same appetite-fulfillment circulates in professional spaces, in the form of semi-public panels on "how to make it in the industry," and in various mentoring and apprenticeship schemes.

A full examination of socioprofessional interactions in the culture of production is beyond the scope of this chapter, and would include everything from network "up-front" meetings, affiliate meetings, trade shows, conventions, program syndication markets, studio mergers or "marriages," and corporate/executive "divorces." Yet even a provisional consideration of a range of socioprofessional practices that I term "cultivation rituals" (recruitment, sponsorship, mentoring, and hazing) reveal determined attempts to establish and construct the notion that the industry is humane, caring, and helpful. Many of the "experts" and seasoned "veterans" of Hollywood tend to explain success – in staged public events – with all of the rhetorical tools that a motivational speaker or revivalist might use. Face-time, humanity, integrity, and personal vision are all regaled on hungry aspirants in "transition" or "how-to-make-it" events sponsored by the DGA, the WGA, the ASC, the Academy, or SMPTE. Even those players now infamous for years of dissolved productions, hubris, and exit strategies due to "irreconcilable creative differences" (Griffin and Masters, 1996) assume in these "half-way spaces" (guild halls, industry conventions, universities), the guiding hand of wise sage and noble moralist. In actuality, high-level show business interactions are highly proprietary and essentially bunkered away from all of the wannabes. But these "cultivation" events ostensibly expose professional "secrets" to the light of day.

One of the best examples of this impulse to theatricalize the intensely private is the "pitchfest." After a lengthy and wearying day on the floor of NATPE2000 selling and buying syndicated programming, 800–1000 professional (and, I would argue, semi- and marginal-professionals) gather for an evening in a convention auditorium. These "participants" comprise an ostensible "audience," and wait to hear whose number has been chosen at random to participate in the pitchfest. As each number and name is called, the audience watches as members (game-show style) "come-on-down" to pitch to heavy-hitter agents on stage from CAA, Universal, and William Morris. The resulting performances on stage and under the severe constraints of time-clock and mocking emcee, provide a riotous range of show, series, and genre pitches, all in an attempt to sell and seduce the big men on stage. If the pitchers are not "gonged" (*Gong-Show* style) and asked to cease, each agent critiques the program concept, offering advice on where to take and how to develop the show or series. A few of the 25 pitches are uniformly praised and awarded, with winners invited to "real" pitch meetings with agents and producers back in Hollywood. Yet many of the other pitches betray the utterly heterogeneous, regional, local, and small-budget competencies of the participants that make up *the* "syndicated programming" production culture. Although NATPE2000 was cast as a high-point of industry "convergence," faux-public "coming-out" events like this show just how contentious and desperate the coalitions of buyers and sellers are on the floor during the day.

As with the "how-to-make-it" and semi-public mentoring events, public pitchfests construe the powerful in moments most candid; now merely sensitive and caring lay colleagues willing to share secrets, and provide the kind of "face-time" never possible in the overpopulated, agent-scarce world of Studio City and Hollywood. Although such pitchfests reveal professional/amateur faultlines at work in professional organizations, the "sharing of secrets" at such events also functions like gossip traditionally has in urban and suburban neighborhoods. Special disclosures of this sort serve as a way to create solidarity and a (perhaps false) sense of empowerment through organizational or guild knowledge.

In addition to cultivation rituals, another set of socioprofessional rituals also work to fabricate solidarity and consensus. "Maintenance rituals" include yearly meetings by networks to cultivate alliances with advertisers (upfront meetings), nervous affiliates (affiliate meetings), and fence-sitting but influential TV critics associations (TV Critics meetings and press junkets). Press tours and the talk show circuit, for example, exploit both the cultivation and maintenance mode, by bringing the hidden spaces and personalities of the production culture into the daylight; in essence, providing face-time for the lay, but implicitly hungry populace. Affiliate and upfront meetings do the same sort of thing for nervous local stations and ad-agencies that hope to be comforted about the financial prospects that come with their contractual and corporate relationships, or the program "pipeline" for the season ahead. These recurrent attempts to solidify and create consensus, however, always play out in a climate of less-hyped socioprofessional interactions that achieve the opposite effect.

*Monitoring Rituals.* Solicitation, cultivation, and maintenance rituals all work in public relations to build consensus, solidarity, and a sense of commonality, and by so doing cover over the anxieties that threaten productive corporate relations. Other workaday rituals in the production culture, however, work in antithetical ways by producing and instilling *anxiety* in the community of production professionals. The process of "giving notes" occurs when an executive or producer sends suggestions to directors or writers about how to "improve" the direction of an ongoing project, program or series. While such incursions by "the suits" into the aesthetic domain rankle most directors, the process has a far more fundamental function. The now-ubiquitous ritual of giving notes underscores the sense that the proprietary and private world of the studio and soundstage is actually very much in doubt, monitored as it is daily by an amorphous but ever-expanding ensemble of seldom seen but always present producers, executives, and their assistants. Production personnel internalize this sense of being watched, much as the prisoners of Bentham's "panopticon" (Foucault, 1977) are disciplined by the continual threat (real or imagined) of always being under surveillance. Curse the notes if you will, but you are being watched and evaluated.

Other monitoring rituals always keep the production space and enterprise from stasis and balance. Many independent program productions involve the daily reconciliation of costs spent versus projected budget estimates. The obligatory production and post-production meetings during works-in-progress also inculcate the personnel with the sense that the project is always "incremental"; that their future is always tied to successfully meeting projected benchmarks throughout the shooting schedule. Most independent program productions also contractually tie financial disbursements to the necessary approval of each major stage in the production by executive producers, or studios. Television ratings, like box-office, have also become an ever-present monitoring ritual – terra firma for all competitors, for accurate viewing numbers and demographics are the basis for rationalizing the success or failure of a show or series. For this reason, endless ways are devised to spike or hypo ratings across the country. The high season for this kind of ritual interchange occurs three times a year during "sweeps weeks," where viewer numbers are codified as the basis for ad rates for the months that follow.

Other monitoring rituals spin out from these kinds of ever-present forms of ritualized surveillance. Each May and June, after the Fall season has been unveiled for advertisers and affiliates, bets are taken on which network programming heads will roll first. This sense of an "executive revolving door" ritual further underscores that fact that, despite all of the overdetermined attempts to build consensus among industrial participants, the daily spaces of the production and producing worlds are characterized by great instabilities and anxieties about duration of employment. Inculcating this impending sense of inevitable temporariness works perfectly to legitimize the vast system of "contract" rather than employee labor that has come to be known as the "Hollywoodization" of American business.

Spatially, monitoring rituals unsettle the ostensibly private and proprietary nature of studio and production space. Studio and soundstage walls evoke walled-off privacy. But note giving, ratings, endless in-progress production meetings, daily budget reconciliations, incremental production funding and disbursement, and the executive revolving door all betray just how "porous" those proprietary walls are. This porosity – providing a one-way vantage point to those controlling both the bottom-line and the possibility of project green-lighting – serves to discipline the community of production in cost-effective ways.

While maintenance rituals transport the truly private and proprietary executive suites out into a semi-public space of reconciliation, monitoring rituals do not need ritualized reconciliation, for the complicated network of contract labor that defines Hollywood knows just how precarious their futures are and will be as long as economic conditions remain the same.

*Therapeutic Rituals.* In *Come On, Trust Us* (2000) – a feature film that played on the low standards of a local television station – a character played by John Travolta attempted to explain to his employee what a corporate retreat was: "I'm not sure what a retreat is ... I think it's a religious thing." Although played for comedy, the off-handed remark showed how trends in management development have infiltrated popular depictions of media and business. In recent years, the alienations and antagonisms of neo-Fordist production, contract labor, technical obsolescence, and ageism have taken their toll on popular perceptions of industry management practice. As a result, a new phalanx of business consultants and corporate players has begun institutionalizing therapeutic discourse into corporate practice. Retreats, for example, promise above-the-line and producer personnel the chance to "escape" the claustrophobic confines of the offices and executive suites in Hollywood and Century City for the group sessions, mud-baths and clear air of Palm Springs. Retreats promise to allow media players to "step-outside-of-the box"; to brainstorm; to make creative decisions that are innovative, and/or to find the inner child. Much less discussed is that retreats also provide an implicit escape from the contentious division-of-labor obligations that undergird the studios and soundstages back in Los Angeles. By turning a cadre of individualist, office-bound executives and producers into a group therapy session, media corporations work hard to produce an industrial space that makes possible creative intimacy and career re-birth. This, of course, is a far less sinister intervention than the panopticon inherent in monitoring rituals. Instead of constantly underscoring the possibility of surveillance, therapeutic rituals are far more deceptive. For while the official bedside manner may be that of psychological "enabling," the discussions and brainstorming nevertheless also proceed under the effaced forms of surveillance. Retreats, that is, look far more benign than the practice of giving notes. But both ritual forms circulate within the constraints of the corporate gaze and sponsorship. Having to deal with network "notes" and soundstage intrusions merely produces less of a tan, and more cynicism than male bonding, than do therapeutic rituals or the corporate retreat.

## Conclusion: Industrial Critical Competencies

*Tinker credits the 18th century Irish playwright Richard Sheridan for giving him a "standard by which to judge literate comedy designed for a mass audience. Sheridan's style was very close to that of the best three-camera comedies on television, the kind on which MTM would later be founded."*

Aesthetic references for MTM sitcoms (Katzman, 1994: E5)

*What is real, really?*

Philosophico-industrial analysis by Brodcasting and Cable (Schlosser and McConnell, 2001: 12)

*I see my background in semiotic theory as the main reason why I've been able to cross-over from such a radical avant-garde position to such a commercial medium ... Godard meets Monterey Pop is my ideal.*

Director Michael Oblowitz (1989) on the industrial utility of high theory

Academics have historically denigrated television for its commercialism and its middle- and low-brow aesthetic and intellectual predilections.

While MTM's workplace application of eighteenth-century drama-turgy may stand in stark contrast to the various radical practices that have enamored cultural studies scholars in the past, a systematic study of the development of primetime forms – one that considers the conscious industrial deployments of aesthetic and cultural princi-ples – would do much to lay bare the cultural capital and "class" dimensions that have been so near and dear to the heart of cultural studies. Similarly, *Broadcasting and Cable*'s musings on the "what is reality?" conundrum may smack of an introductory Philosophy 101 survey, but the actual industry discussion it represents raises all kinds of useful complications for the scholarly study of reality television. By critically arguing the distinctions between "rigging," appearance shots, establishing shots, and recreations – and their impact on regulatory and legal bodies – the trade publication actually suggests ways to pursue or integrate an "institutional study" of the reality aesthetic.

Most cultural studies of production culture fail to acknowledge that the object of academic research (the industry) is also a critical, research-driven enterprise. Although it comes as no surprise to media management, media production cultures are *also* fundamentally guided by critical and cultural analysis. This chapter has considered ways that industry creates a critical understanding of itself through public practices (organizing, marketing, and promotion). Methodologically, the chapter stands between, and at times synthesizes, two approaches that are typically seen as divergent: ethnography and textual analysis. Arguing that either approach fails to account for important aspects of spatial practice (with ethnography susceptible to vested disclosures by industrial informants, and textualism typically blind to industrial and technological determinants), the chapter set out to map the critical spatial practice of production through the close examination of "deep industrial texts." Many of these workaday or "low" texts" – visual icons, social and professional rituals, demo tapes, recurrent trade and union narrativizations, and machine designs – circulate in a greatly delimited public sphere, but a public sphere nevertheless, as promo-tional and industrial artifacts and professional events. All of these "deep texts" precede and pre-figure the kinds of film/TV screen-forms that scholars typically analyze, and all offer dense and overdetermined interpretive schemas that serve to regulate and make sense of the mean-ings and significance of the space of production, and the space of culture.

The industrial competencies that I have described here – and my argument that a great deal of what viewers see in film/TV critically mediates or de-constructs other examples of screen content – may suggest that the newly convergent and conglomerated industry now leads by hyping and selling its critical sophistication and agency to viewers. But this is far from the case. In fact, although deep texts and practices show a constant churn of critical and theoretical ideas among practitioners, actual cases of public disclosure by industry players typically work to deny or disavow any agency or pretense. Far from being crass movers-or-shakers who exploit cultural trends, industry players talk about themselves as simple, honest, and direct men; screen-writers in touch with the universalism of Aristotle's three-part drama and well-rounded characters; producers responsively creating what the common person wants; executives couching even lowest-common denominator programming as opportunities for reflection, consensus, and release. In trade talk, screenplays and films are never ideological, television shows are never racist or about race, and producer-creators never have a cultural axe to grind. But as these recognizable public-relations bells peal to announce that the industry is only about basic human values, "emotional transport" (Guber, 2001) and "enter-tainment," the deep texts, the socioprofessional networking, and the engineering of new technologies and stylistic methods all show some-thing very different. A constantly changing coalition of sub-groups, competitors, and skilled practitioners stand as a collectivity held together by "willed affinity" – but only until the next economic crisis or technological change forces the collective to re-configure once again. Although the same sort of statement could be made in many places, a recent remark by a writer-producer on the long-running primetime series *The Simpsons* demonstrates that this bifurcated culture of public disavowal alongside private-professional critical deployment does very much exist. In rejecting the notion that anything profound was engi-neered into or intended by the series, senior writer Tom Martin suggests that most of the critical-theoretical barbs in the 12-year history of the series were purely the result of "accident." "People think it's mostly a result of some deep effort. Mostly it's just about trying to be funny" (Lobdell, 2001: b20).

Even as creative practitioners assume the same recognizable, but effaced, "aw-shucks" posture, the series itself has generated immense amounts of critical writing that seek to lay bare and address the dense cultural and intellectual intertexts that form the very fabric of the

*Table 5.3*   Manic Disclosure/Non-Disclosure

| DISCLOSURES / AVOWALS | NON-DISCLOSURES / DISAVOWALS |
|---|---|
| *(understood via intentional discourses)*<br>**Industrial Disclosures**<br>**Top-down Intentionality**<br>**Informants, Interviews** | *(understood via embedded industrial practices)*<br>**Deep Textual Analysis**<br>**Actor–Network Performance**<br>**Technologies, Iconographies, Narratives, Rituals** |
| *Myth-cliché from producers*<br>*// Marketing Objective* | *Forms of disavowal from producers*<br>*// Industrial Logic Elided* |
| "Nobody knows anything. . . ."<br>CHANCE | Disavowal of RATIONALITY by execs claiming artistic credit (in industry that is *heavily* rationalized and continuously researched) |
| "Everyone in the industry lies. . . ."<br>SELF-SUFFICIENCY, against all odds | Disavowal of COOPERATIVE nature of work by "players" (when everything career-wise depends upon "who you know") |
| "All information is spin. . . ."<br>PERSUASIVE abilities | Disavowal of basic INDUSTRIAL NEED for producer's product (when media content fills manufacturing need and corporate logic) |
| "I've developed a 'feel' for winners . . ." zones<br>INTUITION and magic-touch | Disavowal of HIERARCHICAL pecking-order in public contact (industry works via "inside deals" and exploitation of work conditions) |
| "I only produce projects I care about. . . ."<br>INTEGRITY | Disavowal of BOTTOM-LINE imperative (even though industry driven by "bottom-feeders" and profit margins) |
| "Our only goal is entertainment . . ."<br>RESPONSIVENESS | Disavowal of CRITICAL INTENTION by successful producers (when artifacts and texts, explicitly deploy theoretical knowledge) |
| "Hollywood is a state of mind . . ."<br>MYSTIQUE legitimized | Disavowal of LEGALIZED CORPORATE RELATIONS (when legal contracting rules corporate business plans) |

series. These include books addressing it as a systematic philosophical treatise (Irwin, Conard, and Skoble, 2001) and as an intervention in theological enquiry (Pinsky, 2001). The process of disavowal can, in fact, be recognized as a rhetorical perspective employed systematically across discursive, technical, and textual registers in the production culture. In many cases, acts of disavowal tame industrial complexity and churn in order to efface economic and ideological dimensions of media on the one hand, and to legitimate long-standing industrial mythologies on the other. Such mythologies have proven lucrative as cultural (and economic) capital over the past century. Interviews with producers and executives tend to reinforce these recognizable mythoi. Critical industrial practice, as I've suggested here however, offers other ways to understand the cultural and ideological significance of practitioners and the culture of production (Table 5.3).

Coming to grips with the extent of the critical industrial competencies considered here challenges some of the favored presuppositions of cultural studies scholars: i.e., that deconstruction necessarily serves a "counter" critical function, that industrial texts must be mined to make visible ideological contradictions; that agency, hybridity, desire, and performativity are subject/audience/user functions. In the new era of media re-conglomeration and multi-channel diversification, industries employ deconstruction, meta-critical textuality, and performativities of identity (racial, ethnic, sexual, hybrid, nomadic, and otherwise). The culture of production acts out these cultural performativities on a daily basis in the contact zones, bounded sanctums and semi-public spaces of the film/video workplace.

## Notes

1   Concerning definitions, throughout this chapter I will use the term "the industry" as it is commonly used by practitioners and critics in Los Angeles; that is, as a term that construes "Hollywood" as a geographically situated cultural phenomenon. Of course, "Hollywood" itself is a misnomer and a construct, since it is typically used to reference a comprehensive set of media activities: the film, television, and digital media activities networked across the greater Los Angeles region. Obviously, there are *many, many* other "cultures of production" apart from Hollywood. So I am choosing to frame my study of "the Industry" and/or "Hollywood" as the study of a very local and specific cultural site; albeit one that expends great effort in promoting and constructing itself as a global production culture.

2   The following discussion of ad campaigns draws on various ads from Panavision (1993), Sony (1997), Quantum (1997), and Wescam (1997).

*John Caldwell*

# References

Abramowitz, Rachel (2000) *Is That a Gun in Your Pocket? Women's Experience of Power in Hollywood* (New York: Random House).

Agre, Phil (1997) *Computation and Human Experience* (Cambridge: Cambridge University Press).

Althusser, Louis (1971) "Ideology and the Ideological State Apparatuses (Notes Towards an Investigation)," in Louis Althusser, *For Marx*, trans. Ben Brewster (New York: Random House), pp. 139–58.

Alvey, Mark (1997) "The Independents: Rethinking the Television Studio System," in Lynn Spigel and Michael Curtin (eds.), *The Revolution Wasn't Televised* (New York: Routledge), pp. 139–60.

Anderson, Tim (1993) *Hollywood Television* (Austin: University of Texas Press).

Andrew, Dudley (1976). *The Major Film Theories* (New York: Oxford University Press).

Balio, Tino (1996) *Grand Design: Hollywood as a Modern Business Enterprise, 1930–39* (Berkeley: University of California Press).

Banks, Miranda (2005) "The Other Woman: Gendered Production Work and the Female Action Hero," dissertation, UCLA.

Baudrillard, Jean (1983) *Simulations* (New York: Semiotext(e)).

Berland, Jody (1992) "Angels Dancing: Cultural Studies and the Production of Space," in L. Grossberg, C. Nelson, and P. Treichler (eds.), *Cultural Studies* (New York: Routledge).

Bierstadt, Robert (1951) "Review of Powdermaker's *Hollywood: The Dream Factory*," *American Sociological Review*, 16(1) (February): 124–5.

Biskind, Peter (1998) *Easy Riders, Raging Bulls: How the Sex, Drugs and-Rock-'n'-Roll Generation Saved Hollywood* (New York: Simon & Schuster).

Bhabha, Homi (1995) "Are You a Man or a Mouse," in Maurice Berger, Brian Wallis, and Simon Watson (eds.), *Constructing Masculinity* (New York: Routledge), pp. 57–68.

Bordwell, David, Kristen Thompson, and Janet Staiger (1985) *The Classical Hollywood Cinema: Film Style and Mode of Production to 1960* (New York: Columbia University Press).

Bowman, James (1998) "The Folks Who Made Hollywood Dark and Dirty," *American Spectator*, 31(9) (September): 78–80.

Brown, Ben (1984) "Tube of Plenty," *American Film*, 9(9) (July–August): 53–6.

Caldwell, John (1993) "Televisuality as a Semiotic Machine: Emerging Paradigms in Low Theory," *Cinema Journal*, 32(4): 24–48.

Caldwell, John (1994) "Performing Style: Industrial Strength Aesthetics," in Nick Browne (ed.), *American Television: New Directions in History and Theory* (New York: Harwood), pp. 193–222.

Caldwell, John (1995) *Televisuality: Style, Crisis, and Authority in American Television* (New Brunswick, NJ: Rutgers University Press).

Caldwell, John (2000) "Theorizing the Digital Landrush," in J. Caldwell (ed.), *Electronic Media and Technoculture* (New Brunswick, NJ: Rutgers University Press), pp. 1–34.

Caldwell, John (2001) "Primetime Fiction Theorizes the Docu-Real," in J. Caldwell (ed.), *Reality Squared* (New Brunswick, NJ: Rutgers University Press), pp. 259–92.

Caldwell, John (2004) "Convergence Television: Aggregating Form and Repurposing Content in the Culture of Conglomeration," in Lynn Spigel and Jan Olsson (eds.), *Television After TV* (Durham: Duke University Press), pp. 41–74.

Caldwell, John (forthcoming) *Production Culture: Industrial Reflexivity and Critical Practice in Film/Television* (Durham, NC and London: Duke University Press).

Cassell, Justine and Henry Jenkins (1998) *From Barbie to Mortal Kombat: Gender and Computer Games* (Cambridge, MA: MIT Press).

Christensen, Mark and Cameron Stauth (1984) *The Sweeps: Behind the Scenes in Network TV* (New York: W. Morrow).

Citron, Michelle, and Ellen Seiter (1985) "The Perils of Feminist Film Teaching," in Peter Steven (ed,), *Jump-Cut: Hollywood, Politics, and Counter-Cinema* (New York: Praeger), pp. 269–77.

Clancey, W. J. (1997) *Situated Cognition* (New York: Cambridge University Press).

Coleman, Tim (1995) "Review of High Concept," *Criticism*, 37(4) (Fall): 653–6.

Comolli, J. (1986) "Technique and Ideology: Camera, Perspective, Depth of Field (Parts 3 and 4)," in P. Rosen (ed.), *Narrative, Apparatus, Ideology* (New York: Columbia University Press), pp. 421–33.

Cooper, Ilene (1996) "Review of Aaron Spelling," *Booklist*, 92(22) (August): 1873.

Couldry, Nick (2000a) *The Place of Media Power: Pilgrims and Witnesses of the Media Age* (London: Routledge).

Couldry, Nick (2000b) "Tracking Down the Media: From the Studio to the Doorstep," Paper presented at the "Crossroads in Cultural Studies" Conference, University of Birmingham, UK, June, 21–5.

Curtin, Michael (1996) "On Edge: Culture Industries in the Neo-Network Era," in Richard Ohmann, ed. *Making and Selling Culture* (Hanover, NH: University Press of New England/Wesleyan University Press), pp. 181–202.

Curtin, Michael (2000) "Producing Public Television, Producing Public Culture (Dornfeld)," *American Ethnologist*, 27(1): 200–1.

D'Acci, Julie (1994) *Defining Women: Television and the Case of Cagney and Lacey* (Chapel Hill, NC: University of North Carolina Press).

Davila, Arlene (2001) *Latinos, inc.: The Making of a People* (Berkeley: University of California Press).

Dornfeld, Barry (1998) *Producing Public Television, Producing Public Culture* (Princeton, NJ: Princeton University Press).

Fiske, John (1986). "British Cultural Studies," in Robert Allan (ed.), *Channels of Discourse* (Chapel Hill, NC: University of North Carolina Press), pp. 254–89.

Foucault, Michel (1977, 1979) *Discipline and Punish*, trans. Alan Sheridan (New York: Random House).

Friend, Tad (2000) "Short Cuts," *New Yorker*, 76(4) (20 March): 34–8.

Gallagher, John (1989) *Film Directors on Directing* (New York: Praeger).

Gans, Herbert J. (1979) *Deciding What's News: A Study of CBS Evening News, NBC Nightly News, Newsweek, and Time* (New York: Pantheon Books).

Geertz, Clifford (1985) *Local Knowledge: Essays in Interpretive Anthropology* (New York: Basic Books).

Gitlin, Todd (1983) *Inside Prime Time* (New York: Pantheon Books).

Goldman, William (1983) *Adventures in the Screen Trade: A Personal View of Hollywood and Screenwriting* (New York: Warner Books).

Goldman, William (2000) *Which Lie Did I Tell?: More Adventures in the Screen Trade* (New York: Pantheon Books).

Gradus, Ben (1981) *Directing the Television Commercial*, Communication arts books (New York: Hastings House).

Gramsci, Antonio (1971) *Selections from the Prison Notebooks*, trans and ed. Q. Hoare and G.N. Smith (London: Lawrence and Wishart).

Gray, Herman (1995) *Watching Race* (Minneapolis: University of Minnesota Press).

Griffin, Nancy, and Kim Masters (1996) *Hit and Run: How Jon Peters and Peter Guber Took Sony for a Ride in Hollywood* (New York: Simon & Schuster).

Gripsrud, Jostein (1995) *The Dynasty Years: Hollywood Television and Critical Media Studies* (London: Comedia/Routledge).

Grossberg, Larry, C. Nelson, and P. Treichler (eds.) (1992) *Cultural Studies* (New York: Routledge).

Guber, Peter (2001) Public comments at "Transition" event, UCLA, April 25.

Hacker, Sally L (1990) *Doing It the Hard Way* (New York: Unwin Hyman).

Hall, Stuart (1980a). "Cultural Studies: Two Paradigms." *Media, Culture, and Society*, 2: 57–72.

Hall, Stuart (1980b). "Encoding and Decoding," In Stuart Hall et al. (eds.), *Culture, Media, Language* (London: Hutchinson), pp. 128–38.

Hayward, Susan (1996) *Cinema Studies: The Key Concepts* (London: Routledge).

Hennion, Antoine (1990 [1983]) "The Production of Success: An Antimusicology of the Pop Song," in Simon Frith and Andrew Goodwin (eds.), *On Record: Rock, Pop, and The Written Word* (New York: Pantheon Books), pp. 185–206.

Hunter, Ian (1992) "Aesthetics and Cultural Studies," in L. Grossberg, C. Nelson, and P. Treichler (eds.), *Cultural Studies* (New York: Routledge), pp. 347–67.

Irwin, William, Mark Conard, and Aeon Skoble (2001) *The Simpsons and Philosophy: The D'oh of Homer* (Chicago: Open Court).

Jones, Kent (1998) "Review of *Easy Riders, Raging Bulls*," *Film Comment*, 34(5) (September–October): 64–70.

Joyrich, Lynne (1996) *Re-Viewing Reception: Television, Gender, and Postmodern Culture* (Bloomington, IN: Indiana University Press).

Katzman, Pat (1994) "Tinker Looks Back on Ups and Downs of TV Career," *San Francisco Chronicle*, 29 August 1994, p. E5.

Kent, Nicholas (1992) "Players at their own Game," *Los Angeles Times Book Review*, May 17, p. 2.

Koszarski, Richard (1976) *Hollywood Directors 1914–1940* (New York: Oxford University Press).

Kuney, Jack (1990) *Take One: Television Directors on Directing*, Contributions to the study of popular culture no. 25 (New York: Greenwood Press).

Latour, Bruno (1986) *Laboratory Life: The Construction of Scientific Facts* (Princeton, NJ: Princeton University Press).

Latour, Bruno (1988) *Science In Action: How to Follow Scientists and Engineers Through Society* (Cambridge, MA: Harvard University Press).

Laurent, Lawrence (1993) "Review of *Prime Time, Prime Movers*," *Television Quarterly*, 26(4) (Spring): 85–8.

Lefebvre, Henri (1979) "Space: Social Product and Use Value," in J.W. Freiberg (ed.), *Critical Sociology* (New York: Irvington Publishers), pp. 285–96.

Lefebvre, Henri (1984) *Everyday Life in the Modern World*, trans. S. Rabinovitch (New Brunswick: Transaction Books).

Lobdell, William (2001) "D'oh God!: The Simpsons and Spirituality," *Los Angeles Times*, September 1, p. b20.

Lumet, Sidney (1995) *Making Movies* (New York: Alfred A. Knopf).

Mamet, David (1991) *On Directing Film* (New York: Viking Press).

Marc, David (1995) *Bonfire of the Humanities: Television, Subliteracy, and Long-Term Memory Loss*. The Television Series (Syracuse: Syracuse University Press).

Marc, David, and Robert J. Thompson (1992) *Prime Time, Prime Movers: From I Love Lucy to L.A. Law – America's Greatest TV Shows and the People Who Created Them* (New York: Little Brown).

Mayer, Vicki (2003) *Consuming Youth, Producing Dreams* (New Brunswick, NJ: Rutgers University Press).

McCarthy, Anna (2001) *Ambient Television: Visual Culture and Public Space* (Durham, NC and London: Duke University Press).

McChesney, Robert (1999). *Rich Media, Poor Democracy* (Urbana: University of Illinois Press).

McDonough, Tom (1985) "Shots Seen Round the World," *American Film*, 10(10) (September): 68–70.

Mellencamp, Patricia (1992) *High Anxiety: Catastrophe, Scandal, Age, and Comedy* (Bloomington, IN: Indiana University Press).

Moloch, H. L. (1996) "L.A. as Product," in Allen Scott and Edward Soja (eds.), *Los Angeles and Urban Theory at the End of the Twentieth Century* (Berrkeley: University of California Press), pp 225–75.

Morley, David (1992) *Television, Audiences, and Cultural Studies* (New York and London: Routledge).

Neale, Steve and Murray Smith (1998) *Contemporary Hollywood Cinema* (London: Routledge).

Newcomb, Horace, and Robert S. Alley (1993 [1983]) *The Producer's Medium: Conversations with Creators of American TV*. New York: Oxford University Press.

Oblowitz, Michael (1989) "Close-ups: Michael Oblowitz," *Millimeter*, February, 196.

Ohmann, Richard (ed.)(1996) *Making and Selling Culture* (Hanover, NH: University Press of New England/Wesleyan University Press).

Papows, Jeff (1998) *Enterprise.com: Market Leadership in the Information Age* (Reading, MA: Perseus Books).

Phillips, Julia (2002) *You'll Never Work in This Town Again* (New York: New American Library).

Pike, Kenneth (1954) *Language in Relation to a Unified Theory of the Structure of Human Behavior* (Glendale, CA: Summer Institute of Linguistics).

Pinsky, Mark J. (2001) *The Gospel According to the Simpsons* (Westminster: John Knox Press).

Powdermaker, Hortense (1950) *Hollywood, the Dream Factory: An Anthropologist Looks at the Movie-Makers* (Boston: Little, Brown).

Raglan, Lord (1952) "Review of *Hollywood: The Dream Factory*," *Man*, 52 (March): 44.

Rifkin, Arnold (2001) Public comments at "Transition" event, UCLA, April 25.

Rosenthal, Alan (1990) *Writing, Directing and Producing Documentary Films* (Carbondale, IL: Southern Illinois University Press).

# John Caldwell

Ross, Andrew (1998) *Real Love: In Pursuit of Cultural Justice* (New York: New York University Press).

Rosten, Leo (1941) *Hollywood: The Movie Colony* (New York: Harcourt, Brace).

Scarry, Elaine (1987) *The Body In Pain: The Making and Unmaking of the World* (New York: Oxford University Press).

Schatz, Thomas (1983) *Old Hollywood, New Hollywood: Ritual, Art, and Industry*. Ann Arbor, MI: UMI Press.

Schatz, Thomas (1988) *The Genius of the System: Hollywood Filmmaking in the Studio Era* (New York: Henry Holt).

Schiller, Dan (1999) *Digital Capitalism: Networking the Global Market System* (Cambridge, MA: MIT Press).

Schlosser, Joe and Bill McDonnell (2001). "What is Real, Really?", *Broadcasting and Cable*, August 27, p. 12.

Scott, Allen (1988) *Metropolis: From the Division of Labor to Urban Form* (Berkeley and Los Angeles: University of California Press).

Scott, Allen (1993) *Technopolis: High-Technology Industry and Regional Development in Southern California, Berkely, and Los Angeles* (Berkeley and Los Angeles: University of California Press).

Scott, A. and Soja, E (1996). *The City: Los Angeles and Urban Theory at the End of the Twentieth Century*. Los Angeles: University of California Press.

Segaller, Stephen (1998) *Nerds 2.0.1: A Brief History of the Internet* (New York: TV Books).

Shattuc, Jane (1997) *The Talking Cure: TV Talk Shows and Women* (New York: Routledge).

Sherman, Eric (1976) *Directing the Film: Film Directors on Their Art* (Boston: Little Brown).

Seiter, Ellen. (1999). *Television and New Media Audiences* (New York: Oxford University Press).

Soja, Edward (1989) *Postmodern Geographies: The Reassertion of Space as a Critical Category in Critical Social Theory* (New York: Verso).

Sova, Dawn B. (1998) *Women in Hollywood: From Vamp to Studio Head* (New York: Fromm International Publishing).

Spelling, Aaron, with Jefferson Graham (1996) *Aaron Spelling: A Prime-Time Life* (New York: St. Martin's Press).

Spielberg, Steven (2000) *Steven Spielberg: Interviews*, edited by Lester D. Friedman and Brent Notbohm. Conversations with filmmakers series (Jackson: University Press of Mississippi).

Stam, Robert, Robert Burgone, Sandy Flitterman-Lewis (1992). *Vocabularies in Film Semiotics: Structuralism, Poststructuralism and Beyond* (London: Routledge).

Starr, Susan Leigh (ed.) (1995) *The Cultures of Computing* (Cambridge, MA: Blackwell Publishers).

Stevens, Jon (ed.) (1997) *Actors Turned Directors: On Eliciting the Best Performance from an Actor and Other Secrets of Successful Directing* (Los Angeles: Silman-James Press).

Streeter, Thomas (1997) "Blue Skies and Strange Bedfellows: the Discourse of Cable TV," in Lynn Spigel and Michael Curtin (eds.), *The Revolution wasn't Televised: Sixties Television and Social Conflict* (London: Routledge).

Storper, Michael, and Robert Salais (1997) *Worlds of Production: The Action Frameworks of the Economy* (Cambridge, MA: Harvard University Press).

Thompson, E.P. (1963; rpt. 1966) *The Making of the English Working Class* (New York: Vintage).

Tinker, Grant, and Bud Rukeyser (1994) *Tinker in Television: From General Sarnoff to General Electric* (New York: Simon & Schuster).

Traube, Elizabeth (1996) "Introduction," in Richard Ohmann (ed.), *Making and Selling Culture* (Hanover, NH: University Press of New England/Wesleyan University Press), pp. xi–xxii.

Turner, Victor, and Edward Bruner (eds.) (1986) *The Anthropology of Experience* (Urbana: University of Illinois Press).

Walker, Joseph B. and Juanita Walker (1984) *The Light on Her Face* (Hollywood: ASC Press).

Wild, David (1999) *The Showrunners: A Season Inside the Billion-Dollar, Death-Defying, Madcap World of Television's Real Stars* (New York: HarperCollins).

Williams, Raymond (1974) *Television: Technology and Cultural Form* (New York: Schocken Books).

Wyatt, Justin (1994) *High Concept: Movies and Marketing in Hollywood* (Austin: University of Texas Press).

# 6

# *Feminism and the Politics of Method*

## Joke Hermes

Second-wave feminism was very important to early audience research in cultural studies. But exactly how feminist thought has informed the study of media audiences has remained something of a blank page, despite interesting suggestions in the work of such authors as Brunsdon (1997), Drotner (1994), and Gray (1999). In this chapter I draw on a small number of key studies and on recent research of my own to show how important feminism's engagement with questions of power has been for the methodology developed early on in cultural studies audience research. The goal of this chapter is to take a closer look at earlier audience studies to understand how they engage with feminist politics at a formative moment. We usually take such moments to have particular *theoretical* significance but the same goes for the methods we use and keep on using.

Early feminist interest in the media was inspired by the work of writers such as Betty Friedan (*The Feminine Mystique*, [1963] 1974) and Germaine Greer (*The Female Eunuch*, 1971). Their fierce criticism of popular women's media is enabled by what Charlotte Brunsdon (1997: 17) has called the "transparent" relationship between feminism and women their work and political outlook assumed. In this early work there is no "otherness"; sisterhood is automatically shared. Friedan's account of women's magazines as disseminators of "the feminine mystique" is grounded in her experience as an editor of women's magazines. Greer quotes her own youthful bad taste in reading and "mooning" over romance novels (1971: 171). With near-Leninist self-assurance these feminist writers take up an *avant-garde* position of enlightenment. Their goal, implicitly, is to divest others of their false consciousnesses as well. A similar feminist "we" in cultural studies work on the media can be found in Dorothy Hobson's early research (1978). According to Brunsdon (1997), Hobson's early work is important for its sensitive questioning of the experience of being a young housewife. The media formed an integral part of this experience but were to be criticized explicitly in cultural studies audience ethnography.

Brunsdon (1997: 118) further suggests in her useful overview that the transparent relation between feminism and women was followed by a recruitment mode. Feminist work on the media in the early to mid-1980s (my time frame) sought explicitly to transform feminine identifications into feminist ones. Janice Radway's (1984) work on the reading of romance novels (which will also be quoted below) is a strong example of a relationship between the feminist author and the female media audience, which Brunsdon terms "hegemonic." As in the first phase of feminist work on the media, the feminist researcher can be understood as one who felt she was ahead of other women and needed them to open their eyes to the price they paid for the pleasures offered by soaps and romances. The difference is that she is aware of the differential positions she and the audience occupy. Authors such as Ien Ang (1985), in her *Dallas* research, try to bridge these positions by reflecting on their own pleasure in particular media texts, rather than dismissing this pleasure as youthful sins. Another example would be Janice Winship's 1980s work, best summarized in her 1987 study. In large part this study is an analysis of the women's magazine text, yet it is informed by Winship's choices as a reader. The combination of feminist and reader, and of writing from what is clearly a double perspective, make work such as Winship's a pleasure to read for someone like me, whose work, in Brunsdon's typology, would be part of a third relationship between feminism and women, which she terms "fragmented." It is founded on the supposition that there is no necessary relationship between women and feminism (Brunsdon, 1997: 120). Although Brunsdon offers a typology rather than a time frame, it is entirely possible to say that this third position becomes common from the early to mid-1990s. All positions or modes can still be found in audience research.

Cultural studies audience research, and the relation between the researcher and the researched, can be situated across these three possible relationships between feminism and women. I would suggest that the formative moment for cultural studies audience research needs to be located between the implicit paternalism of the first category (however sensitive to what were felt to be women's needs and problems) and the second category, of recruitment which does not allow for anyone's unreflexive pleasure in traditional media content. The power to oppress women, to restrict their sense of who they are and who they could be, is laid at the feet of patriarchy and capital, and given a recognisable face in the media. Media texts seduced women to comply with their subservient positions in the world. When feminist researchers invoke power relations they refer to men and the media. Individual texts may question these givens. Angela McRobbie wrote one of the earliest critiques of a feminist sense of superiority, taken up wittingly or unwittingly. She famously pointed out that however well-meaning women researchers were in their approach to groups of less privileged women, they needed to be aware of how their university backgrounds would make them formidable figures in the eyes of others (cf. McRobbie, 1982). Ien Ang showed herself to be wary of any automatic condemnation of media content (Ang, 1985).

Unfortunately, between speaking from personal experience overcome and speaking on behalf of others on the one hand, and feminist condemnation of media texts on the other, feminist sensitivity to power relations in media audience research had taken a particular and somewhat conservative form. Friedan and Greer can hardly be faulted for their seminal work. After all, they wrote from their personal experience and, liberals that we are, we tend not to question such accounts as misguided or limited. Everyone is entitled their interpretation of the media and of media texts. However, the self-evidence of taking up a critical position regarding popular media, and implicitly including others in this criticism, has since thrown its shadow over audience research. Whether audiences (read feminists) could be trusted to have the critical facilities to understand the deeper, conservative, sexist or racist meanings of a text, or not, everyone should be given a chance to express their own opinions. Favorite outcomes, however, would point to the (proto)feminism or the critical readings of these audiences. Thus, the following elements came to define what constitutes acceptable methodology: (1) instead of surveys and questionnaires one should employ ethnography or at least long unstructured interviews that allow all interviewees some measure of agency; (2) textual analysis can never be taken to predict or explain how audiences will read, experience or interpret a text; and (3) method could legitimately be employed to serve critical-political goals.

The impetus behind audience research is precisely motivated by the wish not to speak on behalf of others even though, as a researcher, one does exactly that. In addition, audience research stands in an uneasy relationship to any criticism of the text the researchers might want to voice on their own behalf. Many feminist authors have found themselves entangled in these contradictory positions. They wish to criticize media content and they also want to do justice to how audiences read or experience them. The danger of such efforts can be to offer audience reactions as illustrations of the position taken up by the author. The author, meanwhile, cannot be faulted for either her political position or for her methodology. Good feminist that she is, she has allowed other women's voices to be heard and has made room for them in her text (method). Given that she also has strong feelings about the content of the media text as a reader (politics) and as a researcher (textual analysis), it would make one nostalgic for the days when the positions of reader and of feminist, combined with that of the researcher, could be taken to be seamlessly connected – if not the same. But they are not. Significant numbers of women were not at all interested in embracing feminism. Feminine pleasures remained strongly rooted in everyday practice, with no sign that feminist criticism was making much of a difference.

Despite good intentions, method, politics and the media text refused to align in a comfortable manner. The tenacity of this ideological knot can be deduced from the fact that a number of issues have yet to be resolved. This includes the absence of powerful informants. For example, men are only seldom part of this type of research, even though men – and male-dominated media – are the categories that have been identified as the traditional holders of power. In feminist ethnographic work, male informants have been of little interest to feminist intellectuals. Paradoxically, it would seem to be the case that feminists, made aware of their own power by McRobbie's much-cited article, have chosen to continue as benevolent power-mongers, giving voice to socially weak informants rather than tackling powerful informants. The same position for the researcher is maintained in cultural studies audience research among lower-class informants or youngsters: they too can be understood to be powerless groups who need the researcher to be their advocate (Willis, 1990). Production research, ethnography among media professionals, likewise, has also been very scarce. Another unresolved dilemma has to do with aligning the methodological question of how best to triangulate audience research and textual analysis with the political truth that combining such methods is impossible. A decade ago, while designing my research on women's magazines, I chose to

evade the issue by concentrating solely on how respondents constructed women's magazines subgenres and the meanings they accorded
these subgenres as part of their practices of use (Hermes, 1995). Below
I will offer a more recent example in which I have tried to confront
the methodological implication of what essentially is a political
choice.

Over two decades after the first prominent cultural studies analyses
of media use, it is obvious that cultural studies has become institutionalized (academic courses in cultural studies are rife; journals have been
established). There have also been fierce attacks, many of them directed
precisely at cultural studies' lack of standardized method and its improper
use of "ethnography" as a label for cultural studies audience research.
In fact, most qualitative audience researchers, including myself, are well
aware that we often work with very small samples from which it is
not really possible to generalize, but which we nonetheless often do
(see Geraghty, 1998; Seiter, 1999). Nor do we spend as much time with
our informants as we probably should and as implicitly promised in
our often-voiced allegiance to anthropological or ethnographic principles (Gillespie, 1995: 55). Be that as it may, after two decades I am
still often impressed with work on audiences and how interaction
between academics and those who are not leads to new impulses and
insights, and generally forces intellectuals to broaden their scope and
develop new visions of the (social) world. Also, I see no reason to
change my mind about research that focuses solely on the media text.
It may well be brilliant for the meanings that can be generated from
small bits (or huge corpora) of writing or visual images, but audience-
based work remains more moving and indicates how we tend to
overrate the meaningfulness of any single text once it is part of an
everyday setting, a concept further explored in my 1995 research on
the fallacy of meaningfulness in cultural studies work.

I also tend to hold on to the commitment of early feminist work
to the political project of deconstructing gender and claiming respect
for women. I do see now that these commendable and inspiring goals
came accompanied by a sense of deep concern for woman as audiences.
Concern tends to inspire paternalism. Paternalism – or, in more positive terms, a sense of responsibility – does not combine well with
approaching powerful informants, and the last thing they need is the
researcher's care or advocacy. They will most certainly be able to voice
their own position and defend it. The question is whether such informants have, or have not, done so. And why assume that male or middle-

class informants are free of the kinds of coercion that define all of us as women or men, as black or white, as ... name any of the well-known power inequalities in the Western world.

## Powerful Informants and Field Relations

Recent research gave me pause to rethink what had also become my own standard practice, in line with accepted method in cultural studies. The project initially dealt exclusively with feminist crime fiction (Hermes, 1998) and then gradually expanded to crime and detective fiction more generally (both in books and on television). Central to it were questions of pleasure, of gender construction and gendered identities, but also of how these particular texts might offer social criticism or utopian visions of a better world. This last set of questions was grouped under the label "cultural citizenship." As an audience researcher, I of course felt it was not enough to simply document an interpretation of my own reading. I therefore decided to approach a mixed group of detective and crime readers, biased in terms of gender toward women, and including a number of self-identified gay people (women and men). They, I reasoned, are the readers most likely to consume those thrillers and detective fiction that can be argued to embody a significant part of the women's and gay liberation movements' ideas and visions (Coward and Semple, 1989; Munt, 1994; several authors in Irons (ed), 1995; Whitlock, 1994; Zimmerman, 1990: 63, 210–11), and among whom it would hence be easiest to identify how reading a popular genre may link up with more political forms of knowledge and practice. This linkage is what I understood as a key site of cultural citizenship.

Cultural citizenship is a term introduced in cultural studies in order to address the power of cultural formations (Allor and Gagnon, 1994). In this formulation popular pleasures are neither simply a threat to our individual senses of discernment and judgment or instruments of domination, nor are they to be celebrated as a source of liberation. Reading popular texts both ties us into the rules and structures of societal power and offers reflection on them. This dual process of actively becoming part of and simultaneously taking part in cultural practice, is an aspect of citizenship. It motivates us to take belonging, being part of social groups, seriously and to reflect not only on its pleasures and horrors (e.g. in reading crime fiction), but also on the concomitant rights and obligations of being a member of society, a citizen.

With an assistant and help from a group of students, 19 crime readers were interviewed at some length. They had replied to our postings on two specialized Internet sites, were clients of a thriller bookstore in Amsterdam, or, in a few cases, were relations of our friends and acquaintances. Five were self-identified feminists, four were men and five were gay (four women, one of the men). Although we had not particularly intended this to be the case, most of them had (professional) middle-class backgrounds. Generally, they were a nice and cooperative group of people. Some of the time, however, their elaborate strategies to ward off any suggestion that they were not in full control of interpretations of their own reading and of their positions as men and women, and also, in many cases, of the interview situation, baffled us and, when we were analyzing the material, irritated us. In part this was related to class position and the management of social relations in a research context. But it was also due to a more general lack of terms or access to a repertoire through which to express important parts of what fascinates crime readers in the (sub)genres they like.

One of our two group interviews provides a case in point. My assistant Cindy Stello felt actively excluded by our three informants after she had failed to pick up on a title of a particular novel. She pointed out that the group had subsequently addressed all their remarks to me, and had consistently used terms such as "we," "our group," or "our circle." My own frustration was with how they ridiculed some of my questions, as well as my opening statement in which I tried to point to the difference between high and low culture and the difficult position of crime fiction in the middle. In making these remarks, I had hoped to break the ice and relieve my guests (the interview was at my home address) of any feelings of unease. My question met with near-derision. The cultural status of the detective was totally unproblematic. To think otherwise was too old-fashioned for words. Time was when you had to hide or be ashamed of reading popular books but this was considered to be in the dim and distant past.

Henry (48, civil servant), one of the three interviewees, a few of whose remarks and observations I have singled out for this report, held the view that detectives are no longer seen as "low" culture (applause from the other two participants and this was the first subject broached in the interview). He even felt that: "Detectives today are more an art form than they have ever been. Ten or twenty years ago, they may have been looked down upon but today ..." This was enough to make me feel guilty for forcing an apparently ridiculous and possibly insulting point of view on these readers. Irritation took over later. For all their vehement disagreement with me on the question of the social standing of thrillers and detectives, our three informants did not so much argue that popular culture has become more accepted, rather they were categorizing the popular books they liked as Literature. They took pains to make it clear that they were collectors of a particular author, or subgenre, and also that they were Readers who were aware of the value of Good Books. We, the interviewers, were obviously the barbarians to whom such distinctions needed to be explained, or worse, who were trying to talk them into being readers of trash with all its suspect pleasures. This group interview was not an exception – in the other group interview and in several of the individual interviews we came across the same type of "impression management" (cf. Goffman, 1959).

Irritation is the last thing you need in audience research. After all, our only material is what informants can and will tell us. As Dave Morley has famously suggested:

> In the case of my own research, I would accept that in the absence of any significant element of participant observation of actual behaviour beyond the interview situation, I am left only with the stories that respondents chose to tell me. These stories are, however, themselves both limited and indexical of the cultural and linguistic frames of references which respondents have available to them, through which to articulate their responses. (1989: 24)

If the words of our informants are all we have, then it will not do to allow irritation to cloud our attention to what they say. For irritation not only threatens respect and thus careful and unprejudiced attention to and representation of what respondents have to say, it is very nearly a crime against what Gadamer called *Verstehen* (Gadamer, 1986; Warnke, 1987). *Verstehen*, or understanding, forms the very possibility of building a shared horizon across the divide of research and everyday life.

In retrospect, it is easy enough to see that I had unwittingly chanced upon a group of powerful informants. Anthropologists have documented how difficult it may be to gain access to, or elicit information from, powerful informants (Hammersley and Atkinson, 1995: 139) and, in particular, how gender is a highly important factor in negotiating relations with others (Warren, 1988). For some reason this type of anthropological reflection has not fully informed cultural studies of audiences and readings; but then neither has the tradition of extended periods of fieldwork. We have preferred the series of long interviews, the textually oriented discussion of reflexivity, and ethnographic writing on the discursive power of the intellectual versus the described Other (cf. Marcus and Fischer, 1986; Clifford and Marcus, 1986) to form a view of what ethnography and qualitative work with audiences should be like. It merged well with our feminist sensitivity to power relations, and it strengthened understanding of ourselves as researchers who were representative of the powerful academy. Powerful informants, and especially men, were obviously not part of this self-definition.

Ellen Seiter's (1990) discussion of a difficult interview must stand as the exception to this rule. In "Making Distinctions in TV Audience Research: Case Study of a Troubling Interview" she documents an interview with two middle-class, middle-aged men. Rather than co-operate and work with the two interviewers, as had other interviewees in the soap opera project, these two were especially interested, according to Seiter, in flaunting their knowledge of television and their superior taste. A transcript of the interview accompanies the article and offers a rare opportunity to compare the researcher's interpretation with the source material.

From the transcript it is obvious that Seiter's male co-interviewer was the one addressed by the two men. It is also obvious that the two informants are not only trying to impress the two interviewers with their knowledge of, amongst other things, television technology but also that they are trying to please them. In many ways, I was reminded of my own father, who would have been at least as difficult a subject for research of this kind, and who would not really know how to listen to the questions and understand what was being asked of him. It may be this personal link and the embarrassment I often experience that leads me to think that Seiter is slightly too harsh in her assessment of the two men. At the same time, her irritation and anger are central to her article, and I share her intuition that a certain type of arrogance is also at the root of what troubles her in the interview. Like my own more recent research experience, it is particularly painful to have the pillars of one's identity upset.

Like Seiter, I was trained in feminist research methods and have been left with a particular legacy. Three deep convictions have remained with me over the years. First, that the knowledge produced in research is not just of academic but always and also of political importance. Secondly, that the power inherent in one's position as an academic needs to be wielded with care. Finally, as a woman I have a special obligation in terms of researching questions of gender and femininity. For me, feminist research is synonymous with showing respect. This political position feeds into both methodological and theoretical choices. It is one of the reasons why I came to prefer the use of discourse analysis over more naturalistic and descriptive frameworks, because it sets different parameters for the actual research. The question is, how are you to do justice to the full complexities of another person's life, morally, methodologically or theoretically? The answer is: you cannot. Therefore focusing on individuals is a questionable choice unless you are writing in a biographical mode. Discourse analysis, understood as the reconstruction of funds of shared cultural knowledge (discourses, repertoires, vocabularies), allows for a different but useful type of outcome, although it certainly constitutes a less ambitious project.

Reflection on Seiter's troubling interview and my own interview experiences in the crime fiction project also suggests that discourse analysis may provide the researcher with an anti-paternalist position while allowing the researcher to retain her feminist focus. Discourse analysis need not be motivated by concern, nor does the outcome suggest that the researcher knows better than her respondents what moved them and how popular forms had meaning for them. It is, however, a different type of feminism that does not start from a position of considering informants as vulnerable or (possibly) as victims of social power relations. It takes on board suggestions that individuals may command differential power bases while being underdogs in other respects. It is less of a moral position, though it retains a political commitment albeit in a less personalized and more issue-oriented sense. Methodologically, this means that it is extremely important to find enough respondents and also to collect enough interview material. Of course, afterwards it is always possible to check how social and cultural capital align, or whether we migrate that much more easily in terms of class position that cultural capital comes to be an indicator of how one was raised rather than of one's current station in life. For the discourse analyst it is of the utmost importance to have enough data (interview material) and to develop an analysis of the transcripts by extending the search for tropes, metaphors and the underlying logic of the repertoires or discourses found in the interviews (the discourse analysis proper) to the structure of meaning in media texts. Traditional literary research methods such as semiology and genre analysis can perhaps be employed here. The challenge would be not to subsume the analysis of the interview material under the often very strong logics of such methods.

In the crime fiction group interview cited above I was aiming for a form of subservience to the group process. As a well-meaning feminist researcher I wished to enable the others to feel free to express themselves. I certainly did not want to impose my own frame of reference upon the group. As a discourse analyst I was concerned to tape as much of my informant's discussion as possible. My intentions misfired badly, the interview was not a success. In retrospect, I can see how the dutiful feminist in me was out to get "the real story," as in naturalistic approaches to social reality, while knowing, of course, that there is no real story to be reconstructed. Rather, there are only fragments of stories that allow us in audience research to build a picture of the cultural knowledges interviewees draw on in gaining pleasure from reading crime fiction as well as in making it meaningful. This much becomes clear in light of the fact that the same defensive, but also arrogant, middle-class way of talking was part of the interviews conducted by my students. It was not aimed at me or the other interviewers personally. It is much more a matter of convention, of the discursive construction of talking about popular fiction. It could well be the case that my fears of having imposed myself or my own interpretive framework prevented me from seeing how my "populist" defense was also a provocation.

This is the point where methodology meets theory. How do choices of method act either to enable analysis and theorization or to hinder them? What goals are served by the particular ways in which discussions about crime fiction are organized? How does analysis of field relations enrich – or possibly save – theorization of the material? What else is there in the material that irritation (or joy) may help me see, or has prevented me from seeing?

Some issues were not problematic for our interviewees (if surprising and in some regards disappointing). Women's position in society is an example of this. A majority of our informants stuck faithfully with a notion of women's emancipation as a taken-for-granted feature of today's world. With the exception of only some of the self-identified feminists, feminism was generally seen as over the top, too much, too aggressive and not properly appreciative of women's qualities as women. Emancipation should be our goal. Issues of women, emancipation, and feminism had obviously been given a place on the maps of meaning our informants employed. Apparently a cease fire had been reached over women and femininity, in which a notion of natural differences between men and women continued to win out over more radical feminist suggestions that gender difference is constructed or a performance, rather than a given. The position of men was a different matter. This only became clear when I decided that a more "symptomatic" reading of the interview material was the best way to confront and lay to rest fears of paternalist mismanagement of interview relations, and to use my irritation to reconstruct and subsequently theorize a part of the material that we had mostly left alone: the books referred to in the interviews. To read up on, or familiarize oneself with, the material one has been talking about is not a big step in an audience research project, but how to handle this material is another matter which is at least as problematic, both politically and methodologically, as the management of interview relations.

## Audience Research versus Textual Analysis

I may have described this more phlegmatically in my introduction, but I still feel strongly about the status of audience research versus the somewhat higher status (especially in terms of theory) of textual analysis. When the two are combined (as in older feminist work on popular culture), they jar. It is the researcher's (superior) reading of a set of texts against the partial or non-politicized understanding of audience groups. It blemished, for instance, Janice Radway's (1984) ground-breaking study on romance novels. Taking on board Brunsdon's suggestion that we read *Reading the Romance* as a recruitment exercise, Radway's conclusion (if not the research itself) that romance readers would be feminists if the world were to change and that in the resultant ideal feminist world there would be no further need for romances, still reads as an insult to romance readers. It marks "ordinary" readers as the lesser feminists, and feminists as the better women. It does not take pleasure itself, or the nature of the pleasure of reading a fictional formula text seriously at all (Ang, 1987). (It also does not allow or account for the possibility that feminists, even academic feminists, might derive pleasure from popular consumer culture, including romance novels or soap operas.) Likewise in a study of the history of women's magazines Ballaster et al. (1991) offer a last chapter based on interviews with readers and interpret what these readers have to say in an overly concerned vein. While they tell us they share the pleasure these readers obviously take in the magazines, they counsel that (traditional) women's magazines should only be taken in small doses because, like eating too much chocolate, they would otherwise make you ill.

Feminists have not had a particularly good track record of combining analysis of the text with interpreting audiences' uses of them. Nor have we always been very careful in our text-based work to make clear that without asking audiences, we cannot speak for them, which implicitly is exactly what we have done. The reason for, and legitimation of, work with popular media texts has too often kept to a modernist frame of reference in which popular texts are always dangerous and possibly damaging for the less-tutored. This is paternalism at its worst, and out of line with the respect we feminists otherwise value so highly. More generally, it is obvious that audience research is not easily combined with textual analysis. Apart from the highly different types of analytic tools we have become accustomed to using, there remains a sense of drawing on knowledges that are too disparate.

Apart from highly descriptive introductions of the material the audience research is related to, many recent studies have therefore left the text for what it is and concentrated on the audience (Hagen, 1994a, 1994b; Hermes, 1995; McKinley, 1997). We may have lost something in the process. It should be possible to talk about texts and interviews without talking about identities and personal choices in life. Both types of material are also indicative of shared social knowledges, of what issues we debate, and how we debate them, and the means we have available to do so. The sometimes defensive, sometimes aggressive manner of defending "their" crime novels which we found in our interviews may not be a question of personal style so much as an indication of the constraints inherent in the mechanisms of "middle-class" discourse on popular culture.

Less systematic than Radway (1984), who had her informants give her lists of the best and the worst romances they had read, but inspired by her example, I followed the only clues left over in my crime fiction material, namely the novels referred to in the discussions with which I was unfamiliar. This symptomatic reading cannot stand as more than a speculative undertaking. The texts studied do not answer questions about what the audience is really like, or why, ultimately, they like crime fiction. But the books mentioned in the interviews may provide some idea of what the group of readers we studied felt was important. They have, in Morley's (1989) words, "indexical value." In the light of my search for the links between popular culture, especially popular fiction, and the public sphere, it is important to understand how there may be issues of public and political importance that can only be understood via a roundabout route. After reading the novels mentioned in the interviews, I suspect that the position of men, and of what we understand and would like masculinity to be, is precisely such an issue which is only very partially addressed by existing vocabularies and repertoires.

## Masculinity and the Media Text

It was a long time since I had read a large number of titles by male authors or novels featuring a heterosexual male protagonist (I know, I am a very parochial feminist) and I was amazed by what I found. There is a strong suggestion that although gender studies may have put masculinity on the agenda, this has not reached everyday life. Men and in a sense masculinity are still mostly what detective and thriller fiction is about, notwithstanding the enormous and long-standing popularity of these genres for women as readers and writers (see also Coward and Semple, 1989). The 1999 edition of a yearly authoritative guide for thriller and detective fiction writers and their work in print in the Netherlands, consisting mostly of Anglo-American authors and a small number of translated and Dutch authors, portrays 266 male authors against 108 female authors. More female authors have male protagonists, than male authors have female protagonists. Also the standard for writing a particular type of detective (a private eye, a police officer) is set by older male-dominated genres (the locked room mystery, the noir or the classic private eye, the police procedural, perhaps even the action and adventure thriller can be taken to be part of this group) against which the amateur spinsters of the Golden Age of detective fiction form a – wrongly endearing – contrast (huge numbers of corpses litter Agatha Christie's novels for instance) (Nesaule Krouse and Peters,

1975). Compounding the implicit male dominance in crime fiction is the fact that today's women crime writers have more often than not sought to create professional women as crime fighters, thereby (implicitly) referring to sets of standards that have historical ties to masculinity rather than femininity (cf. Tasker, 1998). My claim therefore that masculinity may be more problematic than femininity in terms of the generic rules of interpretation for crime fiction developed by readers over time, may strike an odd note. It is certainly the case that my own perception of this state of affairs is strongly slanted toward feminist issues, and masculinity has traditionally mostly been an issue because of its undesirability rather than anything else.

I did not (re)read classic noir novels (such as *The Maltese Falcon*) that were mentioned but focused instead on more recently published novels that I had not read before. Amongst the authors I read are Kinky Friedman, David Baldacci, and Ken Follett. The story line in these novels and the positions in which male characters find themselves are exemplary for the confusion over masculinity that can also be found in other genres. Jackson et al. (1999) interviewed men about men's lifestyle magazines and concluded that men tend to fall back on traditional and sexist repertoires of interpretation, for lack of other ways of expressing positions more in line with the changes feminism has wrought in society. Others, too, have underlined how men since the Second Feminist Wave have been faced with the unpleasant task of giving up traditional privileges without any clear reward or evident means and strategies to do so (Tolson, 1978; Seidler, 1991). Gender studies research makes clear how masculinity has operated as the norm, thus making itself invisible and largely unspeakable. Dudink (1998: 430–1) therefore counsels the "outflanking maneuver" rather than an attempt to deconstruct masculinity head on. Undeniably here is a task for cultural critics to show how the absent presence of masculinity (as invisible norm and concretely as room for men to do whatever they liked), has turned, in some fictional genres at least, into a present absence. There hardly seems a role left for them. Poor Jason Archer's death in David Baldacci's *Total Control* (1997) does not even merit narrative space. He just gets lost.

Neither Jackson et al.'s male interviewees, nor my mixed group of respondents, had the means available to do more than hint at male identity as a possible site of trouble and strife. Generally the preference of the few men in my research project was to read thrillers and detectives that do not question masculinity. The male protagonists deal with the burdens of masculinity with sarcasm (the noir detective: whatever you do, it is never good enough; don't ever trust a woman, she will betray you), and with male–female relationships at great distance (women are absent or, if present, seem to be a source of eternal mystification). This is not to argue that the pleasures of the text cannot be explored outside gendered terms, such as in terms of mood or description, but to point out how gender, and especially masculinity, is invisible for the readers I interviewed. Henry did read the thrillers and detectives his female partner likes, but he did not offer any comments on them. He also empathized with the struggle of Jane Tennison in the BBC television series *Prime Suspect* (BBC, 1991–1994). For him she occupied the position of an honorary male. He was not convinced by comments from the two women in the group interview that her "male" strategy of coping with a woman-unfriendly workplace could be interpreted as a loss for women, rather than a gain for them. This suggests that men may be more comfortable with traditional models of masculinity, even when it comes to individual women's struggle to achieve better positions. How this will ultimately affect men's positions and their (remaining) privileges is conveniently left out, even though this question haunts popular genres.

The women in our research were more open to dramatized criticism of masculinity (men as women's enemy, as rapist, as agent of violence, as portrayed by women thriller writers). They also offered off-hand suggestions about the type of man or masculinity they preferred for which television police detectives Morse (*Inspector Morse*) and Frost (*A Touch of Frost*) were given as examples. It strikes me that both Morse and Frost are older and that, although they obviously like to be with women, there is no regular woman in their lives. Morse is a hopeless romantic who is unlucky in love, while Frost is a slightly more pragmatic widower, who nevertheless will take on the cause of women and waifs if necessary. They are seen as gentlemen and even, despite their bullying of their sergeants, as basically gentle men. Neither one of them needs to reconstruct their masculinity, or, for that matter, appears threatened by feminism. As romantics, they both offer Man as an asexual being rather than as a menacing beast driven by lust. They are not merely traditional men, they are traditional men of a highly particular ilk. Given the men's preferences in novels, and the women's in television series, romantic, individualist versions of (gentlemanly) masculinity were a preferred way to read oneself out of the disreputable place masculinity has found itself in since 1970s feminist criticism and its subsequent translation into popular fiction genres.

# Conclusion

Cultural studies can be distinguished from disciplines such as sociology or anthropology by how it combines politics and methodology. In fact, feminist politics provided a formative moment for cultural studies. Although early work at the then CCCS in Birmingham had already taken its cue from anthropological research, the particular form taken by audience research was clearly inspired by the way in which feminist researchers combined the personal, the political, and the methodological. After the youth culture research period at the Centre (the 1970s and 1980s), class analysis lost much of its appeal internationally. However, the implicitly feminist agenda of the small audience research project, focused on gender and based on long interviews rather than an extended stay "in the field," was to gain cultural studies a strong and enduring reputation for engaged social criticism and theory grounded in actual audience practice. Of course, it needs to be added that this type of media ethnography also quickly gained ground because it was a cheap method, available to academic newcomers who were not in a position to command big research budgets (Drotner, 1994: 342). In this chapter I have tried to show how feminist politics as methodology energizes research, but how it may also hinder the further development of strong methodology. Some of the original feminist issues have disappeared from the agenda (we hardly wonder today why women participate in their own oppression), others endure (how does the nexus of pleasure, meaning, and ideology produce discourses that define us and seduce us into taking up particular positions?) and new ones have surfaced (questions of gendered and ethnic identity more generally, the use of media in everyday life). Methodology has been discussed, if at all, in terms of reflexivity: the relation of the researcher to her informants. This has resulted in the paternalist impasse described above. As much as questions of the public sphere, another arguably neglected area in feminist audience studies, methodology should therefore be on the agenda.

Following the rules of conduct of feminist research, I have used my own experience self-reflexively to try and sort out how cultural studies audience research conceives of fieldwork relations, but hardly discusses them, and how we theoretically legitimate combining interview quotations and impressions with other types of material. We should discuss fieldwork relations and we should also find ways and means of re-introducing the text in our work without being stopped beforehand by a fear of paternalism. The fear of paternalism is a fear of overinterpreting what texts and informants have to say. Letting go of this fear while paying close attention to what we feel the material *is* able to tell us, is the only way forward. This also means letting go of naturalist assumptions of the right question to ask, of hopes of "the real story" emerging in favor of radical discourse, theoretical questions, and methods. After all, socially shared knowledges rather than psychologized readings of individuals are what is of especial interest to audience studies. As such, the elements of such socially shared knowledges provide clues toward visualizing the relation between popular culture and the public sphere. The issue may seem to be theoretical, but is in fact methodological: how can we unravel the constitutive distinction between the public and the private and the ways in which it has defined the quality of media texts and the identity of media users, to name but two examples.

The status of the media text is one of offering a certain type of knowledge as well as pleasure and excitement. Readers may use these knowledges or, of course, find their own highly idiosyncratic ways through the text. By using a large enough (rather than very limited) number of books, and by talking to a large enough number of readers it should be possible to find traces of such linkages, of how we (and by "we" I mean all of us users of popular culture, rather than us academics, or even smaller subgroups) come to terms with changing social and cultural conditions. To my mind, then, popular culture provides us with a "peri-political" form of citizenship, that is nonetheless of extreme importance, especially perhaps when it comes to areas that beset us with confusion, as is the case currently with masculinity.

Methodologically, the issue is even more interesting than it is theoretically. How do we gain access to issues that confuse us as audiences? Direct representation of the interview material does not offer much in that respect. Only in linking the interviews (via the titles of books given as examples by informants) and performing a form of triangulation (bringing to bear other research material and/or other research methods on the research question) can we begin to formulate an answer. This neatly avoids the danger of pursuing the paternalist route which would suggest that the quotations given and the books mentioned directly support my argument. This would be to say: "I know what these readers are talking about, even if they do not realize this themselves." And I may have gone further down that road than I intended, unwittingly doing exactly what I criticized Radway and Ballaster et al. for. My goal, however, is simply to suggest that our cultural resources are highly limited when it comes to talking about masculinity and about violence. What was obvious from the interviews is that highly politicized feminist positions on masculinity, violence, and sexuality are much too radical to be palatable for a wide audience, even though our readers felt involved in these issues. I found little evidence of crime fiction offering utopian hope, but I did find traces of how these texts offer a beginning of social criticism. That, perhaps, could be a realizable goal of feminist work with audiences: to trace what binds us to particular forms of culture and to offer not so much explanation or description, but to work with fascination and to develop what can be said about such forms in relation to the social, cultural, political state of affairs we find around us using a variety of methods bearing on a range of sources. Rather than simply use texts we as academics find appealing or fascinating, thereby benefiting a cultural elite, we could extend common knowledge and offer repertoires, vocabularies to take up issues that are of everyday importance but that only find their way to public debate in too shorthand a form to be of much use.

## Acknowledgments

I would like to thank Ann Gray and Pieter Hilhorst. Part of this argument was presented in Joke Hermes, "Of Irritation, Texts, and Men: Feminist Audience Studies and Cultural Citizenship," *International Journal of Cultural Studies*, 3:3 (2000): 331–50.

## References

Allor, M. and M. Gagnon (1994) *Létat de culture. Généalogie discursive des politiques culturelles Québécoises* (Montreal: Grecc [Concordia University/Université de Montréal]).
Ang, I. (1987) "Popular Fiction and Feminist Cultural Politics," *Theory, Culture and Society*, 4: 651–8.
Ang, Ien (1995) *Watching Dallas* (London: Methuen).
Baldacci, David (1997) *Total Control* (New York: Warner).

Ballaster, R, M. Beetham, E. Frazer and S. Hebron (1991) *Women's Worlds: Ideology, Femininity and the Women's Magazine* (Basingstoke: Macmillan).

Brunsdon, Charlotte (1997) "Identity in Feminist Television Criticism," in C. Brunsdon, J. D'Acci and L. Spigel (eds.), *Feminist Television Criticism: A Reader* (Oxford: Oxford University Press), pp. 114–25. Originally published in 1993.

Clifford, J. and G.E. Marcus (1986) *Writing Culture: The Poetics and Politics of Ethnography* (Berkeley: University of California Press).

Coward, R. and L. Semple (1989) "Tracking Down the Past: Women and Detective Fiction," in H. Carr (ed.), *From My Guy to Sci-fi: Genre and Women's Writing in the Postmodern World* (London: Pandora), pp. 39–57.

Craig, P. and M. Cadogan (1981) *The Lady Investigates: Women Detectives and Spies in Fiction* (London: Victor Gollancz).

Drotner, Kirsten (1994) "Ethnographic enigmas: 'the everyday' in recent media studies" in *Cultural Studies* 8(2): 341–57.

Dudink, S. (1998) "The Trouble with Men: Problems in the History of 'Masculinity'," *European Journal of Cultural Studies*, 1(3): 419–31.

Friedan, Betty (1963) *The Feminine Mystique* (New York: Norton).

Gadamer, H.-G. (1986 [1960]) *Wahrheit und Methode. Grundzuege einer philosophischen Hermeneutik* (Tubingen: J.C.B. Mohr).

Geraghty, C. (1998) "Audience Studies," in D. Lusted and C. Geraghty (eds.), *The Television Studies Book*. London: Arnold.

Gillespie, M. (1995) *Television, Ethnicity and Cultural Change* (London: Routledge).

Glaser, B.G. and A.L. Strauss (1967) *The Discovery of Grounded Theory* (Chicago: Aldine).

Goffman, Irving (1959) *The Presentation of Self in Everyday Life* (New York: Doubleday).

Gray, Ann (1999) "Audience and Reception Research: The Trouble with Audiences," in Pertti Alasuutari (ed.), *Rethinking the Media Audience* (London: Sage), pp. 22–37.

Greer, Germaine (1971) *The Female Eunuch* (London: Granada).

Hagen, I. (1994a) "Expectations and Consumption Patterns in TV News Viewing," *Media, Culture and Society*, 16: 415–28.

Hagen, I. (1994b) "The Ambivalences of TV News Viewing: Between Ideals and Everyday Practices," *European Journal of Communication*, 9: 193–220.

Hammersley, M. and P. Atkinson (1995) *Ethnography: Principles in Practice*, second edition (London: Routledge).

Hermes, J. (1995) *Reading Women's Magazines: An Analysis of Everyday Media Use* (Cambridge: Polity Press).

Hermes, J. (1998) "Popular Culture and Cultural Citizenship," in K. Brants, J. Hermes and L. van Zoonen (eds.), *The Media in Question: Popular Cultures and Public Interests* (London: Sage), pp. 157–68.

Irons, G. (ed.) (1995) *Feminism in Women's Detective Fiction* (Toronto: University of Toronto Press).

Jackson, P., N. Stevenson and K. Brookes (1999) "Making Sense of Men's Lifestyle Magazines," *Society and Space*, 17: 353–68.

Marcus, G.E. and M.M.J. Fischer (eds.) (1986) *Anthropology as Cultural Critique: An Experimental Moment in the Human Sciences* (Chicago: University of Chicago Press).

McKinley, E.G. (1997) *Beverly Hills, 90210: Television, Gender and Identity* (Philadelphia: University of Pennsylvania Press).

McRobbie, A. (1982) "The Politics of Feminist Research: Between Talk, Text and Action," *Feminist Review*, 12: 46–58.

McRobbie, Angela, Charlotte Brunsdon, Dorothy Hobson, Janice Winship, Rachel Harrison et al. (eds.) (1978) *Women Take Issue: Aspects of Women's Subordination* (CCCS Women's Studies Group) (London: Hutchinson).

Morley, David (1989) "Changing paradigms in audience studies" in E. Seiter, H. Borchers, E. Warth and G. Kreutzner (eds.), *Remote Control* (London: Routledge), pp. 16–43.

Munt, S. (1994) *Murder by the Book: Feminism and the Crime Novel* (London: Routledge).

Nesaule Krouse, A. and M. Peters (1975) "Why Women Kill," *Journal of Communication*, 25(2): 98–105.

Radway, J. (1984) *Reading the Romance: Women, Patriarchy and Popular Literature* (Chapel Hill, NC: The University of North Carolina Press).

Seidler, V. (1991) *Recreating Sexual Politics: Men, Feminism and Politics* (London: Routledge).

Seiter, Ellen (1990) "Making Distinctions in TV Audience Research: Case Study of a Troubling Interview," *Cultural Studies*, 4(1): 61–84.

Seiter, Ellen (1999) *Television and New Media Audiences* (Oxford: Oxford University Press).

Tasker, Yvonne (1998) *Working Girls: Gender and Sexuality in Popular Cinema* (London: Routledge).

Tolson, A. (1978) *The Limits of Masculinity* (London: Tavistock).

Warnke, G. (1987) *Gadamer: Hermeneutics, Tradition and Reason* (Cambridge: Polity Press).

Warren, C. (1988) *Gender Issues in Field Research* (London: Sage).

Whitlock, G. (1994) "'Cop it Sweet': Lesbian Crime Fiction," in D. Hamer and B. Budge (eds.), *The Good, the Bad, the Gorgeous: Popular Culture's Romance with Lesbianism* (London: Pandora Press), pp. 96–118.

Willis, Paul (1990) *Common Culture* (Buckingham: Open University Press).

Winship, Janice (1987) *Inside Women's Magazines* (London: Pandora).

Zimmerman, B. (1990) *The Safe Sea of Women: Lesbian Fiction 1969–1989* (Boston: Beacon Press).

# 7

# Taking Audience Research into the Age of New Media: Old Problems and New Challenges

## Andrea Press and Sonia Livingstone

### Introduction

It is sometimes thought, for a variety of reasons, that audience research is dead. In the age of multiple screens, it is difficult to pinpoint when people become audiences. And, in the wake of postmodern theorizing about the fluidity of our identities, it is difficult to know how to frame questions about the interaction of media with people so that they can be investigated empirically. In the midst of all this confusion, we have begun a comparative ethnographic project on young people. Foremost in our minds is a consciousness of the continuities and breaks with our previous experience as television audience researchers. So, we are thinking about methodological approaches to audience study, and, in particular, what methods are appropriate for audience researchers to use in the age of the Internet?

In the following discussion, we ask first why was active audience research so significant? Concomitantly, we ask why did media theory come to see empirical, qualitative audience research as important? This sets the scene for our current dilemma: must audience research start all over again with the Internet, or can ideas, methods, and findings be carried forward, so we don't reinvent the wheel? In short, we examine the parallels between researching audiences for television and for the Internet, identifying the similarities and differences in the trajectories of the two bodies of research. Of course, the people are generally the same – the television audience has now transmogrified into the Internet audience. There's some overlap in research communities: although not all television researchers are making this move, many others are joining in the study of Internet use. Most important, the theory of television audiences always involved larger concepts – concerned with people's engagement with mediated texts – that went beyond the phenomenon of television, particularly national mass broadcast television. That theory now needs rethinking in the age of the Internet.

While qualitative, ethnographic work on television took some time to get started, the field has now grown to a substantial size, establishing a recognized tradition of enquiry. Many scholars are now turning their interest to new media, facing some of the same quandaries we ourselves are as we try to translate television audience issues into a new domain. This essay is designed to address the differences, if any, between the issues facing those who attempt to study the audience for new media, and the issues we faced as scholars of the television audience. Are the skills we've developed as scholars of the television audience directly transferable to the study of new media? Are the questions which oriented our study the same? What are the new issues that need to be investigated, the new questions that must be posed? And do these issues and questions require new methodological skills and strategies by audience researchers? We select from each field – qualitative studies of television viewers, and qualitative studies of Internet users – discussing several pioneering works which we argue have been, and continue to be, influential in the field of audience reception. In doing so we attempt to review the answers to these questions that others have given as they've entered this new field of audience research, and to identify some new directions we feel the current research should be taking.

## On the Continued Importance of Audience Research

In an age of new information and communication media, why persist with a theory that was developed in the age of mass broadcasting? The reason is, primarily, that we find huge existing strengths in theory, method, and findings. These strengths are essentially twofold, together accounting for the recent successes of audience research:

- the introduction of the ethnographic tradition into the field of media and communications. The advantages of this work include its interdisciplinarity, the richness of its data and insights, its ability to integrate the study of text and viewer, and contextualization. This leads to the development of a critical tradition of media studies, particularly in integration with a program of empirical studies; and

- the substantive arguments developed within audience research and their critical intervention into theories of dominant media power, which are largely based in either or both of political economy and textual studies, theories including the theory of media imperialism, globalization discussions, etc.

To develop these arguments, we need first to sketch a brief history. To begin, active audience research is significant because it challenged the grand claims about dominant ideology (with the theory of encoding/ decoding; Hall, 1980), media imperialism (Liebes and Katz, 1995), and media power (with Katz's oscillation between powerful media and powerful audiences, 1980). Hence, empirical audience research posed ideas of heterogeneity against homogenization, of active against passive, of resistant against exploited audiences. Theoretically, this was exciting, influential. Methodologically, this set the scene for the ethnographic turn in audience work.

Television audience study emerged out of a concept of the mass audience, and initially the questions posed placed the audience in a passive position. Audience members were surveyed, subjects of experiments, and basically treated as atomized, vulnerable, exploited members of a mass group. In response to what researchers identified as an overly passive characterization of the television audience, the tradition of active audience study emerged. This tradition posed questions about the audience which emphasized the creative response of audience members to the media in question. According to theories of the active audience, sweeping generalizations about the dangers of the media had suffered from the lack of close attention paid to audience activity. The new type of close analysis, carried out by researchers trained in the traditions of qualitative and ethnographic methodologies, indicated that there were subtle aspects to the interaction between audience and the media that could add crucial information to both textual analysis as well as survey research. Audience members sometimes used media, and interpreted media, in diverse, unexpected, and creative ways that belied the hegemonic media influence that textual analysts so often hypothesized. There were some lively, occasionally hostile arguments between those who argued for the importance of audience ethnography, and those who argued that audience ethnography was beside the point, and could not add to the knowledge derived either from sophisticated textual analysis, or from large-scale quantitative survey data (e.g. Seaman, 1992; Neuman, 1991).

One of the most interesting arguments was the exchange between Janice Radway, a pioneer of of the ethnographic investigation of audiences in her widely cited *Reading the Romance* (1984a), and Tania Modleski, a textual analyst who, in a review of Radway's book, tore into what she termed the "empiricist" notion that the researcher could "learn" anything new from a sociological investigation of audience members. Using research findings that she herself had reached using the method of textual analysis, Modleski argued that Radway's own conclusions did not really cover new ground, despite the difference in their research methodology (Modleski, 1986). In what eventually became a heated exchange, Radway (1984b) foreshadowed the conclusion of the field that in fact, ethnographic methods yielded material which supported a much more subversive interpretation of media influence than that garnered through textual analysis, offering her own data as the first in a line of arguments illustrating the active, subversive ways audience members used the mass media to support activities which undermined their hegemony. One of Radway's key arguments had been that women romance readers used their reading time to carve out time away from the demands of their families and the constrictions of their role within the family. For many, this time was their only independent, self-directed time, in a life of extensive demands placed upon them by their families. Moreover, this led them to interpret the romance texts in a particular manner, resolving the polysemy of the texts themselves so as to draw out a message of the heroine's independence and self-worth rather than one of her subordination to the male hero. Without empirical data from audience research, Radway argued, these kinds of arguments would have been neither anticipated nor found convincing.

Radway's arguments foreshadowed a new era, one in which research on what came to be defined as the "active audience" revealed that television audiences could creatively appropriate mass media for their own goals and purposes. While audiences did not always use media in such creative and often subversive ways, the growing body of research based on qualitative studies of the audience increasingly argued that audiences could – and sometimes did – resist the hegemonic impact of the media, precisely because the texts themselves are structurally indeterminate, awaiting the interpretive activities of particular audiences. Thus, the overall active audience tradition radically challenged prior scholarship theorizing the role of the media, particularly those who overestimated, or simply "read off," the extent and nature of media influence from an analysis of media production or texts.

# The Ethnographic Turn: Contextualism and its Relevance Today

The qualities and experiences of being a member of an audience have begun to leak out from specific performance events which previously contained them, into the wider realms of everyday life. (Abercrombie and Longhurst, 1998: 36–7).

As the media environment becomes ever more diverse and complex, and ever more thoroughly embedded in all aspects of daily life, those studying media audiences have become concerned about the charge of media-centrism. The result has been a more systematic exploration of the contexts of media use, moving ever further away from the medium itself in search of the local sites of cultural meaning-making which shape people's orientation to the media. Several arguments led to this shift in focus from text to context, from literary/semiotic analysis to social analysis. As Robert Allen (1987) argued, once textual and literary theorists had made the crucial transition to a reader-oriented approach, context flooded in for two reasons: first, the shift from asking about meaning of the text in and of itself to asking about the meaning of the text as achieved by a particular, contextualized reader (i.e. the shift, in Eco's terms, from the virtual to the realized text); secondly, the shift from asking about the meaning of the text to asking about the intelligibility of the text (i.e. about the diversity of sociocultural conditions which determine how a text can make sense).

Although a crucial transition was made, these should not be posed as either/or options, for the moment of reception is located precisely at the interface between textual and social determinations and so requires a dual focus on media content and audience response. Research must, in short, contextualize the reception of television texts in order to understand how audience activities carry the meanings communicated far beyond the moment of reception into many other spheres of everyday life, and it must also examine the converse process by which reception is shaped through the symbolic practices of everyday life. This argument has taken a more dramatic turn, however, following Janice Radway's (1988) call for "radical contextualism" in audience research, namely the analytic displacement of the moment of text-reader reception by ethnographic studies of the everyday – what she describes as "the kaleidoscope of daily life" (Radway, 1988: 366; see also Ang, 1996: 250–1) or, for Paul Willis, "the whole way of life" (1990).

Following these arguments, the "ethnographic turn" in audience research shifts the focus away from a detailed analysis of the moment of textual interpretation and toward the contextualization of that moment in the culture of the everyday. Starting with an account of the context of media use, rather than with a semiotic reading of a media text, ethnographic audience studies have explored the ways in which media goods are rendered meaningful insofar as they are positioned in a particular kind of place within the home, the domestic timetable, the family's communication ecology. Research shows that this process of active appropriation shapes, enables, or restricts the uses and meanings of the medium for its audience or users, across a wide range of media (see, for example, Moyal, 1995 on the telephone, Kramarae, 1988 and Spigel, 1992 on television, and Flichy, 1995, on the increasingly media-rich home).

An analysis of the trajectory of David Morley's work illustrates the conundrum in which audience research finds itself following the ethnographic turn. Following the analysis of the text of a British current affairs program (Brunsdon and Morley, 1978), in *The Nationwide Audience* (1980) Morley investigated the reception of a particular episode of the show by organizing focus groups of viewers related only by their membership in common socioeconomic and occupational categories (e.g. housewives, bank clerks, etc.). Although we learned little about the role of this program and its meanings in any of their lives, the respondents' interpretation of the episode revealed the interaction between sociodemographic background and the strategies of openness and closure encoded into the text. In his later work, *Family Television* (1986), Morley sought to contextualize the use of television in the routines of daily life by interviewing families from different social class positions and observing the dynamics of their television viewing at home. This revealed a range of subtle and not so subtle gender- and generation-based tactics of power within the home but, in contrast to the earlier project, added little to our understanding of the reception of television texts.

The contrast between these two projects foreshadows divisions which mark the field of audience research today. Through the concept of double articulation, Roger Silverstone (1994) contrasts the media *qua* material objects such as the television or walkman, namely as technological objects located in particular spatio-temporal settings, with the media *qua* texts such as the news or the soap opera, namely as symbolic messages located within particular sociocultural discourses. Broadly, to focus on the media-as-object is to invite an analysis of media use in terms of consumption in the context of domestic practices. On the other hand, to focus on the media-as-text is to invite an analysis of the textuality or representational character of media contents in relation to the interpretive activities of particular audiences. The implication, clearly, is that the audience is also doubly articulated – as the consumer-viewer. Yet, unexpectedly perhaps, researching audiences simultaneously in terms of reception and contexts of use seems hard to sustain methodologically. In the classic figure-ground illustration used by Gestalt theorists, we can see either two heads facing each other with a gap in between, or we can see a vase in what was the space between while the surrounding objects become background. Understanding audiences in terms of either what's surrounding, or what's on, the screen is similar. The further one stands back from the television set to focus on the context of the living room, the smaller the screen appears and the harder it is to see what's showing on it (Livingstone, 2003a). And, as a result, reception studies and ethnographic/ consumption studies – taking as their starting point text and context respectively – seem to diverge rather than complement each other.

But, of course, audiences are both interpreters of media-as-text and users of media-as-object. The activities associated with the symbolic and material uses of media each shape the other as part and parcel of everyday life. Theoretically, ethnographic and reception studies of audiences draw on the same insights – the stress on active audiences making contingent and context-dependent choices, on plurality (or fragmentation) within the population rather than assuming a normative mass audience, on the idea of audiences as co-producers rather than merely consumers of the meanings of media, and so forth. Hence, it should not be so hard as it seems to be to keep both reception and use in the frame simultaneously. Indeed, although this bifurcation continues to haunt current audience research, some of those developing an ethnographic approach can and do address both of these issues simultaneously.

## *Media ethnography: a developing tradition*

Radway's *Reading the Romance* (1984a) is most often cited as the cornerstone of media ethnography for its combined analysis of text, audience reception, and context of use. Radway gathered her informants, conceived as an interpretive community, from the patrons of a local bookstore, run by someone she called "Dot" who wrote a newsletter about new romances for her customers. These women had, for the most part, never met one another before, only coming together when Radway organized them for group interviews, though all had communicated beforehand with Dot and were readers of her newsletter. While Radway's work is universally cited as an example of media "ethnography," it lacks some of the classic features of ethnographic work, the primary one being that the researcher accesses a physically existing community within which its members interact based on some type of socially defined interrelationships. For Radway, the "community" was defined by her respondents' common reception of a media product, in this case, romance novels. They belonged to an imagined community of "fans" or avid readers of these products. Although they lived in a nearby area (which would define their patronage of the particular bookshop that Dot ran), they had no other interconnection with each other in the physical world, except perhaps by chance when they entered Dot's bookstore.

The questions that Radway's project raises, regarding the nature of community as well as the nature of the research process, illustrate some long-term confusions among those studying media audiences regarding the meaning of the term "ethnography" (Nightingale, 1996; Press, 1996). If we look at some of the key texts generally considered to be works of media ethnography, we find that the methods they use, and the treatment of individuals and communities which result, differ in various ways, often radically so from more conventional ethnographic methodology within anthropology. So, for example, Ien Ang's first book, *Watching Dallas* (1985), often cited as one of the first examples of media ethnography, is based on an imagined community of viewers of the prime-time soap opera *Dallas*, and Ang accessed them individually through letters they wrote in response to a newspaper advertisement she placed requesting that fans of the show write to her to explain why they liked watching it. Of course, Ang could not be sure that the respondents to her advertisement had never met one another before, but her method precluded an investigation of this – and other

– aspects of their identity (for example, their race, social class, age, or family circumstances). Years later, Elizabeth Bird appropriated Ang's method in her work, *For Enquiring Minds* (1992), once again sampling through written responses to a newspaper advertisement the opinions of readers of such tabloids as the *National Enquirer*. Bird followed up her research by conducting telephone interviews with some of the respondents, but this does not solve the problem of informant invisibility. Both of these works were sorely lacking in the contextualization necessary for genuine ethnographic work.

So, audience research had in any case encountered some conceptual and methodological problems, even before it turned to face the changing media environment. More recently, there have been more concerted attempts to employ the ethnographic methods of traditional anthropology, interestingly combined with the methods of media reception research. Some of the best examples include Gillespie (1995), who studied how television and video are used to recreate cultural traditions within the "South Asian" diaspora in London, Seiter's (1999) exploration of the meanings of cartoons and other genres for young children – and their teachers – in nursery school, and Mankekar (1999), who looked at issues of women's identity in relation to television viewing in India. In these highly contextualized studies, the bifurcation between media-as-object and the study of media reception is in large part overcome. These books serve as a model of contextualized ethnography, in that they investigate communities of viewers linked in the physical world in other ways besides their media consumption. Based on many months of participant observation coupled with extensive interviewing, in strong contrast to the more usual single or limited series of interviews with unconnected viewers, these authors do succeed in gaining a grounded sense of the role of media in their informants' lives, offering a series of critical insights into the processes of media reception and use.

### Extending the reception tradition to Internet use: the challenges ahead

How shall we take what we know of audiences into the new field of Internet use? Thinking back to the early days of audience research, we note that the field of mass communication distinguished itself from interpersonal or face-to-face communication precisely because of the socially, economically, and culturally institutionalized break between production and reception in mass, but not interpersonal, communication. Historically, as this institutionalized break became more technologically complex, more economically successful and more culturally taken-for-granted, the audience was gradually transformed from what Abercrombie and Longhurst (1998) term the simple audience through the lengthy phase of the mass audience which defined our twentieth-century ideas of media research, to what they now term the diffused audience of the new media environment. For today, as Fornas et al. (2002: 25) argue, interactive media "blur the distinction between production and reception as communication moments, as institutionalized forms of practice, and as research areas." No longer have we clear distinctions between production and reception, between mass and interpersonal communication, or between hitherto distinct forms of media (print, image, music, broadcasting, games, etc.).

The challenge posed to the field of media research by the growth of new forms of media leads some to stress the difficulties to be faced. Jones (2002) addresses the particular difficulties of Internet scholarship – difficulties of interdisciplinarity, of the status of research, of audience research, and so forth. On a more positive note, Fornas et al. (2002: 1) characterize the new field thus:

> …an expanding tribe of cyber-cultural studies, combining media and cultural studies with Internet research. This rapidly growing field crosses and reworks certain traditional borderlines such as those concerning identities, communities, forms of reception or media use, textual genres, media types, technologies, and research methods.

It is on one of these borderlines – that between forms of reception and media use (or between audiences and users, media-as-text and media-as-object) – that we explore the emerging theories and methods for understanding changing media cultures. And, like Fornas et al., we seek research continuities as well as change, agreeing that "just as newer media always connect to older ones, studies of computer media must integrate media and cultural studies to catch what is really bravely new in this digital world" (Fornas et al., 2002: 3). However, we remain cautious in claiming anything as "bravely new" for, as they go on to argue, "tenacious structures in media institutions as well as in everyday-life contexts of use and production work to delimit the transformations first promised by each new medium, reproducing instead certain inherited boundaries in the new media as well" (2002: 3). On the other hand, as they also argue, this delimiting work is never entirely successful, so that to some unpredictable but significant extent, the new always escapes the stabilizing grasp of the old ways – if only through a series of contingent and unintended consequences. In the end, notwithstanding the grand and overarching theorizations which abound concerning the transformative impact of the Internet, Fornas et al. position ethnographic studies as anchoring (old and new) media use in the specifics of actual contexts, thereby resisting technological determinism and legitimating, in the main, contingent, qualified, and differentiated claims.

Clearly, when discussing the newness of the Internet, its capacity to support interactivity on a huge scale is most striking. Interactivity can itself be usefully subdivided into social interactivity (i.e. interactivity or networking among users, e.g. email), textual interactivity (i.e. interactivity between user and documents via hypertext, e.g. the world wide web) and technical interactivity (i.e. interactivity between user and system, e.g. games) (see Fornas et al., 2002; McMillan, 2002). Each is associated not only with particular forms of the Internet (for this is far from a unified medium), but also with different potential practices of meaningful use. When we compare with the practices associated with older media, it becomes clear that different media foreground different forms of interactivity – it not being interactivity in itself that is qualitatively new – although none of these previous media combine all forms of interactivity, that is, until the Internet. So, social interactivity, as defined here, is characteristic of the telephone but not of television, except in the indirect sense that viewers talk to each other about what they have seen. Textual interactivity is characteristic of television – this has precisely been the focus of reception studies as they have sought to reveal the complex interpretative engagement between reader and text: on the world wide web, although the strategies for multiple pathways are more directly built into the structure of hypertext than of the (superficially at least) linear printed text, these are balanced online, as offline, by strategies of closure, preferring and ideological reproduction. Technical interactivity is characteristic neither of the telephone nor television, but has become familiar through video and computer games.

The point we are making is that, in approaching the Internet user, research must draw on its understanding of the use of – or audiences for – a range of hitherto quite distinct media. One cannot keep these separate, arguing that the Internet represents a collection of parallel media, for as studies of use immediately reveal, users adopt a range of strategies precisely to interlink and integrate these multiple media. They chat on instant message while researching an assignment on the web. They play games in the interstices of a slow-to-download piece of music. And, most important, they exploit the intertextual possibilities of the medium through constantly cross-referring across these multiple activities (Livingstone, 2002).

## On Method and New Media

In researching new media, especially the Internet, how far can we learn from the experience of prior audience research, and in what ways must we begin again? First, audience discourses and practices are more elusive because practice is often private – in the bedroom or study – making the audience researcher's presence even more salient than in the days of observing family television in the living room. Media engagement may be even more transgressive or personal – including pornography, intimate conversations, personal advice, etc. And the use of media is harder to chart than in the days of mass communication – filling in a survey to record an evening's viewing is tricky, but by no means as tricky as recording and interpreting an evening's surfing or chat.

This brings us to the as yet little-theorized interpretative relation between text and reader online, which raises both practical and theoretical problems. New media researchers have no stacks of neatly labeled video tapes on their shelves for *Coronation Street* or *The News at Ten*, no stacks of newspapers in the corner of the office, no industry records of audience ratings categorized by demographics; rather, they barely know how to track their "texts" given the threefold problems of overwhelming volume of material, temporary existence of material, and its "virtuality" (hypertext being dependent on users to "actualize" it; c.f. Eco, 1979). Further, there are no easy distinctions to be made in terms of channel, form or genre – indeed, there are few textual studies on the basis of which audience research can formulate its questions about people's interpretation of the texts. Add to this the fact that online, in contrast to the audiovisual domain, people can be producers as well as receivers of content, and the extent of the challenge becomes apparent; how shall we record, catalog and re-present the world wide web? Or Internet chat? How shall we illustrate MUDs or computer games to those who haven't played them? The debates have begun over methods – and ethics – to sample and record a range of online activities, including the conduct of online interviews and surveys (Hine, 2000). And the industry is experimenting with extending television audience measurement to the world wide web at least. But these texts are nonetheless ephemeral; they are nonlinear; we have no established language for units – or genres – let alone for charting people's use of such texts; people may have always read the paper while watching television, but multitasking on the computer is commonplace since the advent of Windows. How are we to capture these activities?

No less problematically, familiar questions of consequences are being asked with some urgency by policy makers and public alike. As with the early days of television (Wartella and Reeves, 1985), this public agenda foregrounds simple effects questions, largely focused on averting harm, and only gradually and reluctantly does it learn to pose more complex questions of meaning and practice. Hence, the research community is asked: does Internet use result in harm to children and young people? – does inadvertent exposure to pornography produce long-term harm, does playing violent games online make boys more aggressive, does immersion in a branded consumer culture produce a more materialistic generation, is the Internet changing the way children think and learn? – all questions which are impossible to "answer" in any simple fashion. Nonetheless, research is making some varied and thought-provoking beginnings in the task of understanding Internet use, as we explore, through selected instances of empirical work, below.

## Researching Internet Use:
## First Generation Studies

We suggest that empirical studies of Internet use currently adopt one or other of two main approaches. These are methodologically distinct – one continues the consumption tradition of audience studies, as discussed above, while the other continues the reception tradition. Both (interestingly) claim to be inheritors of the ethnographic turn, albeit in different ways, although one centers on life in front of the screen while the other centers on life on the screen. Hence, while these studies have much to offer, their initial research choices are tending to continue the bifurcation in audience studies. And problematically so, for we still lack studies which integrate reception and consumption, although there has been some emergent momentum in this direction.

## *Life on the screen*

The first generation of Internet studies begins with the online text, often to the exclusion of the context of its consumption. Sherry Turkle's *Life on the Screen: Identity in the Age of the Internet* (1995) is a founding instance of this extension of audience analysis, centering on the textual discussion of the online community. It also makes some sweeping arguments in favor of arguing for the extensive influence of new media technologies on postmodern life, encouraging a postmodern discourse of fluid identities (Radway, 1988). Given the impracticability of tracing online texts to a particular physical being in any definite manner, researchers are tempted to assert that anything is possible with an online text — those who in "real" life have male gender identities can assume female ones, the rich can assume the demeanor of the poor, the old can assume the personage of a young person, etc. The only characteristics that cannot be consciously hidden are the literacy skills of the participant — one may be judged by the wittiness, and fluency, of one's writing, which is harder to hide. This is why online ethnographies, perhaps much more than traditional ones, lend themselves to a very different language of analysis, one more amenable to current modes of theorizing about the fragmentation of life in the postmodern age, and the concomitant fragmentation of identities. However, although researchers studying online communities are very limited in their ability to assess the physical and socioeconomic characteristics of their informants, the advantage is that online ethnographies are based on texts which are already written, as opposed to interview transcripts or participant observation field notes generated by the research process — like other forms of transcripts or field notes, however, these texts must be edited by the analyst, and, if not entirely created, are nevertheless located and selected by the studies' authors, a not inconsiderable undertaking in most cases.

Turkle adopts a type of ethnographic method to investigate how Internet use facilitates the increasingly 'fragmented, multiple experience of identity prototypical of the postmodern age. Citing a stream of postmodern philosophers and psychologists who argue that our identities are now more fluid than they were half a century ago (she cites Riesman's *Lonely Crowd* and its theory of the "inner-directed" for evidence of the "personalities that were"), Turkle provides an engrossing combination of clinical (she was a therapist in a former life) and ethnographic evidence to ground her claims. In each of a series of case studies, she documents how the use of computers has challenged the type of identity the user had in the pre-computer era, in essence offering him or her a more malleable notion of "self."

One case Turkle discusses gives a clear illustration of what we feel are both the strengths and the weaknesses of her line of analysis. This particular case concerns an 18-year-old college student who obtained an abortion. The abortion deeply offended her mother, who was a religious Catholic, and she subsequently cut off financial support for her daughter. In response to this deeply felt family pain, Turkle argues, the daughter began extensive fantasy play, sometimes for days at a time, on computers. This helped to alleviate the pain of her troubled relationship with her mother, in essence to "work through," in a therapeutic sense, her unresolved family difficulties, and the pain surrounding them. What is not apparent from Turkle's discussion was the material surroundings within which this role-playing occurred. We found ourselves questioning the socioeconomic aspect of this woman's reality, questions which Turkle's emphasis allowed her to evade. How was it possible for the student to spend days in role-playing computer games when her mother had withdrawn all financial support? Wouldn't she have had to increase her work hours in order to support herself? What was happening to her studies, her friends, her housemates? We could not get past the unexplained realities of her situation, details we felt were necessary in order to really understand the significance of computer playing in her life.

Nancy Baym's book *Tune In, Log On* (2000) is another example of an online ethnography which uses the online text as the main unit of analysis, a project that clearly follows from the rich vein of research on television audiences for the soap opera. Baym's work differs somewhat from Turkle's in that she does occasionally visit some of her participants in the physical world – she herself is a participant in the fan group for the daytime soap opera, *All My Children,* and so she physically knows the members of the Champaign group at least, and occasionally gets together with them as a group off-line as well as on-line. This gives her some perspective on their lives outside of the computer group, although she makes little use of this to comment on or contextualize her analysis of the online texts generated by the group.

## Life in front of the screen

A further newly rapidly established tradition of research on how people are appropriating the Internet within their everyday lives – at home, in the family, at work, school and elsewhere – is taking a mainly but not exclusively qualitative, contextualized approach (e.g. Facer et al., 2001; Ribak, 2001; Livingstone, 2003b). The focus has been on locating this new object of consumption within domestic practices of space, time, and social relations to understand how it is becoming integrated within an already complex media environment.

These studies suggest that, for many people, the Internet is still a fragile medium, experienced as unfamiliar, confusing, easier to get wrong than right, far from taken for granted. In the home, for example, we begin to see how parents are developing strategies to manage and regulate the Internet within the home, strongly framed by educational aspirations for their children, even though children themselves value online entertainment centered on fandom, transferring established interests from older media contents – music, stars, sports, television programs. The resultant struggle between parental strategies and children's tactics suggests a "digital generation gap" in which children and teens play a key role in acquiring and understanding the Internet, and this includes explaining it to their parents, although their expertise and influence should not be overestimated.

Research on the social contexts of Internet appropriation and use is beginning to move beyond the descriptive, identifying ways in which the home is changing, becoming the site of content production as well as reception, of education and work as well as entertainment and leisure (Livingstone, 2003b). This raises new questions about the links between different activities, as learning becomes fun, as work blurs into leisure, as online chat may "count" as civic participation, and so forth. Such interlinked and mediated activities serve also to sustain particular, perhaps new, links between people also, this having implications for social codes and regulation, for emergent community or peer cultures, and for changing boundaries and occasions for social exclusion.

At present, however, we have more questions than answers, partly because although it is assiduous in contextualizing Internet use, much of this research has yet to engage thoroughly with the Internet *qua* medium (or, more correctly, a diverse bundle of information and communication technologies, each with distinct possibilities for content): often it fails satisfactorily even to discriminate between the computer and the Internet, treating the computer *qua* object in the living room or bedroom as more significant than it does people's engagement with specifically online contents, services and activities.

## From "Virtual Ethnography" to "Internet Ethnography": Toward the Second Generation Studies

How is research to go beyond "virtual ethnography" to "Internet ethnography," to contextualize interpretation of online texts (reception of what's on the screen) in relation to consumption of a technological good in the domestic setting (in front of the screen)? Methodologically, Fornas et al. (2002) advocate supplementing participation in online interaction ("cyberethnography") with face-to-face and other offline methods, "in order to contextualize their online texts and thereby understand them even better than other participants do" (38). One project which does exactly that is Miller and Slater's (2000) study of Internet use as one aspect of an ethnographically-based study of life in Trinidad. They conclude that computer and Internet use reinforce social meanings and practices already inherent in the offline world. Rather than undermining national identity, for example, and encouraging a more global identification, the Internet is used by Trinidadians to strengthen their national identity, for it gives them additional communicative venues they can use to develop national networks and groups.

Using much simpler methods, but following the same principle of integrating the online with the offline, Sveningsson (2002) inquired into the formation of those romantic or friendship relations in online chatrooms that are then continued offline (to varying degrees, from a phone call to a permanent relationship). Methodologically, hers was a traditional qualitative study, based on in-depth face-to-face interviews, and addressing the Internet as a topic of research, not a medium for research. As the focus was on the medium as a locus for social interaction rather than on direct engagement with the medium as text or technology, the project pursued questions of identity and sociality rather than of audiencehood, except insofar as participants in online chat are involved in a process of interpretation or textual encoding and decoding.

In her interviews, Sveningsson listens particularly for their accounts of why an online meeting differs from an offline one, and for the ways in which the relationships develop both before and after they move to meeting offline; this latter requires an offline rather than online research method. Typically, there was a shift from a textual relationship (seeing the other not as a person but through an engagement with synchronous typed text) in which some aspects of identity could be playfully managed (through nicknames, accounts of appearance, etc.) while others were inadvertently disclosed, or "given off," just as in offline meetings. Crucially, the possibility for playful management of identity was used to increase, rather than decrease, self-disclosure, enabling a careful revealing of the self in ways not easy to manage offline, resulting in an enhancement rather than a lessening of trust in relationships formed online. The offline world, by implication, was widely seen as risky, inhibiting trust, opening one up to embarrassment and loss of face, while a mediated context obviates such risks, liberating through distance. The shift to an offline relationship is thus a tense and tricky one, though Sveningsson argues that until it occurs, participants may become close ("as soul mates," even), but they do not fall in love, the face-to-face therefore indelibly changing the nature of the relationship. As she shows, there is less likely to be a simple shift from online to offline, but rather a carefully staged sequence, mediated through the move from chat to email, then telephone, and then the face-to-face meeting. Interestingly, she found that following the offline meeting, the participants no longer sustain the online chat, though the phone remains part of the relationship, the need for a carefully managed distance no longer being required. In conclusion, Sveningsson suggests that the process of forming relationships is altered when mediated by the Internet – in terms of chronology, pace, control, conditions of trust, and so forth – but that the relationships themselves do not differ from those formed in offline settings.

## Theorizing Internet Use: All Change?

We have seen that the second generation ethnographic research projects are attempting to integrate offline and online analyses of Internet use.

Hence they combine an enquiry regarding users' engagement with what's on the screen (studies extending the text-reader metaphor, or exploring theories of identity and selfhood in relation to particular online forms and genre) with an account of the context of use in front of the screen (exploring the motives for gaining Internet access, the social contexts of use in terms of timetabling of use, location of the computer, etc., and the emerging domestic practices of use in terms of gender, class and generation). These are laudable aims, albeit they demand time-consuming projects often using multiple methods. However, we suggest that the legacy of the contrasting versions of the first generation projects, as discussed above, persists, generating some contrasting rather than complementary conclusions.

In particular, it seems that those conducting purely online ethnographic research are more liable to draw conclusions regarding the transformative nature of the Internet than are those conducting primarily offline ethnographies on the contexts of Internet use. In other words, as was the case for television, it seems that those following in the reception tradition are more likely than those following in the consumption tradition to find evidence hinting at shifts from unified to fragmented identity, from normative to creative meanings, from hierarchical to anarchic sociality – in short, from the modernist world view of mass broadcasting to a postmodern engagement with today's complex and shifting media environment. In so doing, online studies tend to underplay or underestimate the importance of the social context in front of the screen, where this works – in Fornas et al.'s terms – to delimit the transformations promised by the new medium through the conservative and stabilizing consequences of everyday material routines and structures.

On the other hand, those who start with life in front of the screen tend to produce findings which argue against the autonomy of cyberspace and instead insist on the anchoring of life on the screen in the social contexts of use in front of the screen. As is consistent with the sociology of consumption, the findings tend to reveal processes of appropriation rather than change, revealing the incorporation of the new within well-established frameworks and routines of the familiar, the everyday. Offline social norms are transferred online, it is argued, and the online changes little or nothing in the offline world. Hence, this approach tends toward a more conservative view, revealing little that is "bravely new" about the new media and supporting an account of the continuation of (late) modernity rather than the radical shift to postmodernity.

One could conclude from this contrast that methods determine findings. But, of course, there are always exceptions to undermine so straightforward a mapping of methods and findings. For example, from her purely online ethnography of a text-based virtual world, Sunden (2002: 107) draws a conservative conclusion about the re-imposition of traditionally gendered practices in this potentially open space: "instead of using the Net as a place for liberating transgressions and textual deconstructions of the physical body, most WaterMOOers tend to use the text to put the gendered body back into the picture, inevitably dragging a whole battery of cultural meanings with them." So, rather than assert a simple mapping of findings onto the methods that generated them, instead we conclude by flagging, and problematizing, the relationship yet to be unpacked between theory, research findings, and choice of research method in the field of Internet use and its consequences.

For the theory at stake is crucial to this emerging story. In the days of mass broadcasting, television was most often theorized as a homogenizing and monolithic force. As Gerbner and Gross (1976) said, television tells most of the stories to most of the people most of the time and, as those following in the tradition of the Frankfurt School argued, for the most part, it's the same story, offering audiences merely "the freedom to choose what is always the same" (Adorno and Horkheimer, 1977). The same may be said, in this broad-brush review, of theories of powerful media and of ideological or social reinforcement and reproduction (e.g. theories of hegemony, of cultivation, of dominant media, of cultural imperialism, etc.). Since these all positioned the audience as passive, vulnerable and homogenous, reception research was used to challenge well-established theory. Indeed, in this context, reception studies were surely bound to seem radical, for studies of interpretation in practice can generally be relied upon to throw up findings of diversity, nuance and context-dependency which contradict the assertion of a dominant medium, particularly one whose power is encoded into and effective through the workings of a supposedly fixed and unitary (or deterministic) text.

On the other hand, media consumption research has tended instead to illustrate social and economic continuities (as in accounts of when old technologies were new or those stressing the appropriation of potentially new media according to familiar domestic structures; Flichy, 1995, Marvin, 1988). Doubtless this is partly because studies of media use draw on a larger social and economic context than that of local interpretation, rendering them much more sensitive to the deterministic power of the social context, even though they may underestimate that of the text. This bias is supported by their strong concern to avoid anything that smacks of technological determinism (consumption studies being more focused on media *qua* technologies than on media *qua* texts). Hence they perform better than reception-oriented studies in recognizing the importance of embedded social inequalities, long-established practices and other structural factors. However, as a result they tend neither to support theories of media power (and passive audiences) nor of creative interpretation (and active audiences), but rather instead they assert a social determinism (where class and gender inequalities are reproduced and reasserted through media use, just as through education, the family, etc.). And in consequence, they struggle to acknowledge the agency or individuality of media audiences.

Intriguingly, it has once again become fashionable to argue that the media exert a strong influence over those who use them. Specifically, the Internet is being strongly theorized by many once again as a dominant force, although crucially, this time, it is proposed as a force for change, taking society from modernity to postmodernity. As a result, the theory itself foregrounds diversity, alternative and open possibilities, transformation, and radical breaks (Poster, 2001; Castells, 2002; Turkle, 1995) rather than, as was proposed for television, foregrounding the media as a force of conservatism, reproducing traditional dominant ideology and inequalities (although some are beginning to theorize the Internet as another force to reproduce dominant ideologies in the interests of the established capitalist elites; see, for example, Barney, 2000).

The challenge today is therefore to balance textual determinism, social determinism, and the agency of the audience or user. Whether these factors in combination result in a reproduction of the status quo or an opportunity for change depends, clearly, on the theory against which these micro-practices of everyday life are measured. If grand shifts are postulated, audiences will seem more conservative than if a "no change" thesis is favored. In the heyday of television audience research, reception studies suggested diversity and creativity in the face of materialist, Marxist theories that posited no change, while audience consumption research suggested continuity and conservatism in the face of what were often technologically determinist theories positing radical change. Are we now repeating such a bifurcation in Internet studies?

# Looking Ahead

Methodologically, what is interesting in all this is the repositioning of ethnographic and qualitative audience study. Whereas once this work was seen as theoretically radical, challenging an orthodoxy which undervalued the role of the audience in interacting with new technologies and as having some input into the influence these technologies might exert, now empirical audience study, even that of the interpretive, critical kind, functions either in support of, or as a conservative check on the claims that postmodern theorists make about the transformative impact of new media on contemporary life. Indeed, we find in our own work that there is a consistent tension between our attempts to, on the one hand, apply the critical frameworks explaining inequality and difference to explaining the lives of those we study, and on the other our ethnographic commitment to observe their agency, to learn from them some of the complexities of how inequality plays out in the day-to-day realities of concrete lives and consciousnesses. For example, when presenting research that explains some of the structural inequalities some of our informants face, we are sometimes criticized for stating these inequalities as the objective reality of their condition, rather than focusing on the power of their agency as they exercise it from their particular positions. When we focus on agency, some criticize us for not mentioning structural constraints. There is a continuing tension in our accounts between these two poles.

These are, of course, long-standing challenges in ethnographic social research. For, as often argued, culture operates in a complex way in modern societies, sometimes carrying the weight of structural constraint, at other times working for those who seek to thwart the constraints of their position. Ortner (2003) describes this quandary in a forthcoming work she has completed analyzing the class mobility of her high school graduating class in Weequahic, New Jersey:

> I had originally planned to break up the class by class, and compare how the "high capital" kids and the "low capital" kids did, in order to see the degree of class "drag" on their later lives, and also the different structures of discourse and feeling in which their different experiences

were framed and embedded. For reasons which I explained earlier, however, the discussion turned out to be virtually unwritable in that form, since people do not for the most part live class in America as socially naked actors, but via other, more salient, identities. Moreover, to look at both class drag and class mobility abstracted from these other identities is to get locked in a kind of simplistic structure/agency binary – either people's life chances were held back (or facilitated) by the effects of class, or people by their own individual efforts (or failures thereof) managed to pull themselves up or drop down. This binary is real enough, and I have of course used it throughout this book, but used "nakedly" it ignores not only the identities through which people function as class subjects, but the histories of those identities. The last several decades of so-called identity politics have forced us to recognize the ways in which "agency" itself is constrained by collective forms of oppression, and facilitated by collective forms of liberation.

Ortner worries about the ways in which frameworks which stress the structured nature of inequality inevitably lack a certain explanatory power, being characterized by chasms that can be filled only by close observation of the ordinary and everyday, and close connection to the agency which breaks through these structures, if not effectively and constantly, at times and significantly. She also offers a way forward which we are now following – a strategy in which inequality remains the major metanarrative but the empirical work shows how complex inequality is in practice, so that in researching young people and the Internet one needs an account of use-in-context as well as of the facts of diffusion and access and so, as a result, political economy needs ethnography of the everyday. To accommodate these complexities, we and others are turning to draw in other concepts such as capacity, agency, capital, competence, etc. Classes – and cultures, including postmodern culture – do not exist except insofar as they are understood and enacted by the people who live them. With this cornerstone, we proceed to detail the daily lives, thoughts and actions of the new world of Internet users, to straddle objectivist and subjectivist frameworks in the interests of doing justice both to the agency of those who use new media, and the cultural, economic, and social constraints which affect them.

# References

Abercrombie, N. and B. Longhurst (1998) *Audiences: A Sociological Theory of Performance and Imagination* (London: Sage).

Adorno, T. and M. Horkheimer (1977) "The Culture Industry: Enlightenment as Mass Deception," in J. Curran, M. Gurevitch, and J. Woollacott (eds.), *Mass Communication and Society* (London: Edward Arnold), pp. 349–83.

Allen, R.C. (ed.) (1987) *Channels of Discourse* (Chapel Hill, NC: University of North Carolina Press).

Ang, I. (1985) *Watching Dallas: Soap Opera and the Melodramatic Imagination* (New York: Methuen).

Ang, I. (1996) "Ethnography and Radical Contextualism in Audience Studies," in J. Hay, L. Grossberg, and E. Wartella (eds.), *The Audience and its Landscape* (Boulder, CO: Westview Press), pp. 247–62.

Barney, Darin (2000) *Prometheus Wired: The Hope for Democracy in the Age of Network Technology* (Chicago: University of Chicago Press).

Baym, Nancy (2000) *Tune In, Log On: Soaps, Fandom, and Online* (Thousand Oaks, CA: Sage).

Bird, S. Elizabeth (1992) *For Enquiring Minds: A Cultural Study of Supermarket Tabloids* (Knoxville, TN: University of Tennessee Press).

Brunsdon, C. and D. Morley (1978) *Everyday Television: "Nationwide"* (London: British Film Institute).

Castells, M. (2002) *The Internet Galaxy* (Oxford: Oxford University Press).

Eco, U. (1979) *The Role of the Reader: Explorations in the Semiotics of Texts* (Bloomington, IN: Indiana University Press).

Facer, K., R. Sutherland, R. Furlong, and J. Furlong (2001) "What's the Point of Using Computers? The Development of Young People's Computer Expertise in The Home," *New Media & Society*, 3(2): 199–219.

Flichy, P. (1995). *Dynamics of Modern Communication: The Shaping and Impact of New Communication Technologies* (London: Sage).

Fornas, J. et al. (2002) "Introduction," in J. Fornas et al. (eds.), *Digital Borderlands*. (New York: Peter Lang, 2002), pp. 1–48.

Gerbner, G. and L. Gross (1976) "Living with Television: The Violence Profile," *Journal of Communication*, 26(2): 173–99.

Gillespie, M. (1995) *Television, Ethnicity and Cultural Change* (London and New York: Routledge).

Hall, S. (1980) "Encoding/Decoding," in S. Hall, D. Hobson, A. Lowe and P. Willis (eds.), *Culture, Media, Language* (London: Hutchinson), pp. 128–38.

Hine, C. (2000). *Virtual Ethnography* (London: Sage).

Jones, S. (2002) "Forward," in J. Fornas et al. (eds.), *Digital Borderlands* (New York: Peter Lang).

Katz, E. (1980) "On Conceptualising Media Effects," *Studies in Communication*, 1: 119–41.

Kramarae, Cheris (ed.) (1988) *Technology and Women's Voices: Keeping in Touch* (London: Routledge and Kegan Paul).

Liebes, T., and Katz, E. (1995) *The Export of Meaning: Cross-Cultural Readings of DALLAS* (Cambridge: Polity Press).

Livingstone, S. (2002) *Young People and New Media: Childhood and the Changing Media Environment* (London: Sage).

Livingstone, S. (2003a) "The Changing Nature of Audiences: From the Mass Audience to the Interactive Media User," in A. Valdiva (ed.), *The Blackwell Companion to Media Research* (Oxford: Blackwell), pp. 337–59.

Livingstone, S. (2003b) "Children's Use of the Internet: Reflections on the Emerging Research Agenda," *New Media and Society*, 5(2): 147–66.

Mankekar, Purnima (1999) *Screening Culture, Viewing Politics: An Ethnography of Television, Womanhood, and Nation in Postcolonial India* (Durham, NC: Duke University Press).

Marvin, C. (1988) *When Old Technologies Were New: Thinking About Electric Communication in the Late Nineteenth Century* (Oxford: Oxford University Press).

McMillan, S. (2002) "Exploring Models of Interactivity from Multiple Research Traditions: Users, Documents and Systems," In L. Lievrouw and S. Livingstone (eds.), *Handbook of New Media: Social Shaping and Consequences of ICTs* (London: Sage), pp. 162–82.

Miller, D. and Slater, D. (2000) *The Internet: An Ethnographic Approach* (London: Berg).

Modleski, T. (1986) "Femininity as Mas(s)querade," in Colin McCabe (ed.), *High Theory/Low Culture* (Manchester: Manchester University Press), pp. 37–52.

Morley, D. (1980) *The Nationwide Audience: Structure and Decoding* (London: British Film Institute).

Morley, D. (1986) *Family Television: Cultural Power and Domestic Leisure* (London: Comedia).

Moyal, A. (1995) "The Feminine Culture of the Telephone: People, Patterns and Policy," in N. Heap, R. Thomas, G. Einon, R. Mason, and H. Mackay (eds.), *Information Technology and Society: A Reader* (London: Sage), pp. 284–310.

Neuman, W.R. (1991) *The Future of the Mass Audience* (Cambridge: Cambridge University Press).

Nightingale, Virginia (1996) *Studying Audiences: The Shock of the Real* (London and New York: Routledge).

Ortner, Sherry (2003) *New Jersey Dreaming: Capital, Culture, and the Class of '58* (Durham, NC: Duke University Press).

Poster, M. (2001) *What's the Matter with the Internet?* (Minneapolis: University of Minnesota Press).

Press, A. (1996) "Toward a Qualitative Methodology of Audience Study: Using Ethnography to Study the Popular Cultural Audience," In J. Hay, L. Grossberg, and E. Wartella (eds.), *The Audience and its Landscape* (Boulder, CO: Westview Press), pp.113–30.

Radway, J. (1984a) *Reading the Romance: Women, Patriarchy and Popular Literature* (Chapel Hill, NC: University of North Carolina Press).

Radway, J. (1984b) "Review of Tania Modleski's *Loving with a Vengeance*," July/August, September/October, V: 5&6.

Radway, J. (1988) "Reception Study: Ethnography and the Problems of Dispersed Audiences and Nomadic Subjects," *Cultural Studies*, 2(3): 359–76.

Ribak, R. (2001) "'Like Immigrants': Negotiating Power in the Face of the Home Computer," *New Media & Society*, 3(2): 220–38.

Riesman, David (1950) *The Lonely Crowd: A Study of the Changing American Character* (New Haven: Yale University Press).

Seaman, W.R. (1992) "Active Audience Theory: Pointless Populism," *Media, Culture and Society*, 14: 301–11.

Seiter, E. (1999) *Television and New Media Audiences* (New York: Oxford University Press).

Silverstone, R. (1994) *Television and Everyday Life* (London: Routledge).

Spigel, Lynn (1992) *Make Room for TV: Television and the Family Ideal in Postwar America.* Chicago: University of Chicago Press.

Sunden, Jenny (2002) "Cyberspace: Writing Gender in Digital Self-Presentations," in J. Fornas et al. (eds.), *Digital Borderlands* (New York: Peter Lang), pp. 79–112.

Sveningsson, Malin (2002) "Cyberlove: Creating Romantic Relationships on the Net," in J. Fornas et al. (eds.), *Digital Borderlands* (New York: Peter Lang), pp. 48–76.

Turkle, S. (1995) *Life on the Screen: Identity in the Age of the Internet* (New York: Simon & Schuster).

Wartella, E. and Reeves, B. (1985) "Historical Trends in Research on Children and The Media: 1900–1960," *Journal of Communication*, 35(2): 118–33.

Willis, P. (1990) *Common Culture* (Buckingham: Open University Press).

# Part III

# Cultural Studies and Selected Disciplines: Anthropology, Sociology, Ethnomusicology, Popular Music Studies

# Introduction

The essays in this section explore methods of cultural studies (or cultural studies as a method) in relation to traditional and emergent disciplines.

In "Mixed and Rigorous Cultural Studies Methodology – an Oxymoron?" anthropologist Micaela di Leonardo reflects on the strategies of interdisciplinary and multi-methodological research that guided her own research and writing in her *Exotics at Home: Anthropologies, Others, American Modernity* (1998). She identifies six kinds of method that informed her research – ethnography, historical contextualization, literary analysis, quantitative methods, classic cultural studies readings, and reflexivity (or personal narrative) – even though, she notes, she did not set out in advance specifically to use these methods. She also talks about the difficulty of negotiating academic and popular discourse, both as objects to analyze and as contexts for disseminating one's work. While she does not consider her six methods a definitive laundry list, she argues that any readings of culture gain depth and authority from multiple methodological scrutinies.

In "Is Globalization Undermining the Sacred Principles of Modernity?" sociologist Pertti Alasuutari raises questions about globalization and what he calls the sacred principles of modernity. In relation to the common assumptions of sociological theory, he challenges the dominant assumption that modernity lacks sacred principles. Rather, he suggests that certain issues and ideas – the nation, development – function as sacred principles in modernity, unspoken but tacit objects (or objectives) to which individuals maintain an emotional attachment of respect. He also proposes that cultural studies, with its insistence on examining foundational assumptions, offers a way to sustain critical thought along the lines of his own inquiry into modernity and sacred principles. Thus, cultural studies offers a method of sociological critique, challenging the unspoken foundational assumptions and values that guide more traditional disciplinary thought.

In "Engagement through Alienation: Parallels of Paradox in World Music and Tourism in Sarawak, Malaysia," ethnomusicologist Gini Gorlinski examines the Rainforest World Music Festival, hosted by the Malaysian state of Sarawak. In the process, she discerns how the categories of "world music" and "traditional" music function permeably in a larger context of contradictory global and local perspectives, and offer distinctive opportunities and limitations for musicians and the way their music is encountered, performed, and understood. While "world music" seems to provide a global embrace of multiple musical traditions, it also mutes and supplants "traditional" music which is at once more authentic and less accessible, and covers over more particular political, economic, and conceptual disjunctures between musicians and musical practices.

In "For the Record: Interdisciplinarity, Cultural Studies, and the Search for Method in Popular Music Studies," Tim Anderson foregrounds popular music studies as he looks at the relationship between an emergent discipline and cultural studies. He argues that although the development of popular music studies as an academic field has been aided and abetted by cultural studies methods, these same approaches have perhaps held back popular music study from having a distinctive focus that would constitute it as a discipline in its own right. Cultural studies approaches have emphasized fans, reception, and (live) performance and have consequently muted concern for the material objects and apparatuses of popular music culture. At the same time, traditional musicology has considered music in its immaterial state to be the ideal object of analysis. Between these approaches, both of which have been brought to bear on popular music, Anderson proposes the recorded object (the record, the CD, and other such media technologies used to record, store, and disseminate music), literally, as the site where this inquiry might begin – the material object where a series of economic, technological, industrial, aesthetic, and affective investments intersect, the object that has been the major mode of circulation/reception of popular music, and so forth. Obviously new technologies have come to coexist with, if not supplant, the record. Anderson's point is not to elevate the record as fetish object, nor to hypostatize the record per se. Rather, he proposes the recorded object as a material starting point for beginning to theorize popular music as a disciplinary enterprise.

# 8

# *Mixed and Rigorous Cultural Studies Methodology – an Oxymoron?*

## Micaela di Leonardo

Like all interdisciplinary efforts, cultural studies has a problematic relationship to the question of method. The fact that cultural studies
research engages primarily with popular or mass culture, and that it
tends to wear its generally progressive politics on its hybridized little
sleeve, further complicate the method issue with the specter of slippages
into entertainment journalism and accusations of ideology-driven
conclusions.

In the decade-long process of researching and writing *Exotics at
Home: Anthropologies, Others, American Modernity*, I found myself engaging firsthand with these anxieties.[1] *Exotics*, an account of the symbio-
sis between the discipline of anthropology and American popular
political culture over the course of the last century, is, with its heavy
reliance on film, television, cartoons, popular journalism, and advertisements, ripe for the accusation of being "merely" popular critique. At
the same time, its clear left, feminist, and anti-racist politics make it
vulnerable to attack as a purely ideologically driven set of analyses.

I think, however, that the clear set of questions that animate *Exotics*,
and the use of multiple appropriate methods to answer those questions,
render such anxieties and criticisms moot, and should do so with any
parallel cultural studies project. In particular, mixed methodologies,
providing varying optics on the same phenomenon, act as a check on
and a test of the validity of particular interpretations. In addition, they
help to retain the balance among what Donna Haraway labels the Four
Temptations: the equally valid epistemic frames – positivism, feminism/
anti-racism, Marxism, and social construction – that contemporary
scholars often find difficult to entertain simultaneously.[2] As I concluded
in *Exotics*:

I have thus written a work of "blurred genres" not as an escape from a troubled discipline, nor as a solipsistic technique for creating textual *jouissance*, but in the belief that the simultaneous engagement here of cultural criticism, historical political economy, intellectual history, and ethnography does the work of making a cogent argument and documenting its empirical rationale.[3]

Let me elaborate these points through laying out the six kinds of methods used in my project, in the context of the questions they enabled me to answer. In the interests of honesty, though, I should add that I never set out to use all of these methods – or, for that matter, to write on precisely the set of topics I ended in treating. My research process was classically hermeneutical: I used methods that seemed appropriate to answer each question with which I began my work. I then altered my analysis in line with new findings, which led again to new research and thus yet other appropriate methods. As Gadamer writes: "Again, the initial meaning emerges only because [the reader] is reading the text with particular expectations in regard to a certain meaning. Working out this fore-projection, which is constantly revised in terms of what emerges as [the reader] penetrates into the meaning, is understanding what is there."[4]

# Ethnography

While not itself primarily an ethnographic study, *Exotics at Home* is steeped in my two long-term ethnographic projects in Northern California and in New Haven, Connecticut. "Ethnography" has become a trendy methodological claim for some in cultural studies, so it is worthwhile taking some time to explain what this term means in the context of anthropology by that term. Ethnography may have one or more of a variety of entrée points: a household, neighborhood or village, a workplace, an institutional site such as a school, a medical clinic, an organized political or cultural movement, a scattered population united by "consciousness of kind," as Max Weber put it, or by similar life trajectories, as in the cases of individuals jailed for the same offense or patients with the same disease.[5] More recently, ethnographies are increasingly multi-sited in order to offer an adequate account of particular phenomena: the circular migration strategies of Puerto Ricans or Mexicans, the overarching shifts in the training and occupational situations of American psychiatrists, the creation of "ethnic" ties between Miao Chinese in the PRC and Hmong migrants to the United States.[6]

In all cases, though, "ethnography" denotes both intensive and extensive study of a human population. While it may involve formal or informal interviewing, it is distinct from journalism in that it is not "covering a story" but "accounting for lives." Ethnographers may focus, for example, on one class fraction or ethnic or racial population, one age group or one gender, but they do so within the context of over-arching class and racial/ethnic formation, of the specificities of life course, of prevailing gender relations for that population. They may account for lives in the present, but they do so (or at least good eth-nographers do nowadays) in a larger historical context. In other words, while few ethnographers today produce the multiple institutional accounts – kinship, marriage, and reproduction, religion and symbolism, law and politics, economy and division of labor, etc. – of the classic period of British social anthropology, contemporary practice goes forward in the light of that tradition. This methodological rigor is also necessary when the practitioner is not an anthropologist but any other sort of scholar – including of cultural studies – who is laying claim to the cachet of ethnography for purposes of claiming authority on a particular topic.

On the other hand, the British tradition also tended to "airbrush," as it were, signs of colonial occupation from accounts of the lives of particular populations in order to narrate "authentic" lives.[7] (There are many notable early exceptions, of course, such as Clyde Mitchell's important account of the Kalela Dance in the Rhodesian Copperbelt, an institution that clearly both reflected and sent up British colonial power.[8]) Because of this reluctance to detail the exigencies of state control, and Third and Fourth World disciplinary framing – although anthropologists have always engaged in First World research as well – until recent years, members of the guild have been slower than those in other disciplines to acknowledge the importance of studying varying public spheres.

However, I was forced to come to terms with the interpenetration of mass media and daily lives and street-level politics in my first major ethnographic study among cross-class Italian Americans in San Francisco, Oakland, and San Jose.[9] Doing research in the midst of – and even personally inspired by – the white ethnic renaissance of the 1970s – although I only came to an understanding of its historicity after the fact – I found the people with whom I was working to be obsessed with the mass media portrayal of Italian Americans. After some initial confusion, I began asking everyone a standard set of questions about their reactions to the *Godfather* films, to the then-new use of Italian Americans in advertising, and to local manifestations such as a television personality, Joe Carcione, who commented on fresh produce and cooking. As might be expected, individuals' reactions were quite varied, and helped to illuminate their very different social positions. Those who functioned in some way as "ethnic brokers," for example, tended to be most upset about the negative, "crime-ridden" portrayal of Italian Americans in the *Godfather* films, while many working- and professional-class men and women found them amusing and even inspiring. One young clerical explained that she made use of Mafia imagery in joking threats against her non-Italian acquaintances.[10]

I also began to analyze both the shifting portrayals of Italian Americans in social science research from the 1940s forward, and the meanings of new white ethnic representations in mass media in the larger American political context – the beginnings of my later historical political-economic analysis of the invention of white ethnic tradition in reaction against (and in imitation of) Afro-American and other race-minority civil rights organizing and ideology.[11] In so doing – and especially in analyzing text and image as representation across both popular and scholarly genres – I anticipated what has since become a rich cultural studies literature as well as a more ordinary part of ethnographic research.

My current long-term ethnographic project in New Haven, Connecticut engages even more centrally with American popular culture, as I am documenting New Haven as urban imaginary both in the minds of New Haveners since the early 1990s and in the national public sphere since World War II. Thus, as part of doing more ordinary life-historical interviewing, I ask individuals to "draw" symbolic maps of the city for me and to account for all of the ways in which they "take in" visions of city life – newspapers, radio, television. I have also participated in the city's public life across neighborhood, class, and race divides: parks, libraries, bars, laundromats, gyms, street and city festivals, etc.

Ethnography appears formally in *Exotics at Home* both as reference for my material on white ethnicity and in a section on New Haven illustrating the growth and hegemony of underclass ideology over the course of the 1980s – the analysis of which in scholarship and mass media is a key part of my overall argument in the book.[12] In describing the changing life of one working-class neighborhood as the state-sponsored urban immiseration of the Reagan/Bush years took hold, I offered a street-level case study instantiating the analysis I had already offered in terms of national statistical trends. In addition, I was able not only to show how neighborhood life altered as the city became poorer, but how neighbors, black and white, envisioned one another through underclass lenses.

## Historical Contextualization

*Exotics at Home* encompasses the twentieth century, and therefore makes considerable synthetic use of extant (economic, political, cultural, feminist, intellectual) American historical narrative. But although there is a rich "history of anthropology" literature, it tends to focus on the nineteenth century and more on the UK than the United States.[13] The original use of historical contextualization in the book, then, is its application of Americanist historiography to the history of the discipline of anthropology and the life histories of its practitioners.

For example, much ink has been spilled on Margaret Mead's life and work, in anthropological histories, biographies, and of course in attacks such as Derek Freeman's *cause célèbre* of the first Reagan term, *Margaret Mead and Samoa*.[14] But I was able to place Mead's 1910s and 1920s coming of age in the context not only of the establishment of Boasian anthropology at Columbia University, not only in terms of the very invention of the category of "youth" in American scholarship and popular culture, but also in terms of both the rise of professionalism/decline of feminist activism of the 1920s, and the establishment of the culture of consumption in the same years.[15] That is, first, as historian Nancy Cott establishes in *the Grounding of Modern Feminism*, in the early decades of the twentieth century, "diffuse 'professional standards' were being adopted in many occupational areas . . ."[16] Simultaneously, post-Suffrage, feminism lost cachet, and many younger women, Margaret Mead among them, simply rushed to take advantage of the educational and occupational opportunities made possible by the activism of earlier generations without themselves engaging in further activism.

Secondly, no one had previously connected Mead's life and work to the rich American Studies literature on the rise of the culture of consumption. This phenomenon includes not simply the proliferation of goods for sale concomitant upon American capitalist industrialization, and the establishment of urban "palaces of consumption" – department stores – and the advertising industry, but also the shifting of American temperaments, as Warren Sussman has claimed, from a theologically driven "character" to psychologically informed "personality." Mead's connection to these shifts is intimately familial: both of her parents were professionally engaged in celebrating and analyzing American corporate growth and consolidation and the phenomenal rise and entailments of the advertising industry. However, the point to stress here is that Mead herself celebrated commodity consumption. Rather, she made use, from the 1930s on, of the techniques of self-advertisement to constitute herself as, to use Betty Friedan's later label, "a scientific supersaleswoman." What concepts and interpretations she actually "sold" shifted considerably over a half-century of professional practice, but Mead consistently sold herself as the authoritative interpreter of "primitive" and Western cultural mores.[17]

## Literary Analyses

While the first wave of postmodern anthropological writings advocated and engaged in literary re-readings of anthropological texts – particularly with regard to deconstructing their use of literary techniques to underwrite claims to ethnographic authority – Margaret Mead's vast output has not been much analyzed in this light. (Or for that matter, most ethnographic production outside of a handful of classic and recent works, such as Evans-Pritchard's *The Nuer* and Vincent Crapanzano's *Tuhami*, that became fetishized through overwhelming postmodern attention.)

As a part of my narration of anthropology's role in twentieth-century popular culture, I did close "New Criticism" readings of a half-dozen popularly written and relatively bestselling ethnographies spanning the 1920s into the 1980s, including, of course, Mead's 1928 *Coming of Age in Samoa*. Through this process, I was also able to articulate changing American popular-cultural visions of what I labeled the Dusky Maiden – that is, the "exotic" woman of color. The Dusky Maiden is a Western condensation symbol of linked race and gender in the contexts of colonialism/imperialism. My argument was that looking at ethnographies over a relatively long period allowed us to discover the shifting ways in which the Dusky Maiden was represented and read, slipping the trammels of anachronistic assertions.

For example, since the 1960s *Coming of Age* has been much commented on as a romantic account of sexually liberated adolescence, especially female adolescence, in a "primitive" society. And certainly Mead does discuss the relatively early and guilt-free sexual experiences of the Samoan girls among whom she lived. But a careful reading of Mead's actual text, and an accounting of all the popular and scholarly reviews of the book at the time of publication (literary-critical reader response research using reviews as proxies for long-dead readers), presents a very different picture. Mead in fact offered a profoundly unromantic portrayal of Samoan life, which she explicitly termed a "shallow society" that cannot produce "great personalities and important art," a "place where no one plays for very high stakes."[18] And Mead understood herself, and was understood by reviewers, both fellow scholars and middlebrow magazine and newspaper writers, as an anthropologist writing not about women and girls, not about sex, but about *youth*, a category that was recently redefined and newly culturally charged in 1920s America.

## Quantitative Methods

My use of quantification in *Exotics* was fairly unsophisticated, but even very simple and restricted bouts of counting can have profound effects, particularly vis-à-vis contemporary received political wisdom concerning "culture." I learned this lesson in my first study, *The Varieties of Ethnic Experience.* Annoyed with and doubtful of Harvard cliometrician (and future New Rightist) Stephen Thernstrom's racist characterizations of Irish and Italian American family life and child-rearing practices (as opposed to "superior" Jewish patterns) in his study, *The Other Bostonians,* I examined his use of US Census data for 1950 to undergird his points.

Claiming that Boston's Irish "lacked any entrepreneurial tradition," and that its Italians lived in a "subculture that directed energies away from work," Thernstrom considered the 1950 occupations and salaries of a range of ethnic men of two different age groups in order to create an artificial set of "fathers" and "sons." As the Census lacks a "Jewish" category, he used Russian men as a proxy. Thernstrom's findings indeed buttressed his claims of poor economic progress and blue-collar continuity among Irish and Italians, and increasing small business and professional involvement among "Jews."

Asking the question, "Is it the ethnics, or is it Boston?," I simply reproduced Thernstom's measures for the same year for the San Francisco/Oakland Standard Metropolitan Statistical Area. (I also included women, and considered female labor force participation rates for all groups for both Boston and Northern California, which had large effects on the findings, all in my favor, but I will not tell that story here.) My results were dramatically different from those produced by Thernstrom: Irish and Italians simply did far better on the West Coast, were more involved in small business and the professions, etc. I theorized that the difference had to do both with differing regional economies at various points of migrant arrival, and with the very different demographic mix in the two areas. In particular, I noted that East Asians and Mexicans were present early on in California to fill the "despised racial other" slot in the local economy and in popular stereotyping, while Irish and Italians had filled those roles in Boston.[19] Racist cultural presumptions had led Thernstrom, who had crafted a career on the creative use of quantitative methods in historical analysis, to make foolish, elementary errors in the use of Census material.

In *Exotics*, among many other examples of quantification, I followed a hunch that the anthropological concept of cultural relativism had become a deliberate New Right punching bag since the rise of that political formation in the 1970s. In order to test this impression, I did a time-series Lexis–Nexis search for all appearances of the term in mass and middlebrow media from 1970 onwards. Just as I had suspected, the search revealed scattered but increasing – and almost entirely negative – references to the topic in the popular press through the 1970s and into the mid-1980s.[20] At first, in the Carter years, the references are made by moderates, and are used to indict straw people, just off-camera, who are "going too far." For example, in 1978 Christopher Jencks, writing in the *Washington Post*, talks of a "kind of spongy cultural relativism that treats all ideas as equally defensible." In a similar vein, in a 1980 editorial against death by stoning in Khomeini's Iran, *The New York Times* thunders, "Cultural relativism has its limits, and at some point tolerance becomes complicity." But then the gloves come off, and all pretense of reasoned debate is abandoned. In 1981 *The Heritage Foundation Policy Review* denounces cultural relativism's "deep and lasting inroads into society." Pat Robertson asserts in 1982 that the United States "is a socialist society" because "the courts have embraced cultural relativism." And Leonard Kriegel in 1984 approvingly cites William Bennett complaining of American education that "cultural relativism was in; the traditional literary canon was out," while Phyllis Schlafly's Eagle Forum comes out against "secular humanism and cultural relativism" in the schools.[21] Note the slipperiness of "culture" across these references, the way that appreciating Toni Morrison and failing to judge cruel and unusual punishment (and just exactly where were these Western cheerleaders for Khomeini?) are equated in the new all-purpose rightist indictment.

At mid-decade, with Reagan's second term, the pattern of occurrence takes on the mathematical neatness of the wrentit's call: deliberate notes, each incrementally faster than the last, until all individuality is lost in a buzzing trill of noise. References are not as frequent as those to OJ or Madonna, of course, but from the early 1990s into the present, no week has passed without one or two snide print media swipes at cultural relativism.[22] In 1987 *The New Republic* whined that "cultural relativism stops us saying our ways are best." William Pfaff complained in 1988 that cultural relativism allows universities (Orwell is turning in his grave) "to shove truth down the memory hole." Thomas Sowell asserted in 1990 that cultural relativism "says one thing is not better than another." In *The National Review* in 1991, Digby Anderson, not to be outdone, excoriates "repellent cultural relativism" that says "that any culture is as good as any other, you know, black Africans had a Renaissance which outshone the West's, it's just that the West has obliterated it with colonialism." William Henry, in *In Defense of Elitism*, favorably reviewed in *The New York Times*, actually wrote in 1994 that "It is scarcely the same thing to put a man on the moon as to put a bone in your nose."

In order to further enrich this set of findings – to test the effects of popular media on scholars' apprehensions – I reviewed major introductory anthropology textbooks over four decades for the presence and interpretation of the concept of cultural relativism. I found, indeed, first, that no anthropological text came anywhere near the silly "no moral evaluation possible" stance that popular commentators had claimed was prescribed by cultural relativism. Secondly, I found that textbook authors, from the 1970s forward, increasingly distanced themselves from the term, until the late 1980s, when texts simply began omitting it altogether.[23]

Micaela di Leonardo

# Classic Cultural Studies Readings

I also engaged extensively in the now-ordinary "reading" of film, television, cartoons, advertisements, book covers, old photographs, and street scenes so heavily practiced in cultural studies. I think that the "cross-readings" provided by my use of so many different methods helped to enhance the cogency and force of these interpretations of popular cultural phenomena. For example, I begin the book with an account of the "gauntlet of ethnological antimodernism" I encounter on my walk home from work – a small-business strip of road thickly populated by ethnic boutiques, Oriental rug stores, and New Age outlets. I provide photographs of the stores and sidewalk scene I describe, but I also contextualize the phenomenon in terms of the role college towns have played as staging grounds for "selling the offbeat" to consumers "eager to display sophistication through the consumption of the exotic ... Particular commodities – folk music, Indian import women's wear, Balinese jewelry – succeeded first in college town test markets before becoming standard American mall merchandise."[24]

I further contextualize my analysis through comparing the "Dempster Street scene" (of Evanston, Illinois) to the display of the exotic a century earlier just a few miles south, at the Chicago World's Columbian Exposition of 1893. While the overt imperialist racism of the display of living human beings in zoo-like exhibits is obvious to the contemporary reader, I also focus on the ways in which fair planners and the popular press distinguished among different "exotic" populations: Within an overarching racist discourse, popular magazines nevertheless lauded the Japanese, the "Yankees of the East," at the fair; the Javanese, described as "about the color of a well-done sweet potato"; and the Samoans, whom the *Nation* denominated "fine specimens of humanity ... the aboriginal note in its purity."[25]

This historical background helps to illuminate which racial others offer consumable difference in the present – and which do not. The analysis feeds into my critique of the contemporary concept of the black and brown urban underclass, which is then undergirded by an account of underclass ideologues' many empirical falsehoods.

In another part of the book, I do close readings of the apartheid-era popular South African film *The Gods Must Be Crazy*, and the ethnographic film *N!ai*, both concerning the same heavily symbolized

Kalahari population, the San. Again, my readings of popular-cultural phenomena are lodged inside a synthetic account, making use of others' scholarship, of the historical and present political economy and social reality of the San – which itself then motors my critical reading of the late Margery Shostak's bestselling ethnography, *Nisa*.[26] The very mixing of methods here enables a three-dimensional analysis of a complex cultural phenomenon.

# Reflexivity

Finally, as they say nowadays, I insert myself repeatedly in the text in *Exotics*. Some autobiographical instances are simply stylistic, as in my opening Dempster Street vignette, or when I note, in the midst of a close analysis of Oscar Lewis's work and popular reception, that I was urged to read *Five Families* by a classmate in an ordinary working- and middle-class public high school in the mid-1960s. Others are more extensive, and necessitated by the substance of my truth claims, as in my repeated accounting for my own residence, activities, and reactions in the New Haven ethnographic section of chapter 6, "Eastern Seaboard Interlude."[27]

Much of my understanding of this kind of use of autobiography draws on urban studies scholars' considerations of the rise of the notion of the *flaneur*, the privileged urban wanderer, who might be an artist, a social investigator, a political activist, or simply a member of the bourgeoisie gone slumming. Feminist scholars have noted the paradoxes of the role of the *flaneuse*, who, because she is female, cannot always take on the carefree ways of the *flaneur*, must worry about potential sexual violence.[28] I try to indicate, in my first-person accounts, the ways in which my urban wandering is both privileged and endangered. I also include a set of cautionary remarks concerning the over-reliance on autobiographical material in some "postmodern" ethnography and other cultural studies work. My argument is that the "I was there" trope, whether used by journalists or scholars, may be rhetorically productive, but is not always adequate as method. My primary example is the by now richly embroidered construction of the urban underclass, which, as I have noted, is not borne out by empirical material. In the New Haven ethnography section of *Exotics*, I show how neighbors on one hard-pressed block did indeed envision urban shifts through underclass lenses. But I set their understandings into both the actual historical political-economic shifts of that era, and the media onslaught that so shaped public understanding of poverty and crime in the 1980s.

I also use autobiography, in *Exotics* and elsewhere, to comment on my situatedness in a very different way: to narrate my varying encounters with journalists as a measure of the complex and always shifting relationship between scholars and the Fourth Estate. In particular, I have written about the changing popular-cultural scene vis-à-vis the rise to hegemony of the second postwar wave of biological reductionism. Sociobiology Take 2, often referred to as evolutionary psychology or biology, jettisoned the obviously racist and homophobic argumentation of the first wave of 1970s sociobiological writers, leaving only a set of sexist presumptions and arguments. Buoyed both by its increasing presence in psychology and biology departments and by its seemingly commonsensical take on gender relations in an era of failed centrist politics and a stalled feminist agenda, nouveau sociobiology has been wildly successful in popular culture. In particular, journalists call on feminist scholars not for actual logical arguments buttressed by empirical information – not, in other words, in the search for truth – but for stock "angry" quotations to insert into already-written stories.

In *Exotics*, I narrated my most memorable close encounter with this newly hegemonic incarnation of sociobiological orthodoxy: a set of phone conversations and then faxes from *Newsweek Magazine* preparatory to the publication of a 1996 cover story on "the new science of beauty":

> The reporter explained that a number of scientists (psychology, ecology, neuroscience) are now claiming that sexual attraction to "symmetry" is a human universal, explicable with reference to "inclusive fitness," and – non sequitur – that across cultures and human history, men are most attracted to women with a particular waist/hip ratio.

I spent an hour or so talking to this woman, long enough to experience amusement, bemusement, frustration, and rage. I cited my own expertise: work on a *Gender/Sexuality Reader* I had co-edited with Roger Lancaster.[29] I tried to explain to her that human sexual attraction and mating patterns are extraordinarily various, and connected to human social and political institutions layered over – and not reducible to – biology. I noted that this nouveau sociobiology (unlike

E.O. Wilson's original, and embarrassingly silly statements) makes no allowance for ubiquitous human homosexuality. I pointed out that it re-introduces the sexist (and anthropologically absurd) notion of a "bottom line" human nature in which men try to maximize their DNA reproduction through impregnating as many young, nubile women as possible, and women attempt to "capture" male parental support by enhancing their personal attractiveness. I argued that in most of human history we see instead very specific – and widely varying – fertility goals. We have abundant evidence of widespread desires for few, not many children in many sorts of societies; and that individuals do not make mating decisions as Cartesian monads, but rather as social beings embedded in webs of kin, friends, and neighbors who have enormous effects on sexual and marital choices. I pointed out that attempting to find some "essential" human attractiveness beneath skin and eye color, hair type, nose shape, and body type denied both cultur-ally varying aesthetic systems and the long historical effects of Western imperialism.

Finally, I tried to offer the reporter a sense of *déjà vu:* that we had already been down this road multiple times, from overtly racist nineteenth-century Social Darwinism to 1960s pop-Naked Ape to 1970s sociobiology. All of these explanatory frames laid claim to "tough-mindedness" and high science; all denied their obvious political inter-ests. I told her that I still owned a copy of the stupid 1977 *Time* issue whose cover, graced with a white heterosexual couple in half-embrace, dangling from marionette strings, proclaimed, "Why You Do What You Do: Sociobiology. The New Theory of Behavior."[30] I explained that as far as I could tell, these "beauty scientists" were as absurdly reduction-ist and sexist as ever, differing from older sociobiologists in only two respects: their focus on the issue of attraction/beauty, and their efforts to purge sociobiology of its racist heritage through the specious claim of a "more basic" human perception of symmetry beneath physical variations culturally marked as "racial." I introduced her to the phrase "junk science."

The reporter was sympathetic and identified herself as a feminist, but kept returning to two points: her editor wanted a positive story on this "new science"; and didn't contemporary American women's desperate attempts to improve their physical attractiveness through clothing, hair dye, makeup and surgery despite so many years of feminist activism "prove" that there was a point here? I tried to lay out the contemporary American political economy of gender, but she wasn't really listening. In my frustration, I finally exclaimed, "Look, Wonderbras are *not* genetic!"[31]

Of course, while the narration of my failure to communicate with this journalist, and more importantly, to gain access for my critique in the pages of *Newsweek*, is a form of scholar's revenge, it is also an effort to make available an alternative record, a very different take on culture and biology, than is currently hegemonic in American society. It is thus as much itself cultural production (albeit, for a comparatively minuscule audience) as it is an analysis of such.

# Conclusions

I do not offer the six aforementioned methods as an exhaustive list, nor as a magic combination, although I would argue that any reading of texts or other popular-cultural phenomena gains depth and authority from historical contextualization. I am aware of the varying and crucial modes of cultural studies analysis with which I am not engaged. Most importantly, I do not deal, above, with aesthetic apprehensions except insofar as I attempt to satisfy them through artful writing.

I will make the programmatic claim, though, that cultural studies is fundamentally *about* investigating the making of meanings, and we cannot understand such cultural processes in the absence of accounting of their particular historical political-economic contexts. (It is also, of course, the case, that historical political economy that is inattentive to cultural process fails its mandate, but that is another essay.) This formulation is really a restatement of Haraway's Four Temptations from another optic. And, of course, it is also an illustration of Raymond Williams's justly famous conception of "structures of feeling."[32]

Thus, the "methods" question is really a theory question. And here I agree with Frederic Jameson's endorsement of a totalizing vision of cultural studies, one that does *not* attempt to replace marxist analysis but rather continually reinvents it: "...a kind of turning structure, an ion-exchange between various entities, in which the ideological drives associated with one pass over and interfuse the other – but only provisionally, for a 'historically specific moment,' before entering into new combinations."[33] That turning structure is clearly, if anything, a more rather than less rigorous project than an ordinarily disciplinary one. And it has the advantages of both crucial interest and modesty: of attempting to describe actually existing social worlds from admittedly historically contingent Archimedean points.

## Notes

1  Micaela di Leonardo (1998), *Exotics at Home: Anthropologies, Others, American Modernity* (Chicago: University of Chicago Press).

2  Donna Haraway (1989), *Primate Visions: Gender, Race, and Nature in the World of Modern Science* (New York: Routledge), pp. 6–8.

3  Di Leonardo, *Exotics at Home*, p. 23.

4  Hans-Georg Gadamer (1989), *Truth and Method*, second, revised edition. Translation by Joel Weinsheimer and Donald G. Marshall (New York: Continuum), p. 267.

5  Max Weber (1978), "Ethnic Groups," in Gunther Roth and Claus Wittich (eds.), *Economy and Society* (Berkeley: University of California Press).

6  Gina Pérez, "The Near Northwest Side Story: Gender, Migration, and Everyday Life in Chicago and San Sebastián, Puerto Rico." PhD dissertation, Northwestern University, 2000; T.M. Luhrman (2001), *Of Two Minds: The Growing Disorder in American Psychiatry* (New York: Knopf); Louisa Schein, "The Consumption of Color and the Politics of White Skin in Post-Mao China," in Roger Lancaster and Micaela di Leonardo (eds.), *The Gender/Sexuality Reader* (New York: Routledge), pp. 473–86.

7  See *Exotics*, pp. 212 ff.

8  J. Clyde Mitchell (1956), *The Kalela Dance: Aspects of Social Relations Among Urban Africans in Northern Rhodesia*, The Rhodes–Livingston Papers, no. 27 (Manchester: University of Manchester Press).

9  Micaela di Leonardo (1984), *The Varieties of Ethnic Experience: Kinship, Class, and Gender Among Italian-Americans in Northern California* (Ithaca: Cornell University Press).

10  Ibid., pp. 158–90.

11  Micaela di Leonardo (1994), "White Ethnicities, Identity Politics, and Baby Bear's Chair," *Social Text*, 41 (Winter): 165–91.

12  See di Leonardo, *Exotics*, pp. 319–32.

13  See, for example, the History of Anthropology Series, University of Wisconsin Press, and George Stocking (1987), *Victorian Anthropology* (New York: The Free Press).

14  Derek Freeman (1983), *Margaret Mead and Samoa: The Unmaking of an Anthropological Myth* (Cambridge: Harvard University Press).

15  See *Exotics*, pp. 163–83.

16  Nancy Cott (1987), *The Grounding of Modern Feminism* (New Haven: Yale University Press), p. 217.

17  Warren Sussman (1984), "'Personality' and the Making of Twentieth-Century Culture," in Susman, *Culture as History: The Transformation of American Society in the Twentieth Century* (New York: Pantheon), pp. 271–85; Betty Friedan (1963), *The Feminine Mystique* (New York: Bantam Doubleday), p. 147; see *Exotics*, pp. 164–70.

18  Margaret Mead ([1928] 1973), *Coming of Age in Samoa* (New York: American Museum of Natural History), pp. 4, 110, 111.

19  Stephan Thernstrom (1999), *The Other Bostonians* (Cambridge, MA: Harvard University Press), pp. 140, 169; *The Varieties of Ethnic Experience*, pp. 96–108.

20  Actual numbers of citations: 1978, 1; 1979, 0; 1980, 1; 1981, 2; 1982, 2; 1983, 9; 1984, 13; 1985, 7.

21  Christopher Jencks (1978), "The Wrong Answer for Schools Is: b) Back to Basics," *The Washington Post,* February 19; unsigned op-ed (1980), "On 'Understanding' the Abominable," *The New York Times,* July 16; Terry Eastland (1981), "The Prophet Abroad," review of Ronald Berman (ed.), *Solzhenitsyn at Harvard, Heritage Foundation Policy Review,* Spring; David E. Anderson (1982), UPI report on Moral Majority conference, July 27; Leonard Kriegel (1984), "Who Cares about the Humanities?," *The Nation,* December 29; Constance Holden (1984), "Reagan versus the Social Sciences," *Science,* November 30.

22  Actual numbers of citations: 1986, 14; 1987, 26; 1988, 19; 1989, 21; 1990, 31; 1991, 43; 1992, 71; 1993, 137; 1994, 95; 1995, 81, 1996, 83 (including my own "Patterns of Culture Wars: The Right's Attack on 'Cultural Relativism' as Synecdoche For All That Ails Us," *The Nation,* April 8, 1996).

23  *Exotics,* pp. 342–4.

24  Ibid., pp. 1–2.

25  Ibid., pp. 3–6.

26  Ibid., pp. 272–97.

27  Ibid., pp. 319–32.

28  See, for example, Judith Walkowitz's 1992 account of the *flaneuse* in her *City of Dreadful Delight: Narratives of Sexual Danger in Late-Victorian London* (Chicago: University of Chicago Press), chapters one and two.

29  Roger Lancaster and Micaela di Leonardo (eds.) (1997), *The Gender/Sexuality Reader* (New York: Routledge).

30  *Time* Magazine, August 1, 1977, pp. 54–63.

31  *Exotics,* pp. 354–5.

32  Raymond Williams (1980), *Problems in Materialism and Culture* (London: Verso), pp. 22–7.

33  Frederic Jameson (1995), "On Cultural Studies," in John Rajchman (ed.), *The Identity in Question* (New York: Routledge), pp. 251–95, esp. p. 269.

# 9

# *Is Globalization Undermining the Sacred Principles of Modernity?*

## Pertti Alasuutari

## Introduction

The title of this chapter might appear to contain a contradiction in terms. How could globalization – or anything for that matter – undermine the "sacred principles" of modernity, since it is commonly perceived that modernity itself is hostile to everything that is sacred? To talk about the sacred principles of modernity is, of course, a conscious provocation, but I hope you can take it seriously. When one is engaged in doing cultural studies of one's own contemporary society, it is, I argue, extremely important to bear in mind that, contrary to many theories of modernity – I would even say unlike the prevalent notion of modernity would have it – we do have shared sacred principles. Losing sight of this means that we are blinded by our ethnocentric "natural attitude," i.e. that we "stay native" so to speak. This is a very real danger in cultural studies, because in contrast to those traditional anthropologists who study the Other, we typically do not have the advantage of noticing the cultural difference between us and them, the objects of study, which gives the researcher a good starting point for asking questions. When studying one's own culture and society, it is easy to overlook our sacred principles because we take them for granted; that is probably the biggest challenge of contemporary cultural studies. When we study the cultural processes and discourses of contemporary society and how they are related to relations of power (a short definition of cultural studies), it is of course possible to do that without the assumption that certain things are sacred for us, but such a starting point can render the research sterile, as if people were bodiless minds whose link to the common culture would only be cognitive.

In any case, ignoring sacredness leaves us poorly equipped to understand the power of culture.

What do I mean by this statement? Let me refer to the meaning of sacred: it depicts an object or thing that we treat with respect, even fear. In other words, we have an emotionally felt relationship to it. People may think that they have rationally induced the sacred principles they honor, but the bottommost sacred principles are not a matter of reason, because they are the premises on which rational arguments are built. And no matter how sacred principles may be rationally defended, they are, when all is said and done, anchored in the emotions. That makes us truly cultural subjects, not isolated individuals that use culture as a map of meaning. Sacred principles make us tick.

In arguing that there are certain sacred principles in contemporary society, I do not suggest that these are constant and unchanging. On the contrary, I do think that recent decades have witnessed certain developments that are changing them. Hence the question posed at the start of the chapter: is globalization undermining the sacred principles of modernity? But before considering this in full, let me first discuss how the prevalent discourse of modernity and modernization perceives the notion of sacredness.

In the philosophy of history used by sociologists, it is thought that "premodern" traditional societies can be characterized by habitual behavior backed up by the sanctifying force of religion, whereas modernization means that, little by little, the immobilizing fetters of sacred principles are broken and people are free to make up their own minds about how to think and behave. As Marx and Engels put it in their *Manifesto of the Communist Party* (1848), a text that is often also seen as a manifesto of modernization:

> Constant revolutionising of production, uninterrupted disturbance of all social conditions, everlasting uncertainty and agitation distinguish the bourgeois epoch from all earlier ones. All fixed, fast-frozen relations, with their train of ancient and venerable prejudices and opinions, are swept away, all new-formed ones become antiquated before they can ossify. All that is solid melts into air, all that is holy is profaned, and man is at last compelled to face with sober senses, his real conditions of life, and his relations with his kind.

In those lines Marx encapsulates the main observation that later classics of sociology also made about modern times. For instance, Emile Durkheim, Max Weber, Georg Simmel and Ferdinand Tönnies all shared the view that as a result of industrialization, the increased division of labor and the exchange economy, all norms based on religious or otherwise sanctified principles are gradually disappearing. They outline a situation in which traditional social organization based on feudalism and estates is replaced by a new class society, in which individuals' social position depends on how much money they have: other resources or forms of "capital," as Pierre Bourdieu succinctly calls them, follow from this. In this increasingly individualized society, we think we can do whatever we want to, provided that we have the money to realize our dreams. The ever-increasing production of consumer goods also means that, for instance, clothing and other possessions that previously used to signify one's position and social group can now be freely chosen according to one's own individual taste and style. It has even been suggested that modernization has occurred in two phases: the first stage saw the replacement of estate society by class society, whereas the late modernity of the latter part of the twentieth century meant that the markers of class faded in the midst of style and fashion (see, for example, Beck, Giddens, and Lash, 1994).

According to this widely shared view of the essence of historical development, in contemporary modern or late modern society every action or opinion is supposed to be based on rational assessment, preferably backed up by scientific scrutiny. We are gradually entering a society in which every individual has to be prepared to constantly doubt and question everything we are accustomed to, because the world is changing so fast that by the time we have developed certain habits and routines they have become outdated. The fact that every individual does not follow these principles, that in advanced contemporary societies some people still unquestionably observe certain sacred principles, is taken as proof of their backwardness. This is, for instance, the way in which extremist groups are commonly conceived of. For instance, Anthony Giddens (1994: 100) talks about fundamentalism as an "assertion of formulaic truth," and argues that it can be seen as a reaction to the difficulties of living in a world of radical doubt.

Thus, if modernity by definition depicts a continuous break away from all that is solid and sacred, if it equals a deep process of secularization in various spheres, how can we even talk about sacred principles of modernity?

As late as the early 1990s Fredric Jameson (1992: 67) wrote that capitalistic modernity has succeeded in killing religion, yet the rise of religion-based fundamentalism in its various forms has shown that this is unlikely to happen. I suggest that the seeming contradiction in terms between modernity and sacredness resides in a biased conception of both terms. First, we must not equate tacit, unquestioned routines with sacred principles or moral norms. I argue that routines are the founding principle of all orderly life and an essential condition for human intelligence and innovative thought. Therefore, although social conditions nowadays seem to change very rapidly, it cannot and does not mean that reflexivity is continuously increasing. Rather, it means that routinization must also be rapid, because otherwise our life would become unbearably difficult and this would slow the pace of social change. By the concept of sacred we refer to a shared conviction among members of a society that an object, idea, or rule is particularly important and also emotionally binding. Thus, violating it demands an account – or even retribution. As to modernity, it is a false futuristic dream – or rather nightmare – to assume that there ever could be a time or society in which there are no commonly honored, indeed sacred principles. That is, in common with any other era, there are sacred principles that prevail in contemporary modern society.

However, moving on to consider the sacred principles of modernity, let me explain how this essay is organized as a whole. I will first discuss in more detail what I mean by the concepts of habit or routine, and how that relates to the category of sacred. In that instance, I discuss a related term, the concept of ritual. This will then lead us on to a discussion of the role of rituals in contemporary society. Having established this theoretical preparation, I tackle the sacred principles of modernity, which are closely related to certain features of North-Atlantic societies during the latter half of the twentieth century. Then, I will continue to discuss how these societies seem to be changing – and whether these changes might indeed undermine the sacred principles of modernity.

## Habits, Routines, and Rituals

As referred to above, the false conception about the "modernity" we live in is constructed out of two false assumptions. First, we tend to think that, along with modernization, habitual action is gradually replaced by the constant reflexivity that is required by modernity. Secondly, the stories of modernization lead us to believe that sacredness is disappearing in a secularizing process in which we will eventually base our entire worldview on rationality and science.

The first false assumption, according to which habitual action is a thing of the past, arises from the way in which we tend to associate habits with tradition. For instance, in the still influential typology of action Max Weber defines action that is guided by custom as "traditional action":

> Strictly traditional behavior, like the reactive type of imitation discussed above, lies very close to the borderline of what can justifiably called meaningfully oriented action, and indeed often on the other side. For it is often a matter of almost automatic reaction to habitual stimuli which guide behavior in a course which has been repeatedly followed. The great bulk of all everyday action to which people have become habitually accustomed approaches this type. Hence, its place in a systematic classification is not merely that of a limiting case because, as will be shown later, attachment to habitual forms can be upheld with varying degrees of self-consciousness and in a variety of senses. In this case the type may shade over into value rationality. (Weber, 1947: 116)

The problem with Weber's formulation is that he links habit or custom with one way in which such action may be justified – that is, by tradition as something we are supposed to honor. Instead, it is important to make an analytical distinction between these two things. I suggest that by the concept of habit or routine we simply refer to behavior in which we are not reflexive or self-conscious of what we do. If and when we are prompted to give an account of it, it is another matter.

In the social science literature there are several concepts used to depict such modes of action. As said, Max Weber among others has talked about "habits," and Emile Durkheim about "mores" or "*moeurs*." Additionally, the concept of "routines" has been discussed in this sense, for instance, by Anthony Giddens. For Michel Foucault the corresponding concept is "non-discursive" or the "unthought," and Pierre Bourdieu has talked about "*doxa*" in this instance.

By the concept *doxa* Bourdieu refers to the universe of undiscussed and undisputed knowledge, on the basis of which people's discourse, arguments, and attitudes arise: "Because the subjective necessity and self-evidence of the commonsense world are validated by the objective consensus on the sense of the world, what is essential *goes without saying because it comes without saying*" (Bourdieu, 1977: 167). Here Bourdieu talks of "knowledge," but as stated earlier it is questionable in what sense we can in fact talk about knowledge when we are discussing routines and the non-discursive. It is certainly not knowledge in the sense of being something that is consciously known to the participants, waiting to be put into words, because any formulation of it instantaneously transforms it, brings it to the realm of the discursive and in doing so changes its nature. We could perhaps speak about "local knowledge" (Geertz, 1983) or "practical reason" (Sahlins, 1976) – that is, the fact that people master and repeatedly perform certain practices without putting them into words or being able to give an account about them at the sleight of hand.

Following such tacit habits in our activity means that our acts are pretty automated. As long as everything goes smoothly following an accustomed procedure, we do not even need to pay attention to what we are doing – our mind might be wandering. When a large number of people behave in a similar fashion – for instance, when rushing from a train and following their paths to the workplaces – it has clear resemblances to a community of ants or bees. However, in all this insect-like behavior there are smaller or larger moments of reflexivity, when we at least have to choose between alternative options. Our mind is not put away by the monotony of the daily grind, it is rather at rest in order to be alert as soon as that is needed. In that sense routines are not an enemy of reflexivity. Rather, they are a precondition for it. Besides, such automation of mental processes is necessary for all learning. Just imagine what it would be like if when listening to or speaking a language one needed to actively memorize the meaning of each term. Mastering a new language or any other skill means that such memorizing has generally become automatic.

Thus, it is obvious that habitual action must not in any sense be deemed "backward" or "traditional" in contrast to modern. Such confusion often arises because of the way people often react to deviations from the expected: the default line of action is defended in the name of tradition, and breaking it is deemed to be wrong and/or immoral.

Indeed, when someone or something deviates from tacit assumptions, it is quite likely that we may become angry or irritated. This reaction led Harold Garfinkel (1984) to believe that the social order based on a shared tacit understanding of routines we follow has an underlying moral basis. However, let me suggest that a moral reaction is only one of the options within which such a situation is handled. Within it, we disapprove of someone's deviation from the expected lines of action by resorting to a norm one should follow, but, for instance, it may as well doubt whether the deviant actor is in his right mind or a foreigner.

However, the option of moral assessment is interesting here because it leads us to the other common confusion about modernity – which is that sacredness is a thing of the past, traditional society. Yet the fact that deviations from default lines of action often lead to angry, emotionally laden reactions suggest otherwise. Although it is incorrect to state that all of the rules we follow in our behavior have a normative basis, strong emotional reactions to certain kinds of deviations – or certain kinds of interpretations of them – show that the deviance in question has some connection with sacred principle.

In his *The Elementary Forms of the Religious Life* (1954), Durkheim links the category of sacred to rituals. The fact that people ascribe sacredness to a person, object, or idea is due to a ritual by which we learn to respect – and also to show our respect – to it. According to Durkheim, the essence of rituals is that sacred things are approached only in a particular manner. For instance, when entering a church one takes off one's hat, bows, or removes one's shoes. The most sacred objects can be approached only by particular people, such as priests.

One of the most interesting aspects of Durkheim's definition is that the link between sacred and ritual is a circular one: one behaves according to ritual rules when entering a sacred object, and sacred thing can be distinguished by the fact that when dealing with them people resort to ritual behavior. However, the point is that rituals sanctify an object. The sacredness does not reside in the object itself, but rather in the special way in which people behave when encountering it. Yet, through repeated rituals performed each time people approach a sacred thing, such a thing – or the ritual that honors it – achieves a deeply felt position in people's minds. If the ritual rules are violated, people may be extremely angry and hurt or scared about the consequences. Thus ritual is the means by which people learn to attach a special, emotional meaning to a particular thing.

But if there are sacred principles in modern society, and if we believe that ritual is the tool by which certain things are made sacred, where are these rituals to be found? Aren't proper rituals also on the wane?

That is the argument advanced by Erving Goffman (1971). According to him, in contemporary society "rituals performed to stand-ins for supernatural entities are everywhere in decay" (63), and what remains are brief, interpersonal rituals. From his viewpoint, greeting a friend or shaking hands are prime examples of such modern rituals.

Nevertheless, even in adopting this stance Goffman did believe that there are sacred things in modern society, even if they are very different in nature from those perhaps found in earlier times or "traditional society."

## What is Sacred in Modernity?

So what is sacred in modern or late modern society? According to Goffman, the brief, interpersonal rituals characteristic of contemporary society sanctify the individual human being. In modern society, rituals are not impressive religious ceremonies but the small interactions that are part of everyday social etiquette. "In situations where we feel momentarily embarrassed and annoyed as people do not give way in the street, as someone in the lift comes too close or as someone wholly impolite interrupts a joke, we are dealing with the sacred that is ingrained in the etiquette prevailing in modern society" (Heiskala, 1991: 97–8). In everyday interaction the role of the sacred, comparable to divinity, is reserved for the individual person. Goffman (1967: 73) quotes Durkheim, who indeed deals with the same question: "The human personality is a sacred thing; one dare not violate it nor infringe its bounds, while at the same time the greatest good is in communion with others" (Durkheim, 1974: 37).

It would be tempting to assume that in earlier times or in "non-western" societies the human personality is particularly sacred. After all, it is often said that modernity cherishes individualism and individuality. The story of modernization from the sixteenth century onward is also the story of the birth of the individual: people learned to think of themselves as autonomous, separate from each other, and possessing a unique personality. Although the particular ways in which the Americans that Goffman studied express their mutual respect for other human beings probably differ from the pattern observed in other countries, I argue that his field of study only dealt with one version of universal rules of politeness.

So is there anything specifically sacred in modernity? To answer that we must consider what modernity is. I suggest that by it we depict the social systems that were built on both sides of the North Atlantic from the sixteenth century onward. There are probably many sources from which these societies derived influence, and many factors affected their development. For instance, they were primarily Judeo-Christian, and the development of the capitalist exchange economy greatly affected their development. Moreover, by the beginning of the twentieth century the nation-state ideology in its various guises had become an important part of the self-consciousness of the citizens. It also meant that in addition to private enterprise, the state became an important player. From the interplay of these factors emerged a loose cultural system we could call modernity.

This already implies one sacred thing that is characteristic of modernity: the nation. It is tempting to argue that an emotional bond to one's "fatherland" is only peculiar to times of crises or to some particularly nationalistic nations, but history shows that this is not the case. In most cases, we take both the nation-state institution and the nationality institution for granted. It is, for instance, commonplace to assume that each individual has a "nationality." We may deny having particularly strong patriotic sentiments, but it is through numerous rituals, such as flying flags, singing national anthems, and inconspicuous everyday-life practices comprising "banal nationalism" (Billig, 1995) that the self-evidence of nation and nationality is produced and maintained.

Another sacred thing in modernity is actually hidden in the very concept by which we depict these societies. Why is it that we choose to talk about modern society or modernity? I suggest it is because we place so much emphasis on social change. By choosing to depict our societies as modern we imply a single world history in which there is only one possible end result, the modern, and we are there already. Thus, by this concept we give the need to be prepared to continuous change a very positive connotation. The fact that the whole society changes, which means that our everyday life is in a continuous gradual change, is associated with getting ahead, becoming increasingly advanced.

It is obvious that change and development are important for us "moderns," but are they really sacred principles? Aren't there very rational reasons to promote the advance of science and technology? These can be justified by, for instance, showing that development has led to a higher standard of living and better health for the majority of the population. Since there are rational reasons to promote development, one does not need to resort to progress as a sacred principle.

Although development *can* be defended on rational grounds, this does not exclude the possibility that it is also cherished as a sacred principle. We must not fall into the trap of drawing an opposition between religion and science, or between sacred principles and rational arguments. Religion and science have sometimes competed as alternative authorities providing a worldview. For instance, the Judeo-Christian religion has made claims about reality, such as about the way in which the world came into being, and natural science has argued against unsubstantiated arguments. However, at this point I do not refer to religion in that sense. Rather, I adopt the definition advanced by Durkheim, who states that a religion does not need to make claims about reality or to include an idea of afterlife. What is common to all religions is that they draw a distinction between profane and sacred, that which is ordinary and that which is honored and cherished. Thus, sacred principles are not the same as unsubstantiated assertions about reality. Rather, they are principles that the members of the religion in question know they should follow in order to "do the right thing." For those who are socialized into the religion in question, sacred principles are not claims to be reflected on and assessed in light of the empirical evidence. Instead, they are strongly and emotionally felt principles that provide the meaning of life. They are the final argument in the sense that other normative arguments about what to do are assessed against them. Science can never provide such existential answers, and in that sense religion and science do not compete with each other.

But why would we need to raise the need to change and develop into a sacred principle, since it is in individuals' self-interest to keep up with the times? One of the reasons is, I suggest, because as humans we are conservatives in a certain sense. The routines we learn are very rewarding because they make our life much easier and enjoyable, and socially shared routines make our social life much more predictable than is the case under conditions of continuous change. A predictable environment also improves people's ontological security, whereas rapid social change can make us feel threatened. We need to have good reasons to happily welcome constant change, as every computer user changing into the next program version knows only too well.

Thus, newness and renewal are sacred principles for us, and that is because they are functional and because there are institutions that promote them. The nation-state system characteristic of modernity has meant that states compete against each other in the global economic system by at best trying to raise the educational level of the national population. Therefore, because it is in the interest of the leadership of each country that citizens try their best to get ahead in life, all methods will be used. As a way of advancing the popular education project, it is likely that if the leadership's objective to raise the population's educational level can be transformed into a civic religion, it will be more effective than by other means.

So if it is possible that development is a sacred principle in modernity, how is it sanctified? What are the rituals through which it is achieved?

There are, of course, highly visible candidates for rituals within academe, such as graduation rituals, but I suggest that these are generally too internal to the university institution to serve well in sanctifying the inner need to develop amongst the entire population. Therefore, we must look elsewhere.

I got a glimpse of this sacred principle of modernity some years ago when I undertook a study about the ways in which ordinary people talk about watching television. When analyzing the interview material, I soon noted a striking phenomenon. When people talk about their viewing habits and about their favorite TV programs, their discourses on the subject of television, their talk has a clearly *moral* tone. There are very few programs that people will freely and plainly admit they like to watch; with the exception of perhaps the evening news, people seem to feel a compelling need to explain, defend, and justify their viewing habits. A closer examination about the character of this moral talk showed that there is a value hierarchy in which soap operas and other fictional programs are at the bottom and factual, informative programs at the top. Norwegian researcher Ingunn Hagen (1994a, 1994b) observed the same phenomenon from the opposite direction. When she studied *Dagsrevyen*, the main TV news program of the Norwegian public broadcasting corporation, she found out that people tend to give an explanation if they for some reason haven't watched it.

What we have here is an illustration of the distinction between sacred and profane, which, according to Durkheim, is common to all religions in the world. This particular distinction is drawn between art and mass culture, between low and high culture, and it underlies the modern civic religion sanctifying development.

In the example outlined above, the high and low distinction appears in the form of a distinction between educationally good and bad programs, fact and fiction, but within the genre of fiction it assumes another form, in which mass culture and sheer entertainment is contrasted with true, modernist art.

The moral denunciation of serials and "mass culture" serves well the civic religion of modernity, because it symbolizes the basic ideals of modernity and the Enlightenment; a body of thought that both condemns "mass culture" and produces it as a social construction. The central characteristic of a "high culture" artifact, such as a novel, is its expected novelty of form. As soon as a story form is identified as a recognizable genre, it is on its way to becoming "mass culture." A modern author who wants him- or herself to be taken seriously as an artist is not supposed to repeat old forms, and the storylines of high cultural narratives are supposed to be surprising, unpredictable. Over and over again high culture should question old forms and ways of thinking. How well high culture actually lives up to its ideal, succeeds in endlessly surprising its consumers, is a different question. In its never-ending quest for novelty and individuality high culture is a modern artform. That is where it derives its value: it is supposed to enlighten its consumers, to teach new things, create new forms, or at least to question old ones. In the modern, "pure" aesthetic disposition, form becomes more important than content or function. Any object – for instance a photograph of an old woman's wrinkled hands (see Bourdieu, 1984: 45) – becomes an art object when it is perceived from the pure aesthetic point of view, when form takes over from function. But, unless it is presented in a new light or from a new angle, it can be done only once. Simple repetition of old forms makes it mass production and mass culture.

Modern art has provided the mental horizon for assessing traditional art or mass culture. For instance, folk tales belonging to a particular tale type or genre consist of the same abstractly defined narrative events, or "functions" as Vladimir Propp (1975) called them, in the same chronological order, forming a "metanarrative," the variants of which are individual tales. Similarly, individual episodes of a television serial are variants of a serial format, a concept that defines the metanarrative and the properties of the leading characters. Serials are modern tales. Since these story types repeat a familiar format, from a "high culture" perspective they are of minor value or quality.

Because the modern notion of art is capable of expressing the need for constant change so central to modernity, with the Enlightenment and its aftermath, artistic practices have come to be thought of as instruments capable of being utilized to improve specific mental or behavioral attributes of the general population (Bennett, 1992: 28). The public funding of the arts affects the "intellectual climate" of the nation, which is reflected in the discourses within which cultural products are assessed. For instance, state cultural policy institutionalizes the division into "high" and "low" culture: art or other preferred "cultural activity," which (also) gains public subsidy, and "mass culture," which functions according to commercial principles.

The main idea behind the modern conception of high culture, the expectation that cultural products that deserve to be treated as art should not repeat old forms or conventions but should create something new, needs no justification. Instead, the modern category of art lends an unquestioned and compelling sense of sacredness to the same principle needed also in other, more practical areas of life. Because of rapid continuous social changes brought about by a global market economy and technological development related to it, to survive and find employment modern individuals have to be ready to constantly adjust to changing conditions, to develop themselves and to question given truths. Although such an attitude is in the self-interest of any individual who wants to be successful, it is far from a small requirement. It is rather characteristic of humans everywhere that we tend to develop routinized, "traditional" forms of thought and action, and to build a feeling of continuity and self-identity around them. Therefore, in order for modern societies to be successful in instilling a readiness for change to the majority population, it needs a religious grounding (in the Durkheimian sense), and art as a sacred category provides this. It is also in the interest of nation-states that are trying to be globally competitive in the market that they should promote art, which thus serves as an element of popular education and overall behavior modification.

## How does Globalization Affect Modernity?

At the beginning of this essay I asked whether globalization will undermine the sacred principles of modernity. Now that I have outlined what I consider to be those principles, let me address that question, but before doing this I need to define what I mean by globalization.

Actually globalization is in my view a tricky concept. It has been used as a label for certain developmental trends in the world system that became increasingly apparent during the 1980s and 1990s. The discussion was started by economists, who noted rapid increases in cross-border flows of capital and goods during this period. In other words, the world is becoming a single marketplace. Political scientists who joined the discussion emphasized that, alongside the economic developments, there is a political process or trend that favors free trade. In fact, the neoliberalist ideology, which has gained popularity during the last couple of decades, has gained more popularity in many countries is the reason why the interregional and intercontinental flows of money, products, and people have grown and why that has also meant that global companies are more influential than has previously been the case. A similar development has also taken place within nation-states or other political units: in many countries, the state has withdrawn from certain sectors of society and given way to market steering.

It has also been noted that during these two decades, the socialist block fell apart because of the collapse of the Soviet Union. This probably strengthened the neoliberalist political trend since the effectiveness of administrative steering and scientific, state-centered planning of society lost much of its credibility.

Finally, it has been pointed out that if by globalization one refers to the development by which different regions of the world become increasingly dependent on each other, then this is not a particularly novel trend. This development was already evident during the age of exploration several hundred years ago. Thus, if one wishes to argue that globalization is a particularly compelling concept in today's world, it needs to be shown that globalization has occurred in distinct waves and that the most recent wave is somehow particularly intensive and qualitatively different from the previous ones.

I do not think that globalization theorists have been sufficiently convincing in that sense. Besides, as one considers all of the developments that have been associated with globalization, it becomes apparent that it is not a single uniform process. Rather, as stated above, it is a term used to refer to all kinds of recent changes, and one which is more convincing in some contexts than in others. It is, of course, true that parallel developments necessarily interact with each other, but that is not the same as saying that globalization is a single process or that there is a coherent force behind it. Yet, it is treated as a force in itself; instead of wondering how exactly recent trends are related to each other or how they affect each other, globalization is often treated as an explanation to emergent phenomena.

So in that sense it cannot really be said that globalization has affected the sacred principles of modernity, but I do think that some of the changes associated with globalization have had a bearing on the way in which we now think about art and mass culture and human betterment.

The worldwide privatization development through which administrative steering is increasingly replaced by market steering has affected – and continues to affect – the prevalent notions of art and mass culture. This is particularly apparent in European societies, which on the whole have been more state-centered than the United States. This development is due to one additional aspect or function of the high–low distinction.

I argue that cultural policy serves in legitimating the social structure that a state-centered system maintains.

The modern notion of art is at the heart of the legitimating function of cultural policy. In short, the modern concept of art implies a distinction drawn between "art" and "not-art," and that in turn implies people with good and bad taste: a distinction between a cultural elite and common people. The idea of cultural policy is basically a popular education project, wherein the "common people" are refined by teaching them to love "high culture" or what are defined as "cultural activities." This project of popular education is endless, because the modern notion of art is conditioned by popular taste. According to the modern notion, art is supposed to express the artist's "creativity" and "individuality," to question and break traditional forms, or to create a new language of expression. The constant need for renewal within the modern notion of art or "high brow" means that, should a piece of work gain much popularity, in a way it ceases to be art. It is, of course, still appreciated as a single exemplary work and probably put on display in an art museum, but imitating the form in later works is out of the question; the *avant-garde* must already be moving on in its eternal quest for something "new." State cultural policy supports and institutionalizes such a practical definition of art. That is because the general idea of cultural policy is to support such cultural production or activity that would not exist without state sponsorship.

The fact that the distinction drawn between art and not-art is relational, and dependent upon the existing situation of the field of art, means that the underlying division between the cultural elite and the common people is also fluid and relational. To be more precise, the distinction in question is part of a discourse that defines a gallery of subject positions defined by good and bad taste. We can all take different positions in the discussion about art and popular culture, or about particular works of art, but playing with that discourse does not write it out of existence. For instance, an appreciation of a mass cultural product in the form of camp constructs an elite position. Although individuals may have different opinions about what constitutes good and bad art or taste, the idea of high culture expresses at once a symbol and a concretization of the general idea that as individuals we should develop ourselves, and thus that some people, the intellectuals or the cultural elite, are better equipped to make value judgments. By valuing good art, or by acknowledging that there is high culture, we contribute to acknowledging an expert position from which to define and direct the popular education project. In that sense the category of high culture naturalizes and legitimates social hierarchies based on expertise in social affairs.

Now, since the state is withdrawing from many spheres and administrative steering is in those areas replaced by market steering, one might expect that there is also less need to sanctify expertise by supporting high art. Parallel with it, we must also remember that cultural production is one of the spheres in which the position of state-funded activity is challenged by the private, commercial sector.

Although there have been no drastic cuts in the culture spending of states, the fact that social hierarchies are being renegotiated has put the justification of cultural policy, that is the state support for cultural products representing "legitimate taste" (Bourdieu, 1984), in jeopardy. Besides, the changed competitive situation of many European state-owned television companies with their "public broadcasting" ethos has forced them to reconsider their program policy. They may still emphasize their "quality programming," but with their profile they now have to compete for their "market share" of the audience.

Changes associated with globalization might also affect the previous sacredness of high culture via another mechanism. Namely, the last 20 to 30 years have also witnessed increased immigration to countries that previously used to have a negative net migration rate, with Finland as one of several such examples. As a consequence, nationhood and nationalism have been called into question in various ways. For instance, in countries that used to have a fairly homogeneous population it was unquestioned to conceive of the nation in terms of a shared religion, "race," or cultural tradition. Now, such tacit and unproblematic notions of the nation face a crisis in these conditions of increased ethnic diversity. If the nation is defined, for instance, on the basis of a shared cultural heritage, it excludes those new citizens that do not share it. If the state promotes the national culture by, for instance, strongly supporting national art, it in effect contributes to reactionary nationalist sentiments, which are also otherwise on the rise under such conditions.

Therefore, one could assume that nation-states are more careful in promoting national art and culture, but of course this could only mean that one emphasizes international trends and multiculturalism in the state's cultural policy.

However, uncertainty over how to define the nation and what happens to it under increasing global pressures does not necessarily mean that one of the sacred principles of modernity, the civic religion of patriotism, is weakening. The concerns for nation-states and national culture in the globalizing world have also resulted in defensive re-actions. In the face of perceived threats to "national identity," there appears to be a renaissance of national sentiments. For instance, recent years have seen a marked revival of British film production and success at the box office, and a similar phenomenon is now occurring in Finland, where home-produced films are gaining in popularity. Similarly, in Finnish television, both in public and commercial channels, there are now more domestic TV serials than ever before. One might assume that these changes have arisen because the public has changed its mind and become more patriotic, but a more probable explanation is that the films and programs have a greater appeal to popular taste. The "golden years" of cultural protectionism and popular education administered by national states nurtured a "climate of opinion" both among artists as well as art and media critics that preferred "art films" and artistic TV productions.[1] Now that social hierarchies are being renegotiated in many ways, European artistic production also tries to appeal to popular taste.

By way of conclusion, since globalization itself is only a name that depicts many, contradictory parallel developments, it is quite difficult to predict how the times are changing as a whole. One could expect that there are traces of modernity, which promotes the idea that it is the inner duty of every citizen to continuously develop secularization in the state religion and to engage in life-long learning. But it might well be that what we are now witnessing in Europe is a separation of the state and the church of Enlightenment. After all, the gospel of self-improvement is hardly less loudly preached and heard in the United States, although the role of the state as a patron of art and as an agent in general is smaller. It may be that we are witnessing a reformation in which the nation-states are increasingly replaced by private, often global companies as promoters of research and development. Parallel with this process, the national churches of modernity may merge into a global religion.

It might, of course, also be the case that the sacredness of the duty of every individual to develop themselves is gradually fading and giving way to a new conception of the role of individuals on this globe. What this new mentality might be like, I do not know, but whatever it is it will develop its own totems and rituals. In any case, I think it would be an error to assume that all sacredness is disappearing from the world. There will always be sacred principles in the human reality.

If that is the case, how should we relate to it as cultural studies people? At the beginning of this chapter I said that we must be careful not to lose sight of sacred things in our own contemporary society, which is difficult because we can easily overlook what is self-evident. But now that I have pointed out certain sacred principles in modernity, should we take sides for or against them? For instance, is cultural studies for lowbrow or highbrow, somehow a way of negotiating beyond the polarities of this debate?

In my view, truly critical thought, which I consider to be the aim of cultural studies, cannot take sides in such battles. As cultural analysts our outlook on life may sound quite cynical and nihilistic, because given any situation, we can only analyze how certain appealing discourses and related subject positions are constructed, and what consequences it all has to relations of power and politics. And, if not simultaneously, the next day we must be ready to scrutinize our own starting points in that analysis: what were the premises on which the argument was built and what was therefore left unnoticed? I know some cultural studies people think that cultural studies is in the service of good, acceptable values against all bad, but such a starting point all too easily compromises the scholar's readiness to question everything. I suggest we leave final answers to others and instead concentrate on finding new ways to think. To quote Michel Foucault (1986: 9), the primary object must be to "free thought from what it silently thinks, and so enable it to think differently."

## Notes

1 That is how Tytti Soila (1998) explains the developments of Finnish film production. In the 1960s the older generation of film workers still considered themselves as masters of a craft, employed by the film industry, but the younger generation saw it as self-evident that the state would support film production in a similar

manner to its support of other art forms. While a state subsidy system for domestic film was created, the new generation tended to consider the production companies as their antagonists which, to protect their commercial interests, confine all artistic ambitions that the aspiring directors might be capable of. Consequently, the films made became more artistic, but the number of films produced as well as audience figures for domestic films dropped dramatically. It was not until the 1990s, with a renewed state subsidy system and a new generation of film directors, that the audiences for domestic films have begun to rise again.

## References

Beck, Ulrich, Anthony Giddens and Scott Lash (1994) *Reflexive Modernization: Politics, Tradition and Aesthetics in the Modern Social Order* (Stanford, CA: Stanford University Press).

Bennett, Tony (1992) "Putting Policy into Cultural Studies," in Lawrence Grossberg et al. (eds.), *Cultural Studies* (New York: Routledge), pp. 23–37.

Billig, Michael (1995) *Banal Nationalism* (London: Sage).

Bourdieu, Pierre (1984) *Distinction: A Social Critique of the Judgement of Taste* (Cambridge, MA: Harvard University Press).

Bourdieu, Pierre (1977) *Outline of a Theory of Practice* (Cambridge: Cambridge University Press).

Durkheim, Emile (1954) *The Elementary Forms of the Religious Life* (London: Allen & Unwin).

Foucault, Michel (1986) *The Use of Pleasure:* Volume 2 of *The History of Sexuality* (New York: Viking).

Garfinkel, Harold (1984) *Studies in Ethnomethodology* (Cambridge: Polity Press).

Geertz, Clifford (1973) *The Interpretation of Cultures* (New York: Basic Books).

Giddens, Anthony (1994) "Living in the Post-Traditional Society," Ulrich Beck, Anthony Giddens and Scott Lash (eds.), *Reflexive Modernization: Politics, Tradition and Aesthetics in the Modern Social Order* (Stanford, CA: Stanford University Press), pp. 56–109.

Goffman, Erving (1967) *Interaction Ritual: Essays on Face-to-Face Behavior* (New York: Pantheon Books).

Goffman, Erving (1971) *Relations in Public* (New York: Pantheon Books).

Hagen, Ingunn (1994a) "The Ambivalences of TV News Viewing: Between Ideals and Everyday Practices," *European Journal of Mass Communication*, 9: 193–220.

Hagen, Ingunn (1994b) "Expectations and Consumption Patterns in TV News Viewing," *Media, Culture & Society*, 16: 415–28.

Heiskala, Risto (1991) "Goffmanista semioottiseen sosiologiaan" [From Goffman to Semiotic Sociology], *Sosiologia*, 28: 90–107.

Jameson, Fredric (1992) *Postmodernism, Or the Cultural Logic of Late Capitalism* (London and New York: Verso).

Propp, Vladimir (1975) *Morphology of the Folktale* (Austin and London: University of Texas Press).

Sahlins, Marshall (1976) *Culture and Practical Reason* (Chicago: The University of Chicago Press).

Soila, Tytti (1998) "Finland," in Tytti Soila, Astrid Söderbergh and Gunnar Iversen, *Nordic National Cinemas* (London: Routledge), pp. 31–95.

Weber, Max (1947) *The Theory of Social and Economic Organization*, trans. A.M. Henderson and Talcott Parsons (New York: Free Press).

# 10

# Engagement through Alienation: Parallels of Paradox in World Music and Tourism in Sarawak, Malaysia[1]

## Gini Gorlinski

### Prologue: Cultural Studies and the Issue of Ethnography

Students and scholars in the ethnography-based humanities and social sciences are ever more avidly investigating issues of race, class, gender, and sense of identity as formative factors in cultural practices. In this sense, these disciplines have been converging on the terrain of cultural studies, which, as addressed in the introduction to this volume, has from its advent been a fundamentally interdisciplinary undertaking. There remains, however, a significant difference between cultural studies and its kindred ethnographic fields, which lies in the nature of the ethnography itself. As revealed in the commentaries of Chris Rojek and Bryan Turner (2001), John Storey (1996a, 1996b), Charmaine McEachern (1998) and others, the ethnographic practices of cultural studies diverge from those of their humanistic and social scientific counterparts in several, interconnected ways. First, ethnographic work in cultural studies carries an intrinsic political agenda, which often embodies an activist-like mission to expose the manner in which "control and exploitation operat[e] in the present day" (Rojek and Turner, 2000: 633), especially in capitalist societies. Secondly, audience (i.e., consumer) reception of cultural "products" has been the primary emphasis of cultural studies inquiry. When production has been addressed, the "industry," rather than individual makers and creators of cultural commodities (in the broadest sense of the term), has typically held the spotlight. Finally,

241

cultural studies has exhibited a tendency to forward rather ambitious theoretical propositions based largely on research conducted not only in Western urban societies, but also from a solidly Western academic and aesthetic perspective. That non-Western communities might (and often do) perceive these phenomena quite differently is rarely addressed.

One of the drawbacks of the current orientation of cultural studies is its frequent failure to acknowledge on multiple levels the positive, creative outcomes of the activities it addresses. Many have chosen to analyze cultural commodities in terms of the opportunities for resistance they indirectly – if not unintentionally – their respective consumers. Although resistance itself can count as both a positive and creative use of cultural productions, when we consider that (a) any effort to cultivate public awareness of a community that has been shadowed by a more powerful Other constitutes resistance, and (b) the identity of that dominant Other will shift as we move through different levels of a given field of cultural production, then such analyses can be rendered meaningless if not properly qualified. To gain a reasonably "accurate" understanding of the social significance of cultural productions, ethnographic work must address not only how the phenomena are received, but also how they are perceived, especially on the part of their creators. As stressed more than a decade ago by John Street (1987: 26 in Storey, 1996b: 112) when discussing popular music, "[t]he politics of music are a mixture of state policies, business practices, artistic choices and audience responses." The same holds for other popular or commodified cultural practices.

Albeit hardly exhaustive, the following cultural-studies-oriented analysis of the commonalities between world music and tourism in Sarawak, Malaysia addresses on some level each of the formative political elements identified by Street. In contrast to most work in cultural studies, however, the ethnographic emphasis is on the intentions and interpretations of the individual makers and mediators of these cultural productions, rather than on the recipients of them. Indeed, it is the creative force, the first child of resistance, which ultimately carries the capacity to catalyze social change. Until the multiplicity of perceptions on all fronts of cultural production are investigated, acknowledged, and taken seriously, it is likely that cultural studies will remain, as Rojek and Turner (2000: 629) have contended, a politically ineffectual endeavor, despite its claims and intentions to the contrary. Broad-based ethnographic and comparative research would be a step toward seeing the trees for the forest, and ultimately toward the effective and humanistic realization of the social and political reforms so championed by the discipline.

## World Music and Tourism: A Provocative Analogy

"Travel the World with Putumayo." The slogan arches colorfully across the cardboard display rack of world music CDs on the Putumayo label, enriching the international section of the local record store, and also, perhaps, the counter of the hip corner coffee shop. The analogy between world music and tourism offers an appealing image to a broad consumer base, and has indeed been a marketing ploy since the world music trend was recognized (and awarded a market category) in the late 1980s.[2] World music as tourism has also been a thematic thread in much of the academic literature. However, analysis of the analogy has been cursory at best, ultimately yielding to the currently more prestigious frames of transnational capitalist economy, cultural imperialism, and the related tug of war between homogeneity and diversity.[3] Martin Roberts (1992: 233), for instance, clearly recognized the commonly perceived parallel between world music and tourism when he succinctly dismissed the overly cynical stance that "listening to world music is a form of musical tourism whose function, like that of tourism, is to give consumers the illusion of authentic engagement with other cultures while in fact insulating them from their more sober political and economic realities." The conceptual comparison stops there, however, with no time or space for critical assessment of the issue. Having made its momentary visit, then, the metaphor evaporates, a lexical tourist leaving an ephemeral echo in Roberts's analysis, as well as in numerous others that have appeared over the last decade. According to my itinerary, however, the trip is not over. Here, I embark on an expedition into the parallels between world music and tourism, and, in so doing, visit a place where world music and tourism stand not in a relationship of merely metaphoric equivalence, but, in many respects, one of synonymic equation. This place is Sarawak, Malaysia.

On the last weekend of August 1998, the Malaysian state of Sarawak hosted the first Rainforest World Music Festival (RWMF) just outside Kuching, the state capital. Since its inception, the RWMF has been staged annually, always at the same venue. Coordinated by the Sarawak

Tourism Board and held at a major government-supported tourist destination, the RWMF indeed beckons a study of the functional and qualitative overlaps between world music and tourism. While on the surface the event may maintain an appearance of running smoothly,[4] some of the operational undercurrents of the RWMF betray a capricious and rocky river bed that has the power to undermine the cross-cultural or cross-musical connection to which the Festival ultimately aspires. It is such incongruities that, at least for the cynics to which Martin Roberts alluded, relegate both world music and tourism to the status of "illusion," of insubstantial surface phenomena.

The river analogy continually crept into my thoughts throughout the composition of this essay. For those unfamiliar with the character of Borneo waterways, the upper stretches are scattered with rapids that, when the river is high, may become treacherous, but when the river is low, may virtually vanish – or vice versa. The lower portions of Borneo rivers flow with slow-moving, often cloudy water, sometimes inhabited by crocodiles. Just as the upper and lower segments of the rivers contrast, so do the communities who typically utilize them. Borneo is ethnically, culturally, and linguistically a diverse region, and the peoples who live in the lower-lying areas are distinct from those who reside near the headwaters. Regardless of who inhabits and uses which realm, riverine communities maintain an intimate relationship with their host waterways. Necessarily, these people know all of the river's quirks of character. It is only by watching the water and recognizing its subsurface idiosyncrasies – albeit sometimes through negative encounter – that anyone can come to navigate, negotiate, and respect the river as an effective and powerful means to a given destination. We can view tourism, world music, and the Rainforest World Music Festival in the same manner.

My intention here is to assess some of the literal and conceptual links between the RWMF and tourism, predominantly through contemplation of *local* perceptions of the event, especially on the part of the organizers and performing artists. In the first major section of my discussion, "Modes of Engagement," I present examples of some of the means by which audience members, musicians, and Festival organizers have realized a feeling of active encounter – of engagement, of connection – with peoples and musics of different heritages or backgrounds. The second portion of the chapter, "Modes of Alienation," exposes some of the rough sub-surface contours, providing counter-illustrations of ways in which the RWMF has revealed and reinforced cultural distance, thus defusing those cross-cultural connections it has ostensibly generated. By shooting the rapids of the Rainforest World Music Festival, then, I aim to provoke review of the effects and effectiveness of world music, both musically and socially, as well as stimulate re-consideration of the status of world music as a truly global phenomenon (phenomenologically speaking).

## Modes of Engagement

World music luminary David Byrne recently denied any substantive similarity between world music and tourism:

> [The] interest in music not like that made in our own little villages . . . is not, as it's often claimed, cultural tourism, because once you've let something in, let it grab hold of you, you're forever changed. Of course, you can also listen and remain completely unaffected and unmoved – like a tourist. Your loss. (Byrne, 1999)

While Byrne's view appears to be quite the opposite of that of the world music detractors so quickly dismissed by Roberts, both views nevertheless share a notion of the tourist experience as insignificant, if not also illegitimate. For Roberts's cynics, this assumption affirms the affinity between world music and tourism. For Byrne, it negates it. The difference between the two perspectives lies primarily in the placement of "blame" for the perceived negative impact of tourism. The cynics described by Roberts hold the tourist *product* to be homogeneously "inauthentic." Any feeling of cultural connection generated by it, then, would be phony. World music, as another *product* exhibiting functional and aesthetic commonalities with tourism, would therefore fall into the same condemned category. Byrne, as a world music practitioner, faults the *consumer*, rather than the product, for what he considers to be the impotence of tourism. From his perspective, tourists are homogeneously impervious to impression, thereby rendering tourism inconsequential. By contrast, Byrne claims that world music is transformative, in that its musicians and enthusiasts are not only impressed, but are indeed altered by it. Despite recognizing a shared pursuit in world music and tourism of the culturally and aesthetically unfamiliar, Byrne nevertheless finds the two enterprises to be *effectually* incomparable; world music makes an impact, tourism does not.

Like Byrne, those who have either blatantly or obliquely acknowledged the intersections and parallels between tourism and world music,[5] have typically maintained a classic negative stance toward tourism that ultimately precludes exploration of the positive, similarly engaging elements of both enterprises. The fact is that both world music and tourism *are* engaging as products as well as experiences. Why else would tourism have become the world's largest industry by the late twentieth century (Garrisson, 1989 in Wood, 1997: 1),[6] and world music by the same time have become the fastest-expanding section of major record stores (see Taylor, 1997: 1)? The key to weighing the shared characteristics of tourism and world music lies in a non-evaluative approach to the issue. Passing qualitative judgment based on objectivist notions of authenticity or subjective ideas of effectual legitimacy is pointless.[7] Rather, we need to investigate the means by which tourism and world music are authenticated and legitimated – that is, the ways in which they engage their respective, and often overlapping constituencies.

## World music in traditional houses

Since its inception in 1998, the setting of the annual Rainforest World Music Festival has been the Sarawak Cultural Village (SCV), a "living museum" overseen by the Sarawak Ministry of Tourism. Situated about 45 minutes from the capital city of Kuching, the SCV occupies a tract of land flanked by rainforested slopes on one side, and by the Damai Beach Resort on the other. Like similar institutions that have emerged in Southeast Asia over the past 25 years or so,[8] the SCV consists of replicas of houses of the most prominent ethnic groups in the region, "built according to authentic styles and replete with real, traditional artifacts."[9] Upon entering these houses, guests have the opportunity to interact with representatives of (but not necessarily from) the various communities, and thereby gain an idea of the lifestyle that is, or at one time was, characteristic of the diverse peoples of Sarawak. In a single afternoon, for example, a guest could observe a woman weaving in an Iban longhouse, participate in a top-spinning competition outside a Malay house, and dance to *sampé'* plucked lute music on an Orang Ulu ("Upriver People") longhouse veranda. As flavorfully expressed on the SCV website:

> This activity-packed Village seeks to tickle all the human senses – the
> visual impact of the traditional lines of the ethnic houses set against a

dramatic landscape, the enchanting cacophony of traditional sounds and music on the ears, the exquisite taste and aroma of ethnic delicacies, the dexterous feel of finely-crafted handiwork and the excitement of unique games. (http://www.sarawakculturalvillage.com)

It is certainly difficult to imagine a more vivid, more memorable environment in which to hold the RWMF.

In tandem with the unique setting of the Sarawak Cultural Village, the festival strives to engage the guests with an enduring sense not only of having "been there," but also of having "done that." That is, the aim is to evoke a feeling of experience, rather than mere attendance at the Rainforest World Music Festival. Contributing monumentally to the achievement of this objective is the structure of the event itself. The RWMF is not simply a series of staged performances. Rather, it consists of numerous small, interactive afternoon "workshops," as they were called in 1998 and 2001, or afternoon "concerts" (albeit informal ones), as they were called in 1999 and 2000, which complement the larger, longer, formally staged evening shows.[10] The afternoon sessions (23 of them the first year, and 22 in the second) are held concurrently in the various houses, and are intended to provide an arena in which the musicians are not only able to discuss their traditions, but most importantly (and hopefully), to experiment with new sounds and sound structures by combining in spontaneous ensemble with other festival participants. These workshops are by no means a mere garnish to more substantive evening performance entrees. They are central to the RWMF event, and, most significantly, fortify the feeling of engagement that is fundamental to cultural or ethnic tourism, as well as to world music. In the intimate atmosphere of the "authentic ethnic houses," visitors bear witness to popular and traditional musicians "connecting" (either theoretically or actually) in creative interchange. In itself, this impromptu format delivers an impression that "this is *really* happening."

The evening shows take place primarily, if not entirely outside (although the SCV did use its spacious indoor theater for half of the night-time performances in 1999). For some of the festival goers, this outdoor setting greatly enhanced the concert atmosphere. As expressed by one Hong Kong visitor, it is "... far better [to be] here in the open than to be cooped up in an auditorium" (Lugun, 1998: 5). Of course, any event anywhere can take place in an auditorium. The RWMF, on the other hand, fed by the sensations generated by the mountains, the forest, the ocean, the "ethnic houses," the darkness, the tropical heat, the plethora of mosquitoes, and indeed the *rain*, engages its guests in what is hoped to be an unparalleled experience not only of music, but also of people, place, and rainforest environment. This climate, literally and figuratively, has consequently engaged a larger and larger audience in each year of the festival's production.

## World music and tourism: cultivators of the aesthetic

In Malaysia, as well as other "developing" countries, images produced by ethnic tourism can be especially important on account of their power to shape perceptions of local culture, and by extension, the nation, both domestically and internationally. Understandably, such nations have much at stake here, as they struggle to shed what is typically perceived as a negative status – "developing," "pre-modern," "pre-industrial," "agrarian," "Third World" – accorded them by the superpowers in the global arena. The tourism industry, then, along with the images generated by it, is frequently monitored and mediated by the state (see Wood, 1997: 2) to ensure congruity with national ideals. In this context, the concept of culture itself operates differently than it does in a strictly academic setting. Here, "culture" is limited to the aesthetic. As Michel Picard and Robert E. Wood (1993: 90) have articulated:

> "culture" is not understood as the anthropologists' broadly defined conception of the "total range of activities and ideas of a group of people with shared traditions," but is narrowed down to those aspects of culture that are subject to aesthetic appreciation, namely artistic expressions.

Malaysia is in many respects a textbook case. "Culture," as perceived by the state, is essentially reduced here to the "visible, or at least, detachable in some way: handicrafts, performing arts, food, architecture, festivals, sports and pastimes, and folklore" (King, 1992: 33). The marketing blurb from the Sarawak Cultural Village quoted earlier is exemplary of this orientation.

In this monitored environment, a symbiotic relationship obtains between cultural tourism and the music that is promoted as part of it. Music, as one of those ostensibly "detachable" traditions that constitutes culture, feeds the tourist industry, while tourism is considered a channel through which to develop the local arts, as well as instill a sense of pride in local ethnicity.[11] Thus, music becomes a critical element in the maintenance of cultural integrity. It should come as no surprise, then, that music and tourism have both played an active part in Malaysia's national development plans (Chopyak, 1987: 450; King, 1992: 30).[12]

Placed in the context of tourism, musics that carry or project a sense of local ethnicity are aestheticized not only through their detachment from broader sociocultural matrices, but also through efforts to "develop" or "modernize" them in such a way as to resonate with a diverse, cosmopolitan, and international community. This process might entail the commodification of traditional forms with minimal adjustment, or the merging of local musics with globally popular styles.[13] Both modes of development have played a role in the RWMF. Professionalization and popularization of traditional musics were definite aims of Haji Mohammed Tuah Jais, the chairman of the RWMF Organizing Committee in 1999 and 2000. As he explained to the *Borneo Post* (BERNAMA, August 22, 2000), "We want to inject professionalism among local musicians so as not to be left behind by tribes from participating countries in promoting their cultural music." The ideal of modernization through musical mixture, on the other hand, rings clear in the statement of Dublin Unting, Sarawak's Assistant Minister for Culture and the chairman of the 1998 RWMF Organizing Committee:

> We believe that Sarawak has a lot to offer and our rich and colorful cultures have been our main selling point in our promotion of Sarawak as a tourist destination. Blending beautifully with these diverse cultures is the wide variety of melodious traditional music of Sarawak's native people.
>
> The Rainforest World Music Festival will provide a perfect opportunity to bring together our local music forms and fuse them with those of the western world in a style that is hopefully enjoyable for listeners.
>
> The presence of world class musicians made this festival particularly interesting. We hope that in their interaction with local groups, our visitors will be inspired to new heights of creativity and innovation which will mutually benefit both parties. (*The Rainforest World Music Festival*, August 29–30, 1998 program booklet, 2)

It is through such aestheticization that local culture becomes globally accessible, local music becomes "world music," and Sarawak engages and is engaged by domestic and foreign populations. In this way, "tradition" begins to shed its broadly held image of "backwardness" in the cosmopolitan local eye, to be donned as a prestigious symbol of unique identity and heritage at the global table. Such dynamics are not particular to Sarawak, Malaysia. Jocelyne Guilbault (1993a: 42) has also realized in her work in the Caribbean that "for the small and industrially developing countries, world music has in many ways contributed to the redefinition of the local." I would submit that re-definition and re-conceptualization of the local are actually among the primary intentions (not mere epiphenomena) of both the cultural tourism industry, and much of the "world music" emanating from these areas. In Sarawak, world music and tourism indeed seem to epitomize the "new aesthetic form of the global imagination," as Veit Erlmann (1996: 428) has described it, "an emergent way of capturing the present historical moment and the total reconfiguration of space and cultural identity characterizing societies around the globe." At the Rainforest World Music Festival, involvement with aestheticized forms of local music becomes symbolic of global engagement, an enactment of global imagination. It is appealing, it is captivating for locals and non-locals alike.[14]

## Aestheticized culture and educational outreach

Aestheticization and the engagement engendered by it carry a tempting educational hook, often overlooked by academics, yet exploited by world music and tourism industry professionals.[15] By adopting the technological and, to an extent, stylistic resources of the dominant society, less powerful individuals, communities, and nations maximize their exposure, and draw attention to their unique circumstance. More than a decade ago, Peter Jowers had already realized the significance of world music in this context in the UK:

> In an increasingly multi-cultural Britain, diverse ethnic groups and particularly second generation citizens have found 'world music' a way of communicating their difference to a wider British audience and in turn have been attracted to other musics expressive of similar experiences here. (Jowers, 1993: 68)

Similarly, anthropologist Steven Feld acknowledged the educational potential of world music, yet went a step further by tapping that resource – rather than merely identifying it – in his own work. In

1991, Feld produced *Voices of the Rainforest*, a collection of environmental sounds and songs from the Kaluli people of Papua New Guinea, with whom he had undertaken his fieldwork in the 1980s. The CD is unique in two significant ways. First, the recordings were artistically edited and electronically merged to create an uninterrupted sonic impression, rather than left virtually untouched in more typical, academic, documentary format. Secondly, Feld released the recordings through the popular music circuit (Rykodisc), rather than through one of the standard academic channels (Smithsonian Folkways, Nonesuch Explorer, Barenreiter, etc.). His intention was to reach beyond the comparatively thin stratum of intellectuals and academic institutions comprising the consumer base of a primarily ethnographic recording. Working through and with the resources of the dominant society – in this instance, the popular music industry – Feld aimed to generate an awareness of the Kaluli, to stimulate concern about the precariousness of their lifestyle in the late twentieth century, and, ultimately, to catalyze action on their behalf (see Feld, 1994: 284–5).[16]

Especially in developing nations, world music and tourism often share an educational objective. Both industries, it must be recalled, often operate as tools of nation-building, and consequently, are as much, if not sometimes more, directed toward a domestic consumership as an international one. Unfortunately, this fact has been obscured in much of the theoretical literature, where tourism and world music have often been analyzed from a blatantly Western perspective, and depicted as pitched primarily to a Western audience.[17] Such orientations essentially strip non-Western countries, as well as many Western minority communities, of any agency in the employment and re-conceptualization of either tourism or the world music phenomenon to meet their local needs.

The Sarawak Cultural Village and the Rainforest World Music Festival are certainly directed in part toward international visitors in their aestheticization of local practices, but on the domestic front they are also largely propelled by educational ambitions. The educational aim of the SCV is evident in the institution's arrangement as an interactional "living-museum," its staffing procedures (discussed in the next section), its coordination of on- and off-site school programs and other events,[18] as well as its maintenance of the music group, Tuku' Kamé'. Tuku' Kamé', meaning "Our Beat" in local Malay dialect, is a multi-ethnic "world music" ensemble of SCV employees that performs daily at the Village. The group has been featured at each of the RWMF

productions. Under the directorship of Narawi Hj. Rashidi, Tuku'
Kamé' performs compositions that aesthetically synthesize various
aspects of local vocal and instrumental traditions with globally recognized popular music idioms. Jane Lian, resident manager of the SCV
and one of Narawi's supervisors, admiringly articulated the aims and
advantages of his and the group's approach:

> It is his [Narawi's] dream to promote to the world music industry . . . Sar-
> awak traditional instruments. So, they're taking this opportunity to
> promote the interest among the younger generation, and to also the
> tourists, to learn more about . . . Sarawak traditional instruments. (Jane
> Lian, September 7, 1999)

Jane Lian then commented that one of the primary "breakthroughs"
made by the band was to shift the perception of Sarawakian instruments away from any ritual function, to a strictly aesthetic one − "for
pleasure, for relaxation, and for entertainment . . . and for hobbies"
(September 7, 1999). In this way, she continued,

> We, we hope that this is the gimmick to get the younger generations
> particularly . . . to get interested in the traditional instruments. So, once
> they get hooked on it, there will be interest there to know, "where did
> this come from?" . . . How did it all [get] started? Because I enjoy playing
> it so much, I begin to get interested to know the roots of all these
> instruments. (Jane Lian, September 7, 1999)

What gets the young people started, she stressed, is the contemporary
music, not the traditional music: "So, that is another way, I feel, which
is more successful, rather then force them to go and sit for hours with
the old people. I think after half an hour they will want to go to the
toilet or go to the burger stall" (September 7, 1999).

Such a strategy is not unique to Jane Lian, the SCV, or Tuku' Kamé'.
It also characterizes the approach of MITRA, a similar multi-ethnic
band that hails from the traditional music section of the Sarawak Ministry of Social Development. (The name "MITRA" is in fact an
acronym for "Muzik Tradisional.") Like Tuku' Kamé', MITRA brought
to the 1999 RWMF a style of performance that is intended to engage
younger listeners in traditional musics by infusing Sarawakian sounds
into a popular music framework. Shazali Attaelah, one of the members
of MITRA, articulated the band's aspirations:

My reason is you, you want to get people interested in an instrument. It's very difficult. What more, we say we want to get those youngsters to be, you know, involved in traditional music. It's very difficult.

Unless you can bring the *sapé'* [Kayan: plucked lute] to play alternative music. Then they want. "Oh – *sapé'* can play alternative!" Then they want to. They want to learn more about the *sapé'*. So, in that way you can educate them.

In, in the same way you teach them, you educate them that "this is the traditional music." This is – then you tell them, then they want to know about the gongs. You can tell them the Bidayuh music. The Iban music. That is, to me that is the, ahh, one way to, to get people involved. (Mohammed Shazali Attaelah, September 8, 1999)

Shazali Attaelah and MITRA demonstrate the versatility of local instruments such as the *sapé'* by disassociating them from their "traditional," unadjusted, and – to youthful audiences – largely unappealing modes of performance. Ironically, this popularized, "alternative" setting baits the very barb by which MITRA hopes to pull listeners back into the traditions from which the instruments were divorced in the first place.

Is the "gimmick," as Jane Lian labeled it, working? Although it is still too early to assess the full impact of the combined artistic and educational efforts of the SCV and the RWMF, some accomplishments certainly deserve recognition. Tuku' Kamé' has drawn both national and international acclaim as winner of several awards – including the "Breakthrough Award" – in the 1999 MTV competition in Kuala Lumpur. The band has also produced a commercial CD, which is available at the Sarawak Cultural Village. Clearly, Tuku' Kamé' has engaged some influential listeners. But does the engagement stop with the popularized world music product, or does it penetrate to the non-commercialized depths of Sarawakian sonic traditions?

Innovative groups like Tuku' Kamé' and MITRA have been inspiring new interest in and development of local musics, attributable at least in part to their exposure at the RWMF. Randy Raine-Reusch, the Canadian world music consultant to the RWMF from 1998 to 2000, observed that "[t]here is now a resurgence of interest in Sarawak in traditional music and many young people are rediscovering their heritage."[19] Beyond the strictly Sarawakian community, a percussionist from the Canadian group, ASZA, was quoted not only as having "learned a lot" from his participation in the 1998 Festival, but also as having made plans to visit an Iban longhouse to study gongs (Chan, 1998: 10). Government officials in Sarawak have also praised the RWMF both for the boost it has given to tourism, as well the impact it has had on the resuscitation of "Sarawak's dying music traditions" (BERNAMA, 2000). The Sarawak Minister of Tourism (1995–2000), Datuk James Jemut Masing, even declared Sarawakian traditional music currently to be a in a state of revival (see Anonymous, 1999: 3).

Revivals are indicative of renewed engagement, and carry tremendous potential to create, alter, or reinforce images of community, as well as the musics that support them.[20] With the continuation of the RWMF in coming years, the ramifications of revival in Sarawak will come into sharper focus. In the meantime, however, the Sarawak case is already instructive on several counts. It demonstrates that world music and tourism *are* highly engaging phenomena, and that this engagement is no illusion. The two industries also share significant developmental (including educational) agendas, along with similar aestheticizing approaches to implementing them. In light of these commonalities of function and process, it would seem obvious that the combined impact of world music and tourism could be intensified by coupling together the two industries. The Rainforest World Music Festival at the Sarawak Cultural Village is a case in point. Perhaps most importantly, this example from Sarawak, Malaysia cautions scholars and theoreticians of world music and tourism *not* to view these enterprises merely as an invitation to foreign visitors and listeners to attend a local cultural cash bar. Rather, locals and foreigners both staff and stock each side of the counter.

## Modes of Alienation

*alienation: a) a renunciation or transfer to another party of something that is one's own; b) a process of estrangement or isolation from a natural or social context; c) the subjective experience of being in such a condition. (excerpted from* Penguin Dictionary of Philosophy, *1996: 12)*

Alienation is engagement's alter ego. As illustrated by the situation in Sarawak, world music and tourism engage both domestic and foreign audiences in a comparable capacity. However, that engagement goes hand-in-hand with an element of social alienation that precipitates from cross-cultural encounter, the very premise on which the two enterprises operate. I now re-visit the Sarawak Cultural Village and the Rainforest World Music Festival to illuminate the institutions' deceptive – and thus alienating – qualities on various fronts. In other words, I here unveil ways in which audience members, organizers, and musicians, while engaged, are indeed often engaged in an illusion.

Before turning the SCV and the RWMF inside out, I should clarify my use of the term, "alienation." Due to its long association with marxist philosophy, this word undoubtedly triggers expectations of a marxist analysis. Such a discursive frame would certainly be in keeping with much of the critical literature, which assesses world music and tourism in terms of the oppression they perpetuate through entrapment within a transnational capitalist economy. Some aspects of the SCV and RWMF certainly lend themselves to such analysis, especially when alienation is effected through "transfer" of musical material. However, I employ the term in a more general sense of social and cultural distanciation, as I show various facets of the Festival venue, activities, and planning process not only to betray significant cultural and professional gaps, but also in some respects to widen them. Ironically, this alienation occurs under the guise of cross-cultural "connection."

## *Façades of interaction: world music in traditional houses*

The setting of the Rainforest World Music Festival at the Sarawak Cultural Village, coupled with the structure of the event itself, was intended to evoke an experience of communication, of exchange between all the parties involved. Many of the interactions facilitated by the RWMF were definitely inspirational for the festival musicians and visitors. On the other hand, some of the connections that were intended to be most remarkable in their linking of individuals from profoundly diverse environments and lifestyles, happened in *façade* form only. In these instances, neither the SCV nor the RWMF offered a WYSIWYG ("what you see is what you get") experience.

### *At the Sarawak Cultural Village*
One day at the Sarawak Cultural Village, I visited the Orang Ulu longhouse at the very moment a young man dressed in Orang Ulu costume was playing the *sampé'* (plucked lute) on the veranda. His playing was unlike any I had heard before.[21] I listened for a while, and when he paused, I asked his about his Orang Ulu origin. "Actually, I

am not Orang Ulu," he responded, smiling. "At the Sarawak Cultural Village, we move around." So I learned that on a given day, there is no guarantee that the cultural representative in the Bidayuh headhouse is really Bidayuh (although he or she will certainly be dressed to look the part), or that the Penan dart blower is really Penan, or that the Orang Ulu *sampé'* player is either Orang Ulu or a musician in that tradition at all. I must admit that I was initially unsettled by this revelation, having been unaware of the depth of the SCV fantasy.

I later had the opportunity to talk to SCV resident manager, Jane Lian, about this practice of staff rotation. She quite graciously elucidated not only the institution's rationale for adopting such a policy, but also indirectly brought me to a recognition of my own idealism and naivete regarding the culture industry. In response to an obviously anticipated, but undelivered accusation of conscious, deceptive substitution of the "inauthentic" for the "real thing," she immediately began to justify the SCV's actions. "Of course, some like to criticize," she conceded, and proceeded to emphasize the village's dual roles as a tourist attraction, and an educational establishment. In keeping with the educational aims of the institution, the SCV administrators expect most of their "living-exhibit" staff to learn something of the cultures represented in each of the "traditional" houses. One of the principal means by which this is accomplished is through periodic re-stationing of the staff to different sites within the village.

Jane Lian further defended the SCV's position by explaining that, in some instances, it is simply impossible to have "the real thing" staffing the various houses, and immediately raised the issue of the Penan. Until relatively recently, most Penan were nomadic or semi-nomadic forest dwellers. Although the majority of the Penan are now settled, remote, rural agriculturists, the image maintained by the SCV is, predictably, one of a nomadic population. Evidently, the Penan Hut at the Village was indeed staffed by Penan at one time, but, according to Jane Lian, this situation was simply not workable. The Penan staff were too unfamiliar with the expectations associated with employment downriver, as well as the operations and intentions of an institution like the SCV to be able to work effectively (Jane Lian, September 8, 1999).

*At the Rainforest World Music Festival*

Thursday, August 27, 1998: I was summoned in the afternoon by the Sarawak Council for Customs and Traditions (Majlis Adat Istiadat) to meet with a group of Kenyah and Penan musicians, who had just arrived from the upper stretches of the Balui River in the state's mountainous interior. They would all be participating in the first Rainforest World Music Festival, which was to start in just two days' time. The Kenyah *sampé'* players, Asang Lawai and Tegit Usat, were somewhat accustomed to traveling to play their music. They had been taken to France earlier in the year to participate in the WOMEX (World of Music Exhibition) in Marseilles. For the three Penan singers and *sapi'* (*sampé'*) players, however, public performance at the RWMF would be a completely new experience. We passed most of the afternoon in an *ad hoc* recording session in the middle of the Majlis deputy director's office. Weary from a long trip and a draining "studio" stint, the musicians finally set their instruments aside, and the recording equipment was put away. Someone brought in a case of Tiger Beer, out came the cigarettes of homegrown tobacco rolled in coarse *tarit* leaves, and the office quickly filled with aromatic smoke. Everyone began to chat. I was anxious to speak to the musicians, and initiated a conversation.

"Are you doing workshops tomorrow?" I asked.

"What?" One of the Penan performers responded with a countenance betraying confusion.

"Workshops? Are you doing workshops?" I repeated my question, hoping to get a hint of their plans for the workshops that I knew had already been scheduled.

"I don't know," the Penan musician replied, obviously having no idea what I was talking about. "When they tell us to play *sapi'*, then we'll play it." Our conversation – on that topic, at least – went no further.

On the opening day of the festival, I got a ride out to the SCV with one of the staff from the Council for Customs and Traditions. Together, we made our way to the cabin where the Penan and Kenyah musicians were staying for the duration of the event. With festival timetable in hand, I was deposited at the cabin, and charged with making sure the musicians were doing what they were supposed to be doing, at the right places and the right times. What I lacked, however, was the information package that was supposedly supplied to all of the festival participants. A peninsular Malaysian newspaper reporter, present at the Penan and Kenyah cabin to cover the RWMF event, offered to let me look at hers. Inside the package I found a copy of the line-up for the evening concerts, a list of afternoon workshop locations and musicians involved in each, and guidelines and goals for workshop presentations. I took a few notes on the latter:

> "idea is to compare & contrast musical styles"
>
> "everyone w/ instruments sits together & leader introduces them and where they are from, as well as what concept of workshop is"
>
> "leader plays a piece first then tells another to play a piece"
>
> "if have extra time, then might ask them to play another piece – or might ask them all to try to play a piece together, even though insts. [instruments] are diff. [different] – impromptu"

Feeling thus apprised of the general objective of the afternoon sessions, I returned the material to the reporter and set out with the musicians toward the SCV proper, just a short walk from the cabin. After lunch, we reviewed the locations of each of the "traditional" houses where their workshops were to take place, and the musicians then dispersed to their respective performance venues. The workshops ran in concurrent sessions throughout the afternoon.

The afternoon workshops combined groups from different areas of Sarawak, different regions of Malaysia, and different parts of the world. Over the two-day festival weekend, the Penan and Kenyah musicians from the rural interior of Sarawak participated in workshops variously with members of the Canadian world music group ASZA, the Orang Asli (indigenous peoples of peninsular Malaysia) fusion group Anak Dayung, a *gendang Melayu* traditional Malay ensemble from Sarawak, the Malaysian Institute of Art Traditional Ensemble from Kuala Lumpur, the Sarawak-based Malay musician/performance artist Safar Ghafar, and Joey Ayala, a prominent world music figure from the Philippines. Each of these 1998 RWMF workshops had an appointed leader, typically drawn from one of the non-Sarawakian pop-fusion groups. In only one instance did a member of one of the local traditional ensembles lead a workshop.[22] For the most part, each of the leaders conducted his or her session as outlined in the participants' instruction packet, with one obvious exception. The experiments with musical mixture were hardly treated as an "if you have time" program addendum. Rather, much like the early WOMAD Festivals,[23] mixture emerged as one of the principal aims – if not the intended culmination – of each workshop. But why wouldn't this be the case? After all, the workshops were led by cosmopolitan musicians who specialized in musical hybridization. The Kenyah and Penan, on the other hand, had no clue about all of this. Even if they had received the workshop packet that I had borrowed from the reporter, it would have made no difference. The "instructions" were printed in English. By the time I arrived on the scene, there was neither time – nor an instruction packet – provided for me to explain just what was intended with their participation in the Rainforest World Music Festival.

I went back to the United States immediately following the 1998 Festival, and returned to Sarawak in 1999, when I had the opportunity to visit the village of Asang Lawai and Tegit Usat, the two Kenyah musicians from the Balui River basin, who had performed in the RWMF a year earlier. We reminisced about the 1998 Festival, and I asked each of the musicians about his understanding of the event. Had they been informed of the festival's objectives before committing to it? Were they aware of the ultimate agenda of the festival, which was not merely to have everyone play their instruments, but to provide a forum for musical interaction, a space for creating new musical modes of communication through artistic exchange between the participants? "No," Tegit Usat responded, and subsequently reiterated the essence of what I had been told in the previous year: they were called to play their instruments, and that is what they did, when they were told to do so. When I suggested that the idea might have been to mix musics, the Asang Lawai paused, and proclaimed, "Yes! [It was] because they wanted us to mix!" It was a retrospective revelation.

*Engagement on account of alienation*
Los Lobos musicians Cesar Rosas and Louis Perez described their experience of the *Graceland* recording session with Paul Simon:

> So we got into the studio, there were no songs. After a while we started feeling like idiots: "when is he going to show us the song?" . . . We expected him to have a song ready for us to interpret when we met him in Los Angeles, but he said "You guys just play," and we said "Play what?" We just worked up a bunch of stuff that he eventually got a song out of, and that was it . . . We felt a little detached from the finished piece; we didn't have any real involvement in it. (From a 1987 interview in *Musician* magazine, quoted in Keil and Feld, 1994: 244)

Nearly two decades after Paul Simon's seminal collaborative endeavor with the *Graceland* album, world music, both as an activity and an industry, still seems to be stumbling over some of the same old blocks – or hitting that same old rock in the river. Los Lobos' encounter with Simon remarkably parallels the Kenyah and Penan experience with the Rainforest World Music Festival in 1998. None of these musicians were aware of the master plan. What kind of engagement prevails when only half of the party "gets it?"

While some might criticize institutions such as the SCV and the RWMF, not to mention the work of Paul Simon, for intentionally misleading audiences, it would indeed be unrealistic to think that the deceptive elements of any of these undertakings could disappear with anything short of bombing the river bed to make the rapids more manageable. After all, the effectiveness of world music and cultural tourism is largely founded on the sustenance of contradictions. As long as the two enterprises rely on the projection of images of the "traditional," "authentic," or "original"[24] to amplify a sense of cultural, musical, experiential, and even temporal distance (often in the face of physical proximity), the illusion will continue. This is because the "real thing" – i.e, a particular music or individual that actually matches one's imagination of it – typically does not work in these contexts. Jane Lian recognized the predicament in her dealings with the SCV employees, as well as with the relatively unadjusted forms of local music traditions regularly rejected by Sarawak's youth. Jeff Todd Titon (1999: 115) also acknowledged the paradox as he addressed the means by which the Smithsonian Institution strives to subvert it in its annual staging of the Festival of American Folklife in Washington, DC.

One of the most striking ironies of tourism and world music is that, while the industries themselves are centered in the metropolis, the cultures or musics valorized by them typically hail from peripheralized communities and non-urban environments.[25] The name "Rainforest World Music Festival" is in itself indicative of this orientation. What we frequently find, then, in events like the RWMF, and the Festival of American Folklife, as well as the Sarawak Cultural Village and comparable institutions, is an urban showcase of urban perceptions of non-urban life. Moreover, peripheral peoples targeted for tourism frequently capitalize on such metropolitan images of themselves when initiating their own involvement with the industry (Nash, 1989: 42). World music relies on the same kinds of cosmopolitan constructions. Popular music is dependent upon urbanization, and, as I remarked earlier, local music is transformed into "world music" when it is popularized (or aestheticized). Seen from this angle, world music and tourism are twin establishments, both products of a cosmopolitan atmosphere and inclination.[26]

Despite some of the Kenyah musicians' having been taken to France to play their music, the lack of extensive cosmopolitan experience, as well as the mindset that goes along with it, set the Kenyah and Penan apart from most of the other "world(ly) musicians" at the 1998 RWMF. While the cosmopolitan contingent was strongly fusion-oriented, the more provincial Festival participants had never seriously considered such musical mixing. The cosmopolitan musicians exhibited a kind of universalism, which, as many have remarked, is one of the hallmarks of the world music mentality. Moreover, as Immanuel Wallerstein has pointedly expressed, universalism is a quality of the elite, in that it is linked to a position of political or economic privilege, a phenomenon "offered to the world as a gift from the powerful to the weak" (Waller-stein, 1983: 85, in Taylor, 1997: 27).[27] In the world music movement, universalism is manifest in the assumption that diverse musicians, performing diverse musics, can, should, and naturally would want to unite as equals, as one in a common sonic setting. This has indeed been the premise of the RWMF. From the assembly of afternoon encounters featuring musicians and musics from a broad spectrum of backgrounds, to the staging of events in concurrent sessions at a single venue, to the designation of world music fusion artists to lead the workshops in 1998, to the "blend-it-into-a-single-package" penchant of the workshop supervisors and festival organizers as a whole, the RWMF is an exponent of the universalizing tendencies of the world music mindset.

The deficiency in world music savvy on the part of many of the local "traditional" musicians was generally understood by the festival organizers, although it was clearly less tolerated by the Sarawakian planners in the second and third years of the event. (I will expand on this issue in the following section.) As Randy Raine-Reusch, the Canadian world music consultant contracted for the RWMF, remarked in the 1998 program booklet:

> The interest in World Music is a golden opportunity for Sarawak due to its immense wealth in music of the traditional and indigenous cultures found here. However, few musicians in Sarawak are aware of the tremendous opportunities that await them, and much of their music is not yet ready for the world market. It is the intent of the festival Organizers to help stimulate local musicians by putting them on the same stage as touring international World Music artists. Local musicians will quickly learn the wealth of their own music and at the same time be able to experience the standards that the international market demands.

The "unawareness" of opportunities and the "unreadiness" of the music for the world market that Raine-Reusch describes, I would translate as the total absence of the "world music" concept, as so glowingly exemplified by the Penan and Kenyah players from the Balui River basin. Seen in this light, the objective of the RWMF then becomes a reification of Wallerstein's universalism. It is a field for the inculcation of the "world music" mindset – for teaching the rules of the game – for bestowal of that gift from the powerful (the cosmopolitan) to the weak (the provincial). It is an arena in which to cultivate the cultural alien- ation that is so necessary for engagement in and through the world music and tourism industries.

## Politically calculated aesthetic management: more on the limits of world music as a global concept

Illusions of equal, multi-directional musical and cultural exchange not only characterized some of the RWMF workshops, but also generated static within the Festival Organizing Committee itself. Where the inti- mate afternoon encounters assumed a presence and refinability of an essentially cosmopolitan world music concept between performers, the Organizing Committee assumed a common understanding among its members of the definition and scope of "world music." There were, in fact, significant discrepancies between the view of the Sarawak Tourism Board (STB), which headed the Organizing Committee, and that of the Canadian World Music Consultant, who was the festival's connec- tion to the music-aesthetically Western-dominated international music industry.[28] These divergent views triggered shifts in musical emphasis at the second and third RWMFs, for which the consultant was not in residence during the planning stage. Moreover, conflicting perceptions of the scope of world music also provided a rationale for the STB's exclusion of certain government bodies from the Organizing Commit- tee. On a deeper level, the conflict within the Committee is rooted in differing dominant agendas for "world music" between developed and developing (or development-oriented) nations or communities, as well as to the Sarawak Tourism Board's role in state and national image management.

### Scope(s) of world music: met and unmet goals at the Rainforest World Music Festival

I have consciously avoided offering any stylistic definition of "world music" to this point, largely because this is a decision contingent on the political position of the definer. Numerous authors have addressed the character of and distinctions between "world music" and "world beat." Steve Feld, in his well-known "schizophonia and schizmogenesis" article (1994: 265), divided the musics in terms of their discursive categories. "World music" is couched in a rhetoric of " 'truth,' 'tradition,' 'roots,' and 'authenticity'," while "world beat" is addressed in terms of "mixing, syncretic hybridization, blending, fusion, creolization," and "collaboration across gulfs." Feld recognized, too, that "world music" and "world beat" have begun to merge conceptually, largely on account of the establishment of "world music" as a market category. Essentially reflecting this consolidation was the definition of world music offered by the RWMF consultant, Randy Raine-Reusch in both the 1998 and 1999 program booklets. "World Music," he wrote, "can be defined as 'the music of, or resulting from, traditional or indigenous cultures' " (*The Rainforest World Music Festival*, August 29–30, 1998, program booklet, 3).[29] Both Feld and Raine-Reusch, however, are coming from a position of privilege in a "developed" society. This is the foundation that enables them to recognize both the "traditional" and "hybrid" styles as equal and legitimate partners in the world music movement. Conversely, for the principal Sarawakian RWMF organizers, as well some of the non-"traditional" Malaysian fusion artists, the World Music and World Beat conceptual categories have not simply merged. Rather, self-conscious musical fusions have usurped the "world music" label altogether. Musics from the "truth, tradition, and roots" bracket inhabit another realm: that of "culture" or "folk life." They are not generally considered "world music."

The Sarawakian planners did not specify the compass of world music in the RWMF literature, as did the Canadian consultant. Nevertheless, their take on the term was quite clear from their commentaries on the various performers, and their strategies in scheduling them. Recalling the passage quoted earlier from the statement of (then) Assistant Minister of Culture, Dublin Unting, in the 1998 Festival program book, the RWMF was geared toward integration of local traditions with "those of the Western world." For Dublin Unting, this was the essence of musical modernization, and, evidently, the hallmark of world music. Admittedly, the printed remarks of the other Sarawakian coordinators were less explicit, or ambiguous, regarding the issue of musical mixing. However, it cannot be assumed that Dublin Unting's remarks were simply idiosyncratic. A shift in the content of the RWMF in 1999 further conveys a sense that, for the Sarawakian contingent, world music is not "traditional" music, *especially* Sarawakian traditional music.

It is a re-contextualization of traditional instruments and forms into "modern" popular amalgams.

A general rundown of the artists appearing in the 1998 and 1999 RWMF events betrays the priority of musical hybrids among the RWMF organizers. The initial RWMF presented a fairly balanced assortment of Sarawakians performing traditions associated with specific ethnic communities (e.g., Kenyah, Penan, Malay, Melanau, Bidayuh), and domestic and foreign ensembles that self-consciously combined diverse musical practices. Of the three "mixed stock" groups from Sarawak, two performed a kind of pop music blend, while the other offered a primarily Iban-based "modern" orchestral experience, complete with conductor. The remaining musical mixtures hailed from peninsular Malaysia and points beyond. The 1999 Festival, on the contrary, included just four groups from Sarawak. One of these was a city-based *sampé'* duo representing the Kenyah community. The other three were fusion bands.

What would account for this re-distribution of festival emphases? To some extent, the changes were part of a scale-back resulting from pressures of the Asian economic crisis of the late 1990s. But economic considerations were hardly the sole motivation for re-facing the RWMF line-up. Comments from festival coordinators, as well as a number of local performers, indicate that the privileging of local pop conglomerates in 1999 arose from a desire to bring the festival more in line with a particular local idea of world music that had little to do with traditional music, *per se*, but was all about modernization and development.

A recurrent theme in my conversations with various members of the RWMF Organizing Committee was their concern that the event devolve into just another "folk festival" or "culture show." This is what happens, a key Sarawak Tourism Board employee explained, when there is too much dancing, when there are too many people on the stage. All the movement ultimately obscures the sound, when the idea here is to highlight the music. "This is a world MUSIC festival," the STB officer stressed. As the discussion continued, however, it became obvious that the goal here was not simply to spotlight the music that is normally overshadowed by dancing. In the words of that same Tourism Board representative:

> We want to promote the ethnic music ... but blend everything together. Try to blend everything together, not really to play cultural music. No,

we would like still to have cultural music, but blend things together –
start to – to make it look like a world music kind of thing. Be able to
blend in. You can have it in a single group or in various groups . . . This
is the concept for this year: blend all the music . . . like Sayu Ateng [one
of the hybrid Sarawakian pop groups] . . . [it is] easier that everyone
comes in. Every musical instrument was in there . . . So, if there's a blend,
it's Sarawakian. So you get to see everything Sarawakian in one group.
(September 2, 1999)

Along the same line, Dr. Wan Zawawi Ibrahim, an anthropologist,
composer, Malaysian world music fusion artist, and Organizing
Committee member from Universiti Malaysia Sarawak (UNIMAS),
summarized the ideal RWMF performance in terms of creativity,
novelty, and innovation. He recounted the audition and selection
procedure:

We audition those that we feel fit in the frame of what we want . . . We
want something that is "world music." Well, you know it is very arbitrary.
It's very subjective. But we – I think we're concerned that we don't
want just any traditional kind of music. You know, we want a music that
fits in, like – an attempt, basically to – to, to – to bring in ethnic elements, but maybe to – to give it a form that is like a Tuku' Kamé' [one
of the Sarawakian fusion groups] kind of – that way, you see . . . It's a
kind of creative music. Locally, but creative. Not just someone coming
and play *sampé'*, ééé-ééé-éé' [imitates *sampé'* sound]. Or play the, you
know traditional Melanau music, because there's room for that kind of
music. We have other festivals. See? Rainforest Festival is a different kind
of festival. (Dr. Wan Zawawi Ibrahim, September 3, 2001)

Much like the Sarawak Tourism Board representative, Dr. Wan Zawawi
viewed the RWMF as an exposure opportunity for new, popular music
syntheses from Sarawak, not the promotion of traditional music. Traditional music is simply not world music in these commentators' ears.

The STB representative indicated that musical blending was the
theme of the 1999 RWMF, and that "next year could be different." No
official theme was indicated in the 1999 publicity literature. In 2000,
however, Organizing Committee Chair Haji Mohammed Tuah Jais
declared:

With growing concern towards environment especially on the preservation of the rainforest, "Rainforest Rythms" [*sic*] has been chosen as
the theme for our festival this year. To reflect the theme, most of the

musicians or groups participating in the festival are from countries with rainforests. (RWMF 2000 program booklet)

This "theme" in no way delimits musical style, nor does it mean that the musics or musicians have anything to do with the rainforests themselves. It is probably best understood as an aesthetic maneuver to capitalize on the rainforest frenzy currently sweeping the international market. Moreover, it could also be interpreted as a political gesture to demonstrate Sarawak's concern for the viability of its own rainforests, despite attacks from domestic and international environmental activist groups, especially over the past decade. When consultant Randy Raine-Reusch arrived in Sarawak, just a couple of weeks before the start of RWMF 2000, he found only one rural "traditional" group in place for the Festival. Raine-Reusch recounted the story of diving into the "chaos and scrambling" of the local Festival organizers at the last minute:

> Once I got here, I took over as usual, and the program definitely has my influence. The reason they had not gotten many Ulu [Upriver] performers was that they just were not organized enough to find how to contact them. They had done everything by email and if Long Makabah [rural upriver Kenyah village] had email, they would have booked artists from there. An example: I had suggested a group from Long Laput that I had recorded. I had given them some possible contacts, but told them the longhouse and that there was a radio phone there, so just call the longhouse. For six months no one called as the numbers I had given didn't work and there was no "listing" for the longhouse. (Author note: They did find a nose flute player in town though, to try and appease me.) Once I got here I pushed HARD, and within 24 hours, the musicians were contacted and a day later they were coming!! ... I am thinking of getting someone from either the museum or from Majlis Adat [Council for Customs and Traditions] to be on the selection committee next year to ensure local participation. (Randy Raine-Reusch, personal communication, August 12, 2000)

Evidently, had it not been for Raine-Reusch's efforts, "blending" would again have been the unofficial "theme" of the RWMF 2000 – at least for the Sarawakian component. It is difficult to believe that the absence of substantial rural local representation prior to the consultant's arrival was merely a function of disorganization or lack of contacts on the part of the Organizing Committee. At that time, the Sarawak Tourism board was less than one minute's walk within the same building from the Majlis Adat Istiadat (Council for Customs and Traditions), one of the government bodies (along with the Muzium Sarawak), that is most knowledgeable about and well-connected to communities even in the most remote rural regions of the state.

*On again, off again: the Council on Custom and Tradition (Majlis Adat Istiadat)*

During the first year of the Rainforest World Music Festival, the Majlis Adat Istiadat and, for a short time, the Muzium Sarawak were both part of the team of festival organizers. While the Muzium discontinued its involvement quite early in the process for reasons unknown to me, the Majlis played a role throughout the planning and production of the 1998 event. The principal charge of this office was to contact and coordinate "traditional" performers, especially from the rural areas. Such local representation in the festival program was definitely stronger in 1998 than it was in either 1999 or 2000. Not insignificantly, neither the Majlis Adat Istiadat nor the Muzium Sarawak were involved at all in these latter two stagings of the RWMF.

Deputy director of the Majlis Adat Istiadat, Nicholas Bawin, recalled being among the first consulted and subsequently invited by the Sarawak Tourism Board to sit on the RWMF Organizing Committee in 1998. But in 1999, he marveled, "We were not even informed about it, you know? We were excluded from that" (personal communication, September 9, 1999). In an attempt to account for the exclusion of his office, he speculated that the committee was disturbed by Majlis' comments at the 1998 Festival "post-mortem" meeting. At that gathering, the Majlis criticized the committee for the inclusion of a pop musician whose parodic performance style was offensive to some of the local Iban audience members. Nicholas Bawin also suggested that the Asian economic crisis prohibited bringing so many local artists from rural areas or small towns in 1999. However, "if the number [of performers] is a concern," he said, countering his own argument, "we can reduce the number, no problem."

The exclusion of the Majlis Adat Istiadat in the second and third years of the RWMF is most likely attributable to the organization's preservationist orientation, which is antithetical to the aims of most of the local Festival Committee members. As articulated on the first page of the Majlis handbook, the principal objectives of this government body are:

- To preserve the customs and traditions of the Dayak ["natives"] for posterity.[30]
- To nurture the customs and traditions of the Dayak so that they can withstand external pressures of modernization and blend with change and development
- To control and coordinate all activities relating to research on customary laws and adat[31] and other aspects of customs and traditions of the Dayak.
- To advise on the interpretation of customs and traditions of the Dayak to maintain order and development. ("Majlis Adat Istiadat, Sarawak," 1992)

While preservation is the number one priority of the Majlis Adat Istiadat, the organization is not *anti*-development *per se*. The Majlis merely recognizes development of local customs and traditions as a process to be undertaken with caution. Deputy director Nicholas Bawin emphasized the institution's concern to monitor the presentation and representation of "native" traditions (including musical ones), to see that they are performed "correctly," and that they retain as much of their "authentic value" as possible (September 9, 1999). If there is a means by which traditions can be sustained with minimal or no alteration in a rapidly changing environment, that is the goal of the Majlis Adat Istiadat.

The Majlis champions the cause of some of the most politically and economically disadvantaged "fourth world" communities in Malaysia.[32] Viewed in terms of Wallerstein's social criteria of universalism, it is not surprising that the stance of the Majlis was in essence diametrically opposed to that of the Assistant Minister of Culture, the chair of the RWMF Organizing Committee, the resident manager of the Sarawak Cultural Village, the "traditional music" component of the Ministry of Social Development, and the representatives from the Universiti Malaysia Sarawak and the Sarawak Tourism Board quoted throughout this essay. All of these individuals were prominent and influential members of the Organizing Committee. Moreover, all advocated "modernization" of local traditions, or at least perpetuation of them in a "contemporary" form. For the majority of the committee (and, I would submit, the majority of urban Sarawak), the Rainforest World Music Festival offered an opportunity to showcase new, creative, innovative, and, most importantly, modern Sarawakian musics before both a domestic and international audience. The traditional forms were perceived to complicate and detract from this powerful agenda, as well as the image that was to be realized through it. Furthermore, since traditional musics were not viewed as "world music" by the bulk of the Committee anyway, why wrestle with the Majlis Adat Istiadat, or its like-minded counterpart, the Muzium Sarawak?

*On political and economic foundations of the world music concept*
Peter Gabriel, British musician and mover-and-shaker of the world music industry since its inception, identified the twofold aim of his organization, WOMAD (World of Music Arts and Dance) as: (1) "to protect and preserve the seed stock of as wide and varied a base as you can keep alive," and (2) "to try out as many hybrid possibilities as you can that will give you the most vibrant, pulsating new life forms" (Gabriel, as quoted by Sinclair in Taylor, 1997: 51). According to this model, Sarawak's presence in the first year of the RWMF was principally that of "seed stock," that is, non-self-consciously hybrid "traditional" sound. The Sarawak Tourism Board and the more influential members of the local Organizing Committee were evidently (and I would say, understandably) uncomfortable with this. Seeds are, after all, embryos; they are undeveloped. Why, then, would a state in a nation that is striving to achieve a vision of being a "developed" country by the year 2020 (a movement known as *Wawasan* 2020[33]) want to display itself as "embryonic" in the world music arena? Is it not the "pulsating new life forms," usually produced through collaboration between US/UK and "Other" artists, that have consistently commanded the most prestige in the industry?[34]

Traditional music can and does carry a stigma for many of the more progressive, development-minded Malaysians, who consider it backwoods, behind-the-times, and unworthy of attention more a nod and a smile. At best, such traditions are viewed and valued as curiosities, as local color, as substance for the "culture shows" and "folk festivals" to which Wan Zawawi and the Sarawak Tourism Board representative alluded earlier.[35] At the RWMF, however, Sarawak can shed its image as a producer solely of "raw" musical resources ("seed stock"). Instead, Sarawak then stands as a producer of processed and "refined" goods that are globally relevant and viable in the world music arena: popular/traditional music hybrids or fusion bands. Three such groups participated in the RWMF between 1998 and 2000, and two of these were specially groomed for the event. Not surprisingly, one of the groups was sponsored by the Sarawak Cultural Village (under the Ministry of

Tourism), another by the Sarawak Ministry of Social Development, and the third by a private development corporation. Development, development, development. Is this a coincidence? Not likely. In the Sarawakian milieu, where tradition can be perceived as a threat to development, and development itself is an ever-present issue, world music takes shape as a distinct phenomenon with its own agenda. Rather than encompassing traditional music, world music runs counter to it. Moreover, when coupled with the RWMF and the tourism industry, world music emerges as an agent by which traditional forms can be kept in "proper" perspective.

While the current era of post-structural analysis has allowed academics only recently to recognize that musical performance indeed *produces* a society as well as reflects it,[36] Malaysia (including Sarawak) has long been aware of music's social power and potential. This is evident not only in the previously noted historical role of music in Malaysia's official development schemes, but also in the involvement of development or development-related institutions in nurturing local fusion bands at the RWMF. World music at the RWMF in Sarawak is not simply a matter of image. It is very much about creation (and revision) of a people. Music that emerges from the distillation, reconstitution, and recombination of diverse local traditions with globally popular musical styles becomes both metaphor and catalyst of a modern, internationally interactive, multi-ethnically harmonious, developed, and unique Sarawakian society.[37] What kind of society, then, is represented and generated through the performance of *traditional* music, and to what extent is that social product desirable?

This question gets to the heart of conceptions and definitions of world music, and responses to it are contingent upon the social, economic, and political position of the judge. Sarawakian traditional music and culture have had different significance for each of the facets – or factions – of the Organizing Committee, an incongruity that ultimately led to the butting of heads regarding the scope of world music in Sarawak and for the RWMF. While the Majlis Adat Istiadat advocated preservation (or closely monitored development) of traditional forms, the STB and its adherents favored synthesis. The Canadian world music consultant, Randy Raine-Reusch, like Peter Gabriel quoted above, supported all. As would be expected, there is a continuum here from the particular to the universal, which runs alongside a continuum of empowerment within a global context. On the one end, we have champions of those marginalized societies that struggle for a voice even on the domestic level; in the middle we have an urban mainstream in pursuit of international recognition as a developed society; and on the opposite end we have a westerner for whom development has likely never carried the same urgency that it does for many Malaysian citizens. Such diversity of the "world music" concept relative to the breadth and depth of social difference on local, national, and global levels remains little acknowledged.[38] Perhaps on account of the use of a single term ("world music") to refer to an array of conceptual phenomena, the illusion that all parties are on the same page looms quite large. However, the dynamics of the RWMF Organizing Committee quickly suck this genie back into the bottle. Although positive encounters between disparate notions of "world music" have yielded creative compromises and composites, negative encounters have again attested to the precariousness of cross-cultural connection within the RWMF setting.

## *The gloved hand extended: reconsidering the educational activities and intentions of Sarawak's world music groups*

The extent to which world music, tourism, and development are officially intertwined at the Rainforest World Music Festival, and in Sarawak as a whole, should by now seem self-evident. Implicated in the mix is also the educational program identified earlier as an intended means of re-engaging Sarawakians with local traditions. I now return to the issue of education as I examine briefly the *modus operandi* of the two local fusion bands spotlighted earlier, Tuku' Kamé' and MITRA. Aspects of the manner in which repertoire is created for these groups, as well as various musicians' attitudes toward the traditional music resources that they theoretically tap, do indeed raise questions regarding the limits and limitations of the educational outreach initiative.

### *Two sides of Tuku' Kamé*

As the signature music ensemble of the Sarawak Cultural Village, Tuku' Kamé' has appeared in each production of the RWMF. Comprised of employees of the Village, the band may actually vary in size depending on the performance venue and circumstances. Twenty-three instrumentalists and vocalists were listed on their commercial release, *Tuku' Kamé'*. In terms of the group's ethnic formation, the great majority of the band members, including the group's director, are Malay. There are, however, a few performers from other Sarawakian communities (e.g.,

Bidayuh, Chinese). The band's highly visible pop (not traditional) *sampé'* player, for instance, is Bidayuh.

In the printed program of RWMF 2000, Tuku' Kamé' is described as an "innovative ensemble [that] takes its inspiration from traditional music of Sarawak's 27 ethnic groups, World Music and jazz." (Notice the distinction between "world music" and "traditional music.") Narawi Hj. Rashidi, the group's director, is an acclaimed musician, composer, and arranger in the Western idiom, but nevertheless maintains a genuine interest in local music traditions. He enthusiastically investigates each of the musical styles that finds a place in the melodies, rhythms, instrumentation, texture, and lyrics of his arrangements for Tuku' Kamé'. Many of Narawi's (and the group's) human musical resources – in the sense of carriers of the traditions – are present within the diversity of the SCV employee pool. These traditional musicians, while they do not usually perform with the group, are consulted for their input into the Tuku' Kamé' and broader SCV musical offering.

While the gesture to learn from the "masters" might be perceived as respectful by its initiators, that the knowledge imparted is subsequently re-cast to "create an infectious and exciting new sound" (RWMF program, 1998, 1999, 2000) is not always appreciated bilaterally. From the perspective of two senior Kenyah men regularly stationed in the Orang Ulu Longhouse at the SCV, their contribution to this hybrid musical product is not voluntary. They feel required by their jobs to dispense their musical knowledge to other employees, who are then called upon to "perpetuate" those Kenyah traditions not only within the Village (recall the *sampé'*-playing Orang Ulu impersonator), but in the local school programs, as well as cultural events abroad. These musicians only "adopt a superficial character" ("*ala' gaya' tua'*") of *sampé'* playing, one of the Kenyah employees explained. The instrument might be recognizable as Kenyah, but the music is not. "We don't know this music," he continued. "Kenyah cannot dance to this music!" This goes for the Tuku' Kamé' group, as well as the Orang Ulu role-players on the longhouse veranda. The other Kenyah musician was also rather disgruntled. "I don't want to mix Kenyah music with other styles," he declared, and he recounted his calculated refusal to reveal (correctly) the names of his instruments or the tunes that he played on them. Ignorance of the names, he felt, would ultimately limit the access of these musicians to Kenyah traditional music.

Some might dismiss these Kenyah musicians' aversion to the innovative uses of Kenyah instruments and melodies as attributable to generational difference. There is probably an element of truth in this assessment, since most of the members of Tuku' Kamé', as well as the rotating Orang Ulu impersonators, are their juniors by far. But the situation is not that straightforward. Part of the difficulty is that these new directions in Kenyah music do not arise from a grassroots movement on the part of the Sarawakian Kenyah community. On the contrary, Tuku' Kamé', while certainly producing some creative, unique, and engaging material, is perceived neither by the Kenyah musicians, nor by some of the officers at the Majlis Adat Istiadat, to have any real grasp of the traditions that they claim to incorporate (and manipulate). Moreover, the work of Tuku' Kamé' suggests a kind of government initiative, in which (at this point in time) non-Kenyah represent Kenyah. Further complicating the matter is the co-incidence that the band's director is Malay, a member of the politically dominant ethnic group of Malaysia. In some ways, this musical "col-laboration" has ironically led to the exacerbation – rather than the alleviation – of pre-existent ethnic and political tensions. This was made manifest in the interpretation of the activities of Tuku' Kamé' by one of the traditional musicians at the SCV. This player understood the Malays to be taking traditional music, re-working it, selling it, and returning nothing to the communities that (sometimes unwillingly) provided them musical inspiration and source material. (I hear echoes of Wallerstein one more time.)

*MITRA and the "real thing"*
Among the Sarawakian fusion bands performing at the 1999 RWMF was MITRA, a group of musicians and employees of the Traditional Music (**Muzik Tra**ditional) section of the Sarawak Ministry of Social Development (Kementerian Pembangunan Sosial). MITRA, like the Tuku' Kamé' group of the SCV, seeks out Sarawak's traditional music practitioners, studies and documents their performance under the aus-pices of the state government, then re-presents this music in various forms to multifarious audiences at home and overseas. Unlike Tuku' Kamé', however, the hybrid music that MITRA presented at the RWMF 1999 is not normally supported by the ensemble's employer. The primary charge of MITRA, as summarized by the group's leader, Shazali Attaelah, is to perform traditional music: "Traditional. Yeah, yeah . . . We do the original stuff. Because our function is mostly . . . [to] do the authentic thing. We do the real thing. We do the real Iban. We do the real Bidayuh" (Mohamed Shazali Attaelah, September 8, 1999).

273

It is only in an unofficial secondary capacity that MITRA performs "a contemporary kind of thing" (Maslan Minggu of MITRA, September 8, 1999), a fusion of the Sarawakian traditional with the global "modern" sound. In normal work circumstances, however, there is no place for this music. "We can't do things that we did in the Festival ... Because what, what we did ... for this Ministry, is we have to do the real thing ...," Shazali sighed (September 8, 1999). Shazali's colleague, Maslan Minggu, added that the group has been "yearning to perform [their 'contemporary thing'] for quite some time. We just don't have the venue to perform it." Perhaps some of the musicians from the Ministry of Social Development should switch places with their counterparts at the Sarawak Cultural Village.

Ironically, the members of MITRA, like the older Kenyah musicians at the SCV, are required by their jobs to play music that is contrary to what they personally endorse. Shazali continually stressed that increased and more widespread performance of traditional music (the "real thing"), as advocated by the Ministry, is not the key to the perpetuation of interest in traditional instruments. He strongly stood by the effectiveness and educational value of MITRA's "alternative" music as mentioned earlier.

> Otherwise, they see, you know, the late Tusau [Kenyah *sampé'* player] play that – [has] long hair, you know, the ears, very long ... You know, they're, 'eee-, not not not our stuff.' See? ... So, in the end, in ten years time, nobody will want to know, except for guys like you ... foreigners. (Shazali Attaelah, September 9, 1999)

In making reference to the long hair and distended earlobes of older Kenyah men, Shazali indicated that traditional music remains tied to an image that is considered by most younger people to be old-fashioned and undesirable. If the music is going to be appealing to Sarawak's youth, it needs to be divorced from this image, and one of the ways of accomplishing this is to change the sound of the music itself. This is Shazali's and MITRA's motivation in popularizing the local music traditions. Although their program had long gone unsanctioned by the Ministry of Social Development, the appearance of MITRA in RWMF 1999 perhaps foreshadows a change in the Ministry's orientation. MITRA obviously hoped so.

Despite the group's honorable ambitions, the depth of Shazali's (or the "contemporary" MITRA's) educational agenda is unclear. On several occasions, Shazali emphasized his and the Ministry's requirement that none of the traditional instruments they perform be altered in any way. This, then, would theoretically insure some connection to the roots of the traditions from which the instruments hail. A musical tradition, however, is a system that goes beyond the physical body of the instrument. Shazali acknowledged that he himself does not play traditional *sampé'* music, nor does he imitate it in his use of the instrument in the "modern" MITRA ensemble.[39] While I do not suggest that he should adhere to the traditional *sampé'* style, his admission reveals his own musical limitations, much in the same way that he found the traditional players at the RWMF too narrow in their musical experience to engage him. "They cannot adjust to us. We have to adjust to them," he said, commenting that the traditional players were thus not "real" musicians. The problem, it would seem, is that despite his knowledge of the structure of the instrument, the placement of the frets, and the tuning of the strings, he is no more educated in the traditional musicians' system than they might be in his. What, then, is the nature of the modernization of traditional music that the group advocates (and practices)?

Further attesting to the clash of traditional and "modern" musicians and musical systems was Shazali's disappointment with the RWMF workshop in which he was placed with the *sampé'* player from Tuku' Kamé', and two traditional *sampé'* performers. (Neither of the non-traditional players, for the record, was Orang Ulu.) The workshop, he felt, was non-productive in that no musical connection was achieved. Essentially, these musicians could not play together. Not surprisingly, the workshop that Shazali found the most rewarding was the one in which MITRA was paired with Sayu Ateng, another of the Sarawakian fusion bands. All participants, then, were already operating within the same musical and conceptual framework.

Similarly, one of the traditional *sampé'* players also had a negative response to the same workshop. This player's issue was that on account of the lack of designated leaders for the workshops in 1999, Shazali by chance wound up being the first to play at the gathering. "Why was he first to play?," the traditional musician asked. "Then that's what people are going to think *sampé'* is!" Shazali, too, told me that he felt awkward in being invited to initiate playing, and consciously prefaced his performance by saying, "I use the *sampé'* in a different way than they [the Orang Ulu players] do." Perhaps no discomfort would have arisen on either side, however, had there been no suggestion – either directly or indirectly – that the new styles of *sampé'* playing had anything more than a tangential relationship to traditional music and culture of Sarawak. Otherwise, the adamantly articulated fear on the part of the Kenyah musicians at the SCV might indeed be realized: "suggestions" ("*gaya'*") of Kenyah music may so come to supercede the "real" ("*lan*"), historically-grounded tradition, leaving neither non-Kenyah nor Kenyah knowing the difference between the wrapper and the candy.[40] If the purported connection is dissolved, however, then the ideals of development, tourism, and world music are also invalidated. It is a local, national, and global predicament.

## Navigating the Rapids of World Music and Tourism

Winding through the sometimes placid, sometimes turbulent waterways of world music and tourism has not only brought to the surface some striking operational similarities between the two enterprises, but has also exposed some of the submerged obstacles that inhibit passage to the ultimate goal of achieving meaningful cross-cultural connection. In Sarawak, world music is solidly embedded in the tourism industry, in that the Sarawak Tourism Board supplies the primary performance outlet through the Rainforest World Music Festival (RWMF), held at a prominent tourist destination, the Sarawak Cultural Village (SCV). Both world music and tourism, moreover, are deeply embedded in local development schemes that aim to aestheticize, popularize, and modernize "culture" through what are perceived to be its "detachable" traditions, largely music and the arts. The two phenomena also serve a frequently articulated educational agenda. In many respects, then, world music and tourism travel in the same boat.

Where Martin Roberts, quoted at the outset of this chapter, discounted what he obviously considered to be the simplistic notion that world music, like tourism, provides an illusion of engagement, I submitted that a more accurate way to view the problem is one of engagement with an illusion. At the SCV, representation of the various cultures of Sarawak is often undertaken by undisclosed ethnic impersonators. At the RWMF, both musicians and audiences are engaged (or at least motivated) by the illusion that all performers – from cosmopolitan popular music artists to rural traditional musicians – were united by a world music mindset that values self-conscious cross-cultural sonic synthesis. Within the Festival Organizing Committee itself, friction arose from tacit yet significant differences in perceptions of the scope of world music. These incongruities, I argued, were essentially politically grounded. Depending on the socioeconomic association of the judge with advantaged, disadvantaged, developed, or developing communities, the boundaries and emphases of world music shift considerably. Some favor modernization, some favor preservation, some embrace both. Such variation in both the presence and contour of the "world music" concept suggests that its status as a global phenomenon is indeed yet another illusion. Finally, the educational component of both world music and tourism becomes suspect, when traditions are intentionally altered and reinterpreted, often without significant prior grounding in those traditions themselves, for the sake of rejuvenating public interest. But in what, actually, is interest being generated? In an earlier tradition, or a contemporary illusion of it?

World music and tourism in Sarawak, Malaysia – and, I would speculate, in many other regions – certainly harbor parallels of paradox. The most unsettling of all, and the root of my own obvious ambivalence toward the world music movement, is the irony that, despite the veiled conflicts and contradictions, and the inequities that often arise from them, both enterprises are engaging. Throughout this study I have not departed from this stance. Visiting the Sarawak Cultural Village is a worthwhile experience; attending the Rainforest World Music Festival is just plain fun. While I have heard quite a few of the musicians and organizers vent their frustrations about the endeavor, complaining about the unequal treatment of participants, the unsatisfactory representation of local talent, technical difficulties with the performance venue, or the ineffectiveness of this workshop or that concert, a good number of international and domestic artists, as well as local program coordinators, have enthusiastically continued their involvement with the event in subsequent years. I, too, have been so "engaged," working "backstage" for three out of four productions. New musicians and volunteers have also come on board. Why, then, have I bothered to write this commentary? Because I believe, contrary to David Byrne's view, that the RWMF and tourism can be positively transformative. While it is foolish to dump the baby with the bathwater, it is equally impractical, if not unethical, to remain oblivious to the social, economic, and political differences that may impede the cross-cultural connection. The rivers of Borneo can and do link distant communities, but for the uninformed, those same rivers can further divide them.

World music and tourism in Sarawak operate in the same capacity. Both demand shrewd and careful navigation.

## Notes

1   First and foremost, I would like to thank all of the musicians of the Rainforest World Music Festivals 1998–1999 who offered me their thoughts and their music, as well as the employees of the Sarawak Tourism Board, Sarawak Ministry of Social Development, Sarawak Council for Customs and Traditions, Sarawak Cultural Village, and Universiti Malaysia Sarawak, who took time out of their busy schedules to discuss their RWMF experiences with me. This essay has also benefited from numerous revisions as a result of its having been presented in various versions at an array of venues. These include a conference on "Social Theory, Politics, and the Arts" at Vanderbilt University (October 1999), the annual meeting of the Midwest Chapter of the Society for Ethnomusicology at Chicago State University (March 2000), a Friday lunch lecture at the Southeast Asia Center at University of Wisconsin–Madison (April 2000), a conference entitled "Art, Literature, and Travel," hosted by National Sun Yat-sen University, Kaohsiung, Taiwan (May 2000), and a lecture and discussion at the Center for International and Comparative Studies at Northwestern University. Finally, I am fortunate to have received generous and valuable input from a number of friends and colleagues. Ann Armstrong meticulously collected local newspaper commentaries for me both while I was in and away from Sarawak, and offered helpful comments on earlier drafts of this essay. I also thank Richard Miller, Jayl Langub, and Khoo Kay Jin for their valuable insights and encouragement.

2   The advent of the "world music" label as the brainchild of a group of music industry representatives who met at a pub in London in 1987 is frequently recounted in the literature. Timothy Taylor (1997: 2) related the story as printed in Philip Sweeney's *Virgin Directory of World Music* (1991). Another colorful version was offered by Peter Jowers (1993: 62–3).

3   Most works address some or all of these issues to varying extents. Roger Wallis and Krister Malm's *Big Sounds from Small Peoples: The Music Industry in Small Countries* (1984) is a landmark study of the power and impact of the global music business. More recently, Timothy Taylor has published *Global Pop: World Music, World Markets* (1997), which also forefronts problems of transnational capitalism in world music production. These issues are also addressed in Laing (1986), Goodwin and Gore (1990), Roberts (1992), Garofalo (1993), Guilbault (1993a, 1993b), Feld (1994), and Erlmann (1996).

4   Such was the impression of at least one local visitor following the 1998 production. See Nikki Lugun, "Overwhelming Response to Rainforest Music Festival," *Sarawak Tribune*, "Home" section, Wednesday, September 2, 1998, p. 5.

5   See, for example, Wallis and Malm's (1984: 293–4) early analysis of the music industry in small countries, as well as Goodwin and Gore (1990: 76), Jowers (1993: 67), and Feld (1994: 288). Taylor (1997: 19) acknowledges the likeness of world music to tourism, but avoids the derogatory tone.

6  The Asia-Pacific region, moreover, is gaining popularity as a tourist destination faster than any other area of the world (Hall in Wood, 1997: 3).

7  Social scientists such as Robert Wood (1997: 2–3) and Erve Chambers (1997: 5) have stressed that contemporary tourism studies have swung away from the negative rhetoric of "inauthenticity" and "bastardization" that generally typified the scholarship of previous decades. World musicians and popular music scholars, however, never believed in the culturally "pure" sound in the first place (Frith, 1989: 3; cf. Byrne, 1999).

8  *Taman Mini Indonesia Indah* (Beautiful Indonesia in Miniature Park), established in Jakarta in 1972 and officially inaugurated in 1975 (http://www.tamanmini.com), is perhaps the best known of such institutions in Southeast Asia. The Sarawak Cultural Village opened in 1990.

9  I quote here from the "general information" section of the Sarawak Cultural Village website, http://www.sarawakculturalvillage.com.

10  In 1998, the RWMF ran for two days, and involved 19 groups/artists in 23 afternoon "workshops" and two six-hour evening concerts. In 1999, the festival again ran for two days, but hosted only 14 groups, who participated in 22 "daytime concerts" and four four-hour concerts, two running concurrently (one inside, one outside) each night. In celebration of the millennium, RWMF 2000 was somewhat larger in scale. It spanned three days, and included 18 performing groups, 30 "daytime concerts," and three five-hour evening performances. In 2001, the festival engaged 13 performing groups, with all of the Sarawakian traditional musicians organized by the Council for Customs and Traditions treated as a single group in that year. The musicians participated in 31 "workshops" and three five-hour evening concerts.

11  Victor King (1992: 30) has commented on the resurgence of interest in local life as a result of the growth of the cultural tourism industry in Borneo and elsewhere in Southeast Asia.

12  Similarly, Martin Stokes (1994: 10) has observed that "music is intensely involved in the propagation of dominant classifications, and has been a tool in the hands of new states in the developing world, or rather, of those classes which have the highest stakes in these new social formations."

13  I intentionally do not use the term "Westernization" to describe the popularization or modernization of these traditional forms. In Malaysia, "Westernization" and "modernization" are perceived as two distinct phenomena, the former usually negative, the latter positive. In terms of music, the use of diatonic scales, regular phrase and metric structures, and functional harmony is simply identified as "modern" or "international" style. R. Anderson Sutton has found the same situation in Indonesia (personal communication, and also implied in 1998: 5). Moreover, a recent exchange on the SEM-L (Society for Ethnomusicology) listserve revealed this orientation to be prevalent in many non-Western nations.

14  I see my emphasis on the local here as complementary, but not necessarily contradictory, to the work of scholars such as Zygmunt Bauman (1996: 30), who has focused more abstractly on the importance of aesthetic sculpting for the sustenance of tourism and the tourist mentality, without addressing the significance of aestheticization for specific communities in unique circumstances.

15  There are certainly some exceptions here. Peter Jowers (1993: 74, 80), has

recognized education to be a principal objective of Peter Gabriel's World of Music and Dance (WOMAD) festivals since their inception in the early 1980s. World music as an educational medium has also been a recurrent theme in Jocelyne Guilbault's work (1993a, 1993b) on *zouk* music in the French Antilles. Tony Mitchell (1993), in his assessment of Aboriginal musicians in the Australian world music . scene, is another academic to acknowledge the educational significance of the movement.

16  In contemplating Feld's actions here, I cannot help but recall the startlingly cynical advice rendered by Stanley Fish in the opening pages of his *Professional Correctness* (1995: 2): "If you want to send a message that will be heard beyond the academy, get out of it."

17  Consider, for instance, the virtual absence of issues of domestic tourism from much of Dennison Nash's work (e.g., Nash, 1989, 1996), and Erlmann's assertion that. because "world music represents an attempt by the West to remold its image . . . a serious analysis of global musics can only be written from a subject position in the West." While Goodwin and Gore (1990: 67) emphasized a Western directionality of world music by commenting that "for world music to reach Western ears, it must be presented in a way that will enable it to compete in the musical marketplace," they nevertheless recognized that "we have very little idea about what Western pop (world beat or not) actually means in its various global contexts" (1990: 76).

18  The Taman Mini Indonesia Indah ("Beautiful Indonesia in Miniature Park"), after which the Sarawak Cultural Village was clearly modeled, is also "aimed mainly at domestic tourists and promoted through school textbooks as the place to learn about all of Indonesia" (Wood, 1997: 14).

19  This quote comes from a posting made by Randy Raine-Reusch to the Society for Ethnomusicology listserve, SEM-L, August 2, 2000.

20  One only need recall the resurgence and transformation of bluegrass, Cajun fid-dling, zydeco, blues, ragtime, and many other musics by way of the 1970s folk revivals in the US. Another case in point is the famous *kecak* ("money chant") of Bali, which was developed by a resident foreigner, cultivated and expanded by Balinese, and promoted through the tourist industry.

21  The young man's *sampé'* playing was largely what provoked me to ask about his heritage. To anyone who has spent significant time in Orang Ulu communities, or who has listened extensively to *sampé'* music, this performance was obviously an imitation rendered in ignorance of the intricacies of the tradition.

22  The exception here was led jointly by the Kenyah *sampé'* players. Ironically, the only other participants in that workshop were the Penan *sapi' (sampé')* players. Not surprisingly, it was still the more politically and economically prestigious of the participants – the Kenyah – who led the session.

23  See Peter Jowers (1993: 74–83) for a summary of the aims and values of the WOMAD festivals at their outset in the late 1980s.

24  It takes only a few world music albums with their accompanying promotional materials to become versed in this discourse of world music as distilled by Timothy Taylor in the initial chapter of *Global Pop* (1997).

25  Use of images from marginalized communities by empowered ones to represent

the very "whole" from which those communities have often been excluded is hardly unique to the tourism and world music industries.

26  Various writers have addressed the cosmopolitan character of world music and world musicians. See, for example, Roberts (1992: 235), Guilbault (1993a: 43), Langlois (1996: *passim*).

27  For instance, Louise Meintjes (1990) made a similar observation in her important article on the multiple meanings of Paul Simon's *Graceland* album.

28  Timothy Taylor discusses the dominance of North American and British world music artists and ideologies at great length in his book *Global Pop: World Music, World Markets* (1997). Indeed, the virtually unassailable position and influence of Anglo-American music in the global music market has been at the heart of the "cultural imperialism" issue. Even for those who have criticized the "cultural imperialism" approach to understanding world music, the pre-eminence of Anglo-American forms and figures in the industry was never denied. For more in-depth commentaries on world music and cultural imperialism, see the classic articles of Dave Laing (1986), Reebee Garofalo (1993), and Andrew Goodwin and Joe Gore (1990), and, more recently, Veit Erlmann (1996).

29  I don't know the source from which Raine-Reusch drew this definition. It does appear in quotes in both program booklets, but without citation.

30  The term "Dayak" has evidently replaced the term "native" in the most recent activities overview booklet of the Majlis Adat Istiadat. "Native," as it was used in earlier literature, basically referred to Sarawakian communities that were neither Chinese, Indian, Malay, nor Muslim. The current Majlis report specifies Iban, Bidayuh, Melanau, and Orang Ulu ("Upriver People") as its focal groups, with the "Orang Ulu" serving as an umbrella label embracing about 30 distinct peoples (see Jayl Langub, 1994: 7).

31  "Adat," a term present in many Austronesian languages, is commonly yet contro-versially translated as "customary law." I have heard this term or one of its cognates used variously to embrace aspects of custom, tradition, religion, ritual, law, morals, and even personal character or conduct.

32  "Fourth world" has been used by various scholars to describe marginalized populations in post-colonial states. Marina Roseman (2000) has applied this term to the Temiar, an indigenous people of peninsular Malaysia.

33  The Malaysian public is constantly reminded of this national campaign through *Wawasan 2020* billboards, banners, TV spots, and all sorts of messages delivered through the mass media.

34  Just a cursory glance at the history of winners of the Grammy Award in the World Music category tells this story. (See the appendices in Timothy Taylor's *Global Pop* (1997) for a summary of the winners in the category's first decade of existence.)

35  Many of such productions are, in fact, put up by the STB.

36  Simon Frith (1996) has provided a fine theoretical exposition on the musical performance and the production of a people. Mark Mattern (1998) has recently published a collection of ethnographic essays illustrating mutually constitutive nature of music and community.

37  One *Sarawak Tribune* guest writer spoke to this very issue in his comments regard-ing the RWMF event as a whole:

> And so the genius of the artiste is reflected in the holistic genius of the event. A multi-cultural celebration on multiple levels; the workshop performances where the band members jammed on each others' instruments; the venue, the Cultural Village, itself a celebration of multi-ethnic lifestyles; Sarawak, a living lesson in positive pluralism, embodying a model of tolerance, mutual respect and sharing. (Harris, 1999)

38  Ethnomusicologist Veit Erlmann has even gone so far as to argue that "world music represents an attempt by the West to remold its image by localizing and diversifying itself through an association with otherness," and that "a serious analysis of global musics can only be written from a subject position in the West" (1996: 470).

39  This is not entirely the case for all members of MITRA. One of the musicians, a Malay, actually won a *sampé'* competition held a few years ago at the Sarawak Cultural Village. Needless to say, his victory did not go without controversy within the Orang Ulu community.

40  This is reminiscent of a story recounted by A.L. Becker in the introduction to his collection of essays, *Beyond Translation: Towards a Modern Philology* (1995): Becker had gone to peninsular Malaysia to deliver a conference paper outlining his progress in translating the *Hikayat Melayu* (Malay Annals). Following the presentation, a senior Malay scholar complimented Becker on his work, then told him that he hoped the translation would never come to completion. Why not? Because the scholar feared that the English translation would replace the Malay original.

# References

Anonymous (1999) "Bigger Festival to Mark New Millennium," *Borneo Post*, August 28, p. 3.

Bauman, Zygmunt (1996) "From Pilgrim to Tourist – or a Short History of Identity," In Stuart Hall and Paul du Gay (eds.), *Questions of Cultural Identity* (London: Sage Publications), pp. 18–36.

Becker, A.L. (1995) *Beyond Translation: Essays Towards a Modern Philology* (Ann Arbor, MI: University of Michigan Press).

BERNAMA news agency (2000 "Rainforest Music Fest Scores Resounding Success," *Borneo Post*, August 22.

Byrne, David (1999) "Crossing Music's Borders: 'I Hate World Music,'" *New York Times*, "Arts & Literature" section, October 3.

Chambers, Erve (1997) "Introduction: Tourism's Mediators," in idem (ed.), *Tourism and Culture: An Applied Perspective* ( Albany: State University of New York Press), pp. 1–12.

Chan, Francis (1998) "Rain Forest World Music Festival Ends on a High Note," *Sarawak Tribune*, August 31, p. 10.

Chopyak, James (1987) "The Role of Music in Mass Media, Public Education and the Formation of a Malaysian National Culture," *Ethnomusicology*, 31(3): 431–54.

Erlmann, Veit (1996) "The Aesthetics of the Global Imagination: Reflections of World Music in the 1990s," *Public Culture*, 8(3): 467–87.

Feld, Steven (1994) "From Schizophonia to Schismogenesis: On the Discourses and Commodification Practicies of 'World Music' and 'World Beat,'" in Charles Keil and Steven Feld (eds.), *Music Grooves* (Chicago: University of Chicago Press), pp. 257–89.

Fish, Stanley (1996) *Professional Correctness: Literary Studies and Political Change* (Oxford: Oxford University Press).

Frith, Simon (1989) "Introduction," In idem (ed.), *World Music, Politics and Social Change*, Papers from the International Association for the Study of Popular Music (Music and Society Series) (Manchester: Manchester University Press)

Firth, Simon (1996) "Music and Identity," in Stuart Hall and Paul du Gay (eds.), *Questions of Cultural Identity* (London: Sage Publications), pp. 108–27.

Garofalo, Reebee (1993) "Whose World, What Beat: The Transnational Music Industry, Identity, and Cultural Imperialism," *The World of Music*, 35(2): 16–32.

Garrison, Lloyd (1989) "Tourism – Wave of the Future?," *World Development* (UNDP), 2: 4–6.

Goodwin, Andrew and Joe Gore (1990) "World Beat and the Cultural Imperialism Debate," *Socialist Review*, 20(3): 63–80.

Guilbault, Jocelyne (1993a) "On Redefining the 'Local' through World Music," *The World of Music*, 35(2): 33–47.

Guilbault, Jocelyne (1993b) *Zouk: World Music in the West Indies* (Chicago: University of Chicago Press).

Hall, Colin Michael (1994) *Tourism in the Pacific Rim: Development, Impacts and Markets* (Melbourne: Longman Cheshire/Halsted Press).

Harris, Roger (1999) "Rain, Music and Genius: Impressions of the Sarawak Rainforest World Music Festival,." *Sarawak Tribune*, September 3, "Outlook," p. 1.

Jayl Langub (1994) "Majlis Adat Istiadat and the Preservation of the Adat of the Natives of Sarawak." *Sarawak Museum Journal*, 67(68): 7–16.

Jowers, Peter (1993) "Beating New Tracks: WOMAD and the British World Music Movement," in Simon Miller (ed.), *The Past Post: Music After Modernism* (Manchester: Manchester University Press), pp. 53–87.

Keil, Charles and Steven Feld (1994) *Music Grooves* (Chicago: University of Chicago Press).

King, Victor (1992) "Tourism and Culture in Malaysia with Reference to Borneo," in idem (ed.), *Tourism in Borneo: Issuues and Perspectives*, Papers from the Second Biennial International Conference of the Borneo Research Council, Kota Kinabalu, Sabah, Malaysia, July, 1992 (Williamsburg, VA: Borneo Research Council Proceedings Series), pp. 29–43.

Laing, Dave (1986) "The Music Industry and the 'Cultural Imperialism' Thesis," *Media, Culture and Society*, 8(3): 331–41.

Langlois, Tony (1996) "The Local and Global in North African Popular Music," *Popular Music*, 15(3): 259–73.

Lugun, Nikki (1998) "Overwhelming Response to Rainforest Music Festival," *Sarawak Tribune* ("Home" section), September 2, p. 5.

Mattern, Mark (1998) *Acting in Concert: Music, Community, and Political Action* (New Brunswick, NJ: Rutgers University Press).

Mautner, Thomas (ed.) (1997) *Dictionary of Philosophy* (London: Penguin Books).

McEachern, Charmaine (1998) "A Mutual Interest? Ethnography in Anthropology and Cultural Studies," *Australian Journal of Anthropology*, 9(3) (December): 251–64.

Meintjes, Louise (1990) "Paul Simon's *Graceland*, South Africa, and the Mediation of Musical Meaning," *Ethnomusicology*, 34(1): 37–73.

Mitchell, Tony (1993) "World Music and the Popular Music Industry: An Australian View," *Ethnomusicology*, 37(3): 309–38.

Nash, Dennison (1989) "Tourism as a Form of Imperialism," in Valene L. Smith (eds.), *Hosts and Guests: The Anthropology of Tourism* (Philadelphia: University of Pennsylvania Press), pp. 37–52.

Nash, Dennison (1996) *Anthropology of Tourism* (New York: Pergamon).

Picard, Michel and Robert E. Wood (1993) "Preface," in idem (ed.), *Tourism, Ethnicity, and the State in Asian and Pacific Societies* (Honolulu: University of Hawaii Press), pp. vii–xi.

Roberts, Martin (1992) "'World Music' and the Global Cultural Economy," *Diaspora*, 2(2): 229–49.

Rojek, Chris and Bryan Turner (2001) *Society and Culture* (London: Sage).

Roseman, Marina (2000) "Shifting Landscapes: Musical Mediations of Modernity in the Malaysian Rainforest," *Yearbook for Traditional Music*, 32: 31–66.

Sinclair, David (1993) "Peter Gabriel's Secret World," *Rolling Stone*, 663, 19 August, p. 9.

Stokes, Martin (1994) "Introduction: Ethnicity, Identity and Music," in idem (ed.), *Ethnicity, Identity and Music: The Musical Construction of Place* (New York: Berg), pp. 1–27.

Storey, John (1996a) *What Is Cultural Studies: A Reader* (London: Edward Arnold).

Storey, John (1996b) *Cultural Studies and the Study of Popular Culture: Theories and Methods* (Edinburgh: University of Edinburgh Press).

Street, John (1987) *Rebel Rock: The Politics of Popular Music* (New York: Basil Blackwell).

Sutton, R. Anderson (1998) "Local, Global, or National? Popular Music on Indonesian Television," Paper presented at a workshop entitled "Media, Performance, and Identity in World Perspective," University of Wisconsin–Madison. Available online at: http://polyglot.hss.wisc.edu/mpi/workshop98/papers/sutton.htm

Sweeney, Phillip (1991) *Virgin Directory of World Music* (London: Virgin).

Taylor, Timothy (1997) *Global Pop: World Music, World Markets* (New York: Routledge).

Titon, Jeff Todd (1999) "'The Real Thing': Tourism, Authenticity, and Pilgrimage among the Old Regular Baptists at the 1997 Smithsonian Folklife Festival," *The World of Music*, 41(3): 115–39.

Wallerstein, Immanuel (1983) *Historical Capitalism* (London: Verso).

Wallis, Roger and Krister Malm (1984) *Big Sounds from Small Peoples: The Music Industry in Small Countries*. New York: Pendragon Press.

Wood, Robert E. (1997) "Tourism and the State: Ethnic Options and Constructions of Otherness," in Michel Picard and Robert E. Wood (eds.), *Tourism, Ethnicity and the State in Asian and Pacific Societies* (Honolulu: University of Hawaii Press), pp. 1–34.

# 11

# For the Record: Interdisciplinarity, Cultural Studies, and the Search for Method in Popular Music Studies

## Tim Anderson

Even the perfection of knowing everything does not absolve oneself from the question of method:

> The perfect scholar of popular music would know all the relevant literature from popular music studies itself and also from all other disciplines. Furthermore, this perfect scholar would be an expert in music theory, literary criticism, the history of popular music, the entire social and cultural milieu that surrounded the creation of the music in question, and all manner of social and cultural theory...But even if one succeeds at all of this, methodological issues may arise to throw into question the value of a particular study. (Burns, 1997)

In a similar vein, some pioneering scholars of cultural studies recognized that the theoretical perfection of all methodological knowledge does not guarantee the perfect relevance of that knowledge to cultural studies. When it comes to asking as well as answering questions of method, cultural studies has no certain guarantees. Therefore, "no methodology can be privileged or even temporarily employed with total security and confidence, yet none can be eliminated out of hand" (Grossberg, Nelson, and Treichler, 1992: 2).

Essays like this one may – despite my best endeavors – lend themselves to suspicious readings. I find in interdisciplinarity and cultural studies a hope, a significant optimism about what it means to be an intellectual. For those who have an academic interest in popular music, cultural studies and its interest in the critical elements of culture provide a promising pathway for many scholars to explore their research. As George Lipsitz notes in *Dangerous Crossroads: Popular Music, Postmodernism and the Poetics of Place*, the relationship between popular music and place offers a way of starting to understand the social world we are losing – and a key to the one that is being built. "Anxieties aired through popular music illumine important aspects of the cultural and political conflicts that lie ahead for us all" (1994: 3). What Lipsitz identifies as both culturally and politically premonitory is that aspect of popular music that so often charges fans and critics alike: the combination of the perceived allure of hipness (connoting exclusivity) and hearing what is both politically and culturally "inexpressible" in music (connoting community) that so often makes one a listener or musician in the first place. This double edge of hip exclusivity and political/social community builds an affinity between cultural studies and popular music studies. Another reason for the affinity of popular music studies and cultural studies is a shared enthusiastic championing of interdisciplinary scholarship. Because popular music, in distinction to, for example, musicology or film studies, has no comparative set of gatekeepers or methodological limits, the interdisciplinary practice of cultural studies has been an intellectual ally for expanding the number of scholars interested in popular music.

Despite the spirit of goodwill that the interdisciplinary practices and intentions of cultural studies harbor and cultivate, such practices and intentions also instill substantial challenges. As a proponent for post-disciplinarity in the English-speaking world, cultural studies spreads and demands greater and greater methodological appropriation and articulation. Many popular music scholars who work within the terrain of cultural studies risk being swept up into disorientation, because of the current free-wheeling methodological attitudes of cultural studies. This lack of mooring makes it very difficult to identify ways to successfully operationalize scholarship regarding popular music such that it can address both beginning students and seasoned scholars alike. For the problem of this relatively recent field of study and debate[1] rests in the navigation of multiple options, which, when all is said and done, is a challenge that many scholars would find inviting.

Nevertheless, this kind of multiplicity contains a number of dilemmas that demand a concerted ordering and understanding. Popular music studies is now on the cusp of a transition from generalist to specialist, a welcome development as it signifies growth, yet also a development which augurs new thinking about methodological possibilities. We need not only better qualify what our analytic efforts can address in popular music studies, but how this address should be made. This is a vexing issue: methods, whether conscious or not, are ways of organizing the production and consumption of all material and aesthetic goods. Without a method, any method, there is literally no way to produce or consume a piece of music. One must be willing to sit and listen, to dance, go to the concert hall to pay attention to music. Listening to music can be addressed by multiple methods through which it can be accessed and understood. The question of method is a vital one for it addresses the many aspects of musical labor, its materials, and the manners in which they are forged, exchanged, displayed, and enjoyed. In the case of scholarship, an understanding of methods demands and reveals the prioritization of our own labor and research material. It is clear that questions of method are also questions of tradition and legacy. One current challenge in popular music studies is to define ourselves through methodological refinements more as popular music scholars and not simply scholars from other disciplines who happen to study popular music.

This does not mean popular music studies should be any less interdisciplinary. Instead, in the face of the methodological uncertainties of cultural studies, we need to better define what we would like to see methodologically engaged. Throughout this essay I discuss the question of method by interrogating and negotiating the recorded music object as an appropriate unit of analysis. Finally, while musicology employs a number of methods that may strike many non-musicologists as rather limiting in explaining the multiple appeals of popular music, it does have a traditional set of analytic methods that provide means of analytic purchase on musical form and instrumentation. Nevertheless, musicology taken as a whole also has a tradition of generally underdeveloping research areas concerning popular music, and therefore turning to musicology and musicology alone will not fully operationalize the work of popular music scholars. For those from such fields as communication, media studies, sociology, anthropology, or literary studies, popular music exacts an interest for many, a subject of study for some, but a dedicated calling for very few. Instead, many of us find that any dedicated analysis of popular music provides us with the opportunity of aligning ourselves with the interdisciplinary ambitions of cultural studies as one means through which we can enter into an engagement with popular music.

Popular music studies currently endures a practical marginality within the world of the university, including within media studies. Among the numerous reasons why popular music is accorded this fate by media studies is the fact that the "music" portion of "popular music" tends to be emphasized in everyday discourse. There are consequences for this type of emphasis, some of which I will underline later. But the most obvious effect is that this effectively deposits music into a removed, aesthetic terrain that is already researched in music departments throughout the academy. Part of this is due to the fact that music has a substantial history that predates and, is not solely dependent on, modern audiovisual technologies of the nineteenth and twentieth centuries. Yet it is these and other media systems that make popular music "popular," and this focus on the popular means cultural studies has provided many media and communication scholars with a seemingly "legitimate" opportunity to engage popular music.

In fact the force of cultural studies and its interest in the "popular" has had a significant impact upon the realm of musicology. Recently, much has been made about the inability of traditional forms of textual analysis to satisfactorily explain the popularity of a piece of music. For example, Richard Middleton begins his 2000 essay, "Introduction: Locating the Popular Music Text," by noting that:

> Textual analysis has been a subsidiary strand of an expanding field of popular music studies; at the same time, much of the work has been marked by methodological hesitations which suggest deep-lying doubts about the viability of the enterprise itself. There are several reasons for this state of affairs, many of them to do with the particular histories of musical scholarship and of the way in which the study of popular culture has entered the academy. Underpinning all of them, however, is the simple tissue – simple, but running deeply through the tissue of modern societies – of the interrelationship of elite and vernacular values. (Middleton, 2000: 1)

Placing Middleton's focus on "academic worth" and cultural capital to one side, what is worrisome for musicologists is the issue of "the popular" as it exists in "vernacular values." While Middleton recognizes the limitations of speaking in the name of the audience, he also recognizes the huge gulf that exists between popular and academic lexicons. For Middleton, it is the tendency of traditional musicologists "to use inappropriate or loaded terminology" when evaluating pop songs that is a central part of the problem. Musicology's "notational centricity" allows one to speak in terms like "pandiatonic clusters," a language that seems only to widen the gulf between a researcher and the popular.

Cultural studies has had a similar impact on film and broadcasting studies by prodding many of these scholars to readdress the popular. But in contrast to broadcast and film studies, students of popular music from a communication and media studies perspective all too often view cultural studies as the only viable option through which the subject can be discussed. The result is interesting: those students and scholars who take up a cultural studies approach gain a much larger, interdisciplinary terrain of address. But in their search for cultural meaning, social resonance and moments of political articulation, cultural studies tends to obscure the formal qualities of media texts and relegate industrial questions to the realm of the self-evident. Yet the kind of detailed attention paid to film and broadcasting vis-à-vis questions of industrial and textual traditions remains sorely underdeveloped in terms of popular music. This is the case despite the fact that popular music is, to even the most naïve listener, popular as the result of its mass mediation. It should be clear that any appropriation of an analytical technique should be questioned for its suitability to address the objects and systems it wishes to examine. This includes any of those investigative priorities and methods that have been appropriated from one discipline and employed in popular music scholarship. Yet as cultural studies ingests one discipline after another, the question concerning how one should digest these disciplines to begin to study popular music languishes under the increasing ingestion of disciplines.

Larry Grossberg posits that:

> There was never an orthodoxy of cultural studies even within the Centre of Contemporary Cultural Studies (often identified as the origin of British cultural studies); there never was a singular and homogenous pure and unsoiled center. There can be no single linear history ... cultural studies has always proceeded discontinuously and sometimes even erratically. The diversity is often only ritually acknowledged, but it is much more, for it is the very practice ... Every position in cultural studies is an ongoing trajectory across different theoretical and political projects. (Grossberg, 1992: 17)

This focus on discontinuity, this resistance to standardization of cultural studies methods, is demonstrated in the totemic emphasis on the marginal and minoritarian as its objects and subjects of analysis and engagement. This tendency is long pronounced in the manner that cultural studies has tended to examine popular music. In a 1992 essay Simon Frith argues,

> That the cultural study of popular music has been, in effect, an anxiety-driven search by radical intellectuals and rootless academics for a model of consumption – for the perfect consumer, the subcultural idol, the mod, the punk, the cool commodity fetishist, the organic intellectual of the high street who can stand in for them. (Frith, 1992: 180)

Frith is not alone in his criticism and, to be sure, much has been written about cultural studies and the perpetual search for the resistant intellectual.[2] But rather than focus on this aspect of cultural studies, I would rather concentrate on Frith's assertion that this search is somehow "anxiety-driven." Perhaps not mentioned enough is the fact that uncertainty or anxiety is a common part of the academy. Apprehension about one's certitude holds a particular resonance for anyone who reflects on his or her career as a student, teacher, or researcher. Every presentation, particularly those given without precedence, is a leap of substantial faith. As a result, we tend to draw from other, less music-specific, sources in popular culture studies in order to learn how to explore and teach our chosen topic. Still, no matter how inventive the approach, there remains a palpable frustration due to the lack of preceding pathways.

But if I loved popular music, and wanted a methodical education on the subject, then why did I choose to study music in the seemingly unharmonious, interdisciplinary terrain of media and mass communication studies? The reason was simple: after taking a few music history courses it seemed to me that music departments were directed at telling me that I needed to know more about the Western canon of classical music literature and less about my collection of LPs and my two Fender guitars. Yet my LPs and guitars were the very things that I felt I needed to know more about in order to better understand my position vis-à-vis popular music. In particular, I wanted to understand why records were popular, a question that may be viewed as simple, but one which I was convinced would sprawl before me with complexities. In other words, from an early stage in my scholarly career it was clear to me that I wanted and needed to know more about the material systems that made music popular.

The findings of the early 1990s regarding the lack of interest paid by American musicologists to popular music continue to this day. As Roger Johnson notes in a recent essay:

> Reporting on a recent survey of music courses at 58 universities in the United States in *The Chronicle of Higher Education*, Sammie Ann Wicks found that almost 98% of the current courses focused on the "elite Western tradition – that body of music originally written by Europeans for consumption by the upper classes from roughly the medieval era to the early 20th century." Only 1.4% of the courses at these institutions dealt directly with American musical traditions. She also found a similar, though not quite so extreme, bias (only about 80%) in *The Journal of the American Musicological Society* between 1948 and 1997. Even *The Journal of Ethnomusicology* published an overwhelmingly large number of articles on elite non-western musics, as opposed to vernacular or popular forms, with only four articles on jazz and five on other American popular music among their 1,576 articles during the same 50-year period. These numbers tell a familiar but depressing story of cultural and professional apartheid that persists even now at the beginning of the new century. (Johnson 1997–98: 3)

In the same article, Roger Johnson underlines the primary reason why media and mass communication scholarship have made the occasional attempt to engage music as an area of media analysis:

> Music is now one of the electronic arts, having evolved to this point through much of the century. It is produced and experienced predominantly through recording and other electronic media. For music to exist at all in any public or social sense it must be electronically mediated, in effect, a type of popular music. In this form music is highly accessible and portable, accompanying us through our daily lives and providing underscoring for our multilayered, sonically filled, increasingly virtual environments. (Johnson 1997–8: 2)

# On the Flipside: Methodological Refinement in Popular Music Studies

*Most music departments spend the majority of their time directing their students towards musical performances, classical music, and marching bands. The musical performances are considered essential to insure that students have a practical, working knowledge of musical literacy. Classical music is studied when the history of music is presented; and marching bands are where music departments are usually most visible, marching on the football field or in parades.*

Don Cusic (1991), "Why Music Business Programs Should Not Be in Music Departments," p. 118

*The only instruments people like me can play today are their record players and tape-decks.*

Simon Frith (1988), Music For Pleasure, p. 11

David Sanjek recognizes that "Cultural Studies aims to connect texts and artifacts with the lives, emotions and assumptions of their producers and consumers. It perceives those consumers as active co-creators of meaning, not the passive dupes of a corporate culture" (Sanjek, 1992: 521–53). This observation supports those few programs and departments specializing in music industry education and research, rendering those programs less strictly "vocational" and therefore more open to a liberal arts marriage with traditional music departments. Despite this move, Sanjek makes no suggestions for an appropriate set of methodologies (Sanjek, 1992: 53–4). Nevertheless, his suggestions are interesting for they begin to focus us on methods through questions about pedagogy. Of the authors Sanjek suggests, no one is a more strident example of cultural studies work in the United States than Lawrence Grossberg. Still, despite his voluminous research, Grossberg exhibits an evident frustration in his search for a way to teach a course on popular music. Take, for example, the pedagogical challenges he encounters in teaching a course on rock and roll:

> My approach was simple: I would try to describe the texts, interpreting the significance produced by the unique synthesis of musical texture and lyrical content. Then I would suggest correspondences to the situation of its audiences which were mediated through the practices of production and consumption. The music obliquely represented and responded to the structure of experience of at least certain portions of its youth audience. As I sought more adequate readings, the correspondence became increasingly refracted; the music had to be located in an overdetermined context: class, race, subcultures, gender, as well as age exerted unequal pressures on and were represented in rock and roll. Nevertheless, my students – as well as the rock and roll fan in me – were noticeably dissatisfied. While they often assented to my readings, it was

clear that my readings failed to capture something important, something that was intimately connected to rock and roll's power as well as to its cultural politics. (Grossberg, 1997: 29)

Grossberg's acknowledgment of his difficulties in attempting to impart a cultural studies perspective to understanding rock and roll may be due in part to the manner that rock works as an affective space, a genre, or both. Perhaps rock is to remain undisciplined and thus no refined set of methods is worth developing in light of its ever-contingent nature. Still, it is clear that we should not conflate rock with popular music. One is a subset of the other and the key to understanding popular music is what makes it popular. Rock, in many cases, ostensibly works in defiance of these systems while, at the same time, never completely disavowing its attempt to become popular.

Still, both Grossberg's frustrations and other testimonies of pedagogical trial and error such as those published in the *Journal of Popular Music Studies*, volume 9–10 are invaluable for a number of reasons.[3] First and foremost, discussions of pedagogy are discussions of how and what to instruct. In essence, pedagogy involves the deliberate investment in producing ways, in other words methods that elicit an understanding of how effectively one can and should teach a subject. In this manner, the aim of a pedagogical discussion is analogous to that of a concerted discussion regarding the validity of a particular research method: both discussions deal analytically with what should constitute a means for a set of given contingencies in order to discover or impart scholarly analysis. Part of my call for a set of distinct popular music research methods is to help us alleviate our anxieties and frustrations about where to begin our research, what should be examined, and how it should be addressed. At the same time that we are expending energies on discussions regarding how one should teach popular music, I believe that we can parallel these efforts with discussions of appropriate method. Thus, I feel that we should turn to a terrain where culture is systematically parsed out, organized, and often considered the province of a "social science": sociology.

Of all of the sources for an approach to studying popular music, it is the empirical confines of sociology, with its focus on modern bureaucracies and mass society, which have provided the foundational claim that popular music is an area worth studying. It has also provided popular music with the initial institutional spaces through which its serious, academic consideration would occur. As Simon Frith and

Andrew Goodwin point out, "The academic study of pop and rock music is rooted in sociology, not musicology . . . the sociology of pop and rock is, in turn rooted in two non-musical concerns: The meaning of 'mass culture' and the empirical study of youth (and delinquency)" (Frith and Goodwin, 1990/2000: 1).

What is interesting is how many of the methodological focal points of sociology, such as debates between quantitative versus qualitative approaches to the discipline, are shared with one area of media inquiry, broadcast and mass communication studies, in which the quality and reliability of data are continually deliberated. This is particularly true of those mass communication scholars who have adopted many techniques from sociology to better understand statistical evidence that comprise demographics, television ratings, and the neoclassical analyses of media industries. Of course, these scholars have also gained from other social sciences such as economics and psychology, but in the English-speaking world sociology departments have often housed some of the more successful media scholars. Furthermore, media industries have traditionally engaged in research projects that make explicit use of methods generated from the social sciences. In many ways social theory and its need to account for and deal with mass entertainment as a form of social propaganda and pacification has always been forced to engage the "culture industries" of Hollywood film and national networks.

On the other hand, as Frith and Goodwin note, the social sciences have also held an interest in the subcultural delinquent, the group or individual not conforming with or otherwise mollified by mass culture. In many ways this search for the delinquent or social deviant dovetails with many of the "margin obsessed" concerns of cultural studies. Nevertheless, the differences between deviant sociology and cultural studies should be clear: while sociology is ostensibly a scientific discipline whose application of observational and statistical methods holds no openly political agenda, cultural studies makes no similar claim. The result is that sociology engages most mass phenomena through a series of distinct (and somewhat limited) methodologies. Thus, it is not too surprising to read early work on popular music that treats popular music as a somewhat bureaucratic field that is negotiated by a variety of organizations (record labels, fan clubs, bands, etc.), operatives (A&R men, fans, musicians, etc.) and objects (promotional material, recordings, instruments, etc.). This is a tempting manner in which to organize popular music. It even has its benefits and explanatory force and has provided organizing principles to negotiate many of the complex industrial and material conditions of popular music. This empirical focus has a number of consequences, but one that I would like to emphasize for now is the manner in which it forces one to think about data as a type of cultural material.

For example, let us consider the materials that are most pronounced in the production of music in general: the musical instruments. Musicology has a dedicated set of scholars whose work focuses on the historical and cultural traces of musical instruments, yet only recently have popular music scholars begun to similarly dedicate themselves.[4] In some cases the advances made by these scholars provide a refreshingly new concern for musical form. Unlike musicology, the analyses of form that these scholars carry out have more to do with the material rather than textual formations and their cultural significance. To be sure, a materialist account of popular music should detail those formations that make music popular. Yet I would like to suggest that the multi-methodological and trans-disciplinary impulse of a movement such as cultural studies perhaps gives us too many issues, with too few avenues of negotiation as to where to focus our questions. Indeed, it is this underdetermination of a pragmatic view that a concerted focus on the materials most basic to music's popularity would help resolve. At the same time it would help popular music studies rethink its "cultural studies" urges and resolve itself to evaluate just what we want to talk about and how to talk about it. The instrument most fundamental to music's popularization is the one that continues to exist as a sorely uninvestigated blind-spot: the recorded music object. The path to this blind-spot involves recognizing the value of pedagogy in musical instruments, but then transferring and adapting that value from a pedagogy of musical instruments to a pedagogy of recorded music objects.

While music departments continue to teach how to play musical instruments, the most obvious way to produce popular music for most fans and musicians is to play a recorded music object, such as a compact disc, MP3 file, record, or a cassette tape. The fact of the matter is that, as scholars and fans, recorded music objects and musical instruments themselves are both sites of impassioned debate, affection, and attention. Still, it would be hard to deny that modern pop music, if not popular music in general, is directly engaged with the assembly and circulation of recordings. All one needs to consider is how essential recordings and mass mediation are to the creation of a "popular music." In all cases, however "cultural" a music's popularity may seem, as Richard Hamilton stated in 1957, to be "popular" in mass society is to be "designed for a mass audience" (quoted in Walker, 1983: 33). In other words, while not every recording is popular, it is designed through and for a popularizing technology. We need to study the record to better understand how music is designed to "become popular."

While we are beginning to develop a solid understanding of the physical and material limits that affect the production of popular music recordings, what we lack is a similarly refined comprehension of how they operate culturally. We lack ways to negotiate both the methods and the questions that would develop such an understanding. One of the primary contributors to this conundrum has been the aforementioned neglect of music's basic materiality in favor of a more standard vision of music as a transcendent art.

This oversight, this elaborate disavowal, has two immediate and discernible impacts on music criticism in general. The first effect is that the material cultural aspects of the recording and the recording processes are removed and culture is defined as something that exists beyond its recording. In this conception popular music is unhinged from the recording apparatus. Music, conceptually adrift and unanchored to the recording, then becomes the always-privileged site of any cultural concern or investigation. This disregard of the recorded object can then foster a naïve, realist aesthetic that permanently positions recorded music objects as secondary, background materials. The result is that the record is never methodologically negotiated, but rather continually exists beyond negotiation, perpetually positioned at least one step away from analysis – something that in theory can almost always be addressed later, but all too often never is in practice. Positioning the recording outside of the investigational premises of any cultural critique, standard musical criticism continually subordinates this material aspect to an aesthetically non-influential station. The record may have significance as a technology that facilitates the cultural communication of music, but its continual bracketing as a non-cultural entity can set a trap: constructing a very untenable position of naïve realism. In this position, the record, at best, reflects music and circulates it within a specific musical culture; at its worst, the record exudes an artifice that contaminates a somehow purer music culture.

Of course, an understanding of how popular music is designed to become popular could focus on the construction of this disavowal as part of its cultural-materialist organization and ambitions. We need to take these organizations and their desires seriously for they are quite literally designed to make music a popular phenomenon. They are also both instrumental with regards to popular music aesthetics and instruments that have a profound influence on popular musical culture. Thus, by negotiating through the materiality of musical organization, we place popular music into a long-standing tradition of artistic and technological design. In this framework, the insights of Pythagoras as well as those of the latest "techno" disk jockey find purchase between music and the physical sciences. The debates surrounding this linkage between musical and physical territories are various: some are concerned with the transcendental connections that music forges with earthly terrain, while others contain more base formations. These debates have negotiative value because they stand as a countervailing force to more traditional understandings of what it has meant to study music; rather, they have an explicit interest in a facet essential to popular music, namely its mediation by specific material arrangements. In the introduction to his work, *Musica Practica*, Michael Chanan (1994) argues that hiding the material organization of music preserves a Romantic ideology of transcendental musical contact between composer and audience. In Chanan's terms, this bourgeois musicological assumption is produced by a number of ideological institutions that reinforce fantasies of a pure, unhindered music. Music in this ideal form is a pure form of communication that provides an immediate, transcendent form contact that potentially bridges all class and cultural differences. On the other hand, Chanan, Frith, and Goodwin advance an analytical interest regarding popular music as a highly mediated form of communication, a form of communication whose mediation can never be obviated. Indeed, to eliminate the mediation would eliminate the music's popularity. Thus, whether this mediation occurs through cultural or material processes, music is never positioned as simply an autonomous force. Developing an argument proposed by Richard Leppert and Susan McClary, Chanan (1994: 7) values how this ideological position of Romantic transcendence has particular effects on how scholars both understand musical processes and comprehend one's self as a musical subject. While it may be seductive to maintain that music exists as an ideal, transcendental artform, "a form of expression purged of the temporal and contingent concerns of daily life," it is a seduction with significant risks. The most significant risk we take when we adopt this stance is that we fail to negotiate the implications of a more refined, materialist understanding of what it means to be a musical (or artistic) subject, listener or composer, in any social or historical sense (Chanan, 1994: 8). Because the primary material object of exchange in today's musical culture and industry is the recorded object, it makes sense that we frankly have no choice but to consider how this product is and has been produced, distributed, and mediated as a component of negotiating methodological strategies for addressing popular music and cultural studies.[5]

For some, my interest in industrial arrangements may sound like the most anesthetic, asocial, and a-musical form of analysis possible. Pushed to extremes, one could posit a fear that popular music and mass media histories could consist of nothing more than accounts of media fashions, industrial acquisitions, and technological advancements (or failures). However, such extremes also trigger a failure of negotiation, for the recording is not strictly technological in the common-sense understanding of the term. The recording is a product of industry, it is a medium, its distribution can be – and often is – marked by class, race, and gender. In other words it is a cultural material, a social technology with specific histories and contexts, and should always be understood as such. If this call sounds oblique, it is because I feel the recording is best viewed as an assemblage that Felix Guattari identifies as "aesthetic machinery." These assemblages result from and emerge out of forms of social, cultural, and aesthetic engineering (Guattari, 1995). This machinery is not and can never consist of simple, top-down arrangements led by industrial moguls who simply "produce" or audiences who simply "consume." As a technocratic assemblage, our conception of the record as passive "object" or the listener/musician as active "subject" can no longer be maintained. In each case, both object and subject are involved in political formations, economic strategies, social programs, moments of history, aesthetic movements, and individual desires of which an ambition of the popular is a conspicuous construction.[6] These technological assemblages are never static. They can break down, become damaged, need updates, be involved in reformatory movements, or simply be discarded for new aesthetic formations. Most importantly, these assemblages are part of and interact with cultural formations in general. In this framework culture is understood as it connects etymologically to the Latin *cultura*, meaning a tending, care, cultivation. Culture is never a static entity, but rather a generative process that can be altered, is never universal, and must always deal in contingencies. Popular culture and popular music do not emanate out of these fabrications as epiphenomenalistic entities. Rather *they comprise* processes that keep aesthetic machinery performing and operational.[7] All of which makes the recordings, along with other musical instruments, extremely complex objects for negotiation and analysis to study.

We need to know much more than the current and past status of the record industry to understand popular music culture. Take, for example, the issue of popular musical stardom. The issue of stardom is an area that is closely related to the ability to facilitate the flow and exchange of commodities. Furthermore, by somehow treating these commodities as merely common, there is little incentive to theorize about and/or catalog these items. One of the initial problems that I encountered in beginning my research was that, in contrast to my peers who dealt with audiovisual media, I was provided with no means to talk about my primary objects of analysis. There were two main reasons for this inability. The first concerned the lack of an adequate vocabulary, historical understanding, or set of concepts that could help us address the recorded music object.

There were more than a few of us who believed that recordings could no longer be discussed with a naïve realism, where the materiality of the recorded music object is ignored "in the face of a fantasy of an unmediated sonic event or musical performance" (The Chicago Recorded Music Work Group, 1993: 172). Furthermore, we believed that,

> Such an account upholds the realist model and fails to account for the ways that recorded music circulates culturally. Such an approach also ignores the heterogeneous practices involved in production (including multitracking, miking technique, studio effects, and commercial packaging) that crystallize in the recorded object. The extent of this theoretical elision becomes apparent when one considers that while contemporary music scholarship in a variety of disciplines has relied for many years upon the recording as a research tool, systematic investigations of the phenomenon of recording itself have yet to converge to define the recorded text as a formal category in the study of music. (p. 172)

It turns out we were not alone in our frustrations. As mentioned earlier, Johnson notes that while "music is now one of the electronic arts," he also remarks that "several fundamentally transforming, though often ignored, things happen as music becomes electronic. The most obvious is that recording itself becomes the work, the 'text,' the product of reference, value and exchange" (Johnson, 1997–8: 2).

Similar to the thoughts of the Chicago group, Johnson points out that recordings involve their own set of material and aesthetic systems and standards of production. Still, there is a palpable frustration as he leaves us with little more than the obligatory set of general examples of what these are (i.e. close-miking, editing, multi-tracking, analog versus digital recording techniques, etc.). It is this frustration that led the Chicago Recorded Music Work Group (1993) to attentively dedicate our interdisciplinary backgrounds to exploring how popular music is and should be investigated. While no one solution or grand theory could (or was desired) to be divined, we all agreed that our collective inability to talk about a record was something worth noting:

> As an interrelated group of scholars, fans, and musicians, we have yet to find a way to speak of the recorded text that adequately accounts for its variable conditions of production, representation, reproduction, and reception. What is it about the sound recording and existing disciplinary approaches to it that makes the task appear so difficult? Why does the recorded aspect of the music/sound object tend to disappear within academic treatments? (p. 171)

Although the upshot of our questioning was to better identify a way and a language through which we could speak about the "interrelations, contingencies, and partialities" that contribute to the production of recordings, no systematic language was offered. I want to be very clear that our call for language represented steps of negotiation toward a call for operationalizing methods through which this important but ignored popular music object could be discussed. For our purpose, the Work Group found an interesting precedence in the study of narrative film:

> The study of narrative film, for example, has developed general theoretical constructs such as spectatorship and apparatus theory. These form a vocabulary for discussing texts as particular examples of a recognizable form (i.e. classical Hollywood cinema) and describe some specific properties of film as a medium. Although some film analyses assume a realist model grounded in the dramatic elements of theatre, film theory emerges from a recognition of the material specificity of film technology. Questions of technological mediations are never allowed to recede entirely. Many approaches within cinema studies – semiotic, psychoanalytic cognitive, sociological, economic – directly address the technological component of their object of study. (pp. 171–2)

Though this passage focuses on the term "theory," I believe that the reason film studies rarely allows the materials of cinema to withdraw from analysis is due to an engaged focus on developing methods of analysis that systematically deny this possibility. One of the most important contributions of film theory has been an interest in developing not simply a vocabulary, but an efficient manner of addressing cinematic objects, a growing and negotiated lingua franca to address cinema and be investigated if researchers wish to deeply understand the very problems they hope to analyze. Thus, a methodology negotiates a set of conventions and procedures that help initiate scholars and researchers into what the discipline considers to have high value for negotiation. Unlike terms of analysis or criticism, method is more analogous to a grammatical system that knowingly negotiates something of a standardized usage. Like grammar, a method's negotiations for standardized arrangements should produce negotiable structures and concepts, flexible enough to accommodate creative ambitions, and secure enough to foster necessary rearrangements and re-articulations.

Methods operate to organize both the data involved and the researcher into a system of interactive and interpretive limits. The result is that, like the guideposts of language, which negotiate both subject and objects into fields of possible experience and expression, methods are pathways through which we begin to negotiate shared understandings of both the objects we want to study and also the intents and limits of our research.

The second reason why I found my interest in music media thwarted was far more pragmatic and is concerned with the aforementioned lack of energy devoted to the cataloguing and making an archive of popular music recordings available to researchers and popular music enthusiasts. I do not need to detail this situation other than to note the obvious: disciplines and fields that fail to decide that they need certain objects make no systematic attempt to keep those materials archived. Libraries, museums, and archives do not occur through the accidental intentions of their objects. Collections are purposely developed through the methodological demands and assistance of disciplined scholars and enthusiasts, persons trained and motivated to understand what is important to understanding their fields of study. Without a method-driven understanding of a need for recordings, popular music scholars (particularly those in North America) rarely voice their concern about the manner in which libraries pay little attention to archiving, let alone acquiring popular music recordings. As a result, there is no standardized attention paid to the institutional housing of popular music records, let alone restoring or circulating them. Scholars interested in these objects are then left to fend for themselves as they draw from their own personal collections and the collections of other individual record collectors. This brief examination does suggest that archival activity, or lack thereof, is what might be called a "significant variable" in a given scholarly community's negotiation of methodology. Thus, recognition of the current lack of this archival significant variable in popular music studies is also a factor in exploring the question of method in popular music and cultural studies, and implies that other facets of cultural studies may also encounter a similarly missing significant variable in other areas of negotiating method.

Emphasizing the cultural-material processes that makes music popular gives rise to new sets of questions and investigations. This is especially important given the continual temptation of understanding popular music as somehow a-material. It is important to understand both our past and our future. In 1988, Simon Frith noted the following:

> We are coming to the end of the record era now (and so, perhaps, to the end of pop music as we know it) and so what I want to stress here is that, from a historical perspective, rock and roll was not a revolutionary form or moment, but an evolutionary one, the climax of (or possibly footnote to) a story that began with Edison's phonograph. To explain the music industry we have, then, to adopt a much wider perspective than rock scholars usually allow. (Frith, 1988: 12)

Part of this wider perspective is a methodological orientation that demands from us new questions about popular music materials and systems, rather than those questions which other disciplines have invested with a predetermined importance. The interdisciplinarity of a set of analysts can only stand as a scholarly strength if it is truly and respectfully tested by the terrain it subjects to analysis. By ignoring what seems to systematically constitute the terrain of popular music in order to study what another discipline finds interesting, it seems to me that what is specific about popular music as we know it today very rarely gets a chance to exert its own judgment about the appropriateness of methods from other disciplines. The arrival of the MP3 format and the popularity of file sharing do not reduce our need to understand the recorded music object. If anything, just as the disappearance of the Hollywood studio system exacerbated our cultural and scholarly need to understand how its systems of production, distribution, and exhibition operated, the slow recession of the long playing record, the compact disc, and the 45 rpm record from our culture should demand from us a better understanding of their purchase and influence on popular music.

So the question is, then, how do recorded objects act as texts? Furthermore, what is their textual significance, their history, their importance to fans? Shouldn't we as scholars begin to develop means through which we can have a better understanding of how recording formats and packaging contribute to our understanding and experience of popular music? Of course, while my answer is an unequivocal "yes," methodological formations are always collective in origin, development, and operation. In short, it is up to the interdisciplinary actors who roam the field of popular music to decide what is important, what we should collectively share with others and how we should self-consciously proceed. Cultural studies may be the term of the day in popular music studies, but our academic interests should not result solely from the passions of others. For the passions of others will most probably subside, and without a distinct methodological inquiry we risk losing our own footing. If we do not begin to negotiate how and why we want to study what we want to study, when the desires of another discipline or academic movement turns elsewhere our analytic and academic options vis-à-vis popular music will have only been compromised by our failure to fully negotiate questions of methods.

## Notes

1  It is fair to note that scholarship regarding popular music, particularly in the English-speaking world, dates back to the 1950s. The most prominent examples are those of David Riesman and Donald Horton, sociologists who, as Frith and Goodwin note, investigated pop music as a textual force that is used by its audiences (see Frith and Goodwin, 1990/2000). Of course, the work of Adorno is well known as an example of someone who, for very different reasons, finds a critical interest in popular music as early as the 1930s. Yet throughout my discussion the application of the term organization is something that is best understood as a forum of scholars who routinely and predictably come together to share, debate and listen to each other's criticisms and discoveries. It should be noted that at least one scholar feels that the "discipline" of popular music studies may have begun well-before the establishment of IASPM. Gary Burns notes, "If there really is such a "discipline" as popular music studies, it probably began, not coincidentally, at about the same

# Tim Anderson

time [*Popular Music and Society*] did – 1971" (Burns, 1997: 123). While the tentative nature of this claim hardly lends it a convincing air, it bears mentioning if only because the issue of serious academic consideration is clearly established by the existence of the journal. In my opinion, the most prominent academic popular music organization throughout the world is the International Association for the Study of Popular Music. The relative youth of organization and its emphasis on interdisciplinarity makes it both an exciting and valuable academic association for moving our understanding of popular music. To quote liberally from the organization's website:

> IASPM is an international organization established to promote inquiry, scholarship and analysis in the area of Popular Music. Founded in 1981, IASPM has grown into an international network of almost 600 members world-wide. On a national and international level, the organization's activities include conferences, publications, and research projects designed to advance an understanding of Popular Music and the processes involved in its production and consumption. To build a large and diverse body of knowledge of Popular Music, IASPM is interprofessional and interdisciplinary. It welcomes as members anyone involved with Popular Music. To preserve its autonomy, the association remains independent of all commercial and governmental interests. (http://www.iaspm.net/iaspm/)

2  This search for the disruptive consumer, the resistant listener, is indicative of something, that despite Meaghan Morris' identification and critique in 1990, still plagues cultural studies:

> Recent cultural studies offers something completely different. It speaks not of restoring discrimination but of encouraging cultural democracy. It respects difference and sees mass culture not as a vast banality machine but as raw material made available for a variety of popular practices.

> In saying "it", I am treating a range of quite different texts and arguments as a single entity. This is always imprecise, polemically "unifying", and unfair to any individual item. But sometimes, when distractedly reading magazines such as *New Socialist* or *Marxism Today* from the last couple of years, flipping through *Cultural Studies*, or scanning the pop-theory pile in the bookstore, I get the feeling that somewhere in some English publisher's vault there is a master disk from which thousands of versions of the same article about pleasure, resistance, and the politics of consumption are being run off under different names and minor variations. Americans and Australians are recycling this basic pop-theory article, too: with the perhaps major variation that English pop theory still derives at least nominally from a Left popu*lism* attempting to salvage a sense of life from the catastrophe of Thatcherism. Once cut free from that context, as commodities always are, and recycled in quite different political cultures, the vestigial *critical* force of that populism tends to disappear or mutate. (Morris, 1990: 21)

Given the extensive proliferation of publishing "cultural studies" titles throughout the last ten years, Morris' critique has perhaps not received the attention that it deserves. Furthermore, the great amount of attention that writers and publishers have paid to popular products and texts such as toys, television shows, and popular genres gives Frith's point a greater significance. Perhaps all researchers of popular culture should ask themselves whether or not their search has a narcissistic component, if their initial impulse for their research is to find their critical substitute, a surrogate academic audience that confirms that one's pop cultural passions are indeed critical.

3   Frith finds in intellectual anxiety something indicative of the need "to satisfy our own desire to feel that we're part of the real world. Intellectuals spend a lot of time anxious that what they're working on doesn't have any significance for anyone else" (Frith, 1992: 183). Given that the classroom is perhaps the most common and palpable point of contact between a public and their own work, it makes sense that this would be a space where such anxieties tended to surface.

4   There are a number of recent examples of this area of research that I feel are quite compelling, including Waksman (1999), Theberge (1997), and Jones (1992), all of which are wonderful examples where scholars explicitly connect issues of cultural consequence and status to modern, popular music technologies.

5   One of the most common critiques of this position, a position that I feel this study anticipates, is that we are entering a "post-record" era, an era where CDs, tapes, and records are being outmoded by a file-sharing economy of MP3s. Yet this cultural economy of information exchange is only possible due to the high volume and speed of recent hard-drive technologies. Hard drives, we should not forget, are simply high-volume record and playback devices and are only another permutation of the recording object.

6   My use of the term "assemblage" draws directly from Felix Guattari's interest in what he calls "aesthetic machinery." Guattari (1995: 89) conceives of aesthetic machinery as machines of the virtual that "have an important role to play ... as a paradigm of reference in new social and analytic possibilities (psychoanalytic in the broadest sense)." These are particularly odd machines: not only are they diagnostic but they also provide fantastic premonitions, potentials for day-to-day experiences and social formations:

> Strange contraptions, you will tell me, these machines of virtuality, these blocks of mutant percepts and affects, half-object half-subject of the possible. They are not easily found at the usual marketplace for subjectivity and maybe even less at that for art; yet they haunt everything concerned with creation, the desire for becoming-other, as well as mental disorder or the passion for power. Let us try, for the moment, to give an outline of them starting with some of their aesthetic principal characteristics ... The assemblages of aesthetic desire and operators of virtual ecology are not entities which can easily be circumscribed within the logic of discursive sets. They have neither inside nor outside. They are limitless interfaces which secrete interiority and exteriority and constitute themselves at the root of every system of discursivity. They are becomings ... (Guattari, 1995: 92)

7   I am drawing on Raymond Williams' discussion of "culture" as both a decided problem and interest for sociology:

> The history and usage of [culture] can be studied in Kroeber and Kluckholn and Williams. Beginning as a noun of *process* – the culture (cultivation) of crops or (rearing and breeding) of animals, and by extension the culture (active cultivation) of the

human mind – it became in the late eighteenth century, especially in German and English, a noun *configuration* or *generalization* of the "spirit" which informed the "whole way of life" of a distinct people. (Williams, 1989: 10)

For a more detailed discussion see Williams (1989: 10–14).

# References

Allen, Robert C. and Douglas Gomery (1985) *Film History Theory and Practice* (New York: McGraw-Hill Publishing Company).

Altman, Rick (1999) *Film/Genre* (London: British Film Institute).

Bazin, Andre (1985) "Beauty of a Western," trans. Liz Heron. *Cahiers du Cinema: The 1950s: Neo-Realism, Hollywood, New Wave.* Ed. Jim Hillier (Cambridge, MA: Harvard University Press), pp. 165–9.

Burns, Gary (1997) "*Popular Music and Society* and the Evolving Discipline of Popular Music Studies," *Popular Music and Society*, 21(1): 123–31.

Chanan, Michael (1994) *Musica Practica* (London: Verso).

Chicago Recorded Music Work Group (1993) "What Are We Listening To? What Are We Talking About? Recorded Sound As An Object Of Interdisciplinary Study," *Stanford Humanities Review*, 3(2): 171–4.

Corbett, John (1994) *Extended Play: Sounding Off from John Cage to Dr. Funkenstein* (Durham, NC: Duke University Press).

Cusic, Don (1991) "Why Music Business Programs Should Not Be in Music Departments," *Popular Music and Society*, 15(3) (Fall 1991): 117–22.

Descartes, Rene (1996) *Discourse on the Method of Rightly Conducting the Reason and Seeking Truth in the Sciences*, ed. David Weissman (New Haven, CT: Yale University Press).

Fink, Robert (2000) "Music as Object?," *Echo*, 2(2) (Fall): 93–102.

Frith, Simon (1992) "The Cultural Study of Popular Music," in Lawrence Grossberg, Cary Nelson, and Paula Treichler (eds.), *Cultural Studies* (New York: Routledge), pp. 174–86.

Frith, Simon (1988) *Music for Pleasure: Essays in the Sociology of Pop* (New York: Routledge).

Frith, Simon (1996) *Performing Rites: On the Value of Popular Music* (Cambridge, MA: Harvard University Press).

Frith, Simon and Andrew Goodwin (eds.) (1990, 2000) *Rock, Pop and the Written Word* (London: Routledge).

Grossberg, Lawrence (1992) *We Gotta Get Out of This Place: Popular Conservatism and Postmodern Culture* (New York: Routledge).

Grossberg, Lawrence (1997) "Another Boring Day in Paradise: Rock and Roll and the Empowerment of Everyday Life," *Dancing Despite Myself: Essays in Popular Culture* (Durham, NC: Duke University Press), pp. 29–63.

Grossberg, Lawrence, Cary Nelson, and Paula Treichler (eds.) (1992) *Cultural Studies* (New York: Routledge).

Guattari, Felix (1995) *Chaosmosis*, trans. Paul Bains and Johan Pefanis (Bloomington: Indiana University Press).

Hardt, Hanno (1992) *Critical Communication Studies: Communication, History and Theory in America* (New York: Routledge).

Hebdige, Dick (1979) *Subculture, the Meaning of Style* (London: Methuen).

Hebdige, Dick (1987) *Cut 'n' Mix: Culture, Identity, and Caribbean Music* (London: Methuen).

Hebdige, Dick (1990) "Style as Homology and Signifying Practice." In Frith and Goodwin (eds.), *On Record: Rock, Pop and the Written Word* (London: Routledge), pp. 56–65.

Horner, Bruce and Thomas Swiss (1999) "Putting It into Words: Key Terms for Studying Popular Music," in idem (eds.), *Key Terms in Popular Music and Culture* (Malden, MA: Blackwell Publishers), pp. 1–2.

Johnson, Roger (1997–8) "Better Late Than Never: Thoughts on the Music Curriculum in the Late 20th Century," *Journal of Popular Music Studies*, 9–10: 1–6.

Jones, Steve (1992) *Rock Formation: Music, Technology, and Mass Communication* (London: Sage).

Lipsitz, George (1994) *Dangerous Crossroads: Popular Music, Postmodernism and the Poetics of Space* (New York: Verso).

Middleton, Richard (2000) "Introduction: Locating the Popular Music Text," in idem (ed.), *Reading Pop: Approaches to Textual Analysis in Popular Music* (New York: Oxford University Press), pp. 1–19.

Morris, Meaghan (1990) "Banality in Cultural Studies," in Patricia Mellencamp (ed.), *Logics of Television: Essays in Cultural Criticism* (Bloomington, IN: Indiana University Press), pp. 14–43.

Negus, Keith (1997) *Popular Music in Theory: An Introduction* (Hanover, NH: University Press of New England).

Negus, Keith (1999) *Music Genres and Corporate Cultures* (New York: Routledge).

Rodman, Gilbert B. (1996) *Elvis after Elvis: The Posthumous Career of a Living Legend* (New York: Routledge).

Rose, Tricia (1994) *Black Noise: Rap Music and Black Culture in Contemporary America* (Hanover, NH: Wesleyan University Press).

Sanjek, David (1992) "A Department of their Own: A Modest Proposal for the Design of Music Business and Technology Programs," *Popular Music and Society*, 16(4) (Winter): 41–60.

Shuker, Roy (1994) *Understanding Popular Music* (New York: Routledge).

Theberge, Paul (1997) *Any Sound You Can Imagine: Making Music/Consuming Technology* (Middleton CT: Wesleyan University Press).

Waksman, Steven (1999) *Instruments of Desire: The Electric Guitar and the Shaping of Musical Experience* (Cambridge, MA: Harvard University Press).

Walker, John (1983) *Art in the Age of Mass Media* (London: Pluto Press).

Williams, Raymond (1989) *Keywords*, revised edition (Oxford: Oxford University Press).

Wollen, Peter (1982) *Singin' In The Rain* (London: British Film Institute).

# Index